ELIZABETH DE BURGH
LADY OF CLARE
(1295–1360)

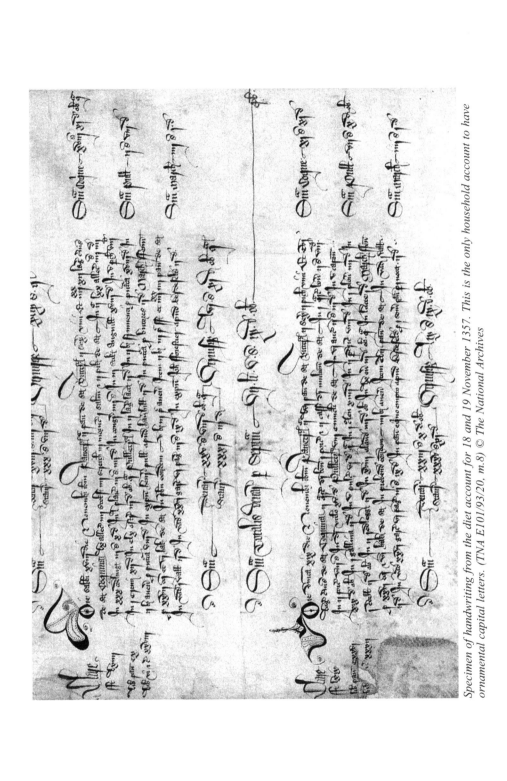

Specimen of handwriting from the diet account for 18 and 19 November 1357. This is the only household account to have ornamental capital letters. (TNA E101/93/20, m.8) © The National Archives

ELIZABETH DE BURGH

LADY OF CLARE

(1295–1360)

HOUSEHOLD AND OTHER RECORDS

Edited and translated by

JENNIFER WARD

General Editor

MARK BAILEY

The Boydell Press

Suffolk Records Society
VOLUME LVII

A Suffolk Records Society publication
First published 2014
The Boydell Press, Woodbridge

ISBN 978–1–84383–891–3

Issued to subscribing members for the year 2013–2014

The Boydell Press is an imprint of Boydell & Brewer Ltd
PO Box 9, Woodbridge, Suffolk IP12 3DF, UK
and of Boydell & Brewer Inc.
668 Mt Hope Avenue, Rochester, NY 14620–2731, USA
website: www.boydellandbrewer.com

The publisher has no responsibility for the continued existence or
accuracy of URLs for external or third-party internet websites referred to
in this book, and does not guarantee that any content
on such websites is, or will remain, accurate or appropriate

A catalogue record for this book is available
from the British Library

Papers used by Boydell & Brewer Ltd are natural, recyclable products
made from wood grown in sustainable forests

Printed and bound in Great Britain

CONTENTS

ILLUSTRATIONS

Frontispiece: Specimen of handwriting from the diet account for 18 and 19 November 1357

Plates

(between pp. 66 and 67)

In memory of my mother
Gladys Amy Ward

PREFACE AND ACKNOWLEDGEMENTS

Elizabeth de Burgh, Lady of Clare, was one of a number of noble widows who made their mark on the social and economic history of fourteenth-century England. Her influence was felt not only in Clare and her estates but in East Anglia as a whole. She was a generous religious patron and her benefactions reflected her strong and determined personality. One of her foundations, Clare College at Cambridge, flourishes at the present day. From the point of view of the historian, it is especially fortunate that many of her household accounts have survived and are now in the National Archives. Her activities and lifestyle can be reconstructed, as can the structure and work of her household and its officials. A vivid picture emerges of her life at Clare and elsewhere as a wealthy member of the higher nobility, exercising her rights, carrying out her responsibilities as a landowner, enjoying the company of family and friends and travelling as a pilgrim to religious shrines.

In selecting and translating the documents for this volume, I have incurred a number of debts. I would like to thank Mark Bailey, the General Editor, and David Sherlock, the Co-ordinating Editor, for their help and advice. I would also like to thank Jim Bolton, Elizabeth Eastlake, Michael Hicks, Jessica Lutkin, Sandra Roe, Julien Ryley, Jenny Stratford, John and Joe Ward, and Elphin and Brenda Watkin for their help on particular points. Any remaining mistakes are mine. I would also like to thank the staff of the National Archives, the British Library and Lambeth Palace Library for their help and for permission to publish documents in their custody. In addition to the Clare accounts and court rolls, and royal government documents in the National Archives, I have made use of the cartularies of Clare and Walsingham priories in the British Library, and of Elizabeth de Burgh's will, copied into Archbishop Simon Islip's register, in Lambeth Palace Library. The Image Library at the National Archives has given permission to reproduce the frontispiece, the Master and Fellows of Clare College, Cambridge, the seal of Elizabeth de Burgh of 1359, Colchester and Ipswich Museums the painting of Clare castle by Thomas Lyus, and John Ward the sketch map of Clare in the fourteenth century.

The Suffolk Records Society is grateful to Clare Ancient House Museum, Clare Historical & Archaeological Society, Clare College, Cambridge, and an anonymous donor for grants towards the cost of publishing this volume.

The volume is dedicated to the memory of my mother, Gladys Amy Ward, who as G.A. Thornton before her marriage wrote *A History of Clare, Suffolk*. She stimulated my interest in Clare and the Clare family and always encouraged me to find out more about Elizabeth de Burgh.

Jennifer Ward
April 2013

ABBREVIATIONS

b.	bushel, bushels
BL	British Library
CCR	*Calendar of Close Rolls*
CChR	*Calendar of Charter Rolls*
CFR	*Calendar of Fine Rolls*
CPR	*Calendar of Patent Rolls*
cwt	hundredweight
d.	penny, pence
fol., fols	folio, folios
lb.	pound, pounds (weight)
m.	membrane
Monasticon	*Monasticon Anglicanum*, ed. J. Caley, H. Ellis and B. Bandinel,
Anglicanum	6 vols (London, 1817–30)
ob.	halfpenny (in Latin, *obolus*)
q^a	farthing (in Latin, *quadrans*)
qr	quarter, quarters (weight)
s.	shilling, shillings
TNA	The National Archives
C47	Chancery Miscellanea
C54	Close Rolls
C66	Patent Rolls
E30	Diplomatic Documents
E101	Exchequer Accounts, Various
SC2	Court Rolls
SC6	Ministers' and Receivers' Accounts
SC11	Rentals and Surveys

INTRODUCTION

Life and Inheritance

Elizabeth de Burgh (1295–1360) is best known today as the founder of Clare College, Cambridge. In her lifetime, she was a well known member of the higher nobility, and her influence was widely felt in Suffolk and further afield. As the heiress to one-third of the inheritance of the Clare earls of Gloucester, and as the niece of Edward II, cousin of Edward III, and kinswoman of many noble families, she played a leading role in the society of her time. In contrast to her chequered life under Edward II, her long widowhood under his son was peaceful and ordered. She never lost her interest in national and local affairs, and exerted influence as a landowner and feudal lord, and as a religious and cultural patron. The survival of many of her household and estate records makes it possible to build up a picture of her wealth, lifestyle and activities, and of the power she wielded over her manors, boroughs and tenants in Suffolk and elsewhere.

Elizabeth was born in 1295, the youngest daughter of Gilbert de Clare, earl of Gloucester and Hertford (d.1295), and his second wife, Joan of Acre, daughter of Edward I.[1] Her brother, Gilbert, born in 1291, succeeded his father as a minor and Elizabeth had two elder sisters, Eleanor and Margaret. Little is known of the children's early years. Joan of Acre remarried, taking as her second husband Ralph de Monthermer, a member of Earl Gilbert's household;[2] she died in 1307 and was buried in the church of the Augustinian friars at Clare.[3] By then, marriages were being arranged for the children. Eleanor married Hugh le Despenser the Younger in 1306, while Margaret married Piers Gaveston, Edward II's favourite, the following year. Gilbert and Elizabeth made alliances with the family of Richard de Burgh, earl of Ulster, and in 1308 the marriages took place at Waltham abbey of Gilbert to Matilda de Burgh, and Elizabeth to the earl's eldest son, John.[4]

Gilbert's death at the battle of Bannockburn in 1314 completely transformed the

---

[1] For the Clare family and Elizabeth de Burgh, see M. Altschul, *A Baronial Family in Medieval England: the Clares, 1217–1314* (Baltimore, 1965); F.A. Underhill, *For her Good Estate. The Life of Elizabeth de Burgh* (Basingstoke, 1999); J. Ward, *English Noblewomen in the Later Middle Ages* (London, 1992); *Women of the English Nobility and Gentry, 1066–1500*, ed. and trans. J. Ward, Manchester Medieval Sources (Manchester, 1995). Lives of Elizabeth de Burgh, her parents and other members of the Clare family are included in *Oxford Dictionary of National Biography* (Oxford, 2004).

[2] Ralph and Joan had two sons and two daughters; Thomas received land from Edward II, Edward fought and died in the early years of the Hundred Years War, Mary married Duncan earl of Fife, and Joan became a nun at Amesbury. Edward was on the closest terms with Elizabeth de Burgh; she died at Clare and was buried in Clare priory. See below, p.43.

[3] *Flores Historiarum*, ed. H.R. Luard, 3 vols, Rolls Series (London, 1890), III, pp.142, 329.

[4] *CPR, 1301–7*, p.43; TNA C47/10/22, no. 10; *The Chronicle of Pierre de Langtoft*, ed. T. Wright, 2 vols, Rolls Series (London, 1866–8), II, p.368; *Vita Edwardi Secundi*, ed. N. Denholm-Young (London, 1957), p.2; *Cronica Maiorum et Vicecomitum Londoniarum*, ed. T. Stapleton, Camden Society, old series, XXXIV (London, 1846), p.251; J.S. Hamilton, *Piers Gaveston, Earl of Cornwall* (Detroit, 1988), p.38; R. Frame, *English Lordship in Ireland, 1318–61* (Oxford, 1982), pp.62–4.

The Family of Elizabeth de Burgh

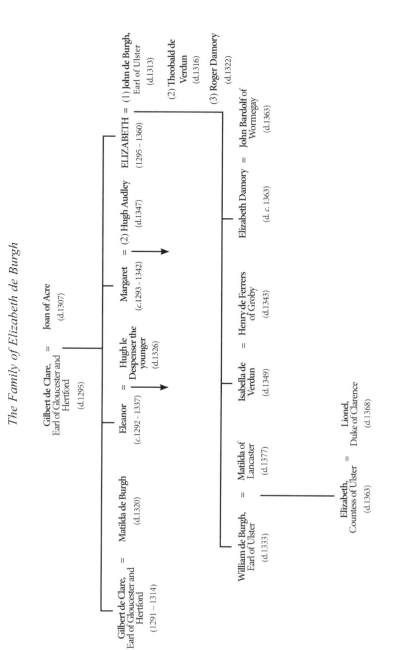

fortunes of his three sisters, and the partition of his inheritance proved to be one of the most acute problems facing Edward II. Because of its political repercussions, he postponed it as long as possible, the countess's claim to be pregnant being used as the excuse well beyond the usual term. For much of this time Elizabeth remained in Ireland where her son William had been born in 1312. She was widowed the following year, but did not return to England until 3 February, 1316, when she resided in Bristol castle. There she made her second marriage to Theobald de Verdun who was accused of abducting her, although Theobald claimed that they had been betrothed in Ireland. Theobald died less than six months after the marriage.[5]

On his death, Edward II wanted to ensure her marriage to one of his court favourites, and she was married to Roger Damory about the end of April, within six weeks of the birth of Isabella, her daughter with Theobald, on 21 March 1317. At about the same time, her sister Margaret was married to another favourite, Hugh Audley, while Eleanor's husband, Hugh le Despenser the Younger, was emerging as the king's most powerful favourite. The Clare inheritance was finally partitioned; Edward II took the husbands' homage on 22 May 1317, and the heirs received their pourparties on 15 November.[6] The total valuation of the inheritance in 1317 came to just over £6,500 and is the best indication of the great wealth and power of the Clare family. Although the Clares were leading members of the nobility from the late eleventh century, their succession to the earldom of Gloucester in 1217 had brought with it a major increase of wealth, since the honour of Gloucester included the lordships of Glamorgan and Gwynllwg in south Wales and extensive lands in west and south-west England. The development of the Welsh lordships in particular during the thirteenth century resulted in their being the most powerful noble family in England.

Elizabeth's and Damory's principal concentration of lands lay in eastern England; they were allotted a large part of the honour of Clare, with its demesne manors, jurisdictional liberties, knights' fees and advowsons.[7] They were also assigned lands in Dorset, of which the most valuable were the manor, borough and hundred of Cranborne, and the lordship of Usk in south Wales, which was held by Earl Gilbert's widow until her death in 1320. In Ireland, County Kilkenny was divided, Elizabeth's most valuable demesne holdings being the manor of Ballycallan, and the borough and mills of Callan. She already held dower in Ireland from her first marriage, but she never revisited Ireland after her return to England in 1316.

Of all these holdings, the honour of Clare had been held by the Clare family since the reign of William the Conqueror. It then comprised two groups of estates, lands in Kent and Surrey centred on Tonbridge, probably granted soon after 1066,[8] and lands in Essex and Suffolk centred on Clare, given to Richard son of Count Gilbert,

---

5   *Chartularies of St Mary's Abbey, Dublin*, ed. J.T. Gilbert, 2 vols, Rolls Series (London, 1884–6), II, pp.294, 338, 342, 343; *Rotuli Parliamentorum*, 6 vols (London, 1783), I, pp.352–3; *Monasticon Anglicanum*, V, p.661. Underhill, *For her Good Estate*, pp.4–24.

6   *Rotuli Parliamentorum*, I, p.355; *Calendar of Chancery Warrants, 1244–1326*, p.470; *CPR, 1313–17*, pp.660–1, 666; *CCR, 1313–18*, pp.414–15, 583; *CFR, 1307–19*, pp.350–1. The shares of each heiress are listed in TNA C47/9/23–5.

7   Altogether, Elizabeth and Damory received just over 201 knights' fees in Essex, Suffolk and Norfolk, about forty and a half in Dorset, fourteen in Wales and about thirteen in County Kilkenny. They received the advowsons of twenty parish churches and ten religious houses. Elizabeth held dower lands from her first two marriages.

8   In 1317, most of the Kent and Surrey lands were granted to Hugh Audley and Margaret de Clare.

the founder of the Clare family, after the rebellion of the earls in 1075.[9] A castle had been built at Clare by 1090, and the castle at Tonbridge was probably erected earlier. Further lands in East Anglia, notably in Norfolk, were added to the honour of Clare during the twelfth century. The Clare lords tended to keep the most valuable manors in demesne, while establishing their followers on the honour in return for knight service.[10] Elizabeth and Damory succeeded to an estate with large demesne manors which they exploited directly and a mass of sub-tenants holding by free or military tenure.[11]

Most of the honour of Clare's demesne manors were in Suffolk, with a few in Norfolk, Essex and Hertfordshire; of these, Clare and Hundon were the most valuable according to the partition of 1317. 1317 was an unusual year when valuations were probably inflated above normal levels owing to the famine raging in England at the time. However, they provide a reliable guide to the relative value of the twelve holdings in the table; these were gross valuations, with no deductions made for expenses.

Demesne valuations of the honour of Clare in 1317[12]

Place-name	County	Valuation
Clare castle and manor	Suffolk	£170 19s. 0d.
Clare borough	Suffolk	£20 7s. 6d.
Hundon manor	Suffolk	£139 6s. 8d.
Lakenheath manor	Suffolk	£15 16s. 6d.
Southwold manor	Suffolk	£15 7s. 3d.
Sudbury borough	Suffolk	£75 0s. 2d.
Woodhall manor in Sudbury	Suffolk	£33 2s. 1½d.
Great Bircham manor	Norfolk	£18 1s. 6½d.
Walsingham manor	Norfolk	£115 0s. 0d.
Great Bardfield manor	Essex	£124 18s. 9d.
Claret in Ashen manor	Essex	£18 1s. 2½d.
Standon manor	Hertfordshire	£66 18s. 6¼d.

In the years after 1317 the retention of these lands posed serious problems, since the grant of Glamorgan to the ambitious Younger Despenser gave him the incentive to extend his estates over the whole of south Wales. This provoked rebellion

---

9   Richard had probably fought with the Conqueror at the battle of Hastings and was one of those responsible for suppressing the 1075 rising. I would like to thank Lucy Marten for information on this point.

10   For more information on the early history of the honour, see R. Mortimer, 'The Beginnings of the Honour of Clare', *Proceedings of the Battle Conference on Anglo-Norman Studies*, III, ed. R.A. Brown (1980), pp.119–41; R. Mortimer, 'Land and Service: the Tenants of the Honour of Clare', *Anglo-Norman Studies: Proceedings of the Battle Conference*, VIII, ed. R.A. Brown (1985), pp.177–97; J. Ward, 'The Lowy of Tonbridge and the Lands of the Clare Family in Kent, 1066–1217', *Archaeologia Cantiana*, XCVI (1980), pp.119–31; J. Ward, 'The Place of the Honour in Twelfth-Century Society: the Honour of Clare, 1066–1217', *Proceedings of the Suffolk Institute of Archaeology and History*, XXXV (1983), pp.191–202.

11   See below, pp.xviii, xxv–vi, 123–8.

12   Some demesne manors of the honour of Clare were assigned to Hugh Audley and Margaret: Desning in Gazeley, Suffolk, and Crimplesham, Warham, Wells-next-the-Sea and Wiveton, Norfolk.

and civil war in 1321–2. Damory and Elizabeth took over the lordship of Usk in 1320. Both Audley and Damory were involved in the Marcher rising of 1321 which resulted in Despenser's banishment. However, on his return, the Marchers were defeated at the battle of Boroughbridge on 16 March 1322; a short time before, Damory died of wounds at Tutbury while Elizabeth was captured at Usk.[13]

Elizabeth was in a serious predicament in 1322, widowed for the third time, with three young children and no family support.[14] She and her children were imprisoned in Barking abbey. Her legal position as a rebel and the widow of a traitor was precarious. As a widow, she had in theory more independence of action than an unmarried woman or a wife, but medieval women, expected to be weak, irrational and subordinate, were at a great disadvantage when faced with a determined king and powerful, ambitious lords. She was determined to stand up for her family, estates and rights, as she recorded in her secret protest against the Despensers, drawn up on 15 May 1326, in her oratory in the small chapel next to her chamber in Clare castle, which recorded her struggle over the lordship of Usk.[15]

Her lands and possessions had been confiscated by the king, but the English and Irish lands were restored on 2 November 1322, apart from the lordship of Usk which she unwillingly quitclaimed to the king. It then passed to Despenser.[16] Before the restoration, her manors on the honour of Clare were stripped of their resources. All grain, livestock, ploughs and carts were sold, as was the wheat growing in the fields for the next year's harvest. Armour, weapons and furnishings in Clare castle were sold so that nothing remained.[17] The keeper of the confiscated lands was Sir Robert de Bures who had previously served Earl Gilbert de Clare, the Lady's brother, as steward of the honour. He subsequently sold at least some of the confiscated livestock back to Elizabeth, and some of the confiscated goods were returned by Edward III early in his reign.[18] The manors had to be restocked and carefully supervised according to the accounts for 1322–3 and 1324–5.[19] Elizabeth was not willing to be driven into retirement, and she welcomed the invasion of Queen Isabella and Roger Mortimer on 24 September 1326, although she regarded it as essential to remain on good terms with Edward II until she was sure that the invasion would be successful. By mid-October, her officials were in Wales and Usk was recovered.[20]

---

13   J. Ward, 'Elizabeth de Burgh and Usk Castle', *Monmouthshire Antiquary*, XVIII (2002), pp.13–22; Underhill, *For her Good Estate*, pp.25–30.

14   *Ibid.*, pp.31–41. Elizabeth, her daughter with Damory, was born in 1320 or 1321. There is a reference to a wet-nurse at Usk castle with the Lady's daughter in the account of the receiver of Usk for 1322–3; TNA SC6/927/31.

15   BL Harley MS 1240, fols 86v–87r. The protest is printed in G.A. Holmes, 'A Protest against the Despensers, 1326', *Speculum*, XXX (1955), pp.207–12, and is translated by J. Ward in *Women of the English Nobility and Gentry*, pp.116–19.

16   TNA E101/332/27, m.5; *CChR, 1300–26*, p.449; *CPR, 1321–4*, p.176; *Cartae et Alia Munimenta quae ad dominium de Glamorgancia pertinent*, ed. G.T. Clark, 6 vols (Cardiff, 1910), III, pp.1100–1; *CCR, 1318–23*, pp.578, 603–4.

17   TNA SC6/1147/9.

18   TNA SC6/992/12; BL Add. MS 60584, fol. 13v; J.C. Ward, 'Sir Robert de Bures', *Transactions of the Monumental Brass Society*, X, part 3 (1965), pp.146–8. I would like to thank Jenny Stratford for drawing my attention to the British Library manuscript.

19   TNA SC6/992/12, mm.2d, 3d; *ibid.*, 1109/19, mm.1–3. See below, pp.63–4.

20   TNA E101/91/11; *ibid.*, 91/12, mm.2d–3d; SC6/928/2. The recovery of Usk was ratified by Edward III soon after his accession; *CPR, 1327–30*, p.32, dated 26 February 1327. See below, pp.1–5. The recovery of Usk also involved a private agreement with Elizabeth's sister, Eleanor Despenser; the

In contrast to the years of turmoil, Elizabeth's third widowhood under Edward III was uneventful, and it is to these years that the household and estate records mainly refer. She never remarried, and styled herself Lady of Clare; she was referred to in the accounts as the Lady. She mostly resided on the honour of Clare but paid long visits to Usk down to 1350, and occasionally to Dorset. Clare castle constituted the centre of her lands in eastern England and the meeting-place of the honour court which was attended by military and free tenants. The castle underwent considerable refurbishing and rebuilding during her widowhood.[21] Down to the 1340s she regularly used her residence at Anglesey priory in Cambridgeshire, but she became increasingly attached to her residence at Great Bardfield, Essex. Her house there was on the site of the present sixteenth-century Bardfield Hall, next to the parish church; a large early fourteenth-century barn lies south of the Hall.[22] In 1352 she built her London house in the outer courtyard of the convent of Minoresses outside Aldgate, and spent part of the year there until the late 1350s.[23]

Wherever Elizabeth de Burgh was residing, she maintained a wealthy lifestyle. Her brother, Earl Gilbert, had been one of the richest members of the nobility with an annual income of about £6,000; there were only six earls in England who received more than £3,000 a year; six received less.[24] Elizabeth's share in the 1317 partition amounted to about £2,000, and in addition she held dower from her first two marriages. She thus enjoyed an income similar to several earls. She derived her income from her demesne manors and boroughs, and from the profits of lordship. Farming was closely supervised by her councillors and auditors, and her interventions referred to in court rolls point to detailed supervision.[25] The main sources of income from the manors comprised rents, mills and farms, profits from arable and livestock husbandry, and the perquisites of the courts. During the 1330s, sheep-farming became increasingly important, and remained so until the Lady's death in 1360. In 1338–9, the largest flocks were at Clare, Hundon and Bardfield, and four years later the receiver of Clare recorded the sum of £61 5s. from the sale of wool to Thomas de Cantebirs, draper and citizen of London.[26]

The Black Death of 1348–9 resulted in some immediate administrative dislocation, as is indicated by the Clare records for those years, and in the attempt in the longer term to maintain the systems in operation before the plague. Even so, there was less land in cultivation and pressure to increase wage rates. In addition, unfavourable weather conditions led to poor harvests between 1349 and 1351, and low

---

Chamber account of 1329–30 recorded that the sum of 500 marks was paid to Lady Despenser and her second husband, Sir William de la Zouche, for the 'fine of Usk'; TNA E101/91/22.

[21] See below, pp.63–5.

[22] J. Bettley and N. Pevsner, *Essex* (New Haven and London, 2007), p.389.

[23] J. Ward, 'Elizabeth de Burgh, Lady of Clare (d. 1360)', in C.M. Barron and A.F. Sutton, eds, *Medieval London Widows 1300–1500* (London, 1994), pp.29–45. In the accounts the residences are referred to by place-name, namely Usk, Clare, Anglesey, Bardfield and London. The Minoresses were Franciscan nuns.

[24] C. Dyer, *Standards of Living in the Later Middle Ages* (Cambridge, 1989), pp.29, 36.

[25] G.A. Holmes, *The Estates of the Higher Nobility in Fourteenth-Century England* (Cambridge, 1957), pp.86–93. See below, pp.100–2, for the close concern with yields of crops and the profit and loss of cultivation. J. Davis, 'Selling Food and Drink in the Aftermath of the Black Death', in M. Bailey and S. Rigby, eds, *Town and Countryside in the Aftermath of the Black Death. Essays in honour of John Hatcher* (Turnhout, 2012), pp.364–9.

[26] Holmes, *Estates of the Higher Nobility*, pp.89–90; G.A. Thornton, *A History of Clare, Suffolk* (Cambridge, 1928), pp.106–14; TNA SC11/roll 801; SC6/1110/10.

harvest yields for the rest of the 1350s.[27] There are few signs of retrenchment in the household accounts, but, overall, it is likely that income was declining.

Elizabeth de Burgh had personal losses among her family and friends; her son William was killed in Belfast in 1333, leaving a daughter, Elizabeth, who, with her husband Lionel duke of Clarence, succeeded to her grandmother's inheritance. Elizabeth's daughter Isabella, married to Sir Henry de Ferrers, died during the Black Death. Her younger daughter, Elizabeth, the wife of Sir John Bardolf, survived her, as did her great friend, Marie de St Pol, countess of Pembroke. As a widow, and therefore as a *femme sole*, Elizabeth was entitled to run her household, manage her estates, and bring cases before the courts. She enjoyed a noble lifestyle, entertained her family and friends, travelled on visits, business and pilgrimage, and made her religious benefactions. All this was achieved with the help of her council, and the household and estate officials and servants whose records have fortunately survived.

Elizabeth de Burgh died on 4 November 1360, and chose to be buried at the abbey of the Minoresses outside Aldgate where she had built her London residence. Her funeral must have been splendid; £200 was bequeathed for it in her will.[28] Her tomb has not survived, but must have been equally lavish. According to his first will, John Hastings, earl of Pembroke (d.1375), wanted a tomb like Elizabeth de Burgh's in St Paul's cathedral, London, and left £140 for its construction.[29] The Lady's executors established a perpetual chantry for prayers for her soul in the Minoresses' church close to her tomb. By the sixteenth century, her tomb had been moved out, probably to the cloister,[30] and it has not survived.

Household Management and its Records

The household provided the focal point for all the Lady's activities and was divided into several departments to which officials and servants of various ranks and functions were attached.[31] On occasion the household split into two; when the Lady changed residences, or travelled, a certain number of the household accompanied her, while the rest were left behind and were entered separately in the accounts.[32] It is likely that for much of Elizabeth's widowhood the household numbered about a hundred people, although it was probably smaller in the 1320s; a list of household members receiving fees contained fifty-eight names.[33] The livery roll of 1343 included estate as well as household personnel, together with local gentry, tradesmen, clerks and others attached to royal government, graded in order of rank.[34] Altogether, the Lady gave livery to 268 people. Of these, about a hundred are known

---

[27] Holmes, *Estates of the Higher Nobility*, pp.90–2; B.M.S. Campbell, 'Grain Yields on English Demesnes after the Black Death', in M. Bailey and S. Rigby, eds, *Town and Countryside in the Age of the Black Death* (Turnhout, 2012) pp.123–9, 144.

[28] See below, p.141.

[29] J. Nichols, *A Collection of All the Wills of the Kings and Queens of England* (London, 1780), pp.92–5. He was in fact buried in the church of the Dominican friars in Hereford, in accordance with his second will; *ibid.*, pp.95–6. His tomb has not survived.

[30] M. Carlin, 'Holy Trinity Minories: Abbey of St Clare, 1293/4–1539', Centre for Metropolitan History, London, 1987, unpublished, p.39.

[31] The structure of the noble household is discussed by K. Mertes, *The English Noble Household, 1250–1600. Good Governance and Politic Rule* (Oxford, 1988).

[32] See below, pp.85–6.

[33] See below, pp.4–5.

[34] See below, pp.69–71.

from other evidence to have been attached to the household. The livery roll can be compared with Elizabeth's will of 1355 which provided for comprehensive bequests to officials and servants, again listed hierarchically.[35] 121 people were named, of whom twenty-one are known to have served on the estates; the household therefore probably still numbered about a hundred members towards the end of Elizabeth's life.

Like other fourteenth-century nobles, the Lady had her council to advise her on major policy decisions. No list of council members survives, but they probably comprised her most important officials and clerks, and a few local knights, who are referred to in the wardrobe and household accounts and in manorial records; members of the council also acted as auditors and advised on legal matters. Individual councillors on occasion represented the Lady, as at the funeral of her cousin, John de Bohun, earl of Hereford and Essex, and at meetings of parliament. Her most important adviser was Thomas de Cheddeworth (d.1352) who was with her when she made her secret protest against the Despensers, and advised her on the state of Ireland before her son, William earl of Ulster, returned there in 1328.[36]

The layout of a residence centred on the hall and chapel, while at the same time providing some privacy for the Lady; the preparation of food and drink and other necessities was carried out in the service areas. Each department had its own location within the residence. The hall was the centre of public life and hospitality, and projected the Lady's status through its furnishings and display of plate. The chapel was richly furnished, with books, altar-vessels, vestments, images and candles, and had its own staff of priests and clerks. Elizabeth's chamber account of 1351–2 testifies to a constant round of services in the chapel.[37] The Lady had a measure of privacy in her own chamber. This was the only place, apart from the laundry, which had a female presence, and it was here that the Lady and her women talked, read aloud, and embroidered; purchases of silk and embroidery thread were entered in the chamber account.

The survival of about a hundred of Elizabeth de Burgh's household accounts, many of them complete, makes it possible to build up a detailed picture of how the household functioned.[38] The term household account covers several different types of document, the purpose in every case being to record the accountability of the official concerned.[39] The Lady's central financial department was the Chamber (not to be confused with Elizabeth's own chamber), with the clerk of the Chamber as the supreme financial official, whose accounts recorded the delivery of money for household expenditure and other purposes, and payments from the receivers, reeves

---

[35] See below, pp.141–3.

[36] TNA E30/1536.

[37] See below, pp.75–7.

[38] The household accounts are listed in the Appendix, pp.151–4 below.

[39] The nature of household accounts is discussed in *Household Accounts from Medieval England*, ed. C.M. Woolgar, 2 vols, British Academy Records of Social and Economic History, new series, XVII (Oxford, 1992–3), I, chapters 1–4. Elizabeth de Burgh's accounts were first discussed by C.A. Musgrave, 'Household Administration in the Fourteenth Century with special reference to the Household of Elizabeth de Burgh, Lady of Clare' (London University M.A. thesis, 1923); this is unpublished. Excerpts from Elizabeth de Burgh's accounts are included in translation in *Women of the English Nobility and Gentry*, ed. and trans. Ward, pp.81, 162–85, 188, 220–2. For the uses made by historians of household records, see C. Dyer, *Standards of Living in the Later Middle Ages*, pp. 27–108; C.M. Woolgar, *The Great Household in Late Medieval England* (New Haven and London, 1999).

and lessees from all the Lady's estates.[40] The Wardrobe, under the clerk or keeper of the Wardrobe, was responsible for provisioning the household and for certain specific supplies, as recorded in the indenture of 1332.[41] The service departments were answerable to the Wardrobe for their purchases and daily expenditure. They comprised the Pantry, providing bread and flour; the Buttery, responsible primarily for wine and ale, but also for cider and drinking-vessels; the Kitchen, dealing with red meat and fish; and the Poultry, with dairy produce, white meat, rabbits, birds of various kinds, and young animals such as piglets. The Larder dealt with the products of hunting, the household having its own huntsmen, and sometimes falconers. The Saucery which provided sauces, the Chandlery candles, and the Scullery dishes, were probably smaller.[42] There was a certain amount of overlap between departments, and officials of one department are found making purchases for others. The department of the Marshalsea comprised the stables and the forge and was involved with all activities concerning horses. Horses were essential for the smooth running of the household, being responsible for the delivery of provisions. The Marshalsea, with its blacksmiths, yeomen, grooms and pages, was probably the most heavily staffed department. The number of grooms and pages fluctuated according to the number of horses in the stables, as can be traced in the diet and stable accounts. Each of the carters had his own cart and horses, and the Lady had her own coach, presumably of the type depicted in the Luttrell Psalter.[43] The department produced its own accounts which were then summarised in the diet accounts.

The Wardrobe kept three main accounts: the wardrobe and household accounts, the diet accounts, and the counter-rolls. Apart from one book,[44] the accounts were of the royal chancery type, with the membranes attached end to end. The membranes measure between 27 and 30 centimetres wide, with the membranes of each roll cut to the same width; the membranes were between 67 and 75 centimetres long, although some were cut shorter to fit the contents of the roll. The majority of the household and estate accounts were written in Latin, with the occasional word in English; French was used for some of the indentures, for the account of the Lady's private expenditure of 1351–2, and for her will of 1355.[45] The financial year ran from the morrow of Michaelmas to Michaelmas. All the accounts were audited after the end of the financial year and it was usual to hold a view of account during the winter, about halfway through the year.[46]

The wardrobe and household accounts recorded purchases of food and drink, cloth and furs, and included expenses connected with the Lady's legal, administrative and political business. The early accounts indicate a period of experiment with

---

40 TNA E101/91/22 (1329–30); *ibid.*, 93/5 (1349–50). From 1351, the chamber account was combined with the wardrobe and household account, and William de Manton served as both Clerk of the Chamber and Clerk of the Wardrobe. The merger may have resulted from the number of debts owed by the last Clerk of the Chamber, William d'Oxwik, amounting to £254 17s. 9d.; TNA E101/93/8, m.3.

41 See below, pp.65–9. Because of possible confusion between names of departments and names of rooms, furniture or livestock, the departments have been given capital letters.

42 For information on food and drink, see *Food in Medieval England*, ed. C.M. Woolgar, D. Serjeantson and T. Waldron (Oxford, 2006).

43 See below, pp.28–35, and the Appendix, pp.151–4; M.N. Boyer, 'Medieval Suspended Carriages', *Speculum*, XXXIV (1959), pp.359–66.

44 TNA E101/91/21.

45 See below, pp.75–7, 141–9.

46 The view of account was an interim account, recording receipts and expenditure up to the date of the account.

the form of the account.[47] They did not always cover the financial year, although this was probably partly due to some confusion at the time of Edward II's deposition. There was some differentiation over the types of goods received, but many items were placed in a miscellaneous list; in 1327–8, for instance, foodstuffs from demesne manors were noted under the name of the manor supplying the goods, but most of the purchases were lumped together and mixed up with payments for Elizabeth Damory's marriage, and items for the passage of William earl of Ulster to Ireland.[48]

Household accounts became more elaborate and systematised during the fourteenth century, and in the Clare accounts differentiation between goods was increasing by the time of the 1331–2 account. By 1336 the arrangement that was to last for the rest of the Lady's lifetime had been adopted.[49] The two accounts of 1336–7 each covered a period of six months; by 1338, it had been decided that the account should cover the financial year. It is possible that Robert de Stalynton, clerk of the Chamber between 1335 and 1344, was responsible for the change to a systematic format; the change to the use of the financial year may also have been the work of Robert de Stalynton, or of John de Lenne, clerk of the Wardrobe between 1337 and 1340. Both men had studied at the university of Cambridge.[50] Although the Lady had been funding the university education of young clerks from at least 1331, there is no evidence that officials before about 1335 had attended university. It was in 1336 that she embarked on her patronage of University Hall at Cambridge.[51]

On the charge or receipts side of the account were listed arrears, receipts from demesne manors, and any sales; on the discharge or expenditure side, the purchase of provisions for people and horses, livery, and 'foreign' expenditure, much of it concerned with payments for messengers and letters; and on the dorse of the roll, the corn and stock account.[52] The rolls after 1336 are particularly informative, with a distinction drawn between provisions from demesne manors or elsewhere, and, as well as the amount and cost of the goods purchased, the name of the seller, the place where the purchase was made, and carriage and transaction costs were normally included.[53]

The diet rolls recorded household consumption for people and horses on a day to day basis, and the format of these rolls changed little over the Lady's lifetime.[54] The account for each day was arranged under household departments, and a distinction drawn between purchases and items from stock. The place of residence and the name of important visitors were inserted in the left-hand margin, together with the number of messes served. The Wardrobe's account for items such as wax and parchment was given each week. Expenditure for people who were left behind at a

---

[47] See the Appendix, below, pp.151–2. TNA E101/91/24 (1330–1) was the only wardrobe and household account to be written in French.
[48] TNA E101/91/17, mm.1–2.
[49] TNA E101/91/27; 92/3; 92/4; 92/9. Household Accounts from Medieval England, ed. Woolgar, I, pp.18–50.
[50] A Biographical Register of the University of Cambridge to 1500, ed. A.B. Emden (Cambridge, 1963), pp.363, 548.
[51] See below, pp.130–1.
[52] See below, pp.6–62, and the Appendix, below, pp.151–4.
[53] J. Ward, 'Noble Consumption in the Fourteenth Century: Supplying the Household of Elizabeth de Burgh, Lady of Clare (d. 1360)', Proceedings of the Suffolk Institute of Archaeology and History, XLI, part 1 (2008), pp.447–60. See below, pp.6–62, 151–4.
[54] See the Appendix, below, pp.151–4.

residence after the Lady's departure, or for some reason were elsewhere, was also included. The account was totalled daily, weekly, monthly and at the end of the year.[55] The information was sometimes incomplete and it is likely that draft copies of the roll were produced before the roll seen by the auditors after Michaelmas.[56]

The counter-roll combined the daily diet roll with the wardrobe and household account; information from the diet roll was summarised on the face of the roll, with the daily, weekly and monthly totals, while the wardrobe account was entered on the dorse.[57] The earliest surviving counter-roll covers the period from 22 March to 29 September 1337, and the introduction of this extra check on household stock and expenditure may again have been the work of Robert de Stalynton, and John de Lenne.[58] Although some counter-rolls covered a year, the normal period was six months. They were drawn up by an official who may have held the office of comptroller, although this term is not used in the surviving rolls.

These three main types of account were written up from rolls of particulars. Each department, such as the Brewery or the Marshalsea, submitted its own account, as did the goldsmiths when employed by the Lady.[59] A distinction has to be drawn between the Chamber, the principal finance department, and Elizabeth's own chamber; both produced their own accounts, and for the latter a roll of the Lady's private expenditure survives for 1351–2.[60] The Wardrobe drew up accounts for particular areas of responsibility such as purchases of cloth for liveries, and the list of those receiving livery dating from 1343.[61] Separate accounts were sometimes drawn up for the Lady's journeys, and for those left behind, as when her children remained at Clare over Christmas and New Year 1327–8 while Elizabeth celebrated the festival at Usk castle.[62] The information in these rolls of particulars was incorporated in the main accounts, but much of the detail was omitted, and it is likely that after the audit most of these rolls were thrown away.

The indenture was used when one official passed on money and goods to his successor; in 1332 the indenture between two clerks of the Wardrobe comprised an inventory of the items in various offices.[63] Until the merger between the Wardrobe and Chamber in 1351, the indenture was used to record the delivery of money by the clerk of the Chamber to the clerk of the Wardrobe for household expenditure.[64]

Elizabeth de Burgh's household rolls comprise about one-fifth of all surviving household accounts in medieval England outside the royal family and the Court.[65] Because of the wealth of information in the Lady's household rolls, it is easy to overlook their deficiencies, and the aspects which, because of their nature and purpose, they did not cover. There is little information on fees and wages, on furnishings and

---

55   Some accounts also have totals every three months. The early rolls covered a period of six months, but from the late 1330s the rolls were drawn up for the financial year.
56   E.g. TNA E101/91/25, where some of the totals and stock accounts are missing, although space was left for them.
57   In some cases, the counter-rolls are incomplete. See the Appendix, below, p.151.
58   TNA E101/92/5.
59   E.g. TNA E101/91/30; *ibid.*, 95/8. See the Appendix, below, pp.151–4.
60   See below, pp.75–7.
61   See below, pp.69–73.
62   TNA E101/91/15.
63   See below, pp.65–9.
64   Once William de Manton was Clerk both of the Chamber and the Wardrobe, there was no call for further indentures.
65   *Household Accounts from Medieval England*, ed. Woolgar, I, p.18.

plate, and on parts of the household, notably the hall and chapel, which were not directly concerned with purchases. It is likely that the accounts give an over-bureaucratic picture of the household, and there was probably greater overlap between departments than is apparent in the records. Although the principal concern of the accounts lay with provisioning, some foodstuffs only received occasional mention; dairy produce was recorded in the diet rolls but not in the wardrobe and household accounts, and home-grown fruit and vegetables are only known about incidentally.[66] How the supplies were cooked and presented was not the concern of the accounts. The impression given is of a large-scale, smooth-running operation and it is likely that this was not always the case. Occasionally, there is mention of a sick servant left behind or an official losing his way; John Gough is recorded as taking the wrong road at night in 1326, and Robert Mareschal as ill at Standon in 1330–1.[67] There is however no indication of difficulties caused by the failure of expected supplies to arrive, or the discovery that certain food had gone bad, or the arrival of unexpected guests. There was no reason to describe domestic crises and the recorded mishaps were ones which entailed financial outlay. Much can be learned from the accounts but their limitations have to be borne in mind.

Estate Management and its Records

The estates had their own hierarchy of officials under the council and the clerk of the Chamber. The Lady's lands were divided into bailiwicks, and the bailiwick of Clare comprised much of the old honour of Clare in the eastern counties of Suffolk, Norfolk, Essex and Hertfordshire.[68] Overall surveys of the estates were compiled by the Lady and her council, one valuation surviving for 1329–30 and another for 1338–9.[69] Through the council and auditors close supervision of the demesne manors was assured.

Two officials were in overall charge of the bailiwick, the steward and the receiver. By this time members of the local gentry were often appointed as stewards, such as Sir Andrew de Bures, whose father had been steward of the honour in the early fourteenth century. He was a member of the council, and his main duty was to hold courts, notably the court of the honour of Clare and courts leet.[70] He also carried out a variety of other business, including auditing accounts. The receiver was responsible for the money paid to him by bailiffs, serjeants and reeves of the demesne manors and boroughs, and bailiffs of fees, and for miscellaneous other receipts which varied from account to account; in 1343–4, he was responsible for the sale of

---

[66] It was usual practice for household accounts not to record fruit and vegetables; Dyer, *Standards of Living in the Later Middle Ages*, pp.63–4.

[67] TNA E101/91/12, m.2d; *ibid.*, 91/24, m.1.

[68] An overall economic analysis of the bailiwick of Clare at this time can be found in Holmes, *Estates of the Higher Nobility*, pp.86–93, and Appendix 3, pp.143–57.

[69] TNA SC1/799, 801. The valuations are printed in Holmes, *Estates of the Higher Nobility*, pp.143–4, with an analysis of profits on pp.145–7. Other surveys can be found in TNA SC6/1109/24 (1332–3) and *ibid.*, /1110/3 (1336–7); Holmes, *Estates*, p.148, analyses the demesne acreage of the Lady's manors in 1332–3. See below, pp.100–2.

[70] For the honour court and its records, see *Court Rolls of the Abbey of Ramsey and of the Honor of Clare*, ed. W.O. Ault (New Haven and London, 1928), pp.xxiv–xxxiii, 73–110. All the court rolls were written in Latin and on parchment, and, like the royal plea rolls, the membranes were fastened at the top.

wool from the bailiwick.[71] On the expenditure side, he was responsible for building work on Clare castle and at Bardfield, payment of various fees and wages, and a range of miscellaneous expenses.[72]

The officials of the demesne manors and boroughs produced their accounts for the financial year from the morrow of Michaelmas to Michaelmas, with a view of account halfway through the year. The accounts were audited, with the auditors making alterations and adjusting totals. The accounts were arranged to show the official's liability, the charge comprising arrears from the previous year and the receipts, and the discharge setting out expenditure; each section was arranged under appropriate headings.[73] The accounts throw light on the local economy, the mortality and temporary disruption caused by the Black Death, and the policies adopted by the Lady and her council, notably the expansion of sheep-farming. The accounts also throw light on the Lady's lifestyle. In particular, the manorial accounts for Clare show how the manor was supplying foodstuffs to the castle, and villein labour services were used to carry out work there.

Each manor and borough held its own courts, and the Lady had rights of leet jurisdiction at Clare and Sudbury.[74] The view of frankpledge was held twice a year to check that all men of twelve years old or older were members of a tithing, and the leet court dealt with minor criminal matters; serious cases were heard before the king's justices. The leet court also fined those who had brewed and baked, and in several cases sold bread and ale, in a manner contrary to the assize of bread and ale, those who had sold leather and bad meat, and hucksters and forestallers. Decisions of the court were enforced by distraint. The manorial court dealt with farming offences, succession to holdings, changes of tenancy and the levy of entry-fines, and matters connected with villain tenure, such as labour services and heriot. The detail provided in the court rolls throws light on the society and economy of manor and borough, and also on the role of the Lady.[75] Petitions were sent to her, pardons issued, and interventions in proceedings took place. The money accruing from fines and licences went to the Lady.

The Lady's jurisdiction over freemen and tenants by knight service was exercised through the honour court held at Clare; the pattern of knights' fees reflects their creation in the late eleventh and early twelfth centuries. With the decline of knight service and the growth of royal justice the honour court's business diminished, but the court was still active in the fourteenth century, although tenants were increasingly finding ways to evade suit of court and feudal obligations, and the cases brought were essentially minor, much of the litigation involving personal actions where damages amounted to less than £2 – cases of debt, detinue, trespass and

---

71 TNA SC6/1110/12, m.2.

72 See below, pp.63–5, 104.

73 See below, pp.102–16. The receivers' and manorial accounts were written in Latin, and the rolls were of the royal chancery type, with the membranes fastened end to end. For information on manorial records, see *Manorial Records of Cuxham, Oxfordshire, c.1200–1359*, ed. P.D.A. Harvey (Historical Manuscripts Commission and Oxfordshire Record Society, L, 1976), pp.1–83, 775–803; D. Stuart, *Manorial Records* (Chichester, 1992); *The English Manor, c.1200–c.1500*, ed. and trans. M. Bailey (Manchester, 2002).

74 See below, pp.117–23.

75 Thornton, *A History of Clare*, pp.31–46, 71–114; Davis, 'Selling Food and Drink in the Aftermath of the Black Death', pp.351–95; J. Davis, *Medieval Market Morality. Life, Law and Ethics in the English Marketplace, 1200–1500* (Cambridge, 2012), pp.274–382 (this also covers the period when the Mortimers were lords of Clare).

covenant.[76] The levying of entry fines testifies to considerable traffic in land, especially among free smallholdings. Of the obligations connected with feudal tenure, the Lady levied an aid for the knighting of her son and the marriage of her elder daughter in 1327 at the rate of £2 for a knight's fee.[77] Homage was generally postponed, but reliefs on a tenant's succession were due and were calculated at the rate laid down by Magna Carta of £5 for a knight's fee. The court was closely involved in the action taken on the death of a tenant. The holding was taken into the Lady's hands, a jury summoned to enquire into his lands, the services due, and the name and age of the heir. The court had copied the royal procedure of inquisition *post mortem* at least by the early 1300s when honour court rolls begin. Dower was allocated to the widow. If the heir was under the age of twenty-one he came into the Lady's wardship, unless he also held land of the Crown. The Lady is found making occasional interventions in business and the orders of the court were enforced by distraint, made by the bailiffs of fees in Norfolk, Suffolk, Essex and Cambridgeshire who also made attachments, summoned juries and carried out enquiries.

Clare and the Lady's Influence in East Anglia

During Elizabeth de Burgh's lifetime, Clare was flourishing as a small seigniorial borough. It had a variety of trades, and the woollen cloth industry was developing at the same time as the Lady was increasing sheep-farming on the demesne manors. Agricultural activity on the manor of Clare was stable down to the time of the Black Death; although hard hit by the plague, farming was recovering by the 1360s.[78] The Lady exerted her influence by the exercise of active lordship, particularly through the courts of both borough and manor. Although most of her provisioning was done elsewhere, some purchases were made from Clare traders. Probably more important for Clare people were the opportunities for employment at the castle, and this had probably been the case since it was built in the late eleventh century. Places of origin of servants and officials are rarely known, although some guesses can be made from surnames derived from place-names. Local people may well have been employed for the numerous casual jobs of building and repairs, cleaning and working in the service departments and stables. Servants and grooms would have been needed at the times when there were a large number of visitors and some work would still have been available when the Lady was residing elsewhere.

Trade in the town may well have benefited from purchases by members of the household and by the retainers and servants accompanying guests. None of the frequent visitors – whether family, friends, churchmen, or men on business – would have travelled on their own. Suitors to the honour court, officials from other bailiwicks, and men bringing provisions from demesne manors may also have done business and spent money in the town. Quite apart from basking in the glory of visits from the de Bohuns, the de Veres, and Edward III and his family, the town probably reaped a material profit.

The Lady's patronage extended across East Anglia. The livery roll of 1343[79] shows that she had among her retainers tradesmen, clerics, gentry and esquires

---

[76] J. Ward, 'The Honour of Clare in Suffolk in the Middle Ages', *Proceedings of the Suffolk Institute of Archaeology*, XXX (1964), pp.94–111. See below, pp.123–8.

[77] *Inquisitions and Assessments relating to Feudal Aids*, VI, pp.555–7.

[78] Thornton, *A History of Clare*, pp.169–79; Holmes, *Estates of the Higher Nobility*, pp.88–93.

[79] See below, pp.69–71.

who wore her livery and carried out a range of services, usually on a casual basis. She retained several men who supplied provisions to the household, such as Nigel Tebaud of Sudbury, Thomas Coteler of Ipswich, and Bartholomew Thomasin and Robert de Eynesham of London. Knights and clerics working in the royal government were valued by the Lady for expediting her legal and financial business, such as Sir John Shardlow, justice of the Court of Common Pleas, William Everdon and William Stowe, both barons of the exchequer, and John de St Pol, who often acted as deputy for the chancellor between 1334 and 1340 and became archbishop of Dublin. The knights and esquires who were retained by the Lady were often appointed to royal commissions as well as holding office and acting as her councillors, such as Sir Andrew de Bures and Sir Warin de Bassingbourne.[80] In addition to receiving livery, members of the household, both men and women, received grants of land, leases and rents. The Lady had in her gift several advowsons of parish churches which were given as rewards to councillors and officials, such as Thomas de Cheddeworth, who received Great Gransden church; John de Lenne received a grant of Ilketshall in Suffolk.[81]

Additional patronage for laymen, clerics and religious houses was facilitated by her close relationship with the king. The only time she successfully secured patronage from Edward II was in 1317, about the time of her marriage to Roger Damory, when Robert de Scales was granted exemption from taking up county offices.[82] Her petitions were more numerous under Edward III when men, such as Sir Andrew de Bures and Sir Warin de Bassingbourne, received what to them were useful concessions from the Crown.[83]

The Lady was well known for her patronage of religious foundations, and here again her close relationship with the Crown was important in enabling her to obtain the mortmain licences which were essential for her donations.[84] Her patronage ranged from the houses founded and supported by her ancestors, such as Anglesey priory where she often resided in the 1330s and early 1340s,[85] to the houses for the friars. Clare priory had been founded by her grandfather in 1248 and the Lady had a two-way relationship with the Augustinian friars: she made use of the friars in her chapel, while contributing to their sustenance, and building the chapter-house, refectory and dorter.[86] Her foundation of a Franciscan priory at Walsingham drew a vigorous protest from the Clare ancestral priory of Augustinian canons there.[87] Like many of her contemporaries, she was particularly drawn to the friars, and she patronised Franciscan nuns, the Minoresses, especially in London, and at Denny, Cambridgeshire, where the house was established by Marie de St Pol, countess of Pembroke.[88]

In establishing Clare Hall at Cambridge, Elizabeth de Burgh was initiating a new area of patronage for the Clare family; education for her was a major concern, at

---

[80] See below, pp.132–3.
[81] See below, p.133.
[82] See below, p.132.
[83] See below, pp.132–3.
[84] The Statute of Mortmain of 1279 forbade grants of property to the church, but this could be circumvented by royal licence.
[85] See below, pp.39, 134–6.
[86] *Monasticon Anglicanum*, VI, pp.1600–1602. See below, p.134.
[87] See below, pp.137–8.
[88] See below, pp.139, 143–4.

least from early in her long widowhood.[89] She was initially called on in 1336 by the university chancellor, Richard de Badew, founder of University Hall, to help his foundation financially, and she responded with the grant of the advowson of Litlington church, Cambridgeshire. She was unwilling to offer further help until Richard de Badew handed over to her all his rights as patron, and this was not achieved until 1346.[90] The Lady then acted quickly to grant two more advowsons to Clare Hall, as it was then and subsequently called, and to secure a licence for the Hall to acquire property worth up to £40 a year.

Looking at her religious patronage as a whole, she made a significant contribution to religious life in East Anglia. Much of the information on religious patronage is drawn from mortmain licences and charters for individual houses. In addition, her will displays the wider extent of her benefactions to all the houses connected with her Clare ancestors and herself in England and Wales.[91] Her respect for and generosity to the friars is apparent in her readiness to support many houses with which she had no earlier connection. She included in her list of gifts one monastery with which in the past her ancestors had sometimes had tense relations,[92] namely the abbey of Bury St Edmunds which received three cloths of gold.

Taken altogether, the Lady exercised patronage in East Anglia over the whole area of the bailiwick of Clare to the benefit of those people and communities connected with her ancestors and her own household. Although the licences and grants are written in formal language, the tone of the Lady's will and of the statutes of Clare Hall indicate that she had a clear idea of what she wanted; as was written in the statutes, 'We specially reserve to ourselves the power of interpreting, explaining and on reasonable grounds of adding to or taking from the said ordinances ... We ought as long as we live to know better than others what our intentions are.'[93] Her determination to make her power felt is apparent in her protest in 1360 over the activities of commissions of array on her manors in Essex and Suffolk.[94] Clare castle constituted the hub of her activities, and during her lifetime Clare itself enjoyed a prominence which made it well known among the people of Suffolk, East Anglia and the kingdom of England.

---

[89] See below, p.130.

[90] A.C. Chibnall, *Richard de Badew and the University of Cambridge, 1315–40* (Cambridge, 1963), pp.37–41.

[91] See below, pp.143–6.

[92] Tension had arisen from time to time in the twelfth and thirteenth centuries over the Clares' seizure of land and jurisdictional privileges.

[93] J. Heywood, *Early Cambridge University and College Statutes* (London, 1855), pp.113–40; the quotation is taken from p.140.

[94] See below, pp.139–40.

EDITORIAL CONVENTIONS

In this collection of documents, the emphasis has been put on Elizabeth de Burgh and Suffolk, although the structure of the bailiwick of Clare and the Lady's life and connections inevitably entail making reference to other regions. Documents have been chosen to illustrate the main types of household and estate accounts generated by the Lady's household, to show how the household functioned on a daily and yearly basis, and to throw light on the Lady's lifestyle. The wardrobe and household account of 1339–40 has been given in full: the account is complete and only minimally damaged, and it covers all aspects of the household for a year when the Lady was resident in the eastern counties, at Clare, Anglesey and Bardfield.[1] Otherwise, excerpts have been chosen from the household accounts to illustrate various aspects of the Lady's life during her widowhood, notably hospitality and food, journeys, patronage, education and almsgiving. Officials, servants and retainers were essential to the household, and the livery list of 1343 and the Lady's will of 1355 have therefore been included. Several excerpts refer to Clare castle, including the account for the autumn of 1326, and information on building work and furnishings. The choice of Clare manor and borough to illustrate the estates was dictated by the close links between manor and castle, and the information provided on the Lady's vigorous exercise of lordship.

Excerpts in Latin have been given of some types of household account which are also given in English translation. The translation has been kept fairly literal, but punctuation, the use of capital letters, and the use of I and J and U and V have been modernised. Place-names are given in their modern form. Surnames have been kept in their original spelling, but where a person occurs several times the surname has been standardised to a single original spelling. Where the name is clearly occupational, it has been translated. Marginal notes have been omitted where they repeat information in the text; otherwise they have been incorporated in the text, as have marginal headings. Dates are given as in the original document, with the modern form in square brackets.

The following conventions have been used:

\	/	for insertions in the document
~~agreement~~		for a word or phrase in the document which has been deleted
[*sic*]		for all editorial insertions
[*illeg.*]		illegible words or sentences
[*deleted*]		deleted and unreadable sections
[*damaged*]		damaged and unreadable sections
[*?*]		for a reading which is not certain

---

1   See below, pp.6–62. For the complete list of household accounts, see Appendix, below, pp.151–4.

The following measurements were used in the accounts:

Money
4 farthings = 1 penny (d.), in Latin quadrans = ¼d. and denarius = penny
2 halfpennies = 1 penny (d.), in Latin obolus = ½d.
12 pennies = 1 shilling (s.), in Latin solidus = shilling, today 1s. = 5p.
20 shillings = 1 pound (£), in Latin libra = pound, today £1 = 100p.
1 mark = 13s. 4d., in Latin marca = mark

Weight
16 ounces (oz.) = 1 pound (lb.), today 1lb. = 0.453 kilogram
1 stone = various weights (7–20lb.)
For grain and certain other commodities:
4 pecks = 1 bushel (b.)
8 bushels = 1 quarter (qr)

Area
40 square poles = 1 rood
4 roods = 1 acre, today 2.47 acres = 1 hectare

Length
12 inches = 1 foot, today 1 inch = 25.4 millimetres, 1 foot = 30.48 centimetres
3 feet = 1 yard, today 1 yard = 0.91 metre
5½ yards = 1 rod, pole or perch

Liquid measures
1 sester = usually 4 gallons, but 1 sester of ale might contain 12–14 gallons
1 pipe = 126 gallons, today 4.55 litres = 1 gallon
1 tun = 252 gallons

Roman numerals have been used in the extracts in the original language of the document; they have been given as Arabic numerals in the translation:

J = 1
iiij = 4
v = 5
x = 10
L = 50
iiij^{xx} = 80
c = 100[2]
m = 1,000

---

[2] For certain goods the long hundred was used, with c = 120. Where this occurs, v^{xx} = 100; c also denoted occasionally 112, 144, and 184. Figures in the text are calculated according to the long hundred where this is indicated.

I

ELIZABETH DE BURGH AND CLARE
Autumn 1326

Excerpts from the Chamber Account, 28 September to 19 October 1326[1]

[TNA E101/91/12]

[m. 3] [*Clare*] Wednesday, 15 October, there. Pantry: 145 loaves from stock. Buttery: 58 gallons of ale from stock. And 1 sester and 3 \gallons/ of wine from stock. Kitchen: 150 herring, 1s. 7d. by tally. Item 60 herring, 7½d. by tally. Item 6 stockfish and 3 cod from stock accounted for. Item 25 whiting, 7½d. by John de London. Item plaice and whiting, 1s. 8d. by John de London. Item ½ carcass of mutton from stock accounted for. Item delivered for the provisions of Sir William de la Beche and Robert de Cheddeworth and others from the household going to the Queen,[2] 40 cod from stock accounted for. Poultry: 1 capon, 3d.; 2 hens, 3d.; 5 pullets, 6¼d.; 8 chickens, 5d.; garlic, 1d.; 3 young doves, 1d.; cheese, 6d.; 50 eggs, 9d.; milk, 1d. Marshalsea: horses and grooms as on the previous day [*44 horses*] but there departed 3 coach-horses of the Lady, and 2 horses of William de Burgh, and 3 grooms of the Lady viz. Lorchoun, Thomas de Rushton, Colle de Routon \and David the page/, and 5 carthorses of the Lady and Walter the carter and Hailles \with his 2 grooms/ with the same. Item there departed Sir William de la Beche with 4 horses, John de Horslee with 1 horse and 1 groom, John de Glatton with 1 horse and 1 groom, Henry de Lucy with 1 horse and 1 groom, John de Scales with 1 horse, Thomas le Norreys with 3 horses, 1 horse of the Earl of Oxford,[3] Roger Tailor with 1 horse, Philip clerk of Brandon with 1 horse; there arrived Robert Mareschal with 1 horse and 1 groom. Sum of horses 21, of which 9 horses each took ½b. of oats and 4 horses ⅓b. each, and 8 horses 5 loaves each. Hay \for/ the said horses from the stock of Erbury.[4] Oats for the same, 5½ and ⅓b. and 40 loaves. Item for \1/ packhorse of William de Burgh arriving and departing that day, ⅓ [b.] of oats from the same stock. Wages of 1 yeoman, 9 grooms and 1 page, 1s. 4½d.

Sum of diet 8s. 9¾d. Pantry nothing. Kitchen 4s. 6d. Poultry 2s. 11¼d. Marshalsea 1s. 4½d.

[m. 1d] Wardrobe. For the expenses and wages of Thomas Catoun, sent to the King[5] with the Lady's letters, for 5 days ending on 30 September, receiving 2d.

---

1   The diet account was written on the face of the roll, and one day's account has been translated. Miscellaneous household information was entered on the dorse and this has been translated in full.

2   Queen Isabella, wife of Edward II.

3   The de Vere family, earls of Oxford, established the centre of their estates at Castle Hedingham, Essex, a few miles to the south of Clare.

4   Erbury was the name given in the fourteenth century to the manor of Clare.

5   Edward II.

a day, 10d. To William Pikerel for a German saddle bought from him in June last past for the use of William de Burgh, £1 4s. To the same for 1 saddle given by the Lady to Sir Nicholas de Clare in the same month, 18s. To the same for 3 coursers' saddles delivered to the Wardrobe in September, £1 16s. To the same for 1 saddle \for/ William de Burgh's courser purchased on 30 September, 15s. On the same day to William's servant by the Lady's gift for his expenses from London and returning, with the carriage of the said courser's saddle, 2s. On the same day for alms to Sir Robert the chaplain on the part of the Lady, 5d. On the same day for money delivered to William de Burgh for leather from 3 carcasses purchased to line his basinet and *skynebald*, 2s. To Simon Courier sent with the Lady's letters to the King, for his expenses for 3 days ending on 1 October, receiving 1s. a day, 3s., by her own hands. Offerings of the Lady and some of her Household at 2 masses celebrated on 4 October for the soul of Robert de Scales, 1s. 2d. To Thomas Ryot sent in haste to Cranborne [*Dorset*] to inform Sir William de la Beche and others there of the Queen's arrival, for his expenses and for 1 hackney of the Lady, for 3 days in going, ending on 27 September, because he returned in the company of Sir T[*homas*] de Cheddeworth, 1s. 3d. To Henry de Lucy for his expenses for 11½ days ending on 3 September, going from Clare to Portchester [*Hampshire*] with the Lady's letters addressed to the King, staying and returning, receiving 1s. a day, 11s. 6d. On 4 October to William de Burgh for repairing cord for hanging up his armour, 6d. by her own hands.

Sum £5 15s. 8d.

[m. 2d] Wardrobe. To a groom of Sir Robert de Wateville on 6 October of the Lady's gift, 1s. Item to Master Richard de Plessys for 1 book purchased by him in March, year 19 [*1326*] for the use of Nicholas Damory concerning the text of the civil law,[6] by her own hands, £2. Item to John de Horslee going twice to Cambridge and [*?*] Barkway on the Lady's private business, for his expenses without his groom, ending on 5 October, 1s. 4d. To Alexander le Bowier on 9 October for 10½lb. of wicks made by him for the office of the Chandlery, 1s. 1¼d. Item to the Prior of Walsingham's groom bringing 1 horse to the Lady on the part of the Prior and returning, for the same horse's expenses and his own expenses in going and returning, on the same day, 1s. On the same day to a groom of Sir E[*dward*], the King's son,[7] of William de Burgh's gift, 1s. To John de Horslee for\expenses/ of 2 horses for 1 night taking \Brother/ Richard de Conyngton[8] and his companion from Clare to Cambridge on 3 October with 1 groom's expenses looking after the said horses, 6d. To Matthew Clerk for 2 dozen and 3 skins of parchment, of which 3 skins for his writing and the rest for the Wardrobe, bought by him at Cambridge on 2 October with 2d. for ink, 5s. 3d. To the same for his wages for 5 days staying in Cambridge both because of illness and waiting for the sellers, receiving 2d. a day, ending on 2 October, 10d. To Robert Mareschal sent from Bardfield to Portchester to the King and staying there waiting for a reply and expediting his business, for his expenses for 10½ days ending on 18 September, receiving 1s. a day, 10s. 6d. To Walter de Cornerthe for 20lb. of candles of paris, price 2d. a lb., bought from him on 10 October, 3s. 4d. On 11 October to Danwe who was with Robert de Cheddeworth taking the Lady's

---

6   I.e. Roman law.
7   The eldest son of Edward II, who became king in 1327.
8   Richard de Conyngton was a Franciscan friar and theologian who was Provincial Minister of the order in England from 1310 to 1316. He spent the last years of his life at the Franciscan priory in Cambridge where he died in 1330.

letters to Robert de Islep, for his expenses, 10d. To Sir William de la Beche, sent on 5 October on the Lady's secret business, for his expenses delivered to him on the Lady's special order, ½ mark. To John Gough sent on similar business of the Lady for his expenses and 1 hackney of his for 2 days ending on 6 October with 3d. paid by him for horseshoes and guiding because he got lost at night, 1s.

Sum £3 14s. 4¼d.

[m. 3d] Memorandum of 1 horse-hide delivered to Robert de Middilton, John de Hailles and Walter Carter on 30 September for mending their carthorses' harness. Memorandum of 2 bridles delivered to John de Horslee for the horses sent with [*members of*] the Lady's household going to the Queen, 14 October, year 20 [*1326*]. Item for horseshoes delivered to John Smith on the same day for the same horses. 3 coursers' saddles delivered to John de Horslee on the same day. Wardrobe: To Henry de Lucy for 4¾ ells of camaca bought by him and delivered in the Lady's Chamber on 13 October for the use of William de Burgh, 18s. To him for 1¼ ounces of silk fringe for the same, 2s. To William de Burgh on 13 October for mending 1 sheep-skin for covering his basinet, 4d. To Roger Tailor coming from Brandon to Clare with 35lb. of pennies, for the expenses of 2 horses and 2 grooms coming, and his expenses of 1 horse and \1/ groom returning, ending on 15 October, 3s. Item on 14 October for alms distributed on the way by Roger Cook on behalf of the Lady going to Hedingham, 3d. On 15 October to the Earl of Oxford's servant returning with the Earl's palfrey, by gift of the Lady, 2s. On the same day to Thomas le Norreys for 1 black horse bought from him for mounting 1 man-at-arms going to the Queen, £8. On the same day to a groom sent to Robert de Cheddeworth to report rumours from the King's court, for his expenses in going, with 5d. delivered to him for shoe-repair, 1s. 2d. To Robert de Pentriz for money paid by him on occasion, viz. of the Lady's gift, to John Athel, £1. To William le Mereman, of similar gift, 10s. To Sir John Dyn for the forfeiture of 1 horse by which Robert de Scales died, £1. To the coroner of Essex for the said Robert, ½ mark. Item to the coroner's clerk, 2s. For summoning the suitors of the hundreds, 2s. And for 1 cloth lined with silk to put Robert's body in, 3s. 1d. Item to the same Robert for money paid by him of the Lady's gift to Master Richard Carpenter, £5. And to William le Pondere by similar gift, £1. Simon Courier sent to parts of Gloucestershire with the Lady's letters addressed to the Lord King for his expenses for 11 days ending on 15 October receiving 1s. a day, 11s. To the same for 1 hackney hired because his horse failed on the road, by the Lady's order, 1s. 3d. On 16 October to Alan de Medefeld's groom, of the Lady's gift, 1s. On the same day to Thomas de Braynford's groom by similar gift 6d. On the same day to John de London for the sewing of 4 canvas bags to put money in, 1d. To Walter de Cornerthe for 15lb. of candles of paris, price 2d. a lb., bought for the provisions of the Lady's household on 17 October, 2s. 6d. On the same day to Margaret de Lucy for the sewing of 2 pairs of linen sheets for the Lady's Chamber, 5d. On the same day to Thomas de Scales for ½ day's expenses going to the sacrist of Bury St Edmunds to fine for a horse, for his expenses, 6d. On the same day to Thomas de Braynford's groom carrying Thomas's letter to the Lady, of the Lady's gift \another time/, 6d. To John de Godeford for his wages for 5½ days between 14 March year 19 [*1326*] and 18 October year 20 [*1326*] on which he went on occasion to Sudbury for certain provisions there, receiving 6d a day, on the same day, 2s. 9d. To the same for the pay of Elias his groom sewing armour in the Lady's Wardrobe for 13 weeks ending on 18 October, receiving 2d. a week, 2s. 2d. Item to William Buntyng reeve of Hundon for making 15,600 faggots for the offices of the Bakehouse and Brewhouse at the beginning of the present year for the winter to come, £2 12s. To the same for felling large firewood in Hundon wood for the offices of the Kitchen and Chambers, 5s. 10d. To the same for providing 6b. of oats for the manor of Hundon's horses obtaining malt and lime in year 19 in Sir Alan's time and not previously allowed, 1s. 6d. To John Chamberlain for his expenses in going to Ipswich in September to provide black cloth for William de Burgh, 3½d. Item for the stitching of 2 pairs of linen sheets given to Stephen the Franciscan, 2d. To Matthew Clerk dismissed for an offence, for pay for his work for J[ohn] de London of the Lady's gift, 10s. To John Thony for his expenses for 39 days in August, September and October going on 2 journeys from Clare to Hugh de Courtenay and to Lady Maria and to others,[9] and to Sir John Gough to obtain money at Cranborne, receiving 6d. a day, with 1s. paid for 2 men escorting the money to Reading, according to the account made with him on 28 October, £1 0s. 6d.

Sum £24 3s. 5½d.

Wardrobe[10]   To Peryn of the Chamber sent to Ireland last August with the Lady's letters addressed to divers lords for part of his expenses in going, by her own hands, 1 mark. To William atte Halle for 11lb. of wicks bought by him and delivered in the Lady's Wardrobe on 17 October, 1s. 3d. To David Page for excess of his wages for 8 days in October going on 1 occasion to London with the Lady's letters and another time to Walsingham to obtain horses, by the Lady's letter, receiving ½d. a day, 4d. To Gilbert Robert for 9 gallons of verjuice bought from him in Sir Alan de Medefeld's time and not previously allowed, price 3d. a gallon, 2s. 3d. To the same for carriage of 2 tuns of wine bought from him last year and not previously allowed, 7d. To John de Whatefeld of the Lady's old debt from the time of Philip Clerk by the hands of Roger of the Buttery of £20 which Roger transferred to him in November, year 19 [1325], £8. To Sir Thomas de Cheddeworth, Sir John Gough and John de Horslee for divers gifts given by them to divers knights, serjeants and others in the business of obtaining a writ of oyer and terminer in Dorset regarding the prosecution of Sir William de Stoke and other trespassers, and for the expenses of Sir John de Stonor, justice in that business, and for the expenses of Sir William de la Beche, Sir T[homas] de Cheddeworth and others of the Lady's household with their horses and grooms going from Clare to Cranborne to prosecute the said business and their expenses in returning, as appears in the schedule attached to this roll and delivered to the Wardrobe by the said Sir Thomas, £52 16s. 8¼d.[11]

Sum £61 14s. 5¼d.

Fees   To Lady Ada la Brune for her fee for Michaelmas term last by her own hands on 18 October, 1 mark. To Matilda de Scales, Margaret de Lucy, Sir Robert the chaplain, Henry de Colingham, Sir John the chaplain, John de Scales, Thomas de Scales, John de Glatton, Henry de Lucy, Simon Courier, John de London, Robert Mareschal and John de Godeford, to each similarly for the fee for the said term 10s., £6 10s. To Master Roger Cook for the same, £1 10s. To Adam le Heaumer for the same, 2 marks. To Alice the laundress, \Robert Poulterer/ and Roger of the Buttery, ½ mark each, £1. Item to Elizabeth de Haliwell, Muriel de Melkele and

---

9   Hugh de Courtenay, styled earl of Devon from 1335; his son Hugh, earl of Devon, 1341–77, married Elizabeth de Burgh's cousin, Margaret de Bohun. Lady Maria was Marie de St Pol, countess of Pembroke, a close friend of Elizabeth de Burgh.

10   The paragraphs concerning the Wardrobe and Fees are in a different hand and format.

11   The schedule attached to the roll has not survived. Four commissions of oyer and terminer were issued on 18 July 1326, to Hugh de Courtenay, John de Stonor and others concerning hunting in Cranborne Chase and fishing in the Lady's fishery at Wareham; CPR, 1324–7, pp.347, 349, 351.

Ibote of the Chamber, 3s. 4d. each, 10s. To Peryn of the Chamber, Richard Petit, John Chamberlain, John Baker, John Porter, Robert Lusser, Robert de Middilton, John Gough, Simon Janitor, Henry le Whatte, Matthew Clerk, Thomas Catoun, and Richard Larderer, 5s. each for their similar fee, £3 5s. To John le Corour, Thomas Ryot, John le Foridere, Robert de Shirewode, Richard de Ottokeshath, Lorchoun le Stedman, Godwyn of the Wardrobe, Thomas de Rushton, Robert of the Nursery, John de Stafford, John de Hailles, Walter Carter, Richard Brewer, Adam of the Bakery, John de London of the Stable, James le Hunte, Nicholas of the Buttery, Robert of the Kitchen, John Wot \and Nicholas de Rompton, [*and*] Roger groom of Robert de Middilton/, 3s. 4d. each for their similar fee on the same day, £3 10s.

Sum £18 5s.

To John de Ingham for the arrears of all his fee except for Michaelmas term last, by the hands of Thomas Catoun handing the money over to him, £2. To John Barri, groom of John de Hailles, carter, serving for the whole year and looking after cart and carthorses for his fee and clothing, because he had received nothing previously except only wages by her own hands, 10s.

Sum of the Wardrobe for this week £106 12s. 10¾d.

II

THE WARDROBE AND HOUSEHOLD ACCOUNT
13–14 Edward III (1339–40)

[TNA, E101/92/11]

[m. 1] Computus Johannis de Lenne \custodis Garderobe domine E[*lizabethe*] de Burgo domine de Clare/ ab ultimo die Septembris\computatus/ anno regni Regis Edwardi tertii post conquestum xiij° usque xxix diem eiusdem mensis anno quartodecimo per unum annum integrum.

Idem oneratur de xxxvjli. xjs. ixd. ob. de arreragiis Gilberti de Cardoil et Domini Johannis Darre nuper custodum Garderobe domine respictis de tempore suo. Et de xvijli. iiijs. iijd. ob. de diversis rebus venditis super officia tempore eiusdem Johannis de Lenne unde officiarii de tempore suo tenentur ipsum acquietare tamen ut patet inferius domina fecit gratiam omnibus officiariis tam tempore dictorum Gilberti et Domini Johannis Darre quam tempore dicti Johannis de Lenne de omnibus superoneratis et venditis super compota sua tempore elapso.

Summa Liiili. xvjs. jd.   probatur

Halghton Idem respondet de Lxxvjs. receptis de Johanne atte Lye preposito de Halghton per unam acquietantiam in diversis emptis de eodem ut patet inferius.

Summa Lxxvjs.   probatur

Catthorp Idem respondet de vjli. xiiijs. vjd. receptis de Thoma preposito [*de*] Catthorp in diversis emptis de eodem pro expensis hospitii per unam acquietantiam.

[m. 1] The account of John de Lenne \Keeper of the Wardrobe of Lady E[*lizabeth*] de Burgh, Lady of Clare/ \counted/ from the last day of September in the 13th year of the reign of King Edward III after the conquest until the 29th day of the same month in the 14th year, for one whole year.

Arrears The same man is debited with £36 11s. 9½d. of the arrears of Gilbert de Cardoil and Sir John Darre, formerly Keepers of the Lady's Wardrobe, respited from their time. And of £17 4s. 3½d. from divers things sold on account in the time of John de Lenne for which the officials from his time are bound to acquit him, but as appears below the Lady pardoned all officials, both in the time of the said Gilbert and Sir John Darre and in the time of John de Lenne for their debts and sales on account in the time elapsed.

Sum £53 16s. 1d.   audited

Holton The same man answers for £3 16s. received from John atte Lye reeve of Holton by one acquittance for divers purchases from the same as appears below.

Sum £3 16s. 0d.   audited

Caythorpe The same answers for £6 14s. 6d. received from Thomas reeve [*of*] Caythorpe for divers things bought from the same for the provisions of the household by one acquittance.

Summa vjli. xiiijs. vjd.   probatur Cranebourne Idem respondet de xvs. receptis de Stephano Bonde preposito de Cranebone in carriagio [*bestiarum*] venaticarum et aliorum ut patet inferius per unam acquietantiam. Item de xxxijs. iijd. receptis de eodem per aliam acquietantiam.

Summa xlvijs. iijd.   probatur Farnham Idem respondet de xxs. iijd. ob. receptis de Edmundo Edward preposito ibidem in cunulis et expensis factis circa captionem dictorum per unam acquietantiam.

Summa xxs. iijd. ob.   probatur Honyden Idem respondet de vijli. xvs. xd. receptis de Ricardo atte Hache preposito ibidem in diversis receptis de eodem pro expensis hospitii per unam acquietantiam. Item de Ljli. iiijs. xd. receptis de eodem in frumento et aliis victualiis per aliam acquietantiam.

Summa Lixli. viijd.   probatur Luttirworth Idem respondet de vijli. xs. receptis de Henrico de Braundon preposito de Luttirworth in diversis receptis de eodem pro expensis hospitii per unam acquietantiam.

Summa vijli. xs.   probatur Staundon. Idem respondet de xxijli. xjs. \xd./ ~~ob.~~ qᵃ receptis de Willelmo Buntyng serviente de Staundon in frumento, ordeo et aliis per unam acquietantiam. Item de xli. ijs. iiijd. receptis de eodem per aliam acquietantiam. Item de vs. receptis de eodem de v multonibus de cronagio sine acquietantia.

Summa xxxijli. xixs. ijd. qᵃ. probatur Erbury Idem respondet de cxijli. xiijs. xd. receptis de Johanne Segor preposito de Erbury in frumento et aliis victualiis receptis de eodem per unam acquietantiam.

Summa cxijli. xiijs. xd.   probatur Wodehall Idem respondet de cijs. viijd. receptis de Ricardo atte Pole serviente de Wodehalle [*illeg.*] receptis de eodem per unam acqietantiam.

Sum £6 14s. 6d.   audited Cranborne The same answers for 15s. received from Stephen Bonde reeve of Cranborne for the carriage of venison and other things as appears below by one acquittance. Item for 32s. 3d. received from the same by another acquittance.

Sum £2 7s. 3d.   audited Farnham The same answers for £1 0s. 3½d. received from Edmund Edward reeve there for expenses incurred in the capture of rabbits by one acquittance.

Sum £1 0s. 3½d.   audited Hundon The same answers for £7 15s. 10d. received from Richard atte Hache reeve there for divers things received from the same for the provisions of the household by one acquittance. Item for £51 4s. 10d. received from the same for wheat and other victuals by another acquittance.

Sum £59 0s. 8d.   audited Lutterworth The same answers for £7 10s. received from Henry de Braundon reeve of Lutterworth for divers things received from the same for the provisions of the household by one acquittance.

Sum £7 10s. 0d.   audited Standon The same answers for £22 11s. \10d./ ½ ¼d. received from William Buntyng serjeant of Standon for wheat, barley and other things by one acquittance. Item for £10 2s. 4d. received from the same by another acquittance. Item for 5s. received from the same for 5 old sheep weeded out, without acquittance.

Sum £32. 19s. 2¼d.   audited Erbury The same answers for £112 13s. 10d. received from John Segor reeve of Erbury for wheat and other victuals received from the same by one acquittance.

Sum £112. 13s. 10d.   audited Woodhall The same answers for £5 2s. 8d. received from Richard atte Pole serjeant of Woodhall [*illeg.*] received from the same by one acquittance.

Summa cijs. viijd.   probatur

Berdefeld   Idem respondet de xviijli. xvjd. ob. receptis de Ricardo Warner serviente de Berdefeld in pis, ordeo et drageto receptis per unam acquietantam. Item de cvs. receptis de eodem in xxviij bovettis, boviculis, juvenculis et vitulis venientibus de Wodham pro expensis hospitii sine acquietantia.

Summa xxiijli. vjs. iiijd. ob.
[probatur]

Clarethall   Idem respondet de ciijs. iijd. receptis de Roberto Wulwy et Willelmo Cole prepositis de Clarette in diversis victualiis sine acquietantia.

Summa ciiijs. iijd.   probatur

Tonebrughall   Idem   respondet   de xxxjli. xixs. vjd. receptis de Roberto de Waldingfeld serviente de Tonebrughall in   diversis   victualiis   pro   expensis hospitii domine sine acquietantia.

Summa xxxjlb. [sic] xixs. vjd.
probatur

Usk   Idem respondet de viijli. viijs. vd. ob. receptis de Rogero de Wetherisfeld Receptatore de Usk in xxv bobus cronatis et expensis factis circa [bestiarum] venaticarum captione ibidem ut patet per unam indenturam sine acquietantia.

Summa viijli. viijs. vd. ob. probatur

Vendicio   apud   [Hempsted]   Idem respondet de xijs. vd. de foragio vendito apud Hempsted pro sufficientia bovibus domine.

Summa xijs. vd.   probatur

Vendicio   frumenti   Idem   respondet de cxs. receptis de Willelmo Buntyng serviente de Staundon pro xxj quarteriis frumenti venditis per eundem cum j quarterio de avantagio, pretium quarterii vs.vjd. Item de cxviijs. ijd. receptis de Rogero de Panetria pro xx quarteriis frumenti venditis Londinii. Item de Liijs. iiijd. receptis de predicto Willelmo Buntyng pro x quarteriis v bussellis frumenti cum v bussellis de avantagio venditis per eundem. Item de iiijli xixs. iiijd. in xxxix quarteriis vij bussellis frumenti venditis Margarete

Sum £5 2s. 8d.   audited

Bardfield   The same answers for £18 1s. 4½d. received from Richard Warner serjeant of Bardfield for peas, barley and dredge received by one acquittance. Item for £5 5s. 0d. received from the same for 28 steers, bullocks, heifers and calves coming from Woodham for provisions of the household without acquittance.

Sum, £23 6s 4½d.
[audited]

Claret   The same answers for £5 4s. 3d. received from Robert Wulwy and William Cole reeves of Claret for divers victuals without acquittance.

Sum £5 4s. 3d.   audited

Tunbridge Hall   The same answers for £31 19s. 6d. received from Robert de Waldingfeld serjeant of Tunbridge Hall for divers victuals for provisions of the Lady's household without acquittance.

Sum £31 19s. 6d.
audited

Usk   The same answers for £8 8s. 5½d. received from Roger de Wetherisfeld Receiver of Usk for 25 old oxen and for expenses incurred in the capture of venison there as appears by one indenture without acquittance.

Sum £8 8s. 5½d.   audited

Sale at [Hempstead]   The same answers for 12s. 5d. for the sale of fodder at Hempstead for the maintenance of the lady's oxen.

Sum 12s. 5d.   audited

Sale of wheat   The same answers for £5 10s. received from William Buntyng serjeant of Standon for 21qr of wheat sold by the same with 1qr from increment, price of qr 5s. 6d. Item for £5 18s. 2d. received from Roger of the Pantry for 20qr sold in London. Item for £2 13s. 4d. received from the said William Buntyng for 10qr 5b. with 5b. from increment sold by the same. Item for £4 19s. 4d. for 39qr 7b. wheat sold to Margaret Gregg, deficient out of 210qr wheat bought from the same in the year last past. Item for 6s. received for 1qr

Gregg deficientibus de ij^{c}x quarteriis frumenti emptis de eadem anno ultimo preterito. Item de vjs. receptis de j quarterio frumenti vendito custodi boviculorum de manerio apud Honised[en].

Summa xixli. vjs. xd.   probatur

Vendicio ordei   Idem respondet de xls. receptis de Ricardo Warner serviente de Berdef[eld] de xij quarteriis ordei debilis venditis per eundem.

Summa xls.   probatur

Vendicio brasei ordei   Idem respondet de xxxijs. receptis de viij quarteriis brasei ordei venditis per Hugonem le Charer pretium quarterii iiijs. Item de xijd. receptis de Domino Willelmo d'Arderne pro iij bussellis ordei deficientibus de mensura brasei ordei recepta apud Queye. Item de Ljs. vd. ob. receptis de xj quarteriis vij bussellis brasei ordei venditis per Ithel pretium quarterii iiijs. iiijd. Et de iiijs. iiijd. receptis de j quarterio brasei ordei vendito per eundem. Et de xijs. iijd. de ij quarteriis vj bussellis dj brasei ordei venditis [illeg.]¹

~~Summa~~

Summa cjs. ob.   probatur

Vendicio [avene] Idem respondet de xxxixs. receptis de xiij quarteriis v bussellis avene cum v bussellis de avantagio venditis per W Buntyng servientem de Staundon.

Summa xxxixs.   probatur

Vendicio allecis albi   Idem respondet de xxxs. receptis de iiij barellis allecis albi venditis per W de Manton Ebercto Buntyng de Clare.

Summa xxxs. probatur

Vendicio ferri, veteris ferri carectarum   Idem respondet de ixs. q^a receptis de iiij paribus rotarum carectarum ferratarum venditis Petro Fabro de Clare. Item de iiijs. vjd. receptis de c ferris Ispaneis venditis. Item de j pare rotarum vendito preposito de ~~Erbury~~ \Clarette/ pretio ijs. vjd.

Summa xvjs. q^a.   probatur

wheat sold to the keeper of the bullocks of the manor at Hundon.

Sum £19 6s. 10d.   audited

Sale of barley   The same answers for £2 received from Richard Warner serjeant of Bardfield for 12qr of poor-quality barley sold by the same.

Sum £2.   audited

Sale of malt barley   The same answers for £1 12s. received for 8qr of malt barley sold by Hugh le Charer, price of qr 4s. Item for 12d. received from Sir William d'Arderne for 3b. of barley deficient out of the measure of malt barley received at Quy. Item for £2 11s. 5½d. received for 11qr 7b. sold by Ithel, price of qr 4s. 4d. And for 4s. 4d. received for 1qr sold by the same. And 12s. 3d. for 2qr 6½b. sold to [illeg.].³

~~Sum~~

Sum £5 1s. 0½d.   audited

Sale [of oats]   The same answers for £1 19s. received for 13qr 5b. of oats with 5b. from increment sold by W[illiam] Buntyng serjeant of Standon.

Sum £1 19s.   audited

Sale of white herring   The same answers for £1 10s. received for 4 barrels of white herring sold by W[illiam] de Manton to Eberct Buntyng of Clare.

Sum £1 10s.   audited

Sale of iron, old iron of carts   The same answers for 9s. 0¼d. received for 4 pairs of iron-hooped cart wheels sold to Peter Smith of Clare. Item for 4s. 6d. received from 1 cwt of Spanish iron sold. Item for 1 pair of wheels sold to the reeve of ~~Erbury~~ \Claret/ price 2s. 6d.

Sum 16s. 0¼d.   audited

---

¹   The last two sentences of the entry were added.   ³   The last two sentences of the entry were added.

Vendicio equorum   Idem respondet de ixs. receptis de j hakeno vendito Johanni Gough. Item de ix\s./ receptis de j hakeno griselo vendito per Ithel. Item de xls. receptis de j equo vocato Doun Colyngham vendito per Willelmum Seman. Item de xxvjs. viijd. de j dextrario vocato Morel Notthern vendito per eundem.

Summa iiijli. iiijs. viijd.   probatur
Vendicio coreorum bovum, exitus bovum   Idem respondet de vs. receptis de j bovetto de Wodham vendito per Ricardum Warner servientem de Berdef[eld]. Item de xxvijli. xviijs. xjd. receptis de clxxix coreis bovum, vaccarum et boviculorum venditis per Dominum Willelmum de Manton. Item de Lxiiijs. ijd. receptis de cviij exitibus bovum, vaccarum et boviculorum venditis per eundem.

Summa xxxjli. viijs. jd.   probatur
Vendicio exitus porcorum   Idem respondet de xxs. vd. qᵃ receptis de exitibus cxix porcorum venditis per dictum Dominum W.

Summa xxs. vd. qᵃ.   probatur
Vendicio pellettarum   Idem respondet de vjli. xs. jd. receptis de pellibus et pellettis iiijᶜlxxvj multonum venditis per dictum Dominum W et de xijs. xjd. qᵃ receptis de exitibus cxl multonum venditis per eundem.

Summa vijli. iijs. qᵃ.   probatur
Vendicio lane et pellium cuniculorum   Idem respondet de xvjs. receptis de xxx velleribus venditis Domino Johanni Capellano de Thrillowe per dictum Dominum W et de xvs. xjd. receptis de ijᶜxxxiij pellibus coniculorum \c computatum per vjˣˣ/ venditis apud Clare per eundem.

Summa xxxjs. xjd.   probatur
Exitus Lardarii   Idem respondet de cxvijs. xd. ob. receptis de iiijˣˣviij petris cepi et cxliiij lagenis crasse \c per vˣˣ/ venditis per eundem.

Summa cxvijs. xd. ob.   probatur
Exitus bracine   Idem respondet de xlvjs. viijd. receptis de drassis venditis

Sale of horses   The same answers for 9s. received for 1 hackney sold to John Gough. Item for 9\s/. received for 1 grey hackney sold by Ithel. Item for £2 received for 1 horse called Doun Colyngham sold by William Seman. Item for £1 6s. 8d. for 1 destrier called Morel Notthern sold by the same.

Sum £4 4s. 8d.   audited
Sale of oxhides, entrails of oxen   The same answers for 5s. received for 1 steer from Woodham sold by Richard Warner serjeant of Bardfield. Item for £27 18s. 11d. received for 179 hides of oxen, cows and bullocks sold by Sir William de Manton. Item for £3 4s. 2d. received for the entrails of 108 oxen, cows and bullocks sold by the same.

Sum £31 8s. 1d.   audited
Sale of entrails of pigs   The same answers for £1 0s. 5¼d. received for the entrails of 119 pigs sold by the said W[illiam].

Sum £1 0s. 5¼d.   audited
Sale of sheepskins   The same answers for £6 10s. 1d. received from skins and pelts of 476 sheep sold by the said Sir W[illiam] and for 12s. 11¼d. received from the entrails of 140 sheep sold by the same.

Sum £7 3s. 0¼d.   audited
Sale of wool and rabbitskins   The same answers for 16s. received from 30 fleeces sold to Sir John Chaplain of Thurlow by the said Sir W[illiam] and for 15s. 11d. received for 273 rabbitskins \100 counted as 120/ sold at Clare by the same.

Sum, £1 11s. 11d.   audited
Issues of the Larder   The same answers for £5 17s. 10½d. received from 88 stones of suet and 144 gallons of grease \100 counted as 100/ sold by the same.

Sum £5 17s. 10½d.   audited
Issues of the Brewery   The same answers for £2 6s. 8d. received from

per Adam Braciatorem per tempus istius compoti.

~~Summa~~

[m. 2] Summa xlvjs. viijd.probatur

Minora recepta Idem respondet de iiijli. xijs. receptis de diversis proficuis de rebus emptis de vicario de Fynchingfeld apud Cokefeld ut patet per parcellas hunc rotulum consutas. Et de vs. receptis de Nigello Tebaud. Et de xxjd. receptis de Panetario.

Summa iiijli. xviijs. ixd.   probatur

Recepta denariorum Idem respondet de m^{l}vj^{c}lxxvjli. xs. jd. ob. q^a receptis de Domino Roberto de Stalynton per j indenturam.

Summa m^{l}vj^{c}lxxvjli. xs. jd. ob. q^a.

probatur

Vendicio super compotum Idem oneratur de lxxiiijs. iiijd. ob. de diversis rebus deficientibus et venditis super compotum.

Summa lxxiiijs. iiijd. ob.   probatur

~~Summa totius recepte preter arreragia et vendita super compotum m^{l}m^{l}lxvjli. viijs. xd. q^a~~[2]

Summa totius recepte cum arreragiis m^{l}m^{l}cxxiijli. xixs. iijd. ob. q^a probatur

Excessus In excessu ultimi compoti sui anni precedentis Lixli. xvijs. vd.

Summa Lixli. xvijs. vd.   probatur

---

malt dregs sold by Adam the brewer for the time of this account.

~~Sum~~

[m. 2] Sum £2 6s. 8d.   audited

Lesser receipts The same answers for £4 12s. received from divers profits from things bought from the vicar of Finchingfield at Cockfield as appears by the particulars sewn to this roll.[4] And for 5s. received from Nigel Tebaud. And for 1s. 9d. received from the Pantler.

Sum £4 18s. 9d.   audited

Money received The same answers for £1,676 10s. 1¾d. received from Sir Robert de Stalynton by 1 indenture.

Sum £1,676 10s. 1¾d.

audited

Sold on account The same is debited with £3 14s. 4½d. from divers things missing and sold on account.

Sum £3 14s. 4½d.   audited

~~Sum of all receipts except arrears and sales on account £2,066 8s. 10¼d.~~[5]

Sum of all Receipts with Arrears £2,123 19s. 3¾d.   audited

Surplus In surplus on his last account of the preceding year £59 17s. 5d.

Sum £59 17s. 5d.   audited

---

[2]   Marginal totals have only been included when they differ from the total in the main body of the document. In this case, as is usual with marginal totals, it has been crossed out.

[4]   This schedule has not survived.

[5]   This marginal total differs from the main total.

Purchase of wheat from the manors   The same accounts for 20qr of wheat bought from William Buntyng serjeant of Standon on 17 May and sent to Stepney against the Lady's arrival there, price 6s. a qr, £6. 21qr with 1qr from increment bought from the same on 5 August, price 5s. 6d. a qr, £5 10s. 10qr 5b. with 5b. from increment bought from the same on 5 August, price 5s. 4d. a qr, £2 13s. 4d. Item 125qr 6b. bought from Richard atte Hache reeve of Hundon on 27 September, price 6s. a qr, £37 14s. 6d. 208qr 4b. bought from John Segor reeve of Erbury on 27 September, price 6s. a qr, £62 11s. 1qr bought from the same on the same day 4s. 8d. Item 60qr bought from Robert de Waldingfeld serjeant of Tunbridge Hall, price 6s. 6d. a qr, £19 10s.

Sum 446qr 7b.; £134 3s. 6d.   audited

Purchase of wheat in the region   The same accounts for 9qr of wheat bought from Edmund Wymer bailiff of Stebbing in January, price 6s. a qr, £2 14s. Item 7qr bought at [North] Weald in June, price 7s. a qr, £2 9s. 20qr bought at Yeldham from the bailiff of Henry \Dars'/ there, price 5s. 6d. a qr, £5 10s. Item 10qr 4b. with 4b. from increment bought from the rector of Birdbrook in September, price 3s. 4d. a qr, £1. 13s. 4d.

Sum 46qr 4b.; £12 6s. 4d.   audited

Purchase of peas, beans, vetch and maslin from the manors   The same accounts for 2qr 1b. of peas bought from Richard atte Hache reeve of Hundon for the Marshalsea on 27 September, price 3s. a qr, 6s. 4½d. 11qr 4b. of peas, of which 8qr were for the Marshalsea, bought from John Segor reeve of Erbury on 27 September, price 3s. a qr, £1 14s. 6d. 4b. of peas bought from Richard Warner serjeant of Bardfield on 27 September, price 6d. a b., 2s. 4qr 4b. of peas bought from Robert Waldingfeld serjeant of Tunbridge Hall for the pigs of the Larder coming from Brandon, price 2s. 4d. a qr, 10s. 6d. 1qr 4b. of maslin bought from William Cole serjeant of Claret for provender of the horses, 6s. 5d. 1qr 4b. of peas bought from the same, 4s. 6d. 3qr 4b. of vetch bought from the same, 7s.

Sum 20qr 1b.of peas, ~~beans~~, 3qr 4b. of vetch, 1qr 4b. of maslin; £3 11s. 3 ½d.

audited

Purchase of peas and beans in the region   The same accounts for 2qr of peas bought from Edmund Wymer bailiff of Stebbing in January, price 3s. a qr, 6s. Item 5qr of peas bought from Simon Peek farmer of Woodham, price 3s. 4d. a qr, 16s. 8d. 3qr of beans bought from the same, price 4s. a qr, 12s.

Sum 10qr; £1 14s. 8d.   audited

Purchase of barley from the manors   The same accounts for 15qr of barley bought from William Buntyng serjeant of Standon on 17 May, price 3s. 4d. a qr, £2 10s. 35qr 5b. bought from John Segor reeve of Erbury on 27 September, price 3s.4d. a qr, £5 18s. 9d. 20qr bought from Richard atte Pole serjeant of Woodhall on 27 September, price 3s. 4d. a qr, £3 6s. 8d. 13qr 4b. bought from Richard Warner serjeant of Bardfield, price 4s. a qr on 27 September, £2 14s. 12qr 4b. with 4b. from increment bought from the same on the same day, price 3s. 4d. a qr, £2. 43qr bought from Robert Waldingf[eld] serjeant of Tunbridge Hall, price 3s. a qr, £6 9s. 15qr 4b. bought from Robert Wulwy serjeant of Claret, price 3s. a qr, £2 6s. 6d.

Sum 155qr 1b.; £25 4s. 11d.   audited

Purchase of barley in the region   The same accounts for 100qr of barley bought from Sir Alan and Sir Geoffrey farmers of Swaffham on 16 October, price 2s. 4d. a qr, £11 13s. 4d. 14qr bought from the rector of Wilbraham on the same day, price 2s. 4d. a qr, £1 12s. 8d. 10qr bought from Richard Skilman of Quy on the same day, price 2s. 4d. a qr, £1 3s. 4d. 24qr bought from John de Ludgate and Richard his brother on the same day, price 2s. 8d. a qr, £3 4s. 4qr bought from John Ward of Stoke, price 2s. 8½d. a qr, 10s. 10d. 21qr with 1qr from increment bought from the farmer of Gazeley on the same day, price 2s. 6d. a qr, £2 10s., with 1d. for God's penny.[6] 42qr with 2qr from increment bought from the rector of Shelford on the same day, price 2s. a qr, £4. Item 4qr bought from John Turnecourt on 1 November, price 2s. 10d. a qr minus in total 1d., 11s. 3d. 1qr bought from a man of Bartlow, price 2s. 8d. a qr. 5qr bought from Matthew Skilman on the same day, price 2s. 4d. a qr, 11s. 8d. 6½qr bought at Haverhill on the same day, price 2s. 8d. a qr plus in total 2d., 17s. 6d. 10qr 4b. with 4b. from increment bought from the parson of Ashen, price 2s. 8d. a qr, £1 6s. 8d. 21qr with 1qr from increment bought from John Chapman of Bumpstead, price 2s. 8d. a qr, £2 13s. 4d. For William Butler's wages going from Bardfield to Anglesey and in parts of Cambridge[*shire*]for the aforesaid purchases for 8½ days in the same month, 8s. 6d. Item 10qr 7b. with 4b. from increment bought at Hempstead from Margaret Gregg on 7 November, price 2s. 6d. a qr, £1 5s. 11¼d. 11qr with 1qr from increment bought from the vicar of Finchingfield on the same day, price 2s. 6d. a qr, £1 5s. 15qr bought in parts of Cambridge[*shire*] by William Butler on 8 November, price 2s. 4d. a qr £1 15s. 12qr bought from the parson of Wratting on the same day, price 2s. 8d. a qr, £1 12s. 12qr bought from John de Ludgate and Richard his brother on the same day, price 2s. 8d. a qr, £1 12s. For William Butler's wages going from Bardfield to parts of Cambridge[*shire*] and Clare for the aforesaid purchases, staying and returning, for 3½ days, 3s. 6d. Item 1qr 4b. bought from John de Ludgate on 4 December, price 2s. 8d. a qr, 4s. 21qr with 1qr from increment bought from the vicar of Finchingfield in November, price 2s. 4d. a qr, £2 6s. 8d. Item 10qr bought from Edmund Wymer serjeant of Stebbing in April, price 3s. 8d. a qr, £1 16s. 8d. 10qr 4b. with 4b. from increment bought from the vicar of Finchingfield in September, price 2s. a qr, £1.

Sum 366qr 7b.; £44 6s. 7¼d.   audited

Purchase of dredge from the manors   The same accounts for 13qr 4b. of dredge bought from William Buntyng serjeant of Standon on 17 May, price 3s. a qr, £2 0s. 6d. 23qr bought from Richard atte Hache reeve of Hundon on 27 September, price 2s. 8d. a qr, £3 1s. 4d. 30qr 2b. bought from John Segor reeve of Erbury on 27 September, price 2s. 8d. a qr, £4 0s. 8d. 9qr 6b. bought from Richard atte Pole serjeant of Woodhall on 27 September, price 2s. 8d. a qr, £1 6s. 12qr bought from Richard Warner serjeant of Bardfield on 27 September, price 3s. a qr, £1 16s. 44qr bought from Robert Walding[*feld*] serjeant of Tunbridge Hall, price 2s. 6d. a qr, £5 10s. 5qr 4b. bought from Robert Wulwy serjeant of Claret, price 2s. 6d. a qr, 13s. 9d.

Sum 138qr; £18 8s. 3d.   audited

[m. 3] Purchase of dredge in the region   The same accounts for 31qr of dredge with 1qr from increment bought from John le Baker of Shelford on 16 October, price 1s. 7d. a qr, £2 7s. 6d. For Robert Schirwode's expenses going there for the aforesaid purchase and for paying cash, staying and returning, for 2 days, 6d. Item 2qr 6b. bought at Haverhill on 1 November, price 1s. 8d. a qr, 4s. 7d. 10qr 4b. with 4b. from increment bought from the parson of Ashen on the same day, price 1s. 10d. a qr, 18s. 4d. 21qr with 1qr from increment bought from John Chapman of Bumpstead on the same day, price 2s. 8d. a qr, £2 13s. 4d. Item 10qr 6b. with 4b. from increment bought from Margaret Gregg at Hempstead on 7 November, price 2s. 2d.

---

6   The payment of 1d. for God's penny indicates that the purchase was made on credit.

a qr, £1 2s. 2½d. 6qr bought at Haverhill by William Butler on 8 November, price 2s. a qr, 12s. 2qr bought in parts of Cambridge[*shire*] by the same on the same day, price 1s. 10d. a qr, 3s. 8d. 20qr bought from the rector of Wilbraham, price 1s. 10d. a qr, £1 16s. 8d. 21qr with 1qr from increment bought at Clare in the same month, price 2s. 2d. a qr, £2 3s. 4d. For the expenses of William Butler going there for the said purchase, staying and returning, for 4½ days in the same month, 4s. 4d. For the expenses of the cart of the prior of Anglesey carting dredge from Shelford to Anglesey for 1 day, 3d. Item 23qr with 1qr from increment bought from the vicar of Finchingfield in November, price 2s. 2d. a qr, £2 7s. 8d. Item 6½qr bought from Edmund Wymer serjeant of Stebbing in April, price 2s. 8d. a qr, 17s. 4d. 10qr 4b. with 4b. from increment bought from the vicar of Finchingfield in September, price 2s. a qr, £1.

Sum 165qr 4b.; £16 11s. 8½d.   audited

Purchase of malt dredge from the manors   The same accounts for 62qr 2b. of malt dredge bought from John Segor reeve of Erbury on 27 September, price 3s. 4d. a qr, £10 7s. 6d. 5qr 6b. of \malt/, for multure from 160qr of malt, bought from the same on the same day, price 3s. 4d. a qr, 19s. 2d.

Sum 68qr; £11 6s. 8d.   audited

Making of malt   The same accounts for the wages of Geoffrey maltmaker being at Clare for maltmaking from the last day of September until 30 October, both days counted, viz. for 31 days taking per day 2d., 5s. 2d. Wages of the same being at Clare for maltmaking from the last day of October until 27 November, both days counted, viz. for 28 days at the above daily wage, 4s. 8d. Geoffrey's wages, left at Clare after the Lady's departure, making malt in November and December for 17 days, 2s. 10d. His wages there from 25 December until 22 January, both days counted, viz. for 28 days as above, 4s. 8d. Pay of 1 groom helping him from 18 October until 26 December, both days counted, viz. for 10 weeks taking 6d. a week, 5s. The same man's pay being there from 27 December until 23 January, both days counted, viz. for 4 weeks taking per week as above, 2s. 1 woman's pay drying malt there from 3 November until 26 December, both days counted, viz. for 7 weeks and 5 days taking 5d. a week, 3s. 3d. Her pay there from 27 December until 23 January, both days counted, viz. for 4 weeks taking per week as above, 1s. 8d. Item for the wages of Geoffrey maltmaker being at Clare from 23 January until 30th day of the same month, both [*days*] counted, viz. for 8 days, 1s. 4d. Pay of 1 man helping him from the said 23 January until 19 February, both days counted, viz. for 4 weeks taking per week as above, 2s. Pay of 1 woman drying malt there for the same time taking per week as above, 1s. 8d. Item for 1 cart hired at Anglesey 4 times to cart barley, dredge and malt barley and dredge from Wilbraham, Lode and elsewhere to the granary at Anglesey, 3s. 4d. Pay of divers men loading the said cart, measuring and unloading malt at divers times there, 2s. 2d. Item given to the carters of the priors of Anglesey and Swaffham for divers help given at divers times, 4d. Item given to the winnowers of Anglesey and Wilbraham for cleaning barley and dredge by turns, 4d. Pay of 1 groom going from Anglesey to Shelford to the rector's bailiff there to warn him to prepare barley and dredge on 2 occasions, 2d. For going to the said granary with the keys bought for it, 2d. Item for the wages of Geoffrey maltmaker being at Clare about his office from 28 February until 18 March, both days counted, viz. for 20 days taking as above, 3s. 4d. Pay of 1 man helping him from 20 February until 18 March taking per week as above, 2s. Pay of 1 woman drying malt there for the same time taking per week as above, 1s. 8d. Item for making 263qr malt at Anglesey by view of Sir William d'Arderne at 4d. a qr, £4 7s. 8d. Item for wages of Geoffrey maltmaker left at Clare after the Lady's departure from 20 March to 15 April, both days counted, taking as above, 4s. 8d. Pay of 1 groom helping him for the same time taking per week as above, 2s. Pay of the same woman drying malt there for the same time taking per week as above, 1s. 8d. Item for wages of Geoffrey maltmaker left at Clare after the Lady's departure, the Lady being at Anglesey, from 16 April until 18th day of the same month, both days counted, viz. for 3 days, 6d. Pay of 1 groom helping him from the said 16 April until 13 May, both days counted, taking as above, 2s. Pay of the same woman drying malt there for the same time taking as above, 1s. 8d. Pay of 1 groom helping Geoffrey maltmaker from 14 May until 3 June, both days counted, viz. for 3 weeks taking per week 6d., 1s. 6d. Item given to the same groom remaining in the brewhouse from 18 October until 3 June by agreement made by Roger of the Pantry for his labour for the said time, 2s. Pay of 1 woman drying malt there for the same time taking per week 5d., 1s. 3d. Item given to the same woman staying in the brewhouse from 3 November until 3 June by agreement made by the said Roger for her labour for the whole time, 2s. Item in making 107qr 4b. of malt in the vill of Bardfield at 4d. a qr, £1 15s. 10d. For carting 33qr of malt from Lode to Anglesey after the departure of the Lady in May by Sir William d'Arderne, 6d. For making 14qr of malt by Eva West in the vill of Bardfield at 4d. a qr, 4s. 8d.[7]

Sum £9 15s. 8d.   audited

Purchase of oats from the manors   The same accounts for 1qr 3b. of oats bought from William Buntyng serjeant of Standon for provender for the lady's horses going from Anglesey to London with Lady de Ferrers, staying there for 1 night, and to reward the carthorses taking barley and dredge from there to Bardfield at divers times, price 2s. 2d. a qr, 2s. 11¾d. 13qr 5b. with 5b. from increment bought from the same on 5 August, price 3s. a qr, £1 19s. Item 77qr 6½b. bought from Richard atte Hache reeve of Hundon on 27 September, price 2s. a qr, £7 15s. 7½d. 44qr 3b. bought from John Segor reeve of Erbury on the same day, price 2s. a qr, £4 8s. 9d. 5qr bought from Richard atte Pole serjeant of Woodhall on the same day, price 2s. a qr, 10s. 21qr bought from Richard Warner serjeant of Bardfield on the same day, price 2s. a qr £2 2s. 3b. bought from the same on the same day for the food-allowance of the swans, 9d. 3qr 6½b. bought from the same on the same day for provisions for the waggon-oxen in 305 sheaves, price 2s. a qr, 7s. 7½d.

Sum 167qr 3b.; £17 6s. 8¾d.   audited

Purchase of oats in the region   The same accounts for 43qr 4b. of oats with 3qr 4b. from increment bought from Sir Richard Talworth on 8 October, price 1s. 8d. a qr, £3 6s. 8d. 10qr 4b. with 4b. from increment bought from John Bumpsted by John Gough on 10 October, 13s. 4d. 42qr with 2qr from increment bought from John de Bendisch by John Gough on the same day, price 1s. 6d. a qr, £3. 12qr 4b. with 4b. from increment bought from the vicar of Finchingfield by John Gough, price 1s. 2d. a qr, 14s. 52qr 4b. with 2qr 4b. from increment bought from the rector of Birdbrook on 12 October, price 1s. 4d. a qr, £3 6s. 8d. 2qr 4b. bought from John Bumpsted by John Gough on 17 October, price 1s. 4d. a qr, 3s. 4d. 6qr 2b. with 2b. from increment bought from the bailiff of Sturmer Hall in the same month, price 1s. 4d. a qr, 8s. 26qr 2b. with 1qr 2b. from increment bought from John Houell in the same month, price 1s. 6d. a qr, £1 17s. 6d. 10qr 4b. with 4b. from increment bought from the prior of Dunmow at Poslingford, price 1s. 4d. a qr, 13s. 4d. 21qr with 1qr from

---

7   The last sentence of the entry was added.

increment bought from John Bendisch in the same month, price 1s. 6d. a qr, £1 10s. 21qr with 1qr from increment bought from the rector of Birdbrook on 28 October, price 1s. 4d. a qr, £1 6s. 8d. Item 21qr with 1qr from increment bought from Walter deThaxted, farmer of the rectory of Bardfield,[8] on 1 November. price 1s. 6d. a qr, £1 10s. 10qr 4b. with 4b. from increment bought from the parson of Ashen on the same day, price 1s. 4d. a qr, 13s. 4d. 10qr 4b. with 4b. from increment bought from John Bendisch on the same day, price 1s. 6d. a qr, 15s. \10qr 4b. with 4b. from increment bought from William Bloy, price 1s. 6d. a qr, 15s./ Item 42qr with 2qr from increment bought from John de Gilingham, farmer of Walter de Finchingf[ield] at Finchingfield, price 1s. 6d. a qr, £3. 52qr 4b. with 2qr 4b. from increment bought from John Semoner of Stambourne on 2 December, price 1s. 4d. a qr, £3 6s. 8d. 84qr with 4qr from increment bought from the vicar of Finchingfield on 17 December, price 1s. 4d. a qr, £5 6s. 8d. Item 105qr with 5qr from increment bought from Walter de Greneville on 13 February, price 1s. 6d. a qr, £7 10s. 21qr with 1qr from increment bought from Master Walter de Thaxted, farmer of Bardfield, price 1s. 8d. a qr, £1 13s. 4d. 21qr with 1qr from increment bought from Swetyng, farmer of Bigods iuxta Bardfield, price 1s. 8d. a qr, £1 13s. 4d. 12qr with 4b. from increment bought from the executors of Henry de Thrillawe, price 1s. 6d. a qr, 18s. 7qr 4b. bought in Cambridge market, price 2s. a qr, 15s. For carriage of the said oats to the water and by water to Anglesey with John Gough's expenses on 25 February, 8½d. 5qr bought at Westley by John Gough on 28 February, price 2s. 2d. a qr, 10s. 10d. 16qr bought by the same\there/ in the same month, price 2s. 4d. a qr, £1 17s. 4d. Item 19qr bought at Wisbech on 8 March, price 2s. 1d. a qr, £1 19s. 7d. 16qr bought there on 18 March by Walter Gilbert, £1 14s. 8d. 20qr bought there on 1 April, price 2s. 2d. a qr, £2 3s. 4d. Item 32qr bought at Wisbech on 10 April, price 2s. 3d. a qr, £3 12s. 6qr bought at Westley from Walter Wille on the same day, price 2s. 4d. a qr, 14s. Item 21qr with 1qr from increment bought from Adam de Wetherisfeld on 20 April, price 2s. 4d. a qr, £2 6s. 8d. 20qr bought by John \Gough/ from Richard Hautrich of Sawbridgeworth on the same day, £2 5s. 10qr bought by the same at Birdbrook from John Chapman, price 2s. 6d. a qr, £1 5s. Item 14qr 4b. with 4b. from increment bought from Andrew de Eyton at Sawbridgeworth on 6 June, price 2s. 8d. a qr, £1 17s. 4d. 20qr bought from the same there on 20 June, £3 3s. 4d. 21qr with 1qr from increment bought from Richard atte Pours of Bumpstead in July, price 1s. 6d. a qr, £1 10s. 10qr 4b. with 4b. from increment bought at Bumpstead from Robert Royly on 4 August at the same price, 15s. 2qr with 1qr from increment bought from the rector of Birdbrook on 13 September, price 1s. 4d. a qr, £1 6s. 8d. 10qr 4b. with 4b. from increment bought from the vicar of Finchingfield in September at the above price, 13s. 4d. 31qr 4b. with 1qr 4b. from increment bought from the rector of Birdbrook in the same month, price 1s. 5d. a qr, £2 2s. 6d. 2qr 7b. bought at Wentford fair,[9] price 1s. 4d. a qr plus in total 1d., 3s. 11d. 6qr 5b. bought in Clare and Haverhill markets at divers times, price 1s. 6d. **[m. 4]** a qr, 9s. 11¼d. 126qr bought from Simon Peek, farmer of Woodham, whereof 6qr from increment, price 1s. 6d. a qr, £9. 3qr 7b. bought from Edmund Wymer serjeant of Stebbing, 10s. 4d.

Sum 1,079qr 7b.; £84 17s. 3¾d. audited

Making of wines and verjuice   The same accounts for the grape harvest at Woodham

---

[8] Walter de Thaxted was master of University Hall, Cambridge, which as a result of the Lady's patronage developed into Clare Hall.

[9] Wentford fair was held on the outskirts of Clare on the main road to Bury St Edmunds.

Ferrers for the making of wines and verjuice by William Butler in October, 1s. 4d. 1b. of salt bought for the said sauce, 6d. For William Butler's wages going from Bardfield to Woodham Ferrers twice to oversee the said work, staying and returning, for 4½ days, 4s. 6d. Item for William Butler's wages going from Clare to Woodham Ferrers to oversee the wines there and to make verjuice, going, staying and returning, for 3½ days in September, 3s. 6d. For divers expenses incurred for the grape harvest there for making 1 pipe of verjuice together with expenses for the purchase of the said pipe, 1s. 8d.

    Sum 11s. 6d.   audited

Purchase of wines   The same accounts for 2 tuns bought in London from John Stuteye on 20 November, £10. For God's penny, 1d. For carriage of the same there, 9d. For 2 carts hired to take them from London to Bardfield, £1. For William Butler's wages [*going*]from Bardfield to London for the said purchase, staying and returning, for 5 days, 5s. Item for 3 tuns bought in London from John Fynch on 20 February, £13 6s. 8d. For God's penny, 1d. 2 tuns bought from the same on the same day at £4. 13s. 4d. [*each*], £9 6s. 8d. For God's penny, 1d. 3 tuns bought from John Stuteye there at £4 13s. 4d. [*each*], £14. For God's penny, 1d. For carriage of the said wine from the cellar in the Vintry to the cellar of Robert de Eynesham viz. at 8d. a tun, 5s. 4d. For William Butler's wages going there for the said purchase and staying for 4 days, 4s. For carriage of 4 tuns by cart to Clare at 4d. a tun, 16d. For William's wages going another time with carriage of the said 4 tuns from London to Clare, going, staying and returning, for 4 days, 4s. Item 2 tuns bought at Lynn by William Butler on 22 February, £9 3s. 4d. For carriage of the same to the water, 1s. For carriage of the same by water from Lynn to Anglesey, 3s. Item given to divers helpers putting the said tuns in the cellar there, 6d. For William Butler's wages going there for the said purchase for 5 days, 5s. Item 1 tun bought at Ipswich from Thomas Coteler in May, £4 18s. 4d. 4 tuns bought in London by William Butler in May at £4 each, £16. For God's penny, 1d. 1 tun bought by the same from John Fynch in the same month, £4 6s. 8d. For carriage of the said 5 tuns and 2 tuns and 1 tun of Rhenish wine sent to the Lady by Sir Henry de Ferrers at 4d. a tun, 2s. 8d. For purchase and hooping of the said casks, 3d. For the said William Butler's wages going from Clare to London twice for the said purchases, staying and returning, for 7 days, 7s. For 1 cart hired from Bardfield to London to seek and bring 1 of the said tuns to Bardfield, 8s. 6d. 1 tun bought in London from the said John Fynch by William Butler, the Lady going to Canterbury, [*and*] for his expenses going and returning, £4 6s. 8d. Item 3 tuns bought from Thomas Coteler on 6 July at £3 18s. 4d. [*each*], £11 15s. 1 tun bought there from Richard de Leyham on the same day, £4. For God's penny, 1d. For 2 carts hired from Ipswich to Clare for carrying the said 2 tuns, 8s. For William Butler's wages [*going*] twice from Clare to Ipswich for 2 days for the said purchases 2s. For carriage of the said tuns, 1s. 1d. Item 2 pipes of white wine \bought/ in London from John Fynch on 6 July, £4 13s. 4d. For God's penny with carriage of the aforesaid and 1 pipe of salmon at 3d. a pipe, 10d. For 1 cart hired to carry the said pipes, with empty pots sent to the house of Robert Mareschal, from London to Bardfield, 7s. 6d. For William Butler's wages going to London for the said purchase and the carriage of the 2 pipes, staying and returning, for 3 days, 3s.

    Sum 23 tuns, 2 pipes; £110 7s. 11d.   audited

Purchase of cider   The same accounts for 9 tuns of cider bought from John Segor reeve of Erbury on 27 September of which 1 is for sauce, price in total £2 14s.

    Sum 9 tuns; £2 14s.   audited

Purchase of oxen from the manors   The same accounts for 4 oxen bought from John atte Lye reeve of Holton on 20 November at 8s. a head, £1 12s. 3 oxen bought from Thomas reeve of Caythorpe on 1 December at 10s. a head, £1 10s. 3 oxen bought from Richard atte Hache reeve of Hundon on 24 February at 10s. a head, £1 10s. Item 3 oxen bought from William Buntyng serjeant of Standon on 17 May at 8s. a head, £1 4s. 3 cows bought from the same on the same day at 6s. a head, 18s. Item 3 cows bought from Richard atte Hache reeve of Hundon on 27 September at 8s. a head, £1 4s. 2 oxen bought from John Segor reeve of Erbury on the same day, total price £1. 2 oxen bought from Richard Warner serjeant of Bardfield on the same day, total price 14s. 3 cows bought from the same on the same day, 18s. 10 steers, 10 bullocks and 8 calves from Woodham bought from Richard Warner serjeant of Bardfield, £5 5s. 25 poor-quality cattle bought from manors in parts of Wales, £6 18s. 6d.

Sum, 17 oxen, 34 cows and poor-quality cattle, 28 bullocks and calves; £22 13s. 6d.   audited

Purchase of oxen in the region   The same accounts for 2 oxen bought from Edmund Wymer bailiff of Stebbing in January at 7s. a head, 14s. 2 cows bought from the same in the same month at 5s. a head, 10s. Item 2 oxen bought for the waggon on 6 May by Robert Poulterer at divers prices, £1 7s. 10d. 3 cows bought by the same on 1 June, £1. Item 2 oxen bought on 9 July at Royston fair for the Great Larder for the following year, £1 5s. 1d. 2 oxen bought at Hedingham fair on 24 July, with ½d. for God's silver, £1 3s. 6½d. 2 oxen bought from Philip Lyouns of Stoke on 13 August, £1 9s. 1d. Item 4 oxen bought at Sudbury on 24 August, £2 7s. 4d. Item 22 oxen bought at Wentford fair in September at 11s. 3d. a head, £12 7s. 6d. For God's penny, 1d. 52 oxen and 8 cows bought in the Usk region for the Lady's Larder by Robert Poulterer in July and August, £23. For the pay of 3 grooms going from Caerleon to Lutterworth and looking after the said oxen and returning from there, 5s. For the pay of 2 grooms going with the said oxen from Usk to Clare, viz. 8 days in coming and 4 days in returning, 4s. Item given to the same for shoes, 12d. For Robert's expenses going about the said provisions and returning to Clare, 8s. 10 oxen bought in parts of Wales by Roger de Wetherisfeld, £3 18s. 6d. Item given to a keeper of the said oxen at Usk by the hands of the said Roger, 1s. 10½d.

Sum 98 oxen, 13 cows; £50 2s. 10d.   audited

Purchase of pasture from the manors   The same accounts for 7½ acres of meadow bought from John Segor reeve of Erbury on 27 September for pasturing the waggon-oxen at 4s. an acre, £1 10s.

Sum £1 10s.   audited

Purchase of pasture in the region   The same accounts for 4 acres of meadow bought from Robert de Apthorpe on 10 October for pasturing the oxen of the Lady's Larder, 4s. 2 acres of meadow bought from William atte Stoure for the same, 12d. For Thomas Doubrigge's wages going from Bardfield to Clare twice for the said purchases for 3 days in the same month, 2s. Item 3 acres of meadow bought at North Weald in June at 5s. an acre, 15s. For mowing the same, 1s. 3d. For pasture on 12 acres of meadow bought from Edmund de Sutton in September, 16s. For pasture on 30 acres of meadow bought from Lady de Goldyngton near Sturmer in the same month, 16s.

Sum £2 15s. 3d.   audited

Purchase of pigs from the manors   The same accounts for 16 pigs bought from John atte Lye reeve of Holton on 20 November at 2s. 6d. a head, £2. For expenses incurred in driving them and 4 oxen of the same manor from Holton to Bardfield,

4s. 1 boar bought from Richard atte Hache reeve of Hundon on 24 February, 3s. 4d. 40 pigs bought from the same on the same day at 2s. 6d. a head, £5. 42 pigs bought from Thomas reeve of Caythorpe on 1 December at 2s. 3d. a head, £4 14s. 6d. \1 boar bought from the same on the same day with 5s. for the pigs' expenses from Caythorpe to Clare, 10s./ 60 pigs bought from Henry de Braundon reeve of Lutterworth on 28 February at 2s. 6d. a head, £7 10s. Item 20 pigs bought from William Buntyng serjeant of Standon on 17 May at 2s. a head, £2. 57 pigs bought from Richard Warner serjeant of Bardfield on 27 September at divers prices, £7 7s.

Sum 2 boars and 235 pigs; £29 8s. 10d.[10]   audited

Purchase of pigs in the region   The same accounts for 5 pigs bought at Braintree by Robert Poulterer on 6 December at 1s. 6d. a head, 7s. 6d. 8 pigs bought from Walter atte Bleyes by the same on 16 January, 19s. 37 little pigs and 8 piglets bought from the vicar of Finchingfield in January, £1. 40 pigs bought from Edmund Wymer bailiff of Stebbing in January at 2s. 8d. a head, £5 6s. 8d. 7 pigs bought at Royston fair by Robert Poulterer on 9 July, £1. For the expenses of the said Robert and Thomas Waynman going there for 2 days for the said purchase, 1s. 7d. Item 20 pigs bought in Braintree and Clare markets by Robert Poulterer on 16 July, £2 9s. 6d. For driving 17 of the said purchase at Braintree from there to Clare, 3d. For the expenses of Robert Poulterer going there for 1½ days for the said purchase, 8d. Item 7 pigs bought at Hedingham fair and in the vill of Bardfield on 24 July, 15s. 8d. For the expenses of William de Manton and Hugh Poulterer going for the said purchase, 2½d. 12 pigs bought at Sudbury by William de Manton on 24 August, £1 6s. 5d.

Sum 136 pigs and 8 piglets; £13 7s. 5½d.   audited

Purchase of sheep from the manors   The same accounts for 27 sheep bought from Richard atte Hache reeve of Hundon on 24 February at 10d. a head, £1 2s. 6d. Item 12 sheep bought from the same on 27 September at 1s. 4d. a head, 16s. 7 sheep bought from the same on the same day at 1s. a head, 7s. 77 sheep bought from John Segor reeve of Erbury on 27 September at 10d. a head, £3 4s. 2d. 32 sheep bought from the same on the same day at 1s. 3½d. a head, £2 1s. 4d. 69 sheep bought from the same on the same day, price in total £3 9s. 1 lamb bought from the same on the same day, price 4d. 27 old ewes weeded out bought from Robert Wulwy serjeant of Claret, £1 7s. 5 sheep bought from William Buntyng serjeant of Standon, 5s.

Sum 256 sheep and 1 lamb; £12 12s. 4d.   audited

Purchase of sheep in the region   The same accounts for 50 old ewes weeded out bought from Edmund Wymer bailiff of Stebbing in January at 10d. a head, £2 1s. 8d. Item 30 unshorn sheep bought by Robert Poulterer on 6 May at divers prices, £2 18s. 42 ewes bought in the Clare region by the said Robert Poulterer on 16 July, £3 3s.

Sum 122 sheep; £8 2s. 8d.   audited

Purchase of swans   The same accounts for 15 swans bought from John Segor reeve of Erbury on 27 September at 3s. a head, £2 5s.

Sum 15 swans; £2 5s.   audited

[m. 5] Purchase of rabbits from the manors   The same accounts for 80 [and] \10/ rabbits bought from Edmund Edward reeve of Farnham on 18 February, 15s. For expenses incurred for their capture and carriage on 2 occasions from Farnham to Clare, 5s. 3½d.

Sum 90 rabbits; £1 0s. 3½d.   audited

---

10   The deleted marginal total reads £29 13s. 10d., but the main total is correct.

Purchase of rabbits in the region   The same accounts for 102 rabbits bought at Desning from John Gyne in February and January at 2½d. a head, £1 1s. 3d.

Sum 102 rabbits; £1 1s. 3d.   audited

Purchase of salt   The same accounts for 11qr 4b. bought from Eustace de la Reche in November at 2s. 8d. a qr, £1 10s. 8d. 7qr 4b. bought from the same on 18 April at divers prices, £1 3s. 36qr bought from the same in May, £3 12s. 20qr bought at Stourbridge fair[11] by William de Manton in September at 2s. 1d. a qr, £2 1s. 8d.

Sum 75qr; £8 7s. 4d.   audited

Purchase of red herring   The same accounts for 4 lasts of red herring bought at Yarmouth in November by Robert Poulterer, £12. 2 lasts bought there by the same, £4. For Robert Poulterer's expenses going from Bardfield to Yarmouth for carriage to Clare of the aforesaid purchases and to Acle for the purchase of eels and to Ely and Reach for pike, with 12d. for carriage of pike from Ely to Reach, staying and returning, for 23 days on 3 occasions, 17s. For boat-hire for 2 lasts of red herring from Yarmouth to Colchester, 7s. For 1 building hired for the said herring for 3 weeks while awaiting carriage there, 1s. 3d. For Robert's wages going at another time to Yarmouth to obtain the said 2 lasts, staying and returning, for 8 days, 5s. 4d. Item 1 last of red herring bought at Ipswich from Thomas Coteler by Robert Poulterer, 100 [counted] as 100, £1 13s. 4d. For \Robert's/ wages going there and to Colchester for the aforesaid and other purchases, for 2 days, 1s. 4d. Item 2 lasts bought from Robert Corby bailiff of Southwold in April, £6. 1,000 red herring bought at Stourbridge by William de Manton, 9s.

Sum 9 lasts, 1,000 herring, of which he answers for 1 last [counting] 100 for 100;[12] £25 14s. 3d.   audited

Purchase of white herring   The same accounts for 1 last bought at Yarmouth by Robert Poulterer in November, £1 17s. 8d. 8 barrels bought at Colchester from Robert de Pamfeld in February at 7s. a barrel with God's 1d., £2 16s. 1d.

Sum 1 last, 8 barrels; £4 13s. 9d.   audited

Purchase of stockfish   The same accounts for 700 stockfish bought at Stourbridge fair by William de Manton in September at 12s. per 100, £4 4s. 300 wild fish[13] bought there by the same at 16s. per 100, £2 8s. 200 split ling bought there at £1 6s. per 100, £2 12s. 100 [?]Baltic ling[14] bought there, £1 5s. For porterage of the said fish to the cart, 2d. For the expenses of the said William and Robert Poulterer being there for the said fish and other necessary [purchases] for 2½ days, 2s.

Sum 1,300 stockfish; £10 11s. 2d.   audited

Purchase of cod   The same accounts for 684 cod, 100 counted as 144,[15] bought at Southwold by Robert Poulterer on 27 June at £1 8s. per 100, £6 13s. For Robert's wages going there to supply the said fish, staying and returning, for 2 days, 1s. 4d. For 1 groom's pay carrying 1 letter there to Robert de Corby to forewarn him to keep the said fish until Robert's arrival, 6d. Item 432 cod, 100 counted as 144, bought at Southwold by Robert de Corby in September at divers prices, £3 6s. 8d. 368 pollack and ling \100 counted as 184/[16] bought at Blakeney by Henry de Honyd[en] for provisions of the Lady's household, £9 7s. 1d. For carriage of the same from Blak-

---

11 Stourbridge fair was held on the outskirts of Cambridge in late August and September.
12 c per v^{xx}.
13 *rakelfisch*. See glossary below, under 'stockfish'.
14 *balgherlieng*.
15 c per vij^{xx}iiij.
16 c per ix^{xx}iiij.

eney to Brandon ferry, 2s. 8d. 460 fish bought in the region of Wells and Holkham with 2s. 7d. for carriage as before, £6 13s. 10d. 368 pollack and ling \100 counted as 184/ bought at Blakeney by the said H[enry] with 2s. 6d. for carriage, £7 12s. 6d.

Sum 2,320 cod; £33 17s. 7d. [*8 cod were presumably sold on account.*] audited

Purchase of salmon   The same accounts for 104 salmon bought in London by Robert Poulterer on 20 June, £4 8s. 10d. For porterage of the same there, 6d. 1 pipe bought to put them in, 1s. 10d. 1b. of salt bought to salt them, 7d. For the wages of Robert Poulterer going to London for the said purchase, for 1 day, 8d.

Sum 104 salmon; £4 12s. 5d.   audited

Purchase of pike   The same accounts for 62 pike bought at Swavesey by Robert Poulterer on 9 February, £3. For his wages going to those parts and elsewhere for the said purchases, staying and returning, for 4 days, 9 February the last counted, 2s. 8d. For boat-hire of the same from Swavesey to Anglesey, 1s. Item 53 pike bought in the Cambridge region by Robert Poulterer on 19 July, £2 13s. 4d. For boat-hire and porterage of the aforesaid from there to Anglesey, 6d. For his expenses going for the said provisions for 1½ days, 1s.

Sum 115 pike; £5 18s. 6d.   audited

Purchase of lampreys   The same accounts for 6 lampreys bought at Gloucester on 19 March by Robert Poulterer, £2 8s. Item 6 lampreys of Nantes bought at Ipswich from Thomas Coteler on 18 April, 18s. For 1 groom's pay going from Anglesey to Ipswich to seek them, 5d. 4 lampreys bought at Gloucester in April for Easter-Eve, with baking of the same, £1 5s. For Edmund Kay's expenses going there for the said purchase with expenses of 1 horse for carriage, for 7½ days, 4s. 12 lampreys bought at Ipswich from Thomas Coteler in May, £1 12s.

Sum 28 lampreys; £6 7s. 5d.   audited

Purchase of sturgeon   The same accounts for 1 barrel of sturgeon bought in London by Robert Poulterer on the last day of January, £3. \For God's penny, 1d./ For Robert's wages going to London for the said provisions, staying and returning, for 4 days, 2s. 8d. Item for porterage of the barrel of sturgeon from Thames Street to the house of Robert de Eynesham, 2d.

Sum 1 barrel of sturgeon; £3 2s. 11d.   audited

Purchase of eels   The same accounts for 1,000 eels bought at Chelmsford by Robert Poulterer on 8 October, 15s. 20 sticks of eels[17] bought there by Hugh Poulterer on 23 October, 8s. 7d. 26 large eels bought there by the same on the same day, 3s. 4d. For carriage of the same from Chelmsford to Bardfield, 8d. Item 3,000 eels bought at Acle by Robert Poulterer on 12 November at 12s. per 1,000, £1 16s. 3b. of salt bought for the said salting and 3 barrels bought to put the eels in, 3s. 3d. 40 sticks of eels bought at Cambridge by Hugh Poulterer on 20 March, £1 2s. 8d.

Sum 4,000 eels, 26 large eels; £4 9s. 6d.   audited

Purchases of spices, wax and canvas   The same accounts for 15 sugar-loaves weighing 100lb. bought from Bartholomew Thomasin on 5 October at 1s. 1d. a lb., £5 8s. 4d. 1 piece of Polish wax[18] bought from the same on 17 October weighing 1½ cwt 18lb., at £2 15s. per cwt, plus in total 4d., £4 11s. 6d. 1 piece of wax of Lubeck bought from the same weighing 103qr at £2 12s. per cwt, £4 11s. 5 gallons 1 quart of olive oil with 1 barrel bought from the same on the same day, 7s. 8d. 1 quire of paper bought from the same on 29 October, 4d. Item 12lb. of pine-seeds bought

---

[17]   A stick comprised 25 eels.
[18]   *cera pullana*. Wax was imported from Poland. The Middle English word *pullane* means Polish.

from Bartholomew Thomasin on 8 December, 6s. 6lb. of plums bought from the same on the same day, 3s. ½lb. of sandal-wood bought from the same on the same day, 2s. 6d. 10lb. of dates bought from the same on the same day, 2s. 6lb. of almonds bought from the same on the same day, 1s. 3d. 1 quire of paper bought from the same on the same day, 4d. Item 6lb. of currants bought from Bartholomew Thomasin on 22 December, 6s. 2½ cwt of rice bought from Nigel Tebaud of Sudbury on 18 February, 17s. 6d. For William the confectioner's expenses going there for the said provisions, 1½d. Item 12 loaves of \loaf/ sugar bought from Bartholomew Thomasin on 19 February weighing 83½lb. at 1s. 3d. a lb. minus in total ½d., £5 4s. 4d. 3lb. of red sandal-wood bought from the same on the same day, 18s. 6lb. of currants bought from the same on the same day, 6s. 1 peck of figs of Malaga bought from the same on the same day, 12s. 4lb. of vermilion bought from the same on the same day, 3s. 4d. 20lb. of dates bought from the same on the same day, 5s. 10d. 2lb. of powdered cinnamon bought from the same on the same day, 7s. 28lb. of raisins of Malaga bought from the same on the same day, 7s. 6lb. of pine-seeds bought from the same on the same day, 3s. 27½ gallons of olive oil with 2 barrels bought from the same on the same day, £1 9s. 1 cwt of canvas bought from the same on the same day, £1 16s. 1 barrel to put the small items in bought from the same on the same day, 1s. For carriage of the said items from the house of Bartholomew Thomasin to the house of Robert de Eynesham, 7d. Item 1 peck of figs of Malaga bought from Bartholomew Thomasin on 23 March, 13s. 4d. 14lb. of raisins of Malaga bought from the same at 6d. a lb., 7s. 8lb. of dates bought from the same on the same day 2s. 8d. 1 basket bought to put the aforesaid in, 2d. For the expenses of 1 packhorse obtaining the aforesaid in London, 10d. 1lb. of cloves bought from Bartholomew Thomasin on 3 April, 6s. 1 barrel of olive oil containing 18 gallons bought at Anglesey from a stranger on 8 April, 16s. 12lb. of ginger bought from the same on the same day, 12s. 26lb. of Cyprus sugar bought from the same on the same day at 5d. a lb., 10s. 10d. Item ½ cwt Polish wax bought from Bartholomew Thomasin on 28 April, £1 6s. 1 pannier bought to put the said wax, confections and other things in, 1½d. Expenses of 1 packhorse going to London to obtain the aforesaid, 8d. Item 206lb. Polish wax bought from Bartholomew Thomasin on 7 May, at £2 12s. a cwt, £5 7s. 6 sugar-loaves weighing 37lb. bought from the same on the same day at 1s. 4d. a lb., £2 9s. 4d. 6lb. of pine-seeds bought from the same on the same day, 3s. Item 2lb. of cloves bought from Bartholomew Thomasin on 17 June, 11s. 4 sugar-loaves bought from the same weighing 44lb. at 1s. 3d. a lb., £2 15s. 12lb. of galingale bought from the same on the same day, £1 4s. 3lb. of sandalwood bought from the same on the same day, 16s. 6d. 12lb. of pepper bought from the same on the same day, 14s. 20lb. of cumin bought from the same on the same day, 5s. Item 1qr of almonds bought at Canterbury in June, 4s. 6d. 1qr of rice bought there in the same month, 2s. 4d. 45lb. of wax bought from John Dunkeslee in May at 4d. a lb., 15s. Item 6 sugar-loaves weighing 57lb. bought from Bartholomew Thomasin on 22 July at 1s. 3d. a lb., £3 11s. 3d. 1½ cwt of Polish wax bought from the same on the same day at £2 10s. a cwt, £3 15s. 1 quire of paper bought from the same on the same day, 6d. 2 panniers and 1 sack bought to put the said wax, sugar and other confections in, 8d. Expenses of 1 packhorse of the Lady going to London to obtain the aforesaid, staying and returning, for 2 days, 9d. Item 1 cwt of rice bought at Stourbridge by William de Manton in August, 6s. 4lb. of currants bought from Bartholomew Thomasin on 8 August, 4s. 4lb. of raisins *de Tanill'* bought from the same on the same day, 1s. 2lb. of figs *de Tanill'* bought from the same on the same day, 4d. Item 1,001qr 25lb. of Polish wax bought at St Botolph[19] at the fair there by William the apothecary at £2 7s. a cwt, £24 12s. 3d. 6lb. of saffron bought there at 5s. a lb., £1 10s. 2lb. of cloves bought there at 6s. a lb., 12s. 2lb. of cubebs bought there at 7s. a lb., 14s. 20lb. of ginger bought there at 1s. 1d. a lb., £1 1s. 8d. 20lb. of galingale bought there at 2s. a lb., £2. 30lb. of pepper bought there at 1s. 2d. a lb., £1 15s. 30lb. of cinnamon bought there at 1s. a lb., £1 10s. 4lb. of powdered cinnamon bought there at 3s. a lb., 12s. 12lb. of pine-seeds bought there at 6d. a lb., 6s. 6lb. of mace bought there at 3s. 6d. a lb., £1 1s. 64lb. of loaf sugar bought there at 1s. 3d. a lb., £4. 2 ells of canvas bought there for packing the aforesaid, 6d. 1 hackney hired for the said William the confectioner [*going*] there from Clare, for 6 days taking 3d. each day, 1s. 6d. Item 3½ cwt and 9lb. of wax bought from Nigel Tebaud in September, £8 18s. 11¼d.

[m. 6] Sum £105 7s. 5¼d. audited

Purchase of confections   The same accounts for 2lb. of *madrian* bought from Bartholomew Thomasin on 29 October at 1s. 3d. a lb., 2s. 6d. 2lb. of ginger comfits bought from the same on the same day at 1s. 3d. a lb., 2s. 6d. Item 2lb. of *madrian* bought from Bartholomew Thomasin on 13 November at 1s. 4d. a lb., 2s. 8d. 2lb. of ginger comfits bought from the same on the same day at 1s. 2d. a lb., 2s. 4d. 3½lb. of quince preserve bought from the same on the same day, 4s. 8d. Item 3lb. of *madrian* bought from Bartholomew on 8 December, 4s. 4lb. of ginger comfits bought from the same on the same day, 4s. 8d. 2lb. of clove comfits bought from the same on the same day, 5s. 2lb. of cubeb comfits bought from the same on the same day, 6s. 1 box of royal pastries containing 4⅜lb. bought from the same on the same day, 4s. 10d. 1 box of pine-nut confections containing 7lb. bought from the same on the same day, 3s. 6d. Item 1 box of pistachio-nut confections containing 3¾lb. bought from Bartholomew Thomasin on 22 December, 6s. 4d. 2lb. of powdered cinnamon comfits bought from the same on 19 February, 5s. 2lb. of *madrian* bought from the same on the same day, 3s. 2lb. of ginger comfits bought from the same on the same day, 2s. 4d. 3lb. of *madrian* bought from Bartholomew Thomasin on 23 March, 4s. 6d. 3lb. of ginger comfits bought from the same on the same day, 3s. 9d. 1 box of royal pastries containing 5¾lb. bought from the same on the same day, 5s. 9d. 1 box of pistachio-nut confections containing 5lb. bought from the same on the same day, 6s. 8d. 3lb. of *madrian* bought from Bartholomew Thomasin on 3 April, 4s. 3lb. of date comfits bought from the same on the same day, 3s. 3lb. of ginger comfits bought from the same on the same day, 4s. 2lb. of powdered cinnamon comfits bought from the same on the same day, 5s. For 1 groom's pay going to London to obtain the aforesaid and to carry letters of the Lady to Sir Andrew de Bures, 10d. Item 3lb. of ginger comfits bought from Bartholomew Thomasin on 27 April, 3s. 9d. 2lb. of [?]barley-sugar bought from the same on the same day, 2s. 8d. 3lb. of slab rose sugar bought from the same on the same day, 3s. 9d. 3lb. of slab sweetmeats bought from the same on the same day, 3s. 9d. 3lb. of red anise bought from the same on the same day, 5s. 2½lb. of powdered rose sugar bought from the same on the same day, 3s. 4d. 2lb. of violet sugar in gobbets bought from the same on the same day 3s. Item 1 box of royal pastries bought from Bartholomew Thomasin containing 4lb. on 7 May, 4s. 2lb. of *madrian* comfits bought from the same on 25 May, 2s. 8d. 3lb. of ginger comfits bought from the same on the same day, 4s. 2lb. of powdered cinnamon comfits bought from the same on the same day, 5s. 2lb.

---

19   St Botolph's fair, Boston, Lincs.

of red anise bought from the same on the same day, 3s. 4d. 1lb. of clove comfits bought from the same on the same day, 2s. 6d. 1lb. of cubeb comfits bought from the same on the same day, 3s. For Jordan Skinner's pay going to London to obtain the aforesaid, 8d. Item 3lb. of slab sugar bought from Bartholomew Thomasin on 17 June, 3s. 6d. 2lb. of [?]barley-sugar bought from the same on the same day, 2s. 8d. 3lb. of *madrian* bought from the same on the same day, 4s. 3lb. of ginger comfits bought from the same on the same day, 3s. 6d. 2lb. of powdered cinnamon comfits bought from the same on the same day, 5s. 2lb. of *madrian* comfits bought from Bartholomew Thomasin on 22 July, 2s. 8d. 3½lb. of slab sugar bought from the same on the same day, 4s. 4½d. 3½lb. of white gobbets bought from the same on the same day, 4s. 4½d. 2lb. of powdered cinnamon comfits bought from the same on the same day, 5s. 2lb. of coriander comfits bought from the same on the same day, 2s. 8d. 1¼lb. of citronade bought from the same on the same day, 2s. 1d. Item 2lb. of powdered cinnamon comfits bought from Bartholomew Thomasin on 8 August, 5s. 2lb. of powdered cinnamon comfits bought from the same on 5 September, 5s. 3lb. of slab sugar bought from the same on the same day, 3s. 9d. 3lb. of slab sweetmeats bought from the same on the same day, 3s. 9d. 2lb. of anise comfits bought from the same on the same day, 3s. 9d.

Sum £10 8s. 4d.   audited

Purchase of vinegar and sour wine   The same accounts for 1 pipe of sour wine bought by Robert Poulterer on 6 May, £1 0s. 1d. Expenses of the same going twice for the said purchase and other provisions viz. to Hedingham and elsewhere, 1s. 1d.

Sum £1 1s. 2d.   audited

Purchase of linen cloth   The same accounts for 17 ells of linen cloth bought at Clare on 28 November, 6s. Item 25 ells bought there from John Dunkeslee on 10 May, 10s. 2d. 19 ells bought from the same on the same day, 5s. 4d.

Sum 61 ells; £1 1s. 6d.   audited

Purchase of wicks   The same accounts for 16lb. of wicks bought at Bury St Edmunds by Hugh Poulterer on 20 October, 1s. 8d. 6lb. of pack-thread bought there for the same, 8d. 46lb. of wicks bought by Robert Poulterer and Hugh on 9 December, 5s. ½d. 43lb. of wicks bought by Hugh Poulterer in December at divers prices, 4s. 5d. Item 70lb. of wicks bought by Hugh Poulterer in April at divers prices, 5s. ½d. 26lb. of wicks bought by the same in May, 1s. 10½d. 8lb. of wicks bought by the same, 8d. 29lb. of wicks bought by the same on 25 August, 2s. 1d. Pack-thread bought from John Dunkeslee on 19 September, 5d.

Sum £1 1s. 10½d.   audited

Purchase of parchment   The same accounts for 16 dozen parchment bought at Bury St Edmunds on 28 October at divers prices, 11s. 4d. For Richard the hosier's pay going from Bardfield to Bury for the aforesaid, 2d. 8 dozen parchment bought at Clare on 10 December, 7s. 2 dozen parchment bought on 26 December, 2s. 6d. Item 5 dozen parchment bought on 23 January, 5s. 6d. 8 dozen parchment bought at Clare on 9 February, 6s. 8d. Item 10 dozen parchment bought at Cambridge on 8 April, 10s. 6d. For William de Manton's expenses going there twice for the said purchase, 4d. 10 dozen parchment bought in London on 18 June, 12s. 1d. 6 dozen parchment bought at Clare on 25 August, 4s. 6d. 11 dozen parchment bought at Clare in September, 5s.

Sum £3 5s. 7d.   audited

Expenses of carthorses   The same accounts for the expenses of 5 carthorses of John Prat going from Bardfield to London for 1 cask of salmon there, staying and returning, for 4 days ending on 6 October, viz. for hay, oats, straw, horseshoes and candles, 3s. 1d. Expenses of 5 carthorses of John Prat going from Bardfield to London with venison and bringing back furs and divers items for the Wardrobe, staying and returning, for 4 days ending on 19 October, 4s. 9d. Expenses of 5 coach horses going from Bardfield to Yarmouth for 8,000 white herring, staying and returning, for 6 days ending on 20 October, viz. for bread, hay, oats, straw, candles and horseshoes, 6s. 10d. Item for expenses of 5 coach horses and 15 carthorses of the Lady going from Bardfield to Yarmouth for 4 lasts of red herring, staying and returning, for 7 days ending on the last day of October, viz. for hay, oats, straw, bread and horseshoes and [?]grease for the carts, £1 0s. 3½d. For the wages of John Best going with the said carts for the same time, taking 4½d. a day, 2s. 7½d. Item for expenses of 6 coach horses going from Bardfield to London to obtain the Lady's coach, staying and returning, for 5½ days, viz. for bread, oats, hay, straw, stabling and candles, 4s. 5d. Expenses of 19 carthorses taking wool from Clare to Ipswich and 10 of the said horses obtaining herring at Southwold in January, going and returning, for 5 days, viz. for hay, oats, bread, straw and stabling, 16s. ½d. Item for expenses of 20 carthorses going to London for 4 tuns of wine in February, going and returning, for 5 days, viz. for bread, hay, oats, candles and straw, £1 4s. 3d. Expenses of 10 horses for 2 carts carrying 2 tuns of wine from London to Bardfield in March, viz. for hay, oats, horseshoes, with 9d. for ullage and 8d. for carriage of the said tuns, 8s. 5½d. For John Southam's wages coming with the said carts to store the said wine at Bardfield, for 3 days, 1s. 6d. Item for expenses of the carts of Robert de Middilton, Roger de Hildresham and 1 cart of the prior of Stoke on 1 occasion and 4 carts of the Lady on another occasion going to London for 7 tuns of wine, viz. for bread, hay, oats, horseshoes and candles and other necessary expenses incurred for the same, going and returning in June, 14s. 6½d. For the wages of 2 carters of the prior of Stoke going with 1 cart viz. for 4 days, 1s. 4d. 1½b. of oats bought for reward of the carthorses of Robert de Middilton going at another time for 2 pipes of white wine, 7½d. Item for straw, stabling and candles for the Lady's carthorses obtaining 2 tuns of wine at Ipswich in July, 3d. Expenses of 2 carthorses going to Southwold for 475 fish on 2 occasions in July and September, 5s. 1½d.

Sum £5 14s. 1½d.   audited

Purchase of horses   The same accounts for 1 hackney bought for John Falconer on 29 November, 12s. 1 hackney bought for the same going with the Lady's falconer to Sir Hugh Despenser on 28 November, 11s. 1 horse bought from Robert de Chilton for the office of the Poultry in the same month, £1 2s. Item for 1 palfrey Grisel Pomeld bought from William Seman and given to the earl of Northampton, £7 6s. 8d. 1 black horse bought from the same for the Lady's coach, £13. 1 skewbald palfrey bought from the prior of Tonbridge in July, £13 6s. 8d.[20]

Sum 3 horses and 2 hackneys; £35 18s. 4d.   audited

Purchase of peat and sedge   The same accounts for 30,000 peats bought in Lode by Sir William d'Arderne at divers prices in February, 12s. 1d. 10,000 peats bought there by the same at 4½d. per 1,000, 3s. 9d. 1,350 sedge bought at Anglesey in February by Adam the brewer, 19s. 6d. Item 1,490 sedge bought there by Adam Baker in March, £1 1s. For carriage of the said sedge, viz. 2d. per 100, from Lode to Anglesey, 4s. 8½d. Item given to a groom being there for the provision of peat

---

20   This sentence was added to the entry, not included in the marginal total, and omitted from the number
     of horses in the main total.

on divers occasions by Sir William d'Arderne, 6d. 50,000 peats bought at Anglesey [*and*] Lode by the said Sir William d'Arderne at 5d. per 1,000, £1 0s. 10d.

Sum £4 2s. 4½d.   audited

Purchase of hay from the manors   The same accounts for hay bought from William Buntyng serjeant of Standon for 46 carthorses and other horses of the Lady going to London with Lady de Ferrers on 2 occasions, 5s. 3d. For 25 acres of hay bought from John Segor reeve of Erbury on 27 September at 5s. per acre, £6 5s.

Sum £6 10s. 3d.   audited

Purchase of hay in the region   The same accounts for 6 cartloads of hay bought at Barway near Ely from William son of Nicholas on 11 April with divers expenses incurred from there to Anglesey, £1 0s. 5d. 334 [*cartloads*] of hay bought in the region of Clare and Bardfield by John Gough for stock in the following year, £72. 9s. 4d. For divers expenses incurred about the said hay at Erbury and Bardfield as appears in the particulars, £2 12s. 1d. Expenses of John Gough going about the said [m. 7] provision on divers occasions, 8s. 10d. For 5 acres of grass and hay bought from Sir John Walram, £1 6s. 8d.

Sum £77 17s. 4d.   audited

Making of charcoal and faggots   The same accounts for the making of 6,100 faggots at Hundon in November at 2s. 11d. per 1,000, 17s. 9½d. Making 6qr of charcoal in the same park in the same month at 2½d. a qr, 1s. 3d. 5qr of charcoal bought from Eustace de la Reche for the forge in the same month at 1s. a qr, 5s. For the pay of John Godolf and John le Saghere felling wood and making charcoal for the store of Clare castle for 35 days ending on 19 February, each taking 2d. a day, 11s. 8d. Item for making 27qr of charcoal in Hundon park in December at 2d. a qr minus in total ½d., 5s. 7d. Making 58qr of charcoal in Bardfield park in December and January, 12s. Item for making 4,100 faggots in Hundon park viz. 2s. 11d. for 1,000, 11s. 11½d. Making 8,000 faggots in *Breusgren* near Bardfield park at 2s. 11d. per 1,000, £1 3s. 4d. Making 3,841 faggots in the same park in March, 11s. 1½d. Making 49qr of charcoal in the same park in the same month at the above price per qr, 10s. 2½d. 17qr of charcoal bought from Eustace de la Reche for the forge in the same month, 17s. Item for making 48qr 4b. of charcoal in Hundon park in April at the above price per qr, 10s. 1¼d. Making 4,400 faggots in the same park at 3½d. per 100 in the same month, 12s. 10d. Making 1,530 faggots in Bardfield park in the same month at the above price per 100, 4s. 5d. Item for making 2,000 faggots in Hundon park of the Parker's fee there in May at 2s. 6d. per 1,000, 5s. Making 1,200 faggots in the same park at 2s. 11d. per 1,000, 3s. 6d. Item for making 1,700½ faggots in Bardfield park of the Parker's fee there in May at 2s. 6d. per 1,000, 4s. 4½d. For 6 men hired for 3 days to carry and stack the said faggots, each taking 2d. a day, 3s. Making 1,200 faggots from loppings of oak trees in June, 3s. For 6 men's pay carrying and stacking the said faggots for 2 days, each taking 2d. a day, 2s. Item for making 2,600 faggots from the loppings of oak trees in Hundon park in May and June at 2s. 6d. per 1,000, 6s. 6d. Making 60qr of charcoal in the same park in June at 2½d. a qr, 12s. 6d. Item for making 21qr of charcoal in Hundon park in July at the above price per qr, 4s. 4½d. For 2 men hired to saw and carry wood in Bardfield park for 4½ days, each taking 2½d. a day, 1s. 10½d. Making 300 faggots from the loppings of oaks in Hundon park in September at 3d. per 100, 9d. For 2 men hired in Bardfield park to saw wood as above for 15 days ending on 22 September, each taking 2½d. a day, 6s. 3d. For 2 men hired to saw wood there for 2 days ending on 29 September, each taking 2½d. a day, 10d. 12qr charcoal bought at Stourbridge fair by William de Manton in September at 10d. a qr, 10s. Making

29qr 4b. of charcoal in Hundon park in September, 6s. 1d. 3qr of charcoal for the forge bought from Peter Smith of Clare in the same month, 3s. 8d.

Sum £11 7s. 11¾d.   audited

Writs and clerks' expenses   The same accounts for wax obtained by John Bataille for 13 marked statutes in December, 3s. 4d. For 1 writ purchased on the same by the same, 9d. 1 writ purchased to the sheriff of Kent concerning arrest of outlawry at the Lady's suit, 10d. 1 writ of trespass obtained by the same in the same month against Thomas Sewale, 9d. For 1 groom's pay carrying writs from Bardfield to London, 6d. Item for 3 writs of record to the sheriffs of Kent and Essex obtained by J[ohn] Bataille in Hilary term[21] against W Greneville, W Mart' and others, 2s. 6d. 1 writ of trespass against the community of Wareham[22] for their offence, obtained by the same, 10d. 1 writ of trespass to the sheriff of Kent against Thomas Sewale obtained by the same, 10d. For 1 groom's wages carrying the said writ of record to the sheriff of Essex from London to Hertford, 4d. Item given for the writing of the presentation of the church of Offord Darcy by the same, 2s. 6d. For 1 groom's pay carrying the said presentation from London to Clare to the Lady, 6d. 1 writ patent purchased for John Daroundel, the Lady's attorney in Ireland, in April by John Bataille, 2s. 6d. 1 writ of *dedimus potestatem* for Robert de Cheddeworth about answering to the said John, attorney of the Lady there, 9d. 1 writ like the other of reseisin of the Pembroke lands, 1s.[23] 2 writs about the manor of Holton for Nicholas Damory, 2s. For John Bataille's wages going to London and Windsor for certain business touching the Lady, going, staying and returning, for 8 days, 8s. For Sir Henry de Thetford's expenses going from Bardfield to London and staying there for the Lady's business from 21 September last past until 28th day of the same month, both days counted, 8s. For writing and sealing 1 writ patent obtained from the Chancery by the same by which the King granted murage to the men of the vill of Callan in Ireland for 5 years from Michaelmas term next following, 3s. 2 writs obtained by the same and directed to the sheriff of Lincoln to distrain Robert Breton and arrest Roger de Gretford in the same term, 1s. 6d. Item for 2 writs obtained by the same directed to the sheriff of Lincoln to distrain the said Robert Breton and arrest the said Roger de Gretford as before in Hilary term, 1s. 6d. Item for 2 writs obtained by the same directed to the sheriff of Lincoln to distrain the said Robert Breton and arrest the said Roger de Gretford as before in Easter term, 1s. 6d. 2 writs obtained by the same directed to the sheriff of Lincoln to distrain the said Robert Breton and arrest the said Roger de Gretford as before in Trinity term, 1s. 6d.[24] For writing 1 Chancery writ directed to the Treasurer and Barons of the Exchequer to discharge the Lady of debts entirely according to the form granted of the statutes both great and small of the Kings of England, 2s. 3 writs obtained for Sir Andrew de Bures directed to the said sheriff for pardon of debts to the Lord King, 15s. 3d. For sealing of 1 writ of *dedimus potestatem* directed to Henry de Thetford clerk concerning receipt by Lady Elizabeth de Burgh [?]to her attorneys in Ireland obtained by the said Henry,

---

[21] The Hilary law term began on 20 January, one week after the feast of St Hilary, and finished before Ash Wednesday, the beginning of Lent.

[22] This probably refers to Wareham, Dorset, which Elizabeth de Burgh held in demesne.

[23] Laurence Hastings (b.1320) was recognised as earl of Pembroke on 13 October 1339 while he was still a minor. In the Close Rolls, a letter dated 23 October 1339 to the escheator south of the river Trent ordered him not to deliver to Laurence the lands committed to Elizabeth de Burgh until he came of age; *CCR, 1339–41*, pp.209–10.

[24] The Easter and Trinity law terms were in the spring and summer.

6d. For sealing 2 letters patent of the Lord King from his Chancery concerning Elizabeth's attorneys in Ireland, 4s. For writing the said letters, 1s. For the said Sir Henry's wages being in London to expedite the said writs and other business of the Lady from 1 September until 10th day of the same month, both days counted, 10s.

Sum £3 17s. 8d.   audited

Purchase of straw The same accounts for 6 cartloads of straw bought at Wethersfield by John Gough on 17 October, 6s. 6 cartloads bought from the vicar of Finchingfield by the same on 7 November, 6s. 10 cartloads bought from the same by the same on 20 November, 10s. 9 cartloads bought from the parson of Birdbrook on 5 December, 10s. 3 cartloads bought from the rector of Birdbrook on 26 December, 3s. 6d. For straw and chaff of 6qr of wheat bought at Hempstead on 16 January, 1s. 5½d. 8 cartloads of straw bought at Belchamp and Birdbrook on 11 February, 13s. 4d. 5 cartloads bought at Anglesey by John Gough on 28 February, 10s. 6d. 5½ cartloads bought at Wethersfield and Bardfield on 28 March for the waggon-oxen, 8s. 6d. Item for 8 cartloads bought at Wethersfield in June by John Gough, 7s.

Sum £3 16s. 3½d.   audited

Purchase of Spanish iron   The same accounts for 100[lb.] of Spanish iron bought in London by Hugh le Charer on 12 November, 5s. 6d. 205lb. bought there by William Butler on 20 November, 10s. 3d. Porterage of the same there, 2d. Item for 3,500[lb.] bought from Thomas Coteler at Ipswich on 28 November, £9 5s. 6d. For 1 cart hired from Ipswich to Clare by John Southam for the said carriage, 4s. 6d. 2,000[lb.] bought at Colchester from Robert Couho of Panfield in February at 4s. 6d. per 100[lb.], £4 10s. For 1 groom's pay going there from Clare to warn the said Robert on what day the Lady's carts would be there to carry the said iron, 3d. For the expenses of William Apothecary going there for the said load of iron with expenses of 1 hackney, 4d.

Sum 5,805lb. of iron; £14 16s. 6d.   audited

Provisions and small expenses of the Marshalsea   The same accounts for 7 couplings bought for the long cart on 9 October, 10½d. 4 hurdles bought for the said cart, 1s. 6d. For the purchase of 1 horse-collar for the said cart, 2d. For the purchase of 5 horse-collars for the cart of Robert de Middilton, 10d. 2 couplings bought for the same cart, 3d. 2 couplings bought for the cart of John Prat, 4d. For the purchase of 3 horse-collars for the cart of Richard Loucesone, 6d. 8 couplings bought for the same cart, 1s. 4 couplings bought for the Lady's waggon, 6d. For ox-shoes for 10 oxen for the waggon on 40 feet, 3s. 4d. 3 large nails for the said waggon, 1d. 100 clout-nails bought for removals [*and replacements*], 2d.[25] For the purchase of saddles for 1 palfrey of the Lady, the packhorse of Nicholas de Rampton, the pack-horse of Robert Cook, and the packhorse of William atte Stoure, 9d. Grease and suet for the horses' feet and the Lady's carts, 1s. 11d. Currying the hides of 2 horses called Biter and Skewbald, 1s. 6d. Item for fitting the long cart with axles on 16 October, 3d. 5 couplings bought for the same, 7½d. Purchase of 2 linch-pins and 3 horse-collars for the same cart, 7d. For fitting axle-boxes to the wheel-hubs of the said cart, 1d. 6 couplings bought for Robert de Middilton's cart, 9d. For the purchase of 2 linch-pins [*and*] 2 traces for the same cart, 2d. 7 couplings bought for the cart of Richard Loucesone, 10½d. Purchase of 2 horse-collars for the same cart, 4d. 5

---

[25]   The wardrobe account regularly enters the purchase of clout-nails for removals – *pro remocionibus*, meaning the removal of horseshoes. Occasionally the entry is given as the purchase of clout-nails for removals and replacements.

couplings and 2 saddlecloths bought for John Prat's cart, 10d. For the purchase of 4 horse-collars for the same cart, 8d. 18 large nails bought for the Lady's cart, 6d. 4 couplings and 2 dowels bought for the waggon, 9d. For currying 9 oxhides, 1s. 1½d. Candles bought at Clare for the Lady's carthorses, 1d. Grease bought for Robert de Middilton's cart, 1d. 100 clout-nails bought for removals [*and replacements*], 2d. Item, 193lb. of hemp made into ropes, cart traces, halters, straps, reins and other small cords for the carts, bought on 23 October, 16s. 30 webs for girths bought on the same day, 3s. 6d. Item 10 couplings and 6 large nails bought for the long cart on 30 October, 1s. 5d. Purchase of 2 horse-collars for the same cart, 4d. 6 couplings, 2 hurters and 3 large nails bought for Robert de Middilton's cart, 1s. 1d. For the purchase of saddles for the same cart, 2d. 5 couplings and 1 iron plate bought for John Prat's cart, 9½d. For the purchase of 1 saddle and 3 horse-collars for the same cart, 8d. 16 couplings, 1 hurter and 6 large nails for the cart of Richard Loucesone,2s. 3½d. For the purchase of 2 linch-pins for the said cart, 1d. 2 couplings bought for the waggon, 3d. 1 pair of new wheels bought for the cart of Richard Loucesone, 5s. Tanning 9 ox and cow-hides, 6s. Item, 2 cart-irons with fittings bought in London by Hugh le Charer on 12 November, £1 11s. 14 strakes bought for the coach by the same, 10s. 24 pairs of buckles bought by the same, 2s. 6d. \10 ells for saddlecloths for cart-harness, 2s. 6d./ 2 panniers bought to put the aforesaid in, 2d. Rope bought for the aforesaid and for packing the wheels of the Lady's coach[26] on the waggon, 1d. Straw bought for packing the coach on the waggon, 3d. For Hugh's wages going there for the said purchases, staying and returning, for 7 days, 4s. 8d. 48 clout-nails bought by the same, 6s. 3 couplings bought for the coach, 4½d. 8 couplings bought for the long cart, 1s. Purchase of 2 horse-collars for the same cart, 4d. 3 couplings bought for Robert de Middilton's cart, 4½d. 10 couplings bought for the cart of Richard Loucesone, 1s. 3d. Fitting axles of John Prat's cart, 3d. 5 couplings bought for the same cart, 7½d. Purchase of 2 horse-collars for the same, 4d. 2 couplings and 1 dowel bought for the Lady's waggon, 4½d. Grease bought for the Lady's carts and waggons, 4½d. 100 clout-nails bought for removals [*and replacements*], 2d. Large nails for the Lady's carts, 4d. Purchase of saddles for the packhorses of William Havering, William atte Stoure, Thomas Ponyng and John Men', 10d. Butter bought for the Marshalsea, 2d. 14 couplings and large nails bought for the long cart's old wheels on 28 November, 2s. Purchase of 4 horse-collars, 1 saddle and 1 bridle for the said cart, 1s. 1 pair of new wheels bought for the same cart, 5s. For the pay of Robert the blacksmith of Bardfield fitting iron tyres, 1s. 2 iron hoops and 2 wooden hoops bought for the said wheels, 8d. For fitting axles of the said cart with axle-boxes, 4d. 7 couplings and large nails bought for Robert de Middilton's cart, 1s. ½d. Purchase of 4 horse-collars and 1 linch-pin for 1 trace of the same cart, 9d. For fitting axles of the same cart with axle-boxes, 4d. For the pay of Robert the blacksmith of Bardfield fitting the cart of Richard Loucesone with iron tyres, 1s. 2 iron hoops and 2 wooden hoops for the hubs of the said wheels, 8d. Fitting axles of the said cart, 4d. **[m. 8]** Purchase of 3 horse-collars and 2 linch-pins of the said cart, 7d. 5 couplings bought for John Prat's cart, 7½d. Purchase of 2 horse-collars and 1 pair of traces of the same cart, 6d. 2 couplings bought for the waggon, 3d. 100 clout-nails for removals [*and replace-*

---

26 The Lady's coach was probably similar to that portrayed in the Luttrell Psalter, drawn by five horses harnessed in line. The coach itself was highly decorated. The passengers were able to look out of the front, back and sides. It was unsprung and cushions were provided.

ments], 2d. Purchase of 1 saddle, 1 pervant and 1 pin for the Lady's coach, 6d. Salt with mixed corn and suet bought for the Lady's sick horses by Master William Ferrour, 5d. Purchase of 1 seat for the coach, 1s. 48 clouts bought for the carts on 12 December, 6s. Purchase of 1 saddle for the coach, 2d. Purchase of 1 horse-collar for the same, 2d. 3 couplings bought for Robert de Middilton's cart, 4½d. Purchase of 1 horse-collar for the same cart, 2d. Purchase of 2 horse-collars for the cart of Richard Loucesone, 3d. 100 clout-nails for removals [*and replacements*], 2d. 9lb. of hemp bought for traces for the Lady's coach, 9d. Item, 1 seat bought for 1 coach saddle on 18 December, 6d. Purchase of *le forsadel* of the coach, 1d. 2 hurters for the long cart, 3d. 10 couplings bought for Robert de Middilton's cart, 1s. 3d. Purchase of 1 hame for the said cart, 2d. Large nails for the same cart, 3d. Fitting the cart of Richard Loucesone with axles, 3d. Purchase of 2 horse-collars for the same cart, 4d. Leather bought to cover [?]3 pairs of traces of the Lady's coach, 1s. 8d. Purchase of a saddle for the packhorse of William de Stanford with 1 *fame-bras* for the same, 5d. 100 clout-nails for removals [*and replacements*], 2d. 1qr of butter bought by Henry de Dene, 2d. Mercury, verdigris, copperas and sulphur for the Marshalsea, 5d. 2 pairs of buckles bought by the same, 2d. Fitting 4 pairs of buckles on 4 pairs of girths, 2d. Item for 12 axles bought by Hugh le Charer on 1 January, 3s. 6 pairs of girths purchased, 10d. For 1 hide of a horse called Hobyn the hackney dead of murrain, 10d. ~~Item for 1 coach bought in London with all the chains and harness bosses by Hugh le Charer in November, £13 6s. 6d.~~ Item, fitting axles to the Lady's coach on 8 January, 10d. 6 bosses bought for the same, 1d. 2 small iron bolts for the same, 2d. Fitting axles to the coach, 4d. Purchase of 1 *trusseyn* for the same, 2d. Fitting iron tyres to 4 new wheels for the coach, 1s. 6d. 8 iron hoops for the said coach, 1s. 8d. Pitch and tar for the wheel-hubs of the said coach, 6d. Purchase of 1 saddle for the said coach, 2d. Purchase of a saddle for William Havering's packhorse, 2d. Purchase of a saddle for Robert Cook's packhorse, 3d. Purchase of a saddle for the Bakehouse's packhorse, 4d. 1 pair of buckles for 1 overgirth for the Lady's foals, 1d. 100 clout-nails for removals [*and replacements*], 2d. 4½lb. of *deaute*[27] bought from Bartholomew Thomasin on 8 December, 2s. 3d. 3½lb. of turpentine bought for the same, 1s. 9d. 1 box of poplar-bud unguent bought for the same, 1s. 2 baskets bought to put the same and other things in, 4d. Item, 48 clouts bought for the Lady's carts by Hugh le Charer on 5 February, 6s. 2 iron tyres for the wheels of the long cart, 2d. Purchase of 4 bridles for the same cart, 2d. Purchase of 2 horse-collars for the same cart, 3d. Purchase of 1 saddle for the same cart, 1d. 20 couplings and dowels bought for Robert de Middilton's cart, 2s. 6d. Purchase of a saddle for the same cart, 2d. Purchase of an extension for the same cart, 2d. Purchase of 2 horse-collars for the said cart, 3d. 1 pick-axe bought for the said cart, 6d. Purchase of a saddle for the cart of Richard Loucesone, 1d. Purchase of an extension for the said cart, 2d. 7 couplings bought for the cart of Roger de Hildresham, 10½d. Purchase of 3 horse-collars for the said cart, 6d. 1 rod for the saddle of the said cart, 2d. Purchase of 2 traces for the said cart, 1d. 100 clout-nails for removals [*and replacements*], 2d. Purchase of a saddle for Thomas Ponyng's packhorse, 3d. Purchase of a saddle for Hugh Poulterer's packhorse, 3d. 2 sheep-skins bought for the forge by Hugh Poulterer, 5¼d. 12lb. of hemp as 1 big halter and 4 ropes bought for the forge at 1d. per lb., 1s. Given to the prior of Stoke's carter coming with victuals to Bardfield and returning to Ashen to cart barley to Clare, 6d.

---

[27] *Deaute* was a salve or ointment for horses.

Item 2 new cart-irons bought in London with large nails, iron clamps and grope-nails bought for the same, £1 6s. 4d. Porterage of the said irons to the cart, 1d. 2 panniers bought for packing the said nails and other small items, 2d. For Hugh le Charer's wages going to London for the aforesaid and other purchases for 4½ days in February, 3s. 1 cow-hide bought to mend the harness of the coach, 3s. 6d. Purchase of 2 saddles for the said coach, 3d. For making 7 pervants of the coach, 2d. For fitting the axles of the long cart with axle-boxes, 4d. 10 couplings bought for the cart of Robert de Middilton, 1s. 3d. Purchase of 1 horse-collar and 1 saddle for the same cart, 3d. Purchase of 2 horse-collars and saddles for the cart of Roger de Hildresham, 6d. 5 couplings bought for the same cart, 7½d. Purchase of 2 horse-collars for the cart of Richard Loucesone and 1 saddle for the said cart, 5d. 100 clout-nails for removals [*and replacements*], 2d. Purchase of a saddle for William Havering's packhorse, 2d. Purchase of a saddle for William atte Stoure's packhorse, 2d. Purchase of a saddle for Robert Cook's packhorse, 4d. Purchase of a saddle for William de Stanford's packhorse, 2d. 1 girth with buckles bought in London for the said packhorse, 3d. Purchase of 2 saddles for the packhorses' foals with 2 new unlined covers, 6d. Purchase of 1 currycomb for Robert Mape, ½d. 2 pairs of new wheels bought for Robert de Middilton's and Roger de Hildresham's carts, 10s. Item 2¾lb. of *deaute* bought from Bartholomew Thomasin on 23 March, 1s. 10d. 3lb. of turpentine bought from the same, 1s. 6d. 2lb. of linseed oil bought from the same, 1s. 4d. 48 clouts bought for the carts by Hugh le Charer on 25 March, 6s. Purchase of 4 horse-collars for the long cart, 8d. Purchase of 2 pairs of traces for the said cart, 3d. 12 couplings for Robert de Middilton's cart, 1s. 6d. 1 new body for the said cart with 1 new extension bought at Ridgewell, 4s. For the pay of Peter Smith of Clare fitting iron tyres to 1 pair of wheels for the same cart, 1s. For 2 iron hoops for the wheel-hubs of the said cart, 4d. 4 wooden hoops for the wheel-hubs of the said cart, 4d. 6 iron plates for the shafts of the said cart, 1s. Pitch for the wheel-hubs of the said cart, 3d. Fitting axles to the same cart, 3d. For the pay of Peter Smith of Clare fitting iron tyres to 1 pair of new wheels for Roger de Hildresham's cart, 1s. 2 iron hoops for the wheel-hubs of the same cart, 4d. 2 wooden hoops for the wheel-hubs of the said cart, 2d. Pitch for the wheel-hubs of the said cart, 4d. Fitting axles to the same cart, 3d. 8 couplings for the said carts' old wheels, 1s. Currying 1 cowhide for mending the cart-cover, 8d. Steel bought by Master William Smith for mending the hammer of the forge, 1d. Item, 700 gilt nails bought for the ladies' saddles, 10d.[28] 900 small tacks for the said saddles, 6d. 4 iron bands for the said saddles, 4d. 1 pole for 1 pack-saddle, 3d. For white leather, 2d. 3 hooks for the said saddles, 1d. For thread, 2d. 4 buckles for clothsacks, 3d. 4 unlined covers, 4d. For 1 saddler's pay for mending the Lady's and her ladies' saddles, pack-saddles and clothsacks for 9 days, taking 3d. a day, 2s. 3d. For 1 groom's pay helping the said saddler for 5 days, 5d. Purchase of 4 horse-collars for the coach on 15 April, 8d. Purchase of 1 saddle for the said coach, 1d. Fitting axle-boxes to the wheel-hubs of the said coach, 1d. Purchase of 4 horse-collars for Robert de Middilton's cart, 8d. Purchase of 1 pair of traces for the said cart, 1d. 3 couplings for the same cart, 4½d. Purchase of 3 horse-collars for the cart of Richard Loucesone, 6d. 2 hurters for the same, 3d. Purchase of a saddle for the same cart, 2d. Purchase of 4 horse-collars for Roger de Hildresham's cart, 8d. Fitting 1 cart for firewood with 1 axle at Bardfield, 6d. 4 couplings for the same cart, 6d. Purchase of the body of the said cart, 3d. 2 hurters for the

---

28 This refers to the ladies in attendance on Elizabeth de Burgh.

same cart, 3d. 1 bridle bought for Hugh Poulterer's packhorse, 7d. 4 gallons of herring grease bought for greasing the harness of the Lady's carts, 2s. 4d. 100 clout-nails for removals [*and replacements*], 2d. 1lb. of gum bought from Bartholomew Thomasin in April, 1s. Item fitting axles to the coach on 22 April, 1s. Fitting axle-boxes to 4 wheel-hubs of the said coach, 4d. Purchase of 4 linch-pins for the same coach, 2d. Purchase of 1 crupper for the said coach, 2d. Purchase of 2 bridles for the said coach, 2d. Purchase of 2 pairs of traces for the said coach, 2d. 8 couplings for the old and new carts of Robert de Middilton, 1s. 1 pair of hurters for the same cart, 3d. 1 cover for the said cart's saddle, 1s. 8d. Purchase of 1 pair of traces for the cart of Richard Loucesone, 1d. Pitch for the wheel-hubs of Roger de Hildresh-am's new cart, 3d. 10 large nails bought for the same cart, 4d. 5 couplings for 1 cart for firewood at Bardfield, 7½d. Purchase of a saddle for Thomas Ponyng's pack-horse with 1 new pole, 6d. Purchase of a saddle for Robert Cook's packhorse, 3d. 2 oxhides bought for the cover, with currying, 6s. 6d. 100 clout-nails for removals [*and replacements*], 2d. Copperas bought by Master William Smith for Nicholas Damory's sick horse, 1d. 86lb. of hemp bought as traces, straps, halters, reins and other necessaries for the Marshalsea, 6s. 8d. Item 48 clouts bought for the carts on 29 April, 6s. For a leather cover of the coach, 4d. Purchase of 1 horse-collar for the coach, 1d. Purchase of 1 bridle for the said coach, ½d. Fitting axles of the cart of Robert de Middilton, 3d. Fitting axle-boxes to the wheel-hubs of the said cart, 1d. Fitting axles of Roger de Hildresham's cart, 3d. Fitting axle-boxes to the said cart, 1d. Making 1 cover for the cart of Richard Loucesone, with thread, 8d. Purchase of a saddle for Hugh Poulterer's packhorse, 2d. For currying and mending harness of the Lady's coach, 6d. 100 clout-nails for removals [*and replacements*], 2d. 211lb. of grease bought in Clare market from 1 stranger of Ridgewell on 5 May, 15s. 10d. Item 12 axles bought for the Lady's carts from Robert Algor on 13 May, 3s. 1 rod for the saddle of Robert de Middilton's cart, 2d. Fitting axles of the cart of Richard Loucesone, 3d. 1 coupling for the same cart, 1½d. 8 clouts bought at Bardfield for 2 carts for firewood there, 1s. 4d. 100 clout-nails for removals [*and replacements*], 2d. 2 webs bought for girths, 4d. Item making 2 saddle-cloths for the Lady's great and little coaches on 27 May, 8d. Purchase of 2 horse-collars for the long cart, 4d. Purchase of 1 crupper for the said cart, 2d. Purchase of 1 saddle for the same cart, 1d. Purchase of a bridle for the said cart, 1d. Fitting axles of Robert de Middilton's cart, 3d. Purchase of 2 horse-collars for the same, 3d. 1 linch-pin for 1 trace of the said cart, 1d. Fitting axles of Roger de Hildresham's cart, 3d. 2 hurters for the said cart, 3d. Fitting axles of the cart of Richard Loucesone, 3d. 1 pair of hurdles for the said cart, 9d. 1 wooden hoop for the wheel-hub of the said cart, 1d. Purchase of 1 horse-collar for the said cart, 2d. 2 couplings and 2 dowels bought for the waggon, 7½d. Purchase of a saddle for Hugh Poulterer's packhorse, 2d. 1 pair of new reins for 1 bridle of 1 palfrey of the Lady, 3d. 100 clout-nails for removals [*and replace-ments*], 2d. 12 new axles bought, 3s. For currying 1 hide of a horse called Grisel de Derham, 10d. 6lb. of turpentine bought from Bartholomew Thomasin on 17 June, 3s. 3lb. of poplar-bud unguent bought from the same, 2s. 3lb. of *deaute*, 2s. 3lb. of linseed oil, 2s. 3lb. of *poyruc'* bought from the same, 1s. 2 panniers bought for putting wax, sugar, galingale and other confections in on the same day, 8d. Item purchase of 2 overgirths for the Lady's palfrey at Dartford, ¾d. Purchase of a bridle for 1 destrier of the Lady at Rochester, 1d. Purchase of a saddle for 1 palfrey of the Lady by Geoffrey de Walpole, 1d. 4 clouts bought for the carts at Ospringe, 6d. Purchase of 2 pack-saddles for the Lady at Canterbury, 1½d. 2 halters bought for 2 packhorses from Dereham, 1d. Purchase of 1 saddle for 1 packhorse from Walsingham, 3d. Purchase of a saddle for 1 packhorse from Dereham, 1d. Purchase of 3 saddles for the Lady's coach at Canterbury, 3d. 2 [?]iron cramps bought in London by Hugh le Charer for the Lady's coach, 8d. 2 hames bought there for the Lady's coach, 1s. Fitting axles of the coach at Malling, 1s. 3 couplings bought there for the said coach, 6d. 12 large nails for the said coach, 4d. Clout-nails for the said coach, 1d. Making 2 linch-pins for the said coach, 3d. Grease bought for the Lady's palfrey and for the Lady's coach and carts, on divers occasions, 2s. 4d. Tallow for a cresset for the Lady's destrier, 3d. Large nails for Robert de Middilton's cart, 1d. 100 horse-shoes bought at Malling, 6s. 30 horseshoes bought in London for destriers and palfreys, 3s. 2,000 horseshoe nails bought, 3s. 6d. For the expenses of William the confectioner and William Smith going from Stratford to London to buy the afore-said, 2d. Item 96 clouts bought for the carts on 1 June, 12s. 5 couplings bought for the long cart, 7½d. 1 band for 1 wheel-hub of the said cart, 1d. Purchase of 4 horse-collars for the said cart, 8d. Purchase of 1 saddle for the said cart, 1½d. 2 hurters for the said cart, 3d. 18 large nails bought for Robert de Middilton's cart, 6d. 3 couplings for the same cart, 4½d. Purchase of 3 horse-collars for the same cart, 6d. Purchase of a saddle for the said cart, 1d. Fitting axles of the said cart, 3d. 5 couplings bought for Roger de Hildresham's cart, 7½d. Purchase of 4 horse-collars for the same cart, 8d. Purchase of a saddle for the said cart, 1½d. 2 hurters for the said cart, 3d. Purchase of 2 traces for the said cart, 2d. 12 large nails bought for the said cart, 4d. 3 couplings for the cart of Richard Loucesone, 4½d. Purchase of 4 horse-collars for the said cart, 8d. Purchase of a saddle for the said cart, 2d. 6 large nails for the said cart, 2d. 12 couplings bought for the waggon, 1s. 6d. 2 staples and 2 hasps for the yoke of the said waggon, 4d. 4 wooden hoops for the wheel-hubs of the said waggon, 4d. Shoes for 10 oxen of the said waggon on 20 feet, 1s. 8d. Purchase of 2 saddles for the Lady at Bardfield, 4d. Purchase of a saddle twice for William de Stanford's packhorse, 3d. Purchase of a saddle twice for Thomas Ponyng's packhorse, 3d. Purchase of a saddle for Richard Hauberk's packhorse, 2d. Purchase of a saddle for William Havering's packhorse, 1d. Purchase of saddles for the Bakehouse's packhorse, 4d. 2 new braces for the length of the forge, 4d. 200 clout-nails for removals [*and replacements*], 4d. Tallow for a cresset for the Lady's destrier at Bardfield, 1d. Currying 3 horse-hides, 2s. 8d. Item 1 pair of shafts for the coach bought at Bardfield on 8 July, 2s. Binding seats of the said coach, 6d. 2 couplings for Robert de Middilton's cart, 3d. 3 large nails for the same cart, 1d. Purchase of 2 horse-collars for the same cart, 3d. Fitting axles of Roger de Hildresh-am's cart, 3d. 3 couplings for the cart of Richard Loucesone, 4½d. 2 rakes bought for hay, 1d. 1 iron fork bought for hay, 1½d. Tallow for 1 palfrey of the countess of Northampton, 1d. 228lb. of \hemp/ bought as lunges, reins, thick ropes and halters, 18s. Item purchase of 2 pairs of traces for the long cart on 29 July, 4d. 2 couplings bought for the same cart, 3d. Purchase of 1 horse collar for the said cart, 2d. Purchase of 2 horse-collars for Robert de Middilton's cart, 4d. 3 couplings for Roger de Hildresham's cart, 4½d. Purchase of 2 horse-collars for the same cart, 3d. Purchase of a saddle for the said cart, 3d. 3 couplings for the cart of Richard Loucesone, 4½d. Purchase of 2 horse-collars for the same cart, 3d. Purchase of an extension for the said cart, 1½d. Purchase of a saddle-pad for the Bakehouse's packhorse, 3d. 100 clout-nails for removals [*and replacements*], 2d. 3 calf-hides bought for ornamenting 4 pairs of traces of the Lady's coach, 1s. Ornamenting the said 4 pairs of traces with the said hides, 8d. Oil bought to soften the said hides, 2d. 2 hurters for the said coach, 3d. Tanning 11 oxhides for the cart-cover at 7d. a hide, 6s. 5d. 2 pairs of girths bought in London by William de Stanford for 1 new packhorse-saddle bought there, 4½d. 1 currycomb bought for 1 nag and hackney by Geoffrey de Walpole, 2d. Eggs bought for 1 destrier and 1 coach-horse which are sick, 2½d. Barley bought for the same, ½d. 1 quart of honey bought for 1 palfrey of the countess of North-ampton, 3d. Item **[m. 9]** purchase of a body for the long cart on 12 August, 1s. 4 wooden hoops for the said cart's wheel-hubs, 4d. 2 hurters for the said cart, 3d. 4 couplings bought for the said cart, 6d. Purchase of 3 pairs of traces for the said cart, 3d. Purchase of 2 saddles for the said cart, 3d. 3 couplings for Robert de Middilton's cart, 4½d. Purchase of 2 horse-collars for the same cart, 4d. Purchase of 2 linch-pins for the said cart, 1d. 12 large nails for the same cart, 4d. 7 couplings bought for Roger de Hildresham's cart, 10½d. 6 large nails for the same cart, 2d. Purchase of 2 horse-collars for the same cart, 4d. Purchase of a pair of traces for the said cart, 1d. 3 couplings for the cart of Richard Loucesone, 4½d. Purchase of 2 horse-collars for the same cart, 4d. 9 large nails for the said cart, 3d. 2 couplings bought for the waggon, 3d. 3 large nails for the said waggon, 1d. 100 nails for removals [*and replacements*], 2d. Purchase of a saddle for Richard Hauberk's packhorse, 1d. Purchase of a saddle for Hugh Poulterer's packhorse, 1d. Purchase of a saddle-pad for the Bakehouse's packhorse, 2d. 2 iron forks for hay bought for the long cart and Robert de Middilton's cart, 3d. Eggs bought for a sick destrier of the Lady, ½d. Making 7 hurdles at Bardfield by William le Gardener, 1s. 1½d. Item 2 hurters bought for the long cart on 9 September, 3d. 4 couplings for the same cart, 6d. 2 bands for the shafts of the said cart, 2d. Purchase of 2 horse-collars for the said cart, 4d. Purchase of a saddle for the said cart, 1d. 7 couplings for Robert de Middilton's cart, 10½d. 1 dowel for the same cart, 1½d. 2 iron bands for 1 felloe of the said cart, 2d. Purchase of 1 horse-collar and saddle for the said cart, 3d. 3 couplings for Roger de Hildresham's cart, 4½d. Purchase of 2 horse-collars for the said cart, 3d. Purchase of a saddle for the said cart, 1d. Purchase of 1 trace for the said cart, ½d. 4 couplings for the cart of Richard Loucesone, 6d. Purchase of 3 horse-collars for the same cart, 5d. 1 hurter for the said cart, 1½d. 2 linch-pins for the said cart, 1d. 1 saddle bought for the packhorse of Edmund Kay of the Poultry, 1s. 1d. Purchase of a saddle for William de Stanford's packhorse, 3d. 200 nails for the leather of the Lady's coach, 4d. Purchase of a saddle-pad for the Bakehouse's packhorse, 2d. 100 clout-nails for removals [*and replacements*], 2d. 48 clouts bought for the Lady's carts, 6s. Currying 2 hides of horses called Hartoth and 1 foal from Bardfield park, 2s. Flaying the said foal's hide, 1d. Item 2 hurters bought for the coach on 28 September, 3d. 1 linch-pin for the said coach, 1d. 5 couplings for the long cart, 7½d. Purchase of 4 horse-collars for the same cart, 8d. Purchase of 2 bridles for the said cart, 2d. Purchase of 1 saddle for the said cart, 4d. Fitting axles to Robert de Middilton's cart, 3d. 4 couplings, 1 dowel for the said cart, 7½d. Purchase of 3 horse-collars for the said cart, 6d. Purchase of a saddle for the said cart, 3d. Purchase of 1 pair of traces for the said cart, 1d. 5 couplings for the cart of Richard Loucesone, 7d. Purchase of 2 horse-collars for the same cart, 4d. 4 couplings for Roger de Hildresham's cart, 6d. Purchase of 3 horse-collars for the same cart, 6d. Purchase of a saddle for the said cart, 2d. Currying 11 ox-hides, 1s. 10d. 3 gallons of oil for the said hides, 3s. 7 couplings for the waggon at Bardfield, 10½d. 1 iron band for the tongue of the waggon, 2d. Large nails for the same, 2d. Shoes for 4 feet of the waggon's oxen, 4d. 4 clouts for the said waggon, 6d. 2 pieces of girths bought at Clare, 6d. Item 5,000 \horseshoe/-nails bought at Stourbridge Fair by William de Manton at 1s. 3d. per 1,000 plus in total 1d., 6s. 4d. 5,000 \horseshoe/ nails bought there at 1s. 1d. per 1,000, 5s. 5d. Item expenses of 1 foal Sorel de Honyden, Bayard Bavent 1 nag of

Sir Edward [*de*] Monthermer,[29] and 1 black destrier Baucyn, being in William Seman's custody at divers times as appears in the particulars, £12 1s. 2½d. Shoeing the said horses for the same time as the same man accounted in the Wardrobe, 9s. 6d. Making cart-covers for the Lady's carts at Bardfield, 1s. 6d.

Sum £36. 8s.[30]   audited

Necessary expenses   The same accounts for 60 ash trees bought from Robert Arnold of Bardfield on 6 November at 1½d. each, 7s. 6d. Carriage \of the same/ from Little Bardfield to the manor in the park, 9d. For 1 cooper's pay for 21 days and another cooper for 4 days making hoops from the same, each of them taking 1d. a day, 2s. 1d. 1 cooper's pay mending wine-casks at Bardfield for 4 days, 9½d. Mending 1 hair-cloth at Clare for drying malt on the same day, 5d. Item for 1 carpenter's pay working on the granaries at Bardfield for 1 week in September, 2s. Pay of 2 sawyers sawing studs and boards for the said work for 3 days in the same month each taking 3½d. a day, 1s. 9d. Pay of 2 men plastering and mending partitions in the same granaries for 1½ days, 6d. Pay of 2 grooms driving pigs for the Lady's Larder for 1 day from Clare to Bardfield, 2d. 10lb. of cotton thread bought from Bartholomew Thomasin on 13 November at 8d. a lb., 6s. 8d. Stitching 15 sacks for the Brewhouse and Bakehouse in the same month, 3d. 2 buckets bought for the Almoner by William Butler in the same month, 11d. Item 2 horse-carts purchased at Maldon and Colchester with expenses incurred for them, 6s. 8d. For 1 cart hired from Colchester to Clare by agreement made by John Best for lack of a cart, 4s. 6d. The said J[*ohn*]'s expenses going for the said provisions for 6 days on 2 occasions ending on 23 December, 2s. 4d. 35 boards bought for covering the great leaden vessel in the Brewhouse, 2s. 3d.[31] 4 pairs of garnet-hinges and 300 nails bought for the same, 1s. 4d. For 1 carpenter's pay making the said covering for 9 days taking 1½d. a day, 1s. 1½d. Item 20lb. of cotton thread bought from Richard Panfeld at 6½d. a lb. plus in total 2½d., 11s. Expenses of 2 horses carrying venison from Cranborne to Bardfield for 6 days in coming and 5 days in returning at 4d. a day for each horse, 7s. 4d. 2 grooms' wages going with them for the same time each taking 2d. a day, 3s. 8d. Item given to the aforesaid grooms for shoes by agreement made by Hern bailiff of Tarrant [*Gunville*], 1s. Canvas bought by the reeve of Cranborne for wrapping the said venison, 2s. 2b. of salt, 1s. Item for threshing 133qr of wheat at Hempstead at 2½d. a qr, £1 7s. 8½d. Winnowing the said wheat at 2d. for 5qr, 4s. 5d. Item 21 ells for strainers bought from John Dunkeslee at 2d. an ell, 3s. 6d. Expenses of Hugh le Charer going from Clare to Bardfield with the Lady's coach, going and returning, for 2 days ending on 10 February, 8d. For his wages going to Hempstead and Bardfield to oversee oxen for 1 day, 8d. Item 13 ells of bolting-cloth for strainers bought from John Dunkeslee on 19 February, 2s. Expenses of John Messenger and William Confectioner going ahead from Bardfield to Clare to make wax, confections and other things for the feast of the Purification,[32] 3d. 2 baskets bought by Nicholas de Hull Almoner for the Almonry at Anglesey, 1s. Expenses of William de Stanford's packhorse going from Clare to London to William de War' to bring salmon, porpoise and whelks for Lent, 11d. Item for cleaning 1 pond at

---

[29] Edward de Monthermer was the Lady's half-brother. He died in 1339.
[30] The deleted marginal total reads £49 12s. 10d. The last entries were not included in the main total.
[31] The vessel was presumably used in the brewing process. A description of the process (including the later introduction of hops) is given in William Harrison, ed. G. Edeles, *The Description of England* (Washington and New York, 1994), pp.135–9.
[32] The feast of the Purification of the Virgin Mary on 2 February, better known as Candlemas.

Anglesey and the well in the kitchen there in January, 1s. 4d. Porterage of stockfish and cod there from the cart to the Larder, ½d. Straw bought there to roof the hay-barn, 3d. William Gent's pay working on the bridge there before the Lady's arrival, 4d. Mending the wash-house laver and the lead there, 6d. 2 women's pay cleaning the Chamber and doing other necessary [*work*] for 3 days before the Lady's arrival, 6d. For pay of 1 man plastering and cleaning the stable there for 3 days, 6d. 1 groom's pay going 3 times to Cambridge to obtain nails and laths and other neces-sary items, 1½d. Cutting rushes for the Hall and Chamber, 8d. 2 mats bought to cover meat, 4d. 2 boards and 100 spike-nails bought for the Chamber, Bakehouse and for other necessaries, 7d. 1 lock bought for 1 pot next to the Bakehouse at Anglesey, 1½d. For the pay of Thomas le fisscher for 8 days at 3d. a day, Richard Gent for 2½ days at 2d. a day, Thomas Gent for 10½ days at 2d. a day, John Gent for 10 days at 2d. a day, working on the lead of the ovens in the Bakehouse and Brewhouse at Anglesey in February, 5s. 10d. Pay of 2 pages serving the same for 9 days, 1s. 6d. 1 cart hired for 2½ days to carry clay, 2s. 1d. Pay of 1 man digging clay for the said work for 4 days, 8d. 1 carpenter's pay repairing the said Bakehouse, namely walls, troughs and other necessary things for 3 days, 9d. 1 cooper's pay repairing vessels of the Bakehouse and Brewhouse for 3 days, 9d. Hoops and nails bought for the said vessels, 2d. Item 1 groom's pay keeping the does at Bardfield for 5 weeks in February and March ending on 26 March, taking 4d. a week, 1s. 8d. 1 man's pay helping Adam le Waynman keeping the oxen at Hempstead for 5 weeks in the same months, 6d. Item William le Wodehewere's wages staying behind the Lady at Clare, Hundon and Bardfield for felling and lopping wood and going with the waggon from 28 February to 16 April, taking 1½d. a day, viz. for 49 days, 6s. 1½d. 2 cartloads of rushes bought at Colchester on 23 April with their cutting and collection, 4s. 3d. John de Reveshale's wages going there for 2 days for the said provisions and purchases, 9d. 1 hackney hired for the same from Clare to Colchester for the same time, 5d. Item 114 poplar boards bought by Sir John Chaplain at Bard-field at divers prices in April for making 1 grain-store in 1 cellar there, 14s. 5d. 2 sawyers' pay sawing divers [*?*]tongues for the grain-store for 6 days taking 7d. a day, 3s. 6d. 400 spike-nails bought at 4d. per 100, 500 board-nails at 3d. per 100, 500 lath-nails at 2d. per 100, and 200 hinge-nails at 1½d. per 100, bought for making the said grain-store, 3s. 8d. For a carpenter's pay working on the said grain-store for 4 weeks and 3 days, taking 2s. a week and 1s. for 3 days, 9s. 1 carter's pay going with 1 cart of the Lady to cart the Parker's fee of wood in Bardfield park for 7 days in the same month, 1s. 9d. 1 man's pay collecting [*and*] preparing the said wood for carting for 6 days, 9d. 1 man's pay making 1 gate near *Breusgren*, for making a way for the Lady's cart and carting faggots made in the same grove, 3d. Item for 6 men hired for stacking the faggots made in the same grove for 2½ days, each taking 1½d. a day, 1s. 10½d. 3 women's pay cleaning and preparing the Chamber at Bardfield for 4 days in the same month because they believed the Lady was arriving at that time, 1s. 6d. 1 horse hired to carry does from Bardfield to Clare, 3d. For expenses incurred over 2 carts collecting rushes at Maldon on 13 May by view of John Best, 3s. 2d. John Best's wages going there from Clare for the said provisions for 2½ days, 11¼d. For 1 hackney hired for the same for the same time, 6d. Hugh le Charer's expenses going from Clare to Bardfield and Wethersfield on 2 occasions in the same month to cart oats bought there, 6d. Item threshing 37qr of wheat at Hemp-stead in May at 2½d. a qr, 7s. 8¾d. Winnowing the said wheat, 1s. 2½d. John Chamberlain's wages being there for the threshing of the said wheat, and measuring and delivering it, for 12 days, 2s. Item given to carters of Hempstead and Bardfield for carting part of the said wheat, 2d. 21 bands bought in Clare market to make hoops for the vessels of the Buttery and Larder, 1s. 8d. Making 10 new sacks, 2d. Item expenses of the 4 aforesaid carts carrying wheat from Hempstead to Bardfield in June viz. for bread, drink, fish and other expenses incurred there by Adam Baker, 10d. 1 carpenter's pay repairing the granary at Bardfield for 1 week and 1 day in the said month, 2s. 4d. 150 spike-nails and lath-nails bought for doing the aforesaid and other necessary [works], 4d. 2 men hired for 3 days to daub the said granary, each taking 2d. a day, 1s. Felling 60 oak trees in Bardfield park to make stalls for the stock there, at 1d. per oak, 5s. 4½qr of malt-dregs bought there to feed the boar, sows and piglets living there, from the last day of January to 26 June, at 8d. a qr, 3s. 7 women's pay cutting rushes for 1 day in June before the Lady's arrival, 7d. 2 men's pay cleaning and preparing the Chamber there before the Lady's arrival, 4d. 2 men's pay preparing wood for carting from great trees felled in Hundon park in June for 16½ days ending on 29 June, taking 4d. a day, 5s. 6d. William le Wode-hewere's wages being in the same park to split wood from 22 May to 1 July, both days counted, viz. for 41 days taking 1½d. a day, 5s. 1½d. Item 2 grooms' pay for 3 days ending on 25 July preparing wood for carting in Hundon park, taking 4d. a day, 1s. 9 women's pay collecting rushes at Bardfield for 1 day before the Lady's arrival, 9d. 15 poplar boards bought in the vill of Clare on 5 August to cover the leaden vessel in the Brewhouse, 1s. 8d. 1 pair of old boots with 3 pairs of gloves bought for stacking faggots in Clare Castle by Henry de Colyngham, [m. 10] 1s. ½d. Item 4 cartloads of rushes bought in Maldon by John Best in September, 8s. 5d. For wages of the said John going for 4 days to obtain the aforesaid, 1s. 6d. 1 hackney hired for the same for the same time, 6d. 3 carpenters' pay making the waggon to carry grain at Bardfield for 1 day in August, 10d. 2 sawyers hired to saw the Lady's timber there for 2 days, taking 7d. a day, 1s. 2d. 2 men's pay sawing oaks across and preparing for carting for 15 days, taking 6d. a day, 7s. 6d. 1 man's pay helping the waggons to cart wood there for 9 days, taking 1½d. a day, 1s. 1½d. Item sewing 30 sacks at Clare in September, 6d. For cleaning buildings and stables at Anglesey after the Lady's departure in May by Sir William d'Arderne, 8d. Hoeing the garden and on occasion doing other necessary things in the same by the same, 6d. 1 piece of bolting-cloth bought for strainers from John Dunkeslee in September, 7s. 6d. 1 lanner bought for snaring by John Reveshale on 20 September, 6s. Wages of the said John going to Lynn and Diss for 5 days to buy the said lanner, 1s. 10½d. 1 hackney hired for the same for the same time, 10d. Item, 4 men's pay repairing the floor of the Bardfield grange for threshing wheat on the same, inclusively 1s. 1½d. 1 horse hired to carry 1b. of flour from Bardfield to Clare, 4d. 2 carpenters' pay making a drail there for 1½ days, each taking 4d. a day, 1s. For a butcher's pay slaughtering 30 oxen and 27 bullocks from the feast of Easter to the last day of September at 1d. for an ox and ½d. for a bullock, 3s. 6d. 1 groom's pay going with the drail at Bard-field for 15 days ending on 29 September, 1s. 10d. 1 other man's pay going with another drail newly made for 4 days ending on the same day, 6d. For 1,100 faggots bought from the fee of the Parker of Hundon, £1. 1 hair-cloth bought by Henry Constable of Clare for towels, 12s. 1 piece of bolting-cloth of Rheims measuring 60 ells bought at Stourbridge fair, 12s. 6 pieces of sackcloth bought there on the same day at divers prices, £1 1s. 11d. 3 pairs of garnet-hinges bought from Peter Smith of Clare for the man covering the leaden vessels there, 1s. 8d. 3 boards bought there that the said man lacked, 3d. 1 hackney hired to carry leaden vessels from Bardfield to Clare to make a cistern there, 3d. Item wood bought from the fee of Thomas

Parker of Bardfield for expenses of the household, £1 10s. 9 boots and old table-linen bought from John Bakere who was with Sir Edward de Monthermer, £1 1s. 8d.

Sum £19 10s. 5d.   audited

Wages of falcons and falconers   The same accounts for John de Reveshale's wages going in the region of Hedingham and Clare to take partridges, staying and returning, for 2½ days ending on 20 October, taking 3½d. a day for himself, his page and his dogs, 8½d. For the wages of 2 falcons and 2 lanners in the custody of John Falconer from the last day of September to 30 October, both days counted, viz. for 31 days, the falcon taking ½d. a day, and the lanner ¼d., 3s. 10½d. Wages of 2 lanners in John de Reveshale's custody for the same time, each lanner taking ¼d. a day as above, 1s. 3½d. Wages of 1 goshawk and 1 tercel in John de Claketon's custody at ½d. a day each for the same time, 2s. 7d. John de Claketon's wages going from Bardfield to Bury St Edmunds and elsewhere in those parts to take pheasants, staying and returning, for 10 days ending on 30 October, 10s. Thomas Pulter's wages going with the same for 5 days, 5s. Expenses of William Albon, John Falconer and Nicholas Falconer going from Bardfield to Hedingham with falcons for 1 night in the same month, 5½d. Item John de Reveshale's wages going to take partridges in divers places for 8 days on 2 occasions, taking per day as above, 2s. 4d. Wages of 2 falcons and 2 lanners in John Falconer's custody from the last day of October to 27 November, both days counted, viz. for 28 days, taking per day as above, 3s. 6d. Wages of 2 lanners in John de Reveshale's custody for the same time taking per day as above, 1s. 2d. Wages of 1 goshawk and 1 tercel for the same time, taking as above, 2s. 4d. Expenses of John de Claketon and Thomas Pulter going to take pheasants in the Walden region, staying and returning, for 4 days in the same month, 4s. Expenses of John Falconer and William Albon going from Bardfield to the Hedingham area with falcons for 1 day, 1d. Item John de Reveshale's wages going to take partridges around Clare, Hundon and Stansfield, staying and returning, for 14 days ending on 5 October, taking per day as above, 4s. 1d. Wages of the same going to take partridges in the Dunmow area for 1½ days ending on 11 December, 5¼d. John de Claketon's expenses going to take pheasants around Clare and elsewhere for 14 days in the same month, 7s. Item wages of 2 lanners in John de Reveshale's custody from 28 November to 25 December, both days counted, taking as above, 1s. 2d. Wages of 1 goshawk and 1 tercel for the same time, taking as above, 2s. 4d. John de Claketon's expenses being in the area of Messing to take pheasants for 3 days ending on 24 December, 1s. 8d. Item wages of 2 lanners in John de Reveshale's custody from 26 December to 22 January, both days counted, taking as above, 1s. 2d. Wages of 1 goshawk in John de Claketon's custody for the same time, taking as above, 1s. 2d. Wages of 2 falcons and 2 lanners in John Falconer's custody for 2 days in January ending on 22 January, taking as above, 3d. Item John de Claketon's expenses going to take pheasants with his goshawk in the region of Weald and Waltham, staying and returning, for 14 days ending on 25 January, 7s. Wages of 2 falcons and 2 lanners in John Falconer's custody from 23 January to 19 Februrary, both days counted, taking as above, 3s. 6d. Wages of 2 lanners in John de Reveshale's custody for the same time, taking as above, 1s. 2d. Wages of 1 goshawk in John de Claketon's custody for the same time, taking as above, 1s. 2d. Expenses \of the same/ going to take pheasants in the area of Bradley for 2 days, 1s. Item wages of 2 falcons and 2 lanners in John Falconer's custody from 20 February to 18 March, taking as above, 3s. 6d. Wages of 2 lanners in John de Reveshale's custody for the same time, taking as above, 1s. 2d. The same man's wages being at Clare with the said lanners after the Lady's departure from 28 February to

18 March, both days counted, for 20 days, at 3½d. a day for himself, page and 2 dogs, 5s. 10d. Wages of 4 puppies being there with the same for 20 days as above at 1d. a day, 1s. 8d. Wages of 1 goshawk in John de Claketon's custody from the said 20 February until 18 March, taking per day as above, 1s. 2d. Item wages of 2 falcons and 2 lanners in John Falconer's custody from 19 March to 15 April, both days counted, taking as above, 3s. 6d. The said John's wages being at Clare after the Lady's departure for 12 days with his falcons, the Lady being at Anglesey, 2s. Nicholas Falconer's wages being there with the same men for 17 days ending on 19 April, 2s. 2½d. Wages of 2 lanners in John de Reveshale's custody from 19 March to 15 April, both days counted, taking as above, 1s. 2d. The said John's wages being at Clare with the same men from 19 March to 20 April, the first day counted [*and*] not the last, taking 3½d. a day for himself, page and 2 dogs, 9s. 4d. Wages of 4 puppies of the Lady being there with the same man for 20 days, taking 1d. a day, 1s. 8d. Item wages of 1 falcon and 2 lanners in John Falconer's custody from 16 April to 13 May, both days counted, taking per day as above, 2s. 4d. Wages of 1 falcon in custody of the same from the said 16 April to 27 April, both days counted, and not more because it died of murrain on the same day and wages ceased, 6d. Wages of John Falconer's page being with his master at Clare after the Lady's departure for 12 days, the Lady being at Anglesey, and entered here in the next month because it was forgotten above, 1s. Wages of 1 lanner in John de Reveshale's custody from the said 16 April to 13 May, both days counted, taking as above, 7d. \Wages/ of 1 lanner in the custody of the same from the said 16 April to 8 May, both days counted, viz. for 23 days, taking as above, and wages ceased because on that day it died of murrain, 5¾d. Wages of 1 goshawk in John de Claketon's custody from 19 March to 13 May, both days counted, taking as above, 2s. 4d. Item wages of J[*ohn*] Falconer and 2 lanners in J[*ohn*] Falconer's custody from 14 May to 8 July, both days counted, viz. for 2 months, taking as above, 4s. 8d. Wages of 1 lanner in John de Reveshale's custody for the same time, 1s. 2d. Wages of 1 goshawk in John de Claketon's custody for the same time, taking as above, 2s. 4d. Wages of 1 tercel in Thomas Pulter's custody from 20 May to 8 July, both days counted, viz. for 50 days, taking ½d. a day, 2s. 1d. Item wages of 1 falcon and 2 lanners in John Falconer's custody from 9 July to 5 August, both days counted, viz. for 1 month, 2s. 4d. Wages of 1 lanner in John de Reveshale's custody for the same time, 7d. Wages of 1 goshawk in John de Claketon's custody for the same time, 1s. 2d. Wages of 1 goshawk in Thomas Pulter's custody for the same time, 1s. 2d. Item wages of 1 falcon and 2 lanners in John Falconer's custody from 6 August to 2 September, both days counted, viz. for 1 month, 2s. 4d. Wages of 1 lanner in John de Reveshale's custody for the same time, 7d. Wages of 1 goshawk in John de Claketon's custody for the same time, 1s. 2d. Wages of 1 goshawk in Thomas Pulter's custody for the same time, 1s. 2d. Item wages of 1 falcon and 2 lanners in John Falconer's custody from 3 September to 29 September, both days counted, viz. for 27 days, 2s. 3d. Wages of 1 lanner in John de Reveshale's custody for the same time, 6¾d. Wages of 1 lanner newly purchased in the custody of the same from 24 September to 29 September, both days counted, viz. for 6 days, 1½d. Wages of 1 goshawk in John de Claketon's custody for the same time, 1s. 1½d. Wages of 1 goshawk in \T[*homas*]/ Pulter's custody for the same time, 1s. 1½d.

Sum £6 16s. 8¾d.   audited

Purchase and making of cloths for livery   The same accounts for 2 marbled cloths bought for the knights from a London merchant in November, £8 13s. 4d. Making of 4 long cloths for the Lady at £2 10s. each with 3s. for shearing, £10 3s. Making 8 cloths for the knights at £1 15s. each with 4s. for shearing, £14 4s. Making 12 cloths for the clerks and ladies at £1 15s. each with 12s. for shearing, £21 12s. Making 24 cloths for the esquires at £1 15s. each with £1 4s. for shearing, £43 4s. Making 2 cloths for the serjeants at £1 11s. 6d. each with 2s. for shearing, £3 5s. Silk bought for Robert de Glemisford for making stripes in the said cloths, 9s. Making 3 cloths for the lesser clerks at £1 7s. 6d. each with 3s. for shearing, £4 5s. 6d. Making 10 cloths for the yeomen at £1 11s. 6d. each with 10s. for shearing, £16 5s. Making 12 cloths for the grooms at £1 7s. 6d. each with 12s. for shearing, £17 2s. Making 1 cloth of *solsele* with 1s. for shearing, £1 14s. Making 1 checked cloth for the summer supertunics of the esquires with 1s for shearing, £1 14s. Making 2½ cloths of apple-bloom at £1 11s. 6d. each with 2s. 6d. for shearing, £4 1s. 3d. Item 3 cloths bought in London for the middle clerks with 2s. for shearing, £4 2s. 7 ells of striped [*cloth*] bought for William de Ferrers with 3d. for shearing, £1 12s. 3d. 1 long cloth of azure blue bought in London with 1s. 6d. for shearing, £8 1s. 6d. ½ a striped cloth bought for the yeomen outside the livery with 6d. for shearing, £1 2s. 6d. 1 long russet cloth of *Burcell'* bought for the Lady for the feast of All Saints with 1s. 6d. for shearing, £8 1s. 6d. Item 3 dozens of English cloth bought at Clare for the pages' livery with 6d. for shearing on 20 February, £1 7s. 6d. 40 ells of *candelwyk* bought for the same with 10d. for shearing, £1 12s. 6d. Item 18 ells of English cloth bought in Clare market for Henry the scribe and the page of hunting with 4d. for shearing, 10s. 8d. Item 10 sacks of wool bought for making the Lady's livery, £50, at £5 a sack. Item making 1 cloth for the little clerks by Robert de Glemisford, £1 6s. 8d.

Sum £224 9s. 2d.[33]   audited

[m. 11] Purchase of furs   The same accounts for 2 furs of minever of 9 timbers bought from Robert de Eynesham for the Lady by Sir Robert de Stalynton, £8. 4 hoods pured bought by the same from the same for the Lady, £2. 2 panes of gris bought from the same for the Lady, £8. 2 furs of gris bought from the same for the Lady, £4. 1 hood of gris bought from the same for the Lady, 6s. 8d. 4 furs of grover bought from the same for the Lady's livery, £4. 27 furs of popel bought from the same at 9s. 6d. each, £12 16s. 6d. 6 furs of strandling bought from the same at 9s. 6d. each, £2 17s. 2 furs of popel bought from the same, 19s. Item 2 furs of minever of 9 timbers bought from Adam Aspal by Sir Robert de Stalynton, £6. 1 pane of gris bought from the same by the same for the Lady, £3. 7 furs of minever of 7 timbers bought from the same for the Lady's livery at £1 6s. each, £9 2s. 8 furs of minever of 7 timbers bought from the same by the same at the same price, £10 8s. 3 furs of minever of 8 timbers bought from the same at £1 12s. each, £4 16s. 32 hoods half-pured bought from the same at 6s. 8d. each, £10 13s. 4d. 1 fur of grover bought from the same, £1. 1 fur of popel bought from the same and 3 furs of strandling, price in total, £1 14s. Item 3 furs of minever of 7 timbers and 2 hoods half-pured bought from Thomas Cheiner by Sir Robert de Stalynton, £3 12s. 2 furs of minever bought for Sir Thomas de Bradeston by the same Sir Robert at £1 8s. each, £2 16s. 1 fur of bis bought for the same, £1. 1 hood pured bought for the same, 8s.

Sum £97 8s. 6d.   audited

Purchase of budge   The same accounts for 18 furs of budge bought from Adam Aspal by Sir Robert de Stalynton for the Lady's livery, £3. 44 hoods of budge bought from the same by the same at 1s. 10d. each, £4 0s. 8d. Item 2 hoods of budge bought from Robert de Eynesham, 5s.

---

[33] The marginal deleted total reads £173 2s. 6d. and omitted the last two items in the account.

Sum £7 5s. 8d.   audited

Purchase of lambs' furs   The same accounts for 6 dozen of lambs' furs bought from Adam Aspal at 1s. 8d. each, £6. 6 lambs' furs bought from Robert de Eynesham, 12s. 1 lamb's fur bought from Nigel Tebaud for livery, 2s. 6d.

Sum £6 14s. 6d.   audited

Carriage of venison   ~~The same accounts for the expenses of 2 horses carrying venison from Cranborne to Bardfield on 12 January viz. for 6 days in coming and 5 days in returning, taking 8d. for a day and night, 7s. 4d. 2 grooms' wages going with them for the same time, taking 4d. a day, 3s. 8d. Item given to the same by the hands of Stephen Bonde reeve there by agreement made with the same by the same, 1s. Canvas bought for packing the said venison, 2s. Salt bought for salting the said venison, 1s.~~ \[*Crossed out*] because allowed above./ Item 3qr of salt bought at Cranborne for salting 18 deer, 8s. 4d. 4 ells of canvas bought for packing them, 2s. 1 pipe and 1 barrel bought to put them in with 1 tub and repair of the same, 2s. 6d. John le Hunte's wages staying at Cranborne for salting and preparing the said venison there after the steward's departure, and coming to Clare, for 22 days, 2s. 9d. Expenses of 4 horses from Cranborne carrying the said venison from there to Clare viz. for 4 days, 7s. 3d. Their expenses in returning, 7s. Fitting axles to the said cart on the way, 6d. Item given to a carter by the hands of Stephen Bonde for his labour going and returning, 6d. Horseshoes for the said horses going and returning, 1s. 4 clouts bought for the said cart, 5d. Item expenses of 2 draught-beasts from Usk coming from there with 9 deer, for 8 days in coming and 4 days in returning viz. at 9d. a day for the said draught-beasts and 2 grooms coming with the same, 9s. Item given to the same for shoes, 1s. 1qr of salt bought in the Caerleon area for salting the venison taken there, 6s. 8 ells of canvas bought for packing the said venison 1s. 7d. 2 pairs of panniers bought for carrying the said venison, 6d.

Sum £2 10s. 4d.[34]   audited

Foreign expenses   The same accounts for Robert Mareschal's expenses going from Bardfield to London on the Lady's business, staying and returning, for 2 days ending on 8 October, 1s. 8d. John de Claketon's expenses going from Bardfield to Wimpole and elsewhere in Cambridgeshire to take pheasants, staying and returning, for 8 days ending on 6 October, 4s. 2d. Wages of Edmund page of the Chamber going from Bardfield to London for Master Richard, carpenter,[35] staying and returning, for 3 days in the same month, 4½d. Wages of the same going to Margery Mareschal at North Weald on the Lady's business for 1 day, 1½d. 1 groom's pay going from Bardfield to Walden with the Lady's letters for a plumber, going and returning, for 1 day, 2d. Expenses of 1 packhorse of the Lady going from Bardfield to London to obtain 2 cloths for the knights, staying and returning, for 3 days, 10½d. Thomas Doubrigge's wages going from Bardfield to Thurston on the Lady's business, staying and returning, for 1½ days,1s. Item Richard le Hosier's pay going from Bardfield to Bircham to Master William de Brampton with the Lady's letters, staying and returning, for 5 days ending on 12 October, 8d. Wages of Richard page of the Chamber going from Bardfield to Ripley near Guildford with the Lady's letters to the earl of Gloucester,[36] staying and returning, for 6 days in the same month, 9d. 1 groom's pay going from Bardfield to St Neots to take Nicholas Matoun to Gransden

---

[34]   The deleted marginal total reads £3 5s. 4d. and includes the payments which were crossed out. The crossing out of items in the account was presumably done by the auditors.

[35]   Probably a reference to Master Richard de Felstede who later built the Lady's London house.

[36]   Hugh Audley, the Lady's brother-in-law.

to Sir Thomas de Cheddeworth, staying and returning, for 3 days, 4d. J[*ohn*] de Claketon's expenses going to divers places to take pheasants for 2 days in October, 6d. Item Colinet Picard's wages going from Bardfield to London on the Lady's business and for furs of the Lady's livery, staying and returning, for 4½ days ending on 18 October, 3s. Wages of the same going from Bardfield to Clare to pack the Lady's livery, staying and returning to Bardfield, for 1½ days ending on 22 October, 10d. Roger Skinner's wages going with the same to help him, staying and returning, for 2 days, 3d. Expenses of Richard Chamberlain going from Bardfield to Gransden to Robert de Cheddeworth on the Lady's business, for 2 days, 5d. Wages of Richard page of the Chamber going from Bardfield to Tonbridge and London to the earl of Gloucester on the Lady's business, staying and returning, for 8 days ending on 22 October, 1s. Item Robert Mareschal's wages going from Bardfield to London with 2 horses to parliament on the Lady's business, staying and returning, for 8 days in October, 12s. Henry de Dene's wages going there with him for the same time, 8s. Expenses of 1 packhorse of the Lady and 1 groom going with the same men for the same time, 4s. Hugh le Charer's wages going from Bardfield to London on the Lady's business, staying and returning, for 10 days ending on 29 October, 6s. 8d. His wages going from Bardfield to Clare on the Lady's business and to oversee the Lady's coach there, staying and returning, for 3 days, 2s. Wages of Edmund page of the Chamber going from Bardfield to London to Sir Edmund de Durem with the Lady's letters, staying and returning, for 3 days, 4½d. 1 hackney hired for the same from *Helphing*'to Stratford at the Lady's cost, 5d. Wages of Richard page of the Chamber going from Bardfield to London on the Lady's business, staying and returning, for 2½ days [*ending on*] 26 October, 3¾d. Richard le Hosier's pay going from Bardfield to Gransden to Sir Thomas de Cheddeworth on the Lady's business, staying and returning, for 2 days in the same month, 3d. Wages of Edmund page of the Chamber going from Bardfield to Tonbridge on the Lady's business, staying and returning, for 4 days in the same month, 6d. For his passage twice over the river at Gravesend in going and returning, 2d. His expenses going from Bardfield to North Weald on the Lady's business for 1 day, 1d. Wages of Richard page of the Chamber going from Bardfield to London to John Bataille on the Lady's business, staying and returning, for 5 days in the same month, 7d. Expenses of Roger Cotel going from Bardfield to Gransden to Sir Thomas de Cheddeworth on the Lady's business for 2 days in the same month, 1s. 2d. Item wages of Andrew de Waleden going from Bardfield to London to Sir Warin de Bassingbourne with the Lady's letters, staying and returning, for 2 days in October, 2s. Expenses of William Havering's packhorse going from Bardfield to London to obtain divers things for the Lady's Chamber, staying and returning, for 3 days ending on 7 November, 1s. Item wages of Richard page of the Chamber going from Bardfield to London to Walter Colpeper with the Lady's letters, staying and returning, for 3 days ending on 6 November, 4½d. Expenses of 1 packhorse of the Lady going from Bardfield to London with Margaret Gregg, staying and returning, for 4 days in the same month, 8d. Item wages of Richard page of the Chamber going from Bardfield to the countess of Pembroke[37] at Fotheringhay with the Lady's letters, staying and returning, for 4½ days ending on 30 November, 6¾d. Colinet Picard's wages going from Bardfield to London for furs and other purchases for the Lady, staying and returning, for 4 days ending on 26 November, 2s. 8d. 1 groom's pay going from Bardfield to Wormegay with the

---

[37] Marie de St Pol, countess of Pembroke.

Lady's letters, staying and returning, for 4 days in the same month, 6d. Expenses of Edmund page of the Chamber going from Bardfield to Gransden with the Lady's letters, staying and returning, for 2 days, 3d. 1 groom's pay and expenses of 1 hackney hired from Bardfield to London for Master Martin, the doctor with Sir Edward [de]Monthermer, 8d.[38] Item wages of Richard page of the Chamber going from Bardfield to Wormegay with the Lady's letters, staying and returning, for 3½ days ending on 5 December, 5¼d. Sir Thomas de Cheddeworth's expenses in London to carry out the Lady's business for 5 days in November, 13s. 8d. 1 hackney hired from Clare to Bardfield by Henry de Colingham to carry 1 doe, 4d. William Seman's wages going to the Lady Queen Isabella[39] and Lord Morley with the Lady's letters addressed to them concerning the burial of Sir Edward de Monthermer, for 5 days ending on 12 December, 5s. John de Claketon's wages going with letters to Lord Fitzwalter and other knights in those parts concerning the said business, staying and returning, for 3 days ending on the above day, 3s. Wages of John Bradewey, James the huntsman, John Walisch and Henry page of hunting being at Hundon in the company of Robert Mareschal for hunting does, for 5 days in the same month, 2s. 3½d. Wages of Richard page of the Chamber going from Bardfield to the Abbot of St Edmunds at Redgrave about the business of the said burial, for 3 days in the same month, 4½d. Item wages of Roger Cotel going to the Abbot of St Edmunds, Sir Robert de Causton, Sir John de Loudham and other knights in Suffolk with the Lady's letters touching the burial of the said Sir E[dward] de Monthermer, for 5 days ending on 13 December, 5s. Wages of Thomas de Wodham going with the Lady's letters addressed to Sir Robert Bourchier, Sir William de Well', Sir William de Wauton and others concerning the said business, for 3 days in the same month, 1s. 1½d. Richard Chamberlain's wages going to Sir Thomas de Monthermer at Stokenham with the Lady's letters addressed to him concerning the said business, staying and returning, for 19 days in the same month, 7s. 1½d. 1 hackney hired for him for the same time, 2s. 4d. Henry de Dene's expenses going with William Seman to separate the mares, for 2 days in the same month, 1s. Expenses of the same going to Hundon to take does before Christmas, 8d. Expenses of 2 packhorses going to London with Robert \Mareschal/ concerning the Lady's livery and of 1 packhorse going with them, 2s. 1¼d. Item, expenses of 1 packhorse of the Lady going from Bardfield to London and Barking carrying venison to the wife of Robert Parvyng and Margaret Gregg and carrying other items back for the Lady's Chamber, going and staying, for 3 days ending on 29 December, 1s. 1d. Throm's wages going with the Lady's letter addressed to Warin Martyn on 27 December, staying and returning, for 2 days, 3d. Item given for the soul of Reginald le Ewer at the Lady's order in the price of his robe and 1qr of wheat, 10s. Item Sir Robert de Stalynton's expenses going from Bardfield to London to buy furs in November, with Colinet Picard's expenses and 1 packhorse of the Lady, 10s. 3d. Colinet's wages being at Clare for business touching the Lady for 1½ days, on 6 January, 1s. Wages of Gilbert, chamberlain, being there for the said business for the same time, 6¾d. 2 hackneys hired by Mareschal and Kent coming from Cambridge before Christmas, 1s. 4d. Expenses of the same on the way at Linton, 3d. Expenses of 1 packhorse of William atte Stoure going with the gift of 1 cloth to the Lady Countess of Pembroke at Fotheringhay in November, 8d. Expenses of William the confectioner going to Clare to

---

[38] Sir Edward de Monthermer was the Lady's half-brother.
[39] Isabella, widow of Edward II.

obtain divers items for the Wardrobe on 8 January, 2d. Bothel's wages going to John Moveron at Frating with the Lady's letters addressed to **[m. 12]** him on 7 January, for 2 days, 4d. Item expenses of John Falconer and Nicholas going with the Lady's falconer to Hanley and elsewhere to Sir Hugh Despenser, staying there and returning, in the months of November, December and January, ending on 19 January, 5s. Wages of Richard page of the Chamber going from Bardfield to Gransden with the Lady's letters addressed to Sir Thomas de Cheddeworth on the same day, 3d. Wages \of the same/ going to Wormegay with the Lady's letters addressed to Lord Bardolf, staying and returning, for 4½ days ending on 19 January, 6¾d. Colinet Picard's wages being at Clare for business touching the Lady's Chamber for 2 days, 10d., and not more because his horse was on provender and his groom on wages. Thomas Goldsmith's wages being at Braintree on the Lady's business and at Clare to supervise the finishing of a gold rose and other things, going, staying and returning, for 3 days, 1s. 1½d. Wages of Gilbert, chamberlain, being there with Colinet for 2 days, 4d. 1 hackney hired for the same from Clare to Bardfield on returning, 4d. Wages of Edmund page of the Chamber going to Tonbridge in December with the Lady's letters addressed to the Prior of Tonbridge and Walter Colpeper, staying and returning, for 6 days, 9d. Wages of the same going with robes to John de Goldingham and Walter Colpeper, staying and returning, for 6 days ending on 20 January, 9d. Expenses of 1 hackney carrying the said robes there, 10d. Expenses of Thomas Mareschal and Kent going to Cambridge on 20 January, 9d. Roger Skinner's wages going to Clare on the Lady's secret business, staying and returning, for 4 days, 6d. Item wages of John Walisch going with the Lady's letters addressed to the Bishop of Llandaff and Philip Vaughan in Wales on business touching Sir Thomas de Cheddeworth, staying and returning, for 21 days ending on 27 January, 2s. 7½d. Item given to the page of the Bakehouse for shoes, 4d. 1 groom's pay carrying John de Lenne's letter to Sir John Darre on the same day concerning his arrears, 2d. 1 groom's pay going from Bardfield to Bury St Edmunds for parchment on 28 January, 3d. Wages of Richard page of the Chamber going to London with the Lady's letters addressed to John Bataille, staying and returning, for 4 days ending on the above day, 6d. Colinet Picard's wages going from Bardfield to Clare for business touching his office for 2½ days, 1s. 1d., and not more because his horse was on provender and his groom on wages. Wages of John, chamberlain, being there for the same time to clean the Chamber and prepare for the Lady's arrival, 9¼d., and not more because his horse was on provender for 1 night. Wages of Robert of the Wardrobe being there for the said business for the same time, 3¾d. Wages of Edmund page of the Chamber going to London with the Lady's letters addressed to Sir Andrew de Bures, staying and returning, for 3 days ending on 29 January, 4½d. Item 1 hackney hired from Warblington to Clare to carry 1 bed and table-linen of Sir Edward de Monthermer, with expenses incurred for the same by John Holdich, ending on 30 January, 3s. 6d. Item Richard le Hosier's wages going from Bardfield to London with the Lady's letters addressed to John Bataille on 30 January, 6d. 1 groom's pay going to Haverhill by night to obtain 1 carpenter by the Lady's order announced to William Lengleys, 2d. 10 women's and 10 helpers' pay carrying 5 tuns with 300 bream from Clare to Hundon to stock 1 pond there on 10 February, 1s. 8d. Andrew de Waleden's expenses going to London in the same month for business concerning Sir Peter de Ereswell by order of the Lady, 2s. Wages of Robert groom of the Chamber being at Clare before the Lady's arrival to prepare the Chamber and do divers other things for 6 days, 9d. Pay of 1 labourer working on [*?*]*reng'* clay by view of Colingham before the burial of Sir Edward de Monthermer, 6d. 2 hackneys hired from Clare to Ipswich for Friar Robert de Cotton deputy and his companion, 1s. Expenses of the said friars with the expenses of their horses going and returning, 1s. 2d. Item given to 1 man of Hundon for 1 sheep killed by Thomas Fitzwalter's greyhounds, 8d. Expenses of 2 hackneys going from Clare to Ipswich for Friar Robert de Cotton and his companion with expenses of 1 groom, a stranger, and of the said friars returning on 20 February, 1s. Wages of Edmund page of the Chamber going from Clare to Anglesey with the Lady's packhorse for 4 days to clean the Chamber and do divers other things before the Lady's arrival, 6d. 1 groom's pay going there to forewarn the Lady's carter about carrying 1 table [*or parcel*] from there to Clare, 1d. Item expenses of William Lengleys going from Bardfield to Hundon, Clare and Sudbury to oversee the state of the manors and stock and to levy money, staying and returning, for 3 days ending on 3 February, 3s. Expenses of the same going from Clare to Bardfield, Stebbing, Finchingfield and elsewhere to oversee the said manors, with Henry de Neuton, newly made Constable, for 4 days ending on 24 February, 4s. Wages of Richard page of the Chamber going to the Countess of Pembroke with the Lady's letters addressed to her, for 3½ days ending on 22 February, 5d. Wages of Edmund page of the Chamber going to London with the Lady's letters addressed to Sir Hugh Despenser and for doing other business of the Lady there, staying and returning, for 4 days ending on 23 February, 6d. 1 groom's pay going with letters of the Duke of Cornwall[40] to Lord Bardolf[41] and meeting the same on the way towards Clare, 1d. Item given to 1 shepherd for 1 sheep killed by the Lady's greyhounds in coming from Clare to Anglesey, 1s. 2 hackneys hired for the friars as above in the preceding week and not entered there for lack of presentation on 20 February, 11d. Item divers expenses made concerning the chimney of Lady Bardolf's chamber at Anglesey by Sir William d'Arderne as appears in the particulars in February, 15s. 11d. Wages of Robert of the Wardrobe and Roger Skinner, left at Clare after the Lady's departure, in coming with the carts to Anglesey on 1 March, 3d. Item expenses of Robert Mareschal staying in London for the Lady's business and coming from there, for 3 days ending on 9 March, 3s. 8d. 1 groom's pay carrying the Lady's letters to Sir Ralph de Bocking at Bury St Edmunds, and from there to Clare with letters addressed to the Constable and the community of Sudbury, on the above day, 3d. 1 groom's pay going to London with the Lady's letters addressed to Sir Andrew de Bures on 10 March, 6d. Wages of Richard page of the Chamber going from Anglesey to London and Tonbridge to the said Sir Andrew, staying and returning, for 6 days, 9d. Wages of Edmund page of the Chamber going to Wormegay with the Lady's letters addressed to Lord Bardolf, for 3½ days, 5¼d. Richard le Hosier's pay going with the Lady's letters to find William de Clopton, for 2 days, 3d. Item wages of John Bradewey, James the huntsman, John Walisch groom and Henry page of the aforesaid, being in the region of Desning, Barrow and Dullingham with coursing hounds for 14 days in March ending on 20 March, 6s. 5d. Bread bought for the said dogs for 1 day because of failure to carry bread from Anglesey to the same men in the said region, 10d. Item John Honylee's expenses going from Anglesey to London on the Lady's business with letters concerning the Lady's business in the parts of Wales and Pembroke, staying and returning, for 3 days ending on 18 March, 1s. 5½d. Colinet Picard's expenses going to London to purchase cloth for the poor in March, 8d., and not more

---

[40] Edward, eldest son of Edward III, was created duke of Cornwall in 1337.
[41] Sir John Bardolf, the Lady's son-in-law.

because he was at the costs of [*Robert*] Mareschal. Expenses of 1 packhorse going there to carry the said cloth to Anglesey, 10d. Robert Mareschal's wages going to London at that time to Sir Henry de Ferrers[42] on certain business for 5½ days, 8s. 3d. Expenses of Richard page of the Chamber going from Anglesey to London with the Lady's letters addressed to John Bataille on 25 March, 4d. 1 groom's pay taking the Countess of Ulster's 2 lost spaniels to Whaddon, 4d.[43] Item Colinet Picard's wages going from Anglesey to Clare to supervise his Wardrobe for 1 day, 1 April, 6d., and not more because his horse was on provender. 2 grooms' pay carrying 1 nanny goat from Anglesey to Hundon on the same day, 2d. Wages of Richard page of the Chamber going to London with the Lady's letters addressed to Sir Andrew de Bures on the same day, staying and returning, for 3½ days, 5¼d. Item wages of Richard page of the Chamber going from Anglesey to London with the Lady's letters addressed to Sir Andrew de Bures on 7 April, staying and returning, for 4 days, 5¾d. Sarlyng's pay going to Bury St Edmunds with the Lady's letters addressed to the prior on the same day, 1d. Wages of the groom of Robert de Bassingbourne going from Anglesey to London with the Lady's letters addressed to Sir Warin de Bassingbourne and the said Sir Andrew, staying and returning, for 4 days, 6d. Wages of Robert Mareschal going to parliament in London to prosecute the Lady's business there, for 6½ days, 9s. 9d. Expenses of Master Richard de Plessys and Sir Robert de Stalynton going from Anglesey to Cambridge for the Lady's business concerning the appropriation of Litlington church in the same month, 6s. 2d. Item wages of John Bataille Bataille [*sic*] going to London to speak to Sir Henry de Ferrers for the Lady's business, staying and returning, for 6 days, 6s. Expenses of the same, Philip ap Jevan[*and*] John son of John Beneyt coming from Cambridge, 1s. Thomas le Barbour's wages going from Anglesey to Bury St Edmunds and West Dereham with the Lady's letters addressed to the abbot of St Edmunds, the abbot of West Dereham and the prior of Walsingham, staying and returning, for 3 days ending on 15 April, 1s. 1½d. Hugh le Charer's wages going from Anglesey to Ely on the same day with the Lady's letters addressed to the prior there, staying and returning, for 2 days on 2 occasions, 1s. 4d. Colinet Picard's wages going from Anglesey to Clare for 1 day to supervise his Wardrobe, 4d., and not more because his horse was on provender and his groom on wages. Item wages of John Bradewey, James the huntsman and J[*ohn*] Walisch, groom, and Henry, the said men's page, going to the area of Bradley, Balsham and elsewhere with coursing hounds, staying and returning, for 16 days in the months of March and April, ending on 13 April, taking as above, 7s. 4d. Expenses of 1 destrier of the countess of Ulster going from Clare to Whaddon, with 1 groom's wages going there with the same, in the same month, 1s. 10½d. Roger Cotel's wages going from Anglesey to London to the countess of Ulster with the Lady's letters addressed to her, staying and returning, for 6 days in the same month, 6s. 2 grooms' pay carrying the organs of the friars minor from Cambridge to Anglesey before the feast of Easter, and returning, 8d. Wages of Edmund page of the Chamber going from Anglesey to London with the Lady's letters addressed to Sir H[*enry*] de Ferrers, waiting there for a reply, staying and returning, for 8 days, 1s. 1 groom's pay going to Usk with a letter of Sir H[*enry*] de Ferrers addressed to Robert de Knaresburgh concerning the business of William de Dernford, 1s. 4d. Item wages of John Chamberlain yeoman, Robert of the Chamber and Jevan of the Wardrobe, groom, going

---

42 Sir Henry de Ferrers was the Lady's son-in-law.
43 The countess of Ulster was probably the Lady's daughter-in-law, Matilda of Lancaster.

46

ahead from Anglesey to Clare to make ready their offices before the Lady's arrival, for 1 day, 18 April, 5d. Wages of William de Berchamsted going from Anglesey to Bardfield with the Lady's bed [*and*] making ready there before her arrival for 1 day in the same month, 4½d. John de Claketon's expenses going from Anglesey with the Lady's letters addressed to the abbot of St Edmunds in the same month, 9d. John Falconer's expenses going from Anglesey with the Lady's letters addressed to the prior of Ely in the same month, 6d. Expenses of Richard page of the Chamber going from Anglesey to Wormegay with letters addressed to Lord Bardolf and returning to Clare, for 3 days, 4d. Expenses of 2 friars minor coming from Ipswich to Clare with the expenses of Edmund page of the Chamber going for the aforesaid friars and returning, for 2 days, 6d. Item expenses of Robert Mareschal, Henry de Dene, Henry de Neuton, Edmund Wymer and others going from Clare to Woodham Ferrers to supervise the stock of the manor and other things there in April, for 3 days, 3s. 11d. Wages of the said Henry de Dene going from Anglesey to Windsor taking 1 destrier of the Lady to Sir Henry de Ferrers and [*doing*] other things concerning the Lady's business in the same month on 2 occasions, staying and returning, for 10 days, 9s. 10d., and not more because the horse was on provender for 1 night. Colinet Picard's wages going from Clare to London to purchase 1 cloth of *tiretain* for the Lady and bargaining for part of the livery in the same month, staying and returning, for 4½ days, 3s. 1 hackney hired for John Best going from Clare to Finchingfield with Thomas Giffard for 1 day, 3d. Richard le Hosier's pay going in the same month with the Lady's letters from Clare to Bottisham and elsewhere to find John de Hertford, staying and returning, for 2 days, 2d. Item expenses of Sir Warin de Bassingbourne, Robert Mareschal, Nicholas Damory and others of the Lady's household going on business concerning John Bataille with 17 horses in May, 6s. 6d. Expenses of Edmund page of the Chamber going from Clare to London with the Lady's letters addressed to Sir John Sturmy and returning, for 3 days, 4d. Henry de Dene's wages going from Clare to [*White*] Notley and London with the Lady's letters addressed to Sir John d'Engaine, staying and returning, for 4 days ending on 2 May, 3s. 10d., and not more because the horse was on provender for 1 night. Wages of Richard page of the Chamber going from Clare to London with the Lady's letters addressed to Sir Andrew de Bures and returning, for 4½ days, and his wages going from there to Cambridge with the Lady's **[m. 13]** letters addressed to Sir Warin de Bassingbourne and returning, for 1 day, 5 May, 9d. Item expenses of Walter Darleston and Henry de Dene going to London with money of Sir Henry de Ferrers and returning, for 4 days in May, with 11½d. for the expenses of 2 packhorses carrying the said silver with the same men, 3s. 11½d., and not more because they were at the cost of Sir H[*enry*] in going and at the cost of the land on returning. Hugh le Charer's wages going from Clare to Anglesey to fetch the Lady's little coach and bringing it to Clare, for 1½ days, 1s. Wages of Richard page of the Chamber going to London with the Lady's letters addressed to Henry de Dene and returning, for 3 days, 4½d. Colinet Picard's wages going to London to obtain 1 cloth of *tiretain* for the Lady, and 5 striped cloths bought there for the yeomen, and returning, for 4½ days, 3s. Wages of Edmund page of the Chamber going to London with the Lady's letters addressed to Sir Andrew de Bures, Henry Chener and Stephen Freynch, and returning, for 4 days ending on 10 May, 6d. Item expenses of Sir Andrew de Bures and William Lengleys going to London and staying there on the Lady's business, and going from there to Tonbridge to take the chamberlain's final account and to sell wood, together with the expenses of the prior of Tonbridge, Walter Colpeper and the forester being with the same for the same time, and returning from there to

London to expedite the Lady's business, staying and returning, for 15 days, together with the said William's expenses staying in London after Sir Andrew's departure waiting for money coming from Tonbridge, and returning to Standon, for 5 days ending on 16 March, £2 10s. 2d. Expenses of the same man, Robert de Cheddeworth, John Bataille, Philip ap Jevan, John Beneyt and others of the Lady's council being at parliament in the same month for certain business concerning the Lady against Countess Marshal, £6. Item Henry de Dene's wages going to Whiston with the Lady's letters addressed to the earl of Gloucester, and from there to London to obtain money, staying and returning, for 6 days ending on 16 May, 5s. 8d., and not more because his horse was on provender and his groom on wages for 1 night. Robert de Bassingbourne's expenses with 2 yeomen going from Kent to Whiston with Henry de Dene, 1s. 10d. 1 hackney hired from Ware to London for Henry de Dene because his horse was sick on the way, 6d. Wages of Edmund page of the Chamber going from Clare to Gransden with the Lady's letters addressed to Robert de Cheddeworth to seek out the said Robert, for 2 days, 3d. Loss of 790 gallons of ale bought at Stepney and sold there because the Lady failed to arrive, with the loss on carting and other expenses incurred concerning the said ale in April and March by Roger of the Pantry, 7s. 8d. Roger's wages going there and to London for the said preparations before the Lady's arrival and arranging delivery of the said ale and divers things concerning his office, staying and returning, for 18 days ending on 26 April, 12s. Adam the baker's wages being there concerning his office and helping the said Roger for 17 days, taking 2d. a day, 2s. 10d. Wages of the page of the Bakery being there for the said business for 13 days, 1s. 1d. 1 hackney hired to carry the Bakery's sacks from London to Clare, 1s. 4d. Expenses of the said Roger going from Clare to London another time to account with divers men for the return and sale of victuals, for 3½ days ending on 10 May, 2s. 2d. For carting and divers expenses incurred over hay bought and sold there by John Gough for the said reason, 6s. 9d. Expenses of 10 men and horses for 5 carts from Standon on boonwork going and carting 20qr of wheat-flour from Standon to Stepney viz. for all expenses, 9s. 3d. God's penny given for divers items viz. for hay, wood, charcoal and other purchases there, 4d. The said John Gough's wages going from Anglesey to London twice in April to arrange for and deliver the said provisions, staying and returning, for 15½ days, 15s. 6d. Item expenses of Edmund the clerk going from Clare to London with the Lady's letters addressed to the countess of Northampton on 20 May,[44] staying and returning, for 4 days, 2s. Richard le Hosier's pay going from Clare to Colchester to fetch Roger Scoler before Ascension Day, 1d. Wages of Richard page of the Chamber going to [?]Latton with the Lady's letters addressed to Robert Mareschal, staying and returning, for 2½ days, 3¾d. John de Horslee's wages going from Clare to Groby in May and returning, for 5 days, 5s. 2 grooms' pay getting organs at Bardfield and bringing them to Clare before Ascension Day, 4d. Pay of a stranger from Cranborne carrying writs from London to Dorset for business concerning William de Warham, 6d. Wages of Edmund page of the Chamber going to London with the Lady's letters addressed to Henry Chener and John de Honelee about divers matters concerning the Lady's Chamber over the King's arrival, staying and returning, for 4 days, 6d. Expenses for 1 day of Robert de Bassingbourne in coming from Whiston and of other esquires of Sir Warin de

---

[44] Elizabeth de Badelesmere married (1) Edmund Mortimer and (2) William de Bohun, earl of Northampton.

Bassingbourne, and entered here because not accounted for above in the past week, 9d. Robert Mareschal's wages going to London to Sir H[enry] de Ferrers, staying and returning, for 4 days, 6s. Item expenses of 1 palfrey of the Lady going from North Weald to London to fetch Stokton for 1 night in June, 5d. Expenses of William de Berchamsted, John the chamberlain and 1 horse of William Seman with 1 groom coming from Clare to North Weald for 1 day in the same month, 6½d. Wages of Robert groom of the Chamber going ahead from Clare to North Weald to prepare the Lady's chamber before her arrival, for 1½ days, 2¼d. Wages of Richard page of the Chamber going from North Weald to Tonbridge with the Lady's letters addressed to the countess of Gloucester, the prior of Tonbridge and Walter Colpeper, staying and returning, for 3 days ending on 8 June, 4½d. Wages of the same going from Rochester to Harwich with the Lady's letters addressed to Lady de Ferrers and Sir Andrew de Bures, staying and returning, for 4 days ending on 13 June, with 2d. for the ferry at Tilbury going and returning, 8d. 1 hackney hired for the same on the way on the Lady's order, 5d. Wages of Richard page of the Chamber going with the Lady's letters addressed to Lady de Ferrers, Sir Andrew de Bures and Thomas Coteler to Ipswich, Walton and elsewhere, staying and returning, for 4½ days, 6¾d. Expenses of Edmund page of the Chamber going from North Weald to London to obtain towels and for other business of the Chamber on 18 June, 1½d. Item wages of Robert page of the Chamber going to London with the Lady's letters addressed to Sir R de Sadyngton, staying and returning, for 3 days ending on 25 June, 4½d. Expenses of John Walisch going to *Manewod* with the Lady's letters addressed to John Bataille and returning, for 2 days, 2d. 1 groom's pay for keeping 1 hackney of Thomas Fitzwalter on the journey to Canterbury, going with the Lady for 3 weeks, 6d. Wages of Richard page of the Chamber going to London with the Lady's letters addressed to Sir Robert de Stalynton, staying and returning, for 4 days, 6d. Wages of the same going from Clare to Wormegay with the Lady's letters addressed to Lady Bardolf and returning, for 3½ days, 5¼d. Item expenses of 1 palfrey and 1 packhorse of Lady going from Clare to Cambridge with Katherine de Haliwell in June, for 1 night, 8d. Expenses of Edmund page of the Chamber going from Clare to Rochford to the earl of Northampton with the Lady's letters addressed to him, 2d. Colinet Picard's wages going from North Weald to Clare to fetch 1 robe of the Lady, with 6d. for 1 hackney hired to carry the said robe, 1s. 2d. Wages of the same going from Dartford and Newton to London for certain business concerning the Lady, the Lady going to Canterbury, and from Dartford and North Weald by another way on returning from Canterbury, and for obtaining the Lady's confections at Clare, the Lady staying at North Weald in June, 3s. 9½d. Item wages of Edmund page of the Chamber going from Clare to London with the Lady's letters addressed to Henry Chener concerning certain business touching the Lady's Chamber, staying and returning, for 3 days ending on 16 July, 4½d. Wages of Richard page of the Chamber going from Clare to Wormegay [and] Whinburgh with the Lady's letters addressed to Lord Bardolf, staying and returning, for 3 days ending on 19 July, 4½d. 1 hackney hired for the same to hasten the said business on the Lady's order, 2½d. Item Robert Mareschal's expenses going from Clare to Bardfield to oversee the park there on 20 July, 10d. Colinet Picard's wages going from Clare to London for divers purchases for the Lady's little coach and returning, for 6 days ending on 22 July, 4s. Hugh le Charer's wages going there for the said business, staying and returning, for the same time, 4s. Expenses of John Holdich going from Clare to Bury St Edmunds to buy cloth on 1 occasion, and from Clare to North Weald another time for certain business touching the Lady, for 1 day, 9d. 1 chain bought for the coach in July by Robert de Schirwode, 6d. 10 hackneys from Clare hired for the journey to Canterbury for certain men of the Lady's household, going and returning, for 21 days, viz. 3s. for each hackney, £1 10s. Item John de Claketon's expenses going from Clare to Ipswich and Harwich to meet Lord Fitzwalter coming from overseas, with 1 hackney hired for the same on the way because his horse was sick, 2s. Wages of John Bradewey, John Walisch and James the groom of hunting, going from Bardfield to Cranborne with coursing hounds to hunt there, viz. in going, for 5 days, 1s. 10½d. Item given to the said James the huntsman for shoes on Robert Mareschal's order, 6d. Expenses of 3 greyhounds and 18 coursing hounds going there viz., 8½d. a day, 3s. 6½d. Wages of John de Rston [sic] and John le Hunte going there with the same for the same time, 1s. 3d. Item wages of Hugh le Charer and Colinet Picard going to London for 3 workmen to roof the Lady's coach and buy other necessary items for it, staying and returning, for 7 days, taking 1s. 4d. a day, 9s. 4d. Wages of Edmund page of the Chamber going to London with the Lady's letters addressed to Colinet Picard, staying and returning, for 3½ days ending on 6 August, 5¼d. Master William de Brampton's expenses going from Clare to Fulham to the Bishop of London[45] on certain business concerning the Lady, staying and returning, for 4 days in August, 4s. 2d. William the confectioner's expenses going from Clare to Bury St Edmunds for 1 night to obtain 1 *pinaculum* on the Lady's order, 2½d. Wages of Edmund page of the Chamber going from Clare to London with the Lady's letters addressed to R[obert] de Eynesham and Stephen Freynsch, staying and returning, for 4 days, 6d. Nicholas Falconer's expenses going in the park of *Karlil* to the house of Sir Richard Parvyng to obtain rabbits, 5s. Item Sir William de Brampton's expenses going from Clare to London to find the Bishop of the Augustinian Friars on certain business concerning the Lady, staying and returning, for 3 days ending on 20 August, 2s. 4d. Colinet Picard's wages going to London to obtain certain items missing from the coach and 12 cloths for the livery of the Lady's clerks, staying and returning, for 4 days ending on the above day, 2s. 8d. Expenses of Richard page of the Chamber going to London with the Lady's letters addressed to Master Richard Plessys, staying and returning, for 3 days, 4d. Item Hugh le Charer's wages going to London on certain business concerning the Lady's coach, staying and returning, for 9 days ending on 28 August, 6s. Expenses of 2 packhorses going with him and Colinet Picard to obtain 13 cloths and for the said business concerning the coach, carrying [them] to Clare, staying and returning, for 4½ days, 3s. ¼d. Item hay bought for 28 horses for 37 nights whereof 13 horses for 28 nights, 10 for 7 nights and 5 for 2 nights, at 5b. for each horse for a day and night, at ½d. a b., £2 15s. 6d. 25qr 4b. 2 pecks of oats bought for the said horses' provender, whereof 12 [horses] for 28 nights, 9 for 7 nights and 5 for 2 nights on provender, at 2s. 2d. a qr, £2 15s. 4½d. 1qr 3 pecks of oats bought for 1 hackney's provender staying with the said horses for 35 days, 2s. 4d. 20 grooms' wages staying with the said horses for 36 days whereof 9 grooms for 27 days, 8 grooms for 7 days and 3 grooms for 2 days, viz. 1½d. a day per groom, £1 18s. 1½d. Item expenses of Nicholas[46] Tebaud, Colinet Picard and William the confectioner going from Clare to St Botolph's[47] to buy cloth for the Lady's livery, wax and other necessary items for the Wardrobe, staying and returning, for 6 days ending on 2 September, 19s. 8d. Jordan Skinner's pay going

---

45 Ralph Stratford, bishop of London, 1340–54.
46 *Recte* Nigel.
47 Boston, Lincs. The purchases were probably made at the fair there.

50

from Clare to London to obtain small nails for the Lady's coach, staying and returning, for 5 days waiting for the said nails, 9d. John Iwayn's expenses going from Clare to Little Easton on the Lady's business to Sir Thomas de Loveyn, staying and returning, for 1½ days, 2d. John Falconer's wages going from Clare to *Lyndon* on the Lady's order, Sir H[ugh] Despenser's falconer being ill there, staying and returning, for 2 days ending on 5 September, 9d. Master William de Brampton's expenses going from Clare to Orsett to the Bishop of London on certain business concerning the Lady, staying and returning, for 2 days, 1s. 5d. Monnamy's pay going from Clare to London to obtain nails for the Lady's coach, for 4 days, 8d. Thomas le Barbour's wages going from Clare to London with the Lady's letters addressed to the earl of Arundel, staying and returning, for 4 days, 1s. 6d. William Butler's expenses going from Tewkesbury to Bristol and Usk to purchase 3 tuns of wine and take them to Usk, for 4 days in April, 4s. Loading the said tuns, 1s. 3d. John Bataille's wages going from Clare to London to Sir H[ugh] Despenser on divers business of the Lady, staying and returning, for 3 days ending on the last day of August, 3s. 1 groom's pay going from London to Farnham to Sir H[enry] de Thetford with the Lady's letters and from there returning to Clare with a letter of the said Sir Henry, 8d. Item pay [*damaged*48] going from Clare to divers places with the Lady's letters addressed to Thomas Fabel [*and*] John Gernoun, staying and returning, for 2 days to do this, 4d. [*damaged*] le Hunte yeoman, J[ohn] Bradewey, James the huntsman, John Walisch groom and Henry page of the aforesaid going round Bardfield and Chelmsford [*damaged*] on 17 September to the 23rd day of the same month, the last day counted, viz. for 6 days, 3s. 9d. H[enry] de Dene's expenses [*damaged*] to Cambridge with 1 palfrey and 1 packhorse of the Lady to fetch Katherine de Haliwell, viz. for bread, hay, oats for the said horses, staying [*damaged*] ending on 11 September, 1s. 1¾d. Item expenses of Roger Ewyas going from Clare to Caversham on his way towards his country with the Lady's letters addressed to [*damaged*] Despenser viz. at the Lady's cost to Caversham, for 2½ days, 2s. 6d. Richard le Hosier's pay going to Thomas Fabel with the Lady's letters addressed to him, seeking the said Thomas in divers places, 2d. Colinet Picard's wages going from Clare to Stourbridge fair to purchase cloth for the Lady's livery there, staying there and returning, for 3 days ending on 16 September, 2s. Hugh le Charer's wages going from Clare to London to supervise the making of new harness for the Lady's coach there, staying and returning, for 4½ days, 3s. Expenses of 2 palfreys and 1 packhorse [*damaged*] Clare to Cambridge with Katherine and Margaret de Haliwell for 1 night in the same month, 1s. 1½d. Item wages of Thomas [*damaged*] from Clare to London on the Lady's business, staying and returning, for 3 days ending on 29 September, taking 4½d. a day, 1s. 1½d. Wages of John le Hunte yeoman, John Bradewey, James the huntsman, John Walisch groom and Henry page of the same men hunting in the Bardfield region for 2 days ending on 29 September, 1s. 3d. Expenses of 8 greyhounds and 27 coursing hounds with the same men viz. for bread bought for the same for 1 day, 8d. Item given to Robert the saddler for the repair of his buildings broken by the Lady's pigs, 2s. **[m. 14]** Item expenses of Robert Mareschal being in parts of Dorset to take venison in August, 6s. 1d. And Henry de Dene's expenses in parts of Wales for the same purpose, 4s.

Sum £43 9s. 5½d.49 audited

---

48 The document is damaged for the next six lines on the right-hand side.
49 There is no marginal total for this paragraph and the following paragraphs on the face of the document.

Pay of servants   The same accounts for payment to W[*illiam*] Apothecary for his fee from the feast of Easter year 12 until Michaelmas [*illeg.*], £1 5s. Item to William de Stanford for his fee and robe for 1 year [*illeg.*].

Sum £1 8s. 4d.   audited

Expenses of the household and for diet   The same accounts for the expenses of the household as appears on the Diet Roll for the time of this account, £472 19s. [*illeg.*]

Sum £472 19s. 4¼d.   audited

Delivery of money   Delivered to Sir Robert de Stalynton for horses and issues of the Kitchen and other things sold, by 1 indenture, £58 7s. 10d. Item delivered to the same Robert by the hands of Sir John Darre, formerly Keeper of the Wardrobe, in part payment of £10 of his arrears, £3 6s. 8d. Item delivered to Sir William de Manton for divers things remaining in the Larder after the end of this account, as appears in the indenture, for which he will answer in next year's account, 14s. 1d.

Sum £62 8s. 7d.   audited

Expenses and provisions made for next year   Grain and divers other things purchased ~~purchased~~ from the vicar of Finchingfield at the manor of Cockfield for the Lady's needs as appears in the particulars sewn to this roll, £22 18s. 1d.[50]

Sum £22 18s. 1d.   audited

Pardons and payments   Pardon given by the Lady to Margaret Gregg for wheat bought from her [*which was*] deficient, for which the same John took responsibility above in this account in the sale of wheat and he did not receive it, £4 19s. 4d. Item pardon given by the Lady to Thomas de Doubrigge, formerly Clerk of the Offices, concerning John's responsibility, 18s. 8½d. Item paid to William d'Arderne chaplain, of the Lady's gift at the Lady's order, £1. Pardon given by the Lady in the presence of Sir Andrew de Bures steward and others of the Lady's council to the pantlers, butlers, bakers, brewers, larderers, poulterers and chandlers for divers items deficient in their offices and sold on their account in this year and the 4 preceding years, as appears in the particulars, £43 16s. 9d.

Sum £50 14s. 9½d.   audited

Sum of all expenses and deliveries £2,147 7s. 4¾d. And know that this account is charged with the sum of arrears of Gilbert de Cardoil, formerly keeper of the said Wardrobe, £1. 18s. 8¹₂d.; and £6 13s. 4d. of the arrears of John Darre, formerly keeper of the same Wardrobe; and £1 10s. of the arrears of the same John and William Butler; and 3s. of John Gough's arrears from 1 old cart's iron-work sold by him in the same time.

Sum of arrears £10 5s. ½d. And the total sum of expenses and deliveries with the said arrears is £2,157 12s. 5¼d. And so the said John de Lenne [*is*] in surplus, £33 13s. 1½d. To which he shows creditors up to the total of £37 15s. 5½d.

[Corn and stock account]

[m. 2d] Wheat   The same answers for 275qr 4b. of wheat received from the remainder. And 446qr 7b. received from the manors. And 46qr 4b. received from purchase in the region and 11qr 6b. received from increment.

Sum 780qr 5b.   audited

Of this, baked for provisions of the Lady's household for the time of this account as appears on the Diet Roll, 648qr 6b. And sold as below 92qr 4b.

Sum 741qr 2b. And 39qr 3b. remain in the granary. Item there remains of the

---

50   The particulars sewn to the roll have disappeared.

Cockfield wheat by estimation 55qr in the stack for which William de Manton now clerk of the Wardrobe is to answer \he is not made responsible for it above/.[51]

audited

Loaves   The same answers for 300 loaves received from the remainder. And 142,646 loaves received from the wheat baked as above. And 54 loaves received as gifts.

Sum 143,000.   audited

Of this, for provisions of the household as appears on the Diet Roll, 135,933 loaves. And delivered for horses' provender as appears by tally between Roger of the Pantry and W of the Avenery, 4,160 loaves. Sold on account, 2,027.

Sum, 142,120 loaves. And there remain 880 loaves.   audited

Wine   The same answers for 13 tuns, 1 pipe received from the remainder. And 23 tuns, 2 pipes received from purchase. And 1 sester, 3 pitchers of wine as gifts. And 1 tun of Rhenish wine, a gift of Sir Henry de Ferrers containing 40 sesters by estimate.[52]

Sum 38 tuns, 1 pipe, 1 sester, 3 pitchers of wine whereof 1 tun contains 40 sesters.   audited

Of this, for provisions of the household as appears on the Diet Roll, 30 tuns, 1 sester, 3 pitchers.

Sum 30 tuns, 1 sester, 3 pitchers. And there remain 8 tuns and 1 pipe of Gascon wine.   audited

Maslin   The same answers for 1qr 4b. of maslin received from the manors. And all is accounted for ~~in delivery to the Avener~~ \in bread provided/ for provender of the Lady's horses as below, 1qr. And he is quit.   audited

Item in sale on account, 4b. Afterwards found by examination that this was baked and provided in provender of the horses sojourning at Clare after the Lady's departure to Canterbury. And so this sale on account is void.

Peas, beans and vetch   1qr of beans from the remainder. The same answers for 23qr 5b. of peas and beans \and vetch/ received from the manors. And 10qr of peas and beans received from purchase in the region.

Sum 34qr 5b.   audited

Of this, ~~delivered to the Avener~~ \accounted for in bread/ baked for provisions of the Lady's horses as appears below, 18qr 1b. And for feeding the boars and pigs, 11qr.

Sum 29qr 1b. of peas and beans. And there remain 5qr 4b. of beans and peas.

audited

Barley   The same accounts for 6qr 4b.of barley received from the remainder. And 155qr 1b. received from the manors. And 366qr 7b. received from purchases in the region.

Sum 528qr 4b.   audited

Of this, for making malt as below, 504qr Sold as below, 12qr

Sum 516qr And there remain 12qr 4b. Item barley of Cockfield by estimate, 17qr 5b. \not answered for above; William de Manton, now clerk of the Wardrobe, is responsible./   audited

Dredge   The same answers for 138qr of dredge received from the manors. And 165qr 4b. purchased in the region.

---

[51]   The account of the Cockfield grain was an addition. See also the account for barley, dredge, oats and oxen, pp.53–5 below.

[52]   This sentence was added.

Sum 303qr 4b.   audited

Of this, making malt, as appears below, 293qr And there remain 10qr 4b. And 36qr 2b. in the stack at Cockfield for which William de Manton answers.

Malt barley and dredge   The same answers for 292qr 6b. of malt barley received from the remainder. And of 132qr 5b. of malt dredge received from the remainder. And 68qr malt dredge received from the issues of the mills. And 504qr of \malt/ barley made as above. And 293qr of malt dredge. And 40qr ½b. of malt received from the increase of the said malt in the making.

Sum 1,330qr 3½b.   audited

Of this, malt for ale for provisions of the household as appears on the Diet Roll, 523qr \malt barley/ and 309qr 4b. malt dredge. Sold as below, 24qr ½b. malt barley.

Sum 856qr 4½b. And there remain 473qr 7b. of malt of which 284qr 3b. of malt barley. And 189qr 4b. of malt dredge.   audited

Malt oats   The same answers for 10qr 4b. of malt oats received from the remainder.

Sum 10qr 4b.   audited

Of this, brewed for provisions of the household as appears on the Diet Roll, 10qr. Item the measure made in making as in the granary, 4b.

Sum as above. And he is quit.   audited

Ale   The same answers for 90 gallons received from the remainder. And 46,266 gallons from the malt as above. And 36 gallons received as gifts.

Sum, 46,392 gallons of ale.   audited

Of this, for provisions of the household as appears on the Diet Roll, 47,124 gallons.

Sum 47,124. And nothing remains.   audited

Oats   The same answers for 298qr 2b. of oats received from the remainder. And 167qr 3b. received from the manors. And 1,079qr 7b. received from purchases in the region. And 334qr 6$^1/_3$b. from increment. And 14qr from gifts.

Sum 1,894qr 2$^1/_3$b.   audited

Of this, for provisions of the household \for provender of/ the horses as on the Diet Roll, 1,670qr 3$^1/_3$b. 2 pecks. And in provisions for the Lady's horses going with Lady de Ferrers from Anglesey to London, 1qr 3b. from stock at Standon. And for the swans' food, 3b. And for the oxen of the waggon, 3qr 6½b. And sold as below, 13qr 5b.

Sum 1,689qr 5$^1/_3$b. And there remain 204qr 5b. Item there remains of the oats of Cockfield by estimate in the stack 41qr 4b. for which W[*illiam*] de Manton answers.   audited

Loaves for the Marshalsea   The same answers for 4,160 loaves received from Roger of the Pantry by tally as above. And 3,716 loaves received from 18qr 1b. [*of peas and beans*] baked as above.

Sum 7,876 loaves.   audited

Of this, for provisions of the household for the horses' provender, 7,335 loaves.

Sum 7,335 loaves. And there remain 541 loaves.   audited

Bran   The same answers for 147qr 1b. of bran from the issues of the Bakehouse this year. And 4qr 3b. received from increment in the Avenery.

Sum 151qr 4b.   audited

Of this, for horses' provender, 137qr 7b. For provisions for oxen and pigs, 13qr 5b.

Sum 151qr 4b. And he is quit.   audited

Venison   The same answers for 89 deer received from divers parks of the Lady. And 5 stags and 54 deer received from the remainder. 5 wild deer received as gifts.

Sum 5 stags, 148 deer.   audited

Of this, for provisions of the household, \4 stags/, 94 deer. And 1 stag and 47 deer given by the Lady.

Sum \5 stags/ and 141 deer. And there remain 46 deer [*sic*].   audited

[**m. 3d**] Oxen   The same answers for 130 oxen received from the last account. And 17 oxen, 25 poor-quality \oxen/, 9 cows and 28 bullocks and calves received from the manors. And 98 oxen [*and*] 13 cows received from purchases in the region. And 1 live ox received as a gift.

Sum 293 oxen and cows and 28 bullocks.   audited

Of these, killed for provisions of the household, 163 oxen and cows. And 27 bullocks and calves. And sold as below, 1 bullock.

Sum 163 oxen and cows, 28 bullocks and calves. And there remain 130 live oxen. Item there remain 12 cows at farm at Cockfield not answered for above for which William de Manton, now clerk of the Wardrobe, answers.   audited

Carcasses of oxen   The same answers for 5¾ carcasses of oxen received from the remainder. And 163 carcasses of oxen and 27 of bullocks and calves slaughtered as above. And 4 carcasses of oxen received as gifts.

Sum 172¾ carcasses of oxen and 27 of bullocks and calves.   audited

Of this, for provisions of the household as appears on the Diet Roll, 198⅜ oxen of which 27 of bullocks and calves.

Sum 198⅜. There remains ⅜ ox.   audited

Ox-hides   The same answers for 9 cow-hides received from the remainder. And 163 hides received from oxen slaughtered as above. And 27 from bullocks slaughtered as above.

Sum 172 ox-hides and 27 bullock-hides.   audited

Of this, sold by Sir W[*illiam*] de Manton 152 hides \and 27 bullock-hides/. For mending harness in the Marshalsea with 2 covers made for carts, 10 tanned hides.

Sum 162 hides and 27 bullock-hides. And there remain 10 tanned hides.

      audited

Entrails of oxen   The same answers for 163 entrails of oxen and cows, and 27 of bullocks slaughtered as above. Of these, sold by Sir W[*illiam*] de Manton as below 83 entrails of oxen and cows and 25 of bullocks. And for provisions of the household 80 entrails of oxen and 2 of bullocks. And he is quit.   audited

Pigs   The same answers for 3 boars and 13 pigs received from the remainder. And 2 boars and 235 pigs received from the manors. And 136 pigs \from purchases in the region/ ~~and 8 piglets received from purchases in the region. And 65 piglets received from the sows' issue.~~ And 7 pigs received from the said issue. ~~And 4 piglets received as gifts.~~ And 3 live boars received as gifts.

Sum 8 boars, 391 pigs.   audited

Of these, \slaughtered/ for provisions of the household and made into bacon, 209 pigs and 4 boars. And for provisions of the household as appears on the Diet Roll \slaughtered for provisions as appears below/ 178 pigs and 4 boars. And given by the Lady to Katherine de Haliwell, 2 pigs. ~~Item 64 piglets used.~~

Sum \8 boars/, 389 pigs ~~and 64 piglets~~. And there remain 2 live pigs ~~and 5 piglets~~.   audited

Piglets   The same answers for 8 piglets received from purchases in the region. And 57 received from the sows' issue \besides tithe/. And 4 as gifts.

Sum 69 piglets.   audited

Of these, for provisions of the household as appears on the Diet Roll, 64.

Sum 64. And there remain 5.   audited

Bacon and pigs   The same answers for 8½ bacons received from the remainder. And 395 bacons \and pigs of which 8 boars/ slaughtered as above. And 6 pigs as gifts.

Sum \8 boars/, 401½ bacons and pigs.   audited

And for provisions of the household as appears on the Diet Roll, 408½ pigs and bacons. And sold on account, 1 pig.

Sum 409½ pigs and bacons. And he is quit.   audited

Entrails of pigs   The same answers for 387 entrails from pigs and boars slaughtered as above.

Sum 387 entrails of pigs.

Of these sold by Sir William de Manton, 119 entrails of pigs and boars. And for provisions of the household, 268. And he is quit.   audited

Sheep   The same answers for 98 sheep received from the remainder. And 256 sheep and 1 lamb received from the manors. And 122 sheep from purchase in the region.

Sum 476 sheep and 1 lamb. And all accounted for as slaughtered for provisions of the Lady's household. And he is quit.   audited

Carcasses of sheep   The same answers for 1 sheep-carcass received from the remainder. And 476 carcasses of sheep and 1 lamb from the sheep slaughtered as above.

Sum 477 and 1 lamb.   audited

Of these, for provisions of the household as appears on the Diet Roll, 473 carcasses of sheep and 1 lamb. And sold on account, 4 sheep.

Sum 477 sheep and 1 lamb.   audited

Woolfells and sheepskins   The same answers for 476 woolfells and sheepskins of sheep and 1 lamb's woolfell from the sheep slaughtered as above.

Sum 476 woolfells and sheepskins and 1 lamb's woolfell.   audited

Of these, sold by Sir W[illiam] de Manton as below, 476 woolfells and sheepskins. Sold \on account/ 1 lamb's woolfell.

Sum 476 woolfells and sheepskins and 1 lamb's woolfell. And he is quit.

audited

Entrails of sheep   The same answers for 476 entrails of sheep from the sheep slaughtered as above.

Sum 476 entrails of sheep.

Of these, for provisions of the household, 336. And sold as below by Sir W[illiam] de Manton, 140. And he is quit.   audited

Calves   The same answers for 8 calves received as gifts and accounted for in provisions of the household. And he is quit.   audited

[m. 4d] Herring   The same accounts for 1,820 herring received from the remainder. And 10 lasts, 1,200 \herring/ and 8 barrels containing 8,640 herring whereof 1 last, 100 counted as 100.[53]

Sum 10 lasts, 11,660/ herring, whereof 1 last, 100 counted as 100.   audited

Of these, for provisions of the household as appears on the Diet Roll, 10 lasts, 4,057 herring \whereof 1 last, 100 counted as 100/. And sold as below 4 barrels containing 4,320 herring. And sold on account, 2,293 herring.

Sum 10 lasts, 10,670 herring.[54] There remain 990 herring.   audited

---

[53]   c per v^{xx}.
[54]   The total reads, x lasta, viij^{m}viij^{c}v^{xx}x.

Stockfish   The same answers for 2,364 stockfish, 373 ling and 225[55] *streitfisch* received from the remainder. And 1,200 stockfish and 300 ling-stockfish purchased.

　　Sum 3,564 stockfish, 673 ling and 225 *streitfisch*.　　　　　audited

Of these, for provisions of the household as appears \from the particulars/, 2,397 stockfish,[56] 376 ling, and 237½ *streitfisch*.[57] And sold on account, 3½ stockfish.

　　Sum 3,014 stockfish. And there remain 1,148 stockfish, 300 ling.　　audited

Cod   The same answers for 665 \100 counted as 120/ cod received from the remainder. And 2,320 \100 counted as 120/ received from purchase in the region. And 2 ling received as gifts.

　　Sum 2,987 cod.[58]　　　　　　　　　　　　　　　　　　　audited

Of these for provisions of the household as appears, 1,370 cod and 2 ling.

　　Sum 1,372 cod. And there remain 1,623 cod, 100 counted as 120.　　audited

[*Marginal note*] Thus there is an excess of 8 cod.

Salmon   The same answers for 153 salmon received from the remainder. And 104 salmon received from purchase. And 1 salmon received as a gift.

　　Sum 258 salmon.　　　　　　　　　　　　　　　　　　　　audited

Of these, for provisions of the household as appears, 221[59] \and ¾ salmon/. Sold on account ¼ salmon.

　　Sum 222 salmon. And there remain 36 salmon.　　　　　　　　audited

Pike   The same answers for 146 pike received from the remainder. And 115[60] received from purchase. And 17 received as gifts

　　Sum 278 pike.　　　　　　　　　　　　　　　　　　　　　audited

Of these, for provisions of the household \as appears on the Diet Roll/ 245 pike. And sold on account, 12 pike.

　　Sum 257 pike. And there remain 21 pike.　　　　　　　　　　audited

Lampreys   The same answers for 28 lampreys received from purchase. And 12 received as gifts.

　　Sum 40 lampreys.　　　　　　　　　　　　　　　　　　　audited

And for provisions of the household, 41. And nothing remains.　　　audited

Sturgeon   The same answers for 1¾ barrels of sturgeon received from the remainder. And 1 barrel received from purchase.

　　Sum 2¾ barrels.

Of this, for provisions of the the household, 134 pieces of sturgeon. And there remain 5 pieces.　　　　　　　　　　　　　　　　　　　　　audited

Eels   The same answers for 1,200 eels received from the remainder. And 4,800 [*and*] 60 sticks \which makes 1,560/. And 26 large eels. And 2 large eels received as gifts.

　　Sum 7,560 eels and 28 large eels.　　　　　　　　　　　　audited

Of these, for provisions of the household as appears, 234½ sticks of eels\which makes 5,786 which makes 7,137/, 7 large eels and 28 shaft-eels. And sold on account, 176 eels.

　　Sum 7,348 eels. And there remain 240 eels.　　　　　　　　audited

Swans   The same answers for 15 swans received from the manors. And 10 received

---

55　cv^{xx}v.
56　mix^{c}v^{xx}xvij.
57　cv^{xx}xvij di.
58　ij^{m}iiij^{c}v^{xx}vij.
59　cv^{xx}j.
60　v^{xx}xv.

as gifts. And 2 swans of the issue of the Lady's swans given to her by William Lengleys.

Sum 27 swans.   audited

And for provisions of the household as appears, 27 swans.

Sum as above. And he is quit.   audited

Herons and bittern   The same answers for 17 herons and 1 bittern received as gifts. And accounted for in the provisions of the household. And he is quit.   audited

Pheasants   The same answers for 50 pheasants received from J[ohn] de Claketon. And 3 pheasants received as gifts. And all taken for provisions of the household. And he is quit.   audited

Does   The same answers for 14 does received from the stock in Bardfield park. And all accounted for in provisions of the household. And he is quit.   audited

Rabbits   The same answers for 90 rabbits received from the manors. And 102 received from purchase in the region. And 6 received as gifts. And 81 received from the manors of Bardfield, Woodham and Stebbing.

Sum 279 rabbits.   audited

And for provisions of the household as appears on the Diet Roll, 286 rabbits.

Sum 286 rabbits. And nothing remains.   audited

Rabbit-skins   The same answers for 279 rabbit-skins received from the rabbits as above.

Sum 279 rabbit-skins.   audited

Of these, sold by Sir W de Manton 273. And not more because Master Cook had 6 skins as his fee from the rabbits coming as gifts.

Sum as above. And he is quit.   audited

Partridges   The same answers for 267 partridges received from the Falconer. And 10 received as gifts. And used. And he is quit.   audited

Mallard   The same answers for 78 mallard received from the Falconer. And used. And he is quit.   audited

Capons and hens   The same answers for 77 capons and 12 hens received as gifts. And used. And he is quit.   audited

Suet   The same answers for 1,938 \100 counted as 100/lb. of suet received from the entrails of oxen slaughtered as above. And delivered for making candles of paris. And he is quit.   audited

Candles of paris[61]   The same answers for 909lb. of candles of paris received from the remainder. And 1,125lb. of candles received from tallow made as above.

Sum 2,034lb. of candles of paris.   audited

Of this, for provisions of the household as appears, 1,729lb. of candles of paris.

Sum 1,729lb. of candles of paris. And there remain 305lb. of candles of paris.

                                                       audited

Whole wax   The same answers for 840lb. \100 counted as 112/ of whole wax received from the remainder. And 2,036lb. received from purchase. And 401lb. bought from Nigel Tebaud.

Sum 3,277lb. of wax, 100 counted as 112.   audited

Of this, \delivered/ for provisions of the household, 1,882lb. as torches, large candles [and] candles made as below.

Sum 1,882lb. of wax. And there remain 1,395bs of whole wax.   audited

---

[61] Tallow candles.

Wax made up   The same answers for 224lb. of made up wax from the remainder. And 1,882lb. of wax in made up wax as above. And 441⅝lb. from the wicks.[62]

Sum 2,547⅝lb. of wax.   audited

Of this, for provisions of the household, 1,946⅛lb. of wax.

Sum 1,946⅛lb. of wax. And there remain 601½lb. of made up wax.   audited

[m. 5d]   Almonds   The same answers for 1,865lb. of almonds received from the remainder. And 28lb. received from purchase.

Sum 1,893lb.[63]   audited

Of this, for provisions of the household as appears \from the particulars/, 1,323½lb.

Sum 1,323½lb. And there remain 569½lb., 100 counted as 112.   audited

Rice   The same answers for 224¾lb. from the remainder. And 420lb. received from new provisions.

Sum 644¾lb. of rice.   audited

Of this, for provisions of the household, 430½lb. of rice as appears from the particulars.

Sum 430½lb. of rice. And there remain 214¼lb. of rice.[64]   audited

Sugar   The same answers for 40¼lb. of sugar from the remainder. And 387½lb. received from purchase.

Sum 427¾lb.

Of this for provisions of the household 346¼lb. And there remain 81½lb. audited

Ginger   The same answers for 104½lb. received from the remainder.[65] And 32lb. received from purchase.

Sum 136½lb. of ginger.[66]   audited

Of this, for provisions of the household as appears, 49¾lb. of ginger.

Sum 49³/₈lb. of ginger. And there remain 86⅛lb. of ginger.   audited

Galingale   The same answers for 23¾lb. of galingale received from the remainder. And 32lb. received from purchase.

Sum 55¾lb.   audited

Of this, for provisions of the household as appears, 32½lb. And there remain 23¼lb. of galingale.   audited

Cinnamon   The same answers for 41¼lb. of cinnamon received from the remainder. And 30lb. received from purchase.

Sum 71¼lb. of cinnamon.

Of this, for provisions of the household as appears, 38¾lb. And there remain 32½lb. of cinnamon.   audited

Pepper   The same answers for 30¾lb. of pepper received from the remainder. And 42lb. received from purchase.

Sum 72¾lb. of pepper.

Of this, for provisions of the household as appears, 28¼lb. of pepper. And there remain 44½lb. of pepper.   audited

Cumin   The same accounts for 17lb. of cumin received from the remainder. And 20lb. received from purchase.

Sum 37lb. of cumin.

---

62   iijᶜvˣˣv.
63   mvjᶜvˣˣj. 100 is counted as 112 in this entry.
64   cvˣˣijqr.
65   vˣˣiiijdi.
66   cxxiiijdi; the long hundred, with 100 counted as 112, has been used in this total.

Of this, for provisions of the household as appears, 27lb. of cumin. And there remain 10lb. of cumin. audited

Cloves   The same answers for 3⅛lb. of cloves received from the remainder. And 5lb. received from purchase.

Sum 8⅛lb. of cloves. audited

Of this, for provisions of the household, 4⅜lb. of cloves. And there remain 3¼lb. audited

Cubeb   The same answers for 3½lb. of cubeb received from the remainder. And 2lb. received from purchase.

Sum 5½lb. of cubeb.   audited

Of this, for provisions of the household as appears, 2⅜lb. of cubeb. And there remain 2⅛lb. of cubeb. audited

Mace   The same answers for 9\½/lb. of mace received from the remainder. And 6lb. received from purchase.

Sum 15½lb.

Of this for provisions of the household, 3⅛lb. of mace. And there remain 11⅜lb.[67] audited

Saffron   The same answers for 12½lb. received from the remainder. And 6lb. received from purchase.

Sum 18½lb.

Of this, for provisions of the household, 10lb. of saffron. And there remain 8½lb. audited

Sandal-wood   The same answers for 4lb. of sandal-wood received from the remainder. And 6½lb. received from purchase.

Sum 10½lb.

Of this, for provisions of the household, 7¾lb. of sandal-wood. And there remain 2¾lb. of sandal-wood. audited

Nutmeg. The same answers for ¾[lb.] of nutmeg received from the remainder. And ½lb. used. And there remains ¼[lb.] of nutmeg. audited

Pine-seed electuary   The same answers for 12¼lb. received from the remainder. And 4¼lb. used. And there remain 8lb. audited

Starch   The same answers for ½lb. received from the remainder. And 6lb. received from purchase.

Sum 6½lb. audited

Of this, for provisions of the household, 1½lb. And there remain 5lb.   audited

Anise   The same answers for 8lb. of anise received from the remainder. And for provisions of the household, 4lb. And there remain 4lb. of anise. audited

Alkanet   The same answers for 2lb. of alkanet received from the remainder. Of this, for provisions of the household, ½lb. And there remain 1½lb.   audited

Powdered cinnamon   The same answers for 1¾lb. received from the remainder. And 6lb. received from purchase.

Sum 7¾lb. audited

Of this, for provisions of the household, 3¾lb. of powdered cinnamon. And there remain 4lb. of powdered cinnamon. audited

Canvas   The same answers for 244 ells of canvas from the remainder. And 100 [ells] received from purchase.

Sum 344 ells of canvas. audited

---

[67] ⅛ was added by the auditor.

Of this, delivered to Roger of the Pantry for making table-cloths, 78 ells. To Margery Mareschal for the Lady's Chamber, 65 ells, for the Lady's 2 coaches, 27 ells, and for the day of the burial of Sir E[*dward*] de Monthermer, 20 ells, and for aprons for the officials at the feasts of All Saints, Christmas, Easter and Pentecost, saddlecloths and other necessary items, 167 ells.

Sum 317 ells of canvas. And there remain 27 ells of canvas.   audited

[m. 6d] Linen   The same answers for 3½ ells of linen received from the remainder. And 61½ ells from purchase.

Sum 65 ells.   audited

Of this, delivered for aprons for the officials of the Pantry, Buttery, Vintry and Kitchen to make the aforesaid, 26 ells. And for divers items impending on the day of the burial of the said Sir E[*dward*] and for covering the dresser and the cupboard of the roasting-house and the saucery and for the porters' lodges, 32 ells, and for making other necessary items on the arrival of the Lord King, 7 ells.

Sum 65 ells. And he is quit.   audited

Spanish iron   The same answers for 6,501lb. of Spanish iron received from purchase.

Sum 6,501[*lb.*].   audited

Of this, for making horseshoes, nails and other necessary items, 4,017lb. And sold as below, 112lb.

Sum 4,129lb. of iron. And there remain 2,372lb. of Spanish iron.[68]   audited

Horseshoes   The same answers for 874 horseshoes received from the remainder. And 3,391 horseshoes received from making as above.

Sum 4,265 horseshoes, 100 counted as ~~the long hundred~~ 100.   audited

Of these, for provisions of the household as appears [*from the particulars*], 2,600 horseshoes.

Sum 2,600 horseshoes. And there remain 1,665, 100 counted as the short hundred.   audited[69]

Destriers   The same answers for 6 destriers from the remainder. And 2 destriers \of which 1 grey and the other bay/ which belonged to Sir Edward de Monthermer. And 1 black destrier bought from William Seman for the Lady's coach. And 1 destrier called the son of Bay Bavent received from the Lady's colts. And 1 called Bay Bardolf received from Sir John Bardolf in exchange for Grey of Hundon.

Sum 11 destriers.   audited

Of these, 1 called Haretoht died of murrain at Broxted *hey*. 1 called Bay Monthermer given to the Lord King by the Lady. 1 exchanged with Lord Bardolf as appears above. 1 called Morelnortherne sold by William Seman.

Sum 4. And there remain 7 destriers.   audited

Palfreys   The same answers for 7 palfreys from the remainder. And 2 palfreys bought from William Seman and the prior of Tonbridge of which 1 grey and the other skewbald. And 1 grey palfrey which belonged to Sir Nicholas Damory.

Sum 10.   audited

Of these, 1 dappled grey palfrey given to the earl of Northampton by the Lady. Item 1 called Grey of Stoke given to Sir Henry de Ferrers by the Lady. Item 2 handed over to the carthorses as below of which 1 called Bay Stanford and the other Sorrel

---

68   100 was counted as 112 in this entry.
69   There is a gap in the document at this point. The rest is written in a different hand.

Hobyn. 1 called Sorrel of Hundon [*handed over*] to the packhorses as below. Sold as below 1 called Dun Colingham.

Sum 6. And there remain 4 palfreys.   audited

Packhorses and hackneys   The same answers for 17 \from the remainder/. 1 received from the palfreys as above. And 1 packhorse for the Poultry and 2 hackneys for the falconers received from purchase as appears below. And 1 grey received from the Lady's stud at Hundon. And 1 iron-grey nag received from Nicholas Masoun.

Sum 23.   audited

Of these, 1 grey foal which came from Hundon died of murrain. Item 1 nag which came from Bottisham. Item 1 packhorse called Blauncherd of Walsingham. Item 1 packhorse called Grey Turnebole died of murrain. Item handed over to the cart-horses as below 1 called Grey Rempton. Item handed over to the carthorses 1 called Grey \Ty/ nag. Item handed over to Robert Flemmyng of the Lady's gift 1 iron-grey nag received from Nicholas Masoun. Item 5 handed over of the Lady's gift viz. 1 to William de Ferrers, 1 to Hugh le Charer, 1 to Robert de Middilton, 1 to John le Foridere and 1 to Robert Pouncy. 2 hackneys sold as below.

Sum 14. And there remain 9 packhorses and hackneys of which 1 nag called Dun Ty is in William Seman's custody for which he answers.   audited

Carthorses   The same answers for 19 carthorses from the remainder. And 2 received from the palfreys as above. And 2 received from the packhorses as above. And 3 found in the Lady's stable by examination of the remainder on account and this is testified by indenture between the Wardrobe and Henry de Dene.

Sum 26.   audited

Of these, 4 died of murrain of which 1 is called Bitere and another Skewbald and the 3rd called Grey of Dereham and the 4th Piebald of Huntingdon.

Sum 4. And there remain 22 carthorses.   audited

Hides   The same answers for the hides of 1 destrier, 4 packhorses and 4 carthorses dead of murrain as above. And of the hide of 1 foal dead in the park.

Sum 10.

Of these, in currying for the cart-harness of the Lady's household and used for the same, 2. Sold on account, 2.

Sum 4. And there remain 7 curried horse-hides.   audited

III

CLARE CASTLE

Building and Repairs

Extract from the Account of Robert de Pentrich, Receiver and Constable of the Honour of Clare, from Michaelmas 18 Edward II to Michaelmas 19 Edward II (1324–5)[1]   [TNA SC6/1109/19]

[m. 1] Cost of buildings   For 1 man's pay making the gutter between the Hall and the Lady's Great Chamber and repairing other gutters, for himself and his boy, 4s. 10d. Henry Golde's pay carrying sand for the said man and helping the said plumber for 6 days, 1s. 3d. 1 tiler's pay tiling between the Hall and the Lady's Great Chamber and repairing the porch at the door of the Lady's Great Chamber and fitting the ridge-pieces of the cloister between the Hall and the Chapel for 31 days, 12s. 11d., taking 5d. a day for himself and his helper. 1 groom's pay carrying sand for the said tiler for making mortar \for 3 days/, 6d. For 6,000 tiles purchased, 17s., at 2s. 10d. per 1,000. For 100 \200/ tiles purchased for the ridge-pieces, 5s. 8d., at 2s. 10d. per 100. 10qr of lime purchased, 7s. 6d., at 9d. a qr. 3,000 lath-nails purchased, 2s. 7d. \6d./, at 10d. per 1,000. For Henry le Daubere's pay roofing above the Chapel for 4 days, 1s. 20 iron bars bought for the Chapel-windows, 10d. 8 \large/ iron bars bought for the said windows, 1s. For Henry le Daubere's helper roofing above the Chapel for 4 days, 8d. 100 lath-nails bought for the Chapel, 1d. For glazing the small windows of the Chapel, 2s. 6d. 200 spike-nails bought for making divers things in the Castle, 8d. 200 splint-nails bought for the same, 5d. 100 lath-nails bought for the same, 1d. Henry le Daubere's pay plastering and white-washing the Hall for 1 week, 1s. 6d. His boy's pay for the said time, 1s. 2d. The said H[enry's] pay plastering, pargeting and whitewashing the cloister for 3 weeks and 3 days, 5s. 3d., taking 1s. 6d. a week. For his helper for the said time, 3s. 6d. Henry Golde's pay plastering and whitewashing the part of the wall outside the cloister with his helper for 3 days, 10½d. 1 lock bought for the door of the Granary, 2½d. 1 lock bought for the door of the chamber under the Lady's Great Chamber, 3d. 1 lock bought for the door of the little Larder, 2½d. For 1 thatcher's pay making repairs over the old Hall and elsewhere in the castle for 5 weeks, 14s. 6d., taking for himself and his boy 3s. a week\except in total 6d./. 1 key bought for the little chamber near the Herber, 1d. 1 key for the door of the clerks' office, 1d. 1 key for the door of Margaret de Courteney's chamber, 1d. 1 key for the Lady's Chamber, 1d. 1 lock with key for the door of the Buttery, 2½d. Henry le Daubere's pay roofing above Henry de Colingham's chamber and the Cook's chamber and pargeting the little Chapel and the chamber behind the Hall for 3 weeks and 1 day, 4s. 9d., taking

---

[1]   This roll was not audited.

1s. 6d. a week. For his helper for the said time, 3s. 2d., taking 1s. a week. For 1 ~~boy's~~ \man's/ pay making a piggery for the castle in Hundon park according to a certain agreement, 14s. 120 \blue/ stones bought for the Lady's garden, 15s.[2] Splitting 6,000 laths in Hundon park, 7s. 6d., at 1s. 3d. per 1,000. 32,000 tiles bought, £4, at 2s. 6d. per 1,000. 300 spike-nails bought from a stranger, 10½d. 700 large spike-nails bought from Peter Smith for the Kitchen, cloister, piggery and other necessary places in the castle, 2s. ½d., at 3½d. per 100 because large. 700 splint-nails bought for the same [m. 2] works, 1s. 2d., at 2d. per 100. 1 hinge bought for the castle-gate, 10d. 2 hooks and 2 hinges bought for the door of the Poultry, 2d. 1 hinge bought for a chamber-window, ½d. 3 staples bought for the locks of 3 doors, 1½d. 300 grope-nails bought for repairing the Lady's Chamber, 4½d. 4 hinges with 4 hooks bought for William de Burgh's chamber, 6d. 1 door-latch with all the fittings bought for the said chamber, 1d. 1 lock bought for the gate of the Herber, 3d. 12,000 lath-nails bought for divers works, viz. for the Kitchen, the cloister, the chamber next to the Dernegate, the said gate, and other works in the castle, 12s., at 1s. per 1,000. For John the mason's pay making an oven in the castle, for 1 week, 1s. 6d. His boy's pay for the said time, 10d. Henry le Daubere's pay making a partition in the cellar and a wall between William de Burgh's chamber and the Constable's chamber and other repairs in the castle \in divers places/ for 2 weeks, 3s. For his helper for the said time, 2s. 30,000 tiles for laying over the Kitchen, part of the Esquires' Chamber [and] the pentice, for the paths of the Herber, over the enclosure next to the Kitchen and for divers other places in the castle, £1 2s. 6d., at 9d. per 1,000, and only because the whole was against laths. Lime bought for divers works in the castle, £1 7s. 1d. For 1 man's pay making a new gutter between the Kitchen and the dresser, 6d. Pay of 1 boy helping on occasion to make the said gutter, 1s. 6d.

    Sum £14 14s. 8½d.

Indenture and Extracts from the Works' Account from 1 April, 21 Edward III to Michaelmas in the same year (1347)[3]   [TNA E101/459/26]
[m. 1] This indenture was made between Sir Walter the Chaplain and John Curteys, Constable of Clare castle, concerning divers works done within the Castle viz. from 1 April viz. the feast of Easter in the 21st year of King Edward III until Michaelmas in the same year.
Easter week. ~~Pay~~ \wages/ of Master William Carpenter working on the Lady's new Chamber, 1s. 2d. William Newman's pay for the same, 1s. 6d. John Boltel's pay for the same, 1s. 4d.

    Sum 4s.   audited
Second week. Master William Carpenter's wages working on the said Chamber, 1s. 2d. William Newman's pay, 1s. 6d. Pay of 2 carpenters, strangers, working on the said work, 2s. 8d., according to an agreement made by W[illiam] Lengleys. John Boltel's pay, 1s. 4d. 2 sawyers sawing timber for the same, 2s. 6d. Roger Mason's pay working on the new Wardrobe next to the Lady's Chamber, 1s. 8d. Richard atte Cherche's pay for the same, 1s. 4d. Thomas Mason's pay for the same, 1s. 3d. 3 servants serving the same men, 2s. 6d. Nicholas Leg's pay carrying sand from the mount next to the Lady's Chamber to the garden for 3½ days, 6d. Pay of 3 grooms

---

[2]   Work on the Lady's gardens is discussed by J. Harvey, *Medieval Gardens* (London, 1981), pp.7, 87–8.

[3]   The diet account for 1346–7 [TNA E101/92/30] shows that the Lady was residing at Clare for part of the spring and summer.

helping him in the said work for the same time, 1s. 3¾d., at 1½d. per day to each of them. Pay of 1 carpenter with his boy mending and repairing the scribe's house for 1 day, 4d. Pay of 1 man and his boy plastering, roofing and fitting ridge-pieces and doing other necessary work for 2 days, 6d. Pay of William Virre, carpenter, making 1 chair and 1 bed from boards in the same Chamber for ½ a day, 1d. For 2 boards and ½ a portal bought for the window, door and chair of the said Chamber, 3d. 100 iron nails bought for the same, 2½d. 2 hinges bought for the same building, 1½d. 1 man hired to collect stones for the said Wardrobe outside the mount of sand for 1 day, 1d. For 1 man cleaning the Herber and railing the walks with rods for 2 days, 3d.

Sum 19s. 7¾d.   audited

Fourth week. ~~Pay~~ \wages/ of Master William Carpenter working on the Lady's new Chamber, 1s. 2d. Pay of William Newman and the other 2 aforesaid strangers for the same, 4s. 6d. John Boltel's pay for the same, 1s. 4d. 2 sawyers sawing timber and boards for the same, 2s. 6d. Roger Mason's pay working on the said Wardrobe, 1s. 8d. Thomas Park's pay for the same, 1s. 3d. Simon's pay serving the same men, 10d. Pay of Hugh and John Berchefair serving the same men for 4 \days/ and ½ \a day/, 1s. 2d. Pay of Hayles repairing and turfing in the Great Herber for 2 days, 2d.

Sum 14s. 7d.   audited

[m. 2] Ninth week. For pay of William Newman, carpenter, and the other two strangers working on the said Chamber, 4s. 6d. 2 sawyers' pay sawing timber for the same, 2s. 6d. Pay of 1 plumber for working 2 fothers of lead and laying it above the said Chamber, 6s. 8d. Pay \of Hugh/ cleaning the new buildings and carrying stones out of the little chamber [*and*] for work on the said Wardrobe, for 3 days, 4½d.

Sum 14s. ½d.   audited

[m. 1d] Fourteenth week, viz. after the feast of the Apostles Peter and Paul [*29 June*]. Pay of William Newman and the other [*2 carpenters*], strangers, 4s. 6d. Roger Mason's pay working on the Lady's new Wardrobe, 1s. 8d. Pay of Henry and John Berchefair serving the same man, 1s. 8d. 2 men hired [*to move*] the sand from the said mount to the garden and other places and to make a new wall outside the said Wardrobe, for 2 days, 6d. Hugh's pay cleaning the new chamber and the open space next to it, for 2 days, 3d. 3qr of lime bought at Reach, 1s. 2d. For money paid for the cart hired to carry the same, 8d.

Sum 10s. 5d.   audited

[m. 2d] Twentieth week, viz. after the feast of St Laurence [*10 August*]. Pay of Master William Carpenter working on and raising the bridge of the castle, 1s. 2d. Pay of William Newman and the other 2 carpenters, strangers, working on the same castle-bridge, 4s. 6d. Roger Mason's pay, 1s. 8d. Pay of 1 man serving him for the same time, 10d. Hugh's pay carrying sand from the mount next to Robert Mareschal's chamber and other things within the castle, for 2 days and ½ on Saturday, 4d. Pay of 1 other man for the same for 1 day, 1½d. For making 1 bucket from the Lady's timber and binding it with iron to use in the lime-house, 1½d. 1 wooden bowl bought for the same, 1½d. Nicholas Leg's pay for whitewashing and pargeting outside the new Chamber and within the closet of Anna the maid, for 2½ days, 7½d.

Sum 9s. 6d.   audited

Contents: Indenture made at Clare on 1 October 6 Edward III (1332)

[TNA E101/91/28]

[m. 1] This indenture, made at Clare on 1 October 6 Edward III witnesses that Hugh de Burgh, former Clerk of the Wardrobe of Lady Elizabeth de Burgh, Lady of Clare, delivered to Sir William le Blount the underwritten items in divers offices of the Lady's Household, viz. from [?]Michaelmas of the preceding year.[4]

Wardrobe   Wax at Clare, 356lb.; wax at Anglesey, 326lb.; wicks, 12lb.; coarse cotton, 2lb.; cotton thread, 1lb.; red [*illeg.*], 2¼lb.; saffron, 3½lb.; cubebs, 1½lb.; [*illeg.*] 3lb.; sandal-wood, 4lb.; damsons, 3lb.; alkanet, 1lb.; pepper, 1¼lb.; mace, ¾ [*lb.*]; [*illeg.*], ¾ [*lb.*]; anise, ²/₄ [*lb.*]; vermilion, 3lb.; verdigris, ¾ [*lb.*]; gum for making into powder, 2 pieces; bags for putting the powder in, 10; canvas weighing 4qr, 19 ells; [?]vair of 9 timbers, 1 fur; furs of minever of 8 timbers, 2; furs of minever of 8 timbers, 3; 1 inferior fur of minever, 4 rows; hoods of minever pured, 3; hoods of minever used, 2; fur of grover of 7 timbers, 3; [*next entry illeg.*]; ermine, 10 *best'*; panes of lamb [*illeg.*]; panes of lamb used [*illeg.*]; backs of gris, 11 [*illeg.*] 26 backs; towels of paris [*illeg.*] 4; towels of paris [*illeg.*], 5, £1; towels of paris of 2½ ells, 6, £2; towels of dinant of 5½ ells, 3; towels of dinant of 2½ ells, 3, delivered for the Ewery; towels of paris made of 12 ells, 2; over-tablecloth of paris of 15 ells, 1; an old tablecloth of paris of 8½ ells, 1; 1 silver plate with a foot for spices weighing in total £1 13s. 8d.; 1 silver plate with a foot for the same weighing £1 19s.; 2 silver spoons for the same weighing in total 3s. 8d.; towels of paris for the same of 3 ells, 6; towels of paris for the same of 4¼ ells, 2; 1 iron *spatorium*;[5] silver dishes weighing £13 4s. 2d. with the arms of Ulster and Gloucester, 12; silver shallow bowls weighing £3 10s. 10d., 12; silver basins, enamelled on the base, weighing £7 2s. 1d. and a chest with a lock for the same, 2; of wooden chests at Anglesey 1 long chest; 1 worn out chest there; 1 new chest there; 1 red long chest at Clare; 1 red short chest for spices; item 1 yellow short [*chest*] there for rolls; item 1 brass mortar weighing 78lb.; item 1 broken brass mortar weighing 37½lb.; item 2 iron pestles for the same; item 1 small pair of brass scales; item 2 pieces of brass weighing by estimation 300lb.; item 1 large pair of scales with *schl'* of leather; item 1 weight of 60lb., 1 weight of 16lb., 1 weight of 14lb., 1 weight of 6lb., 1 weight of 4lb., 1 weight of 2lb., 1 weight of 1lb., 1 weight of ½lb., and 1 of ¼ [*lb.*] of lead; item 2 large old baskets which were once in the Pantry; item 1 pair of irons for hosts;[6] item 1 pair of irons for wafers; 8 axes; item 1 saddlecloth for 1 horse with divers arms that was of R Tailor; item 1 pyx with the arms of Gloucester and Ulster that belonged to J Tony; 21 ells of sackcloth of Sandwich, 12 ells expended; cloth-sacks; cart-covers; 65 ells of kitchen-cloth, 41 expended; 8½ \ells/ of bolting-cloth, all expended; 2 ells of black russet for grooms' hose; 2¾ ells of striped cloth remaining of the pages' [*livery*]; 12 new shallow bowls of pewter; old used dishes and broken shallow bowls of pewter, 47lb.; item 637lb. of candles of paris, and 156lb. of tallow; and by the hands of Robert the clerk against the Avenery, £10; and by the hands of Arnold Sely against wax and other things provided by him, £100; item for carriage of wax and fish from St Botolph to Lakenheath, 13s. 4d.; item by the hands of Richard de Berkyng against the Lady's livery, £66 13s. 4d.; for shearing 1 cloth of the same livery for the Lady, 3s. 4d.

Chamber   2 pegs for splitting firewood.

Bakehouse   12 used sacks of Sandwich; item 3 fire-grates, 10 sieves, 2 wicker containers and 1 [?]wedge for malted dough; 1 worn out pair of scales for weighing dough, and 2 canvases measuring 16 ells for covering dough.

---

[4]   The indenture was arranged in two columns, with the name of the household department at the top of each list.

[5]   Probably a utensil for mixing medicines.

[6]   The hosts were consecrated at mass in the chapel by the priest.

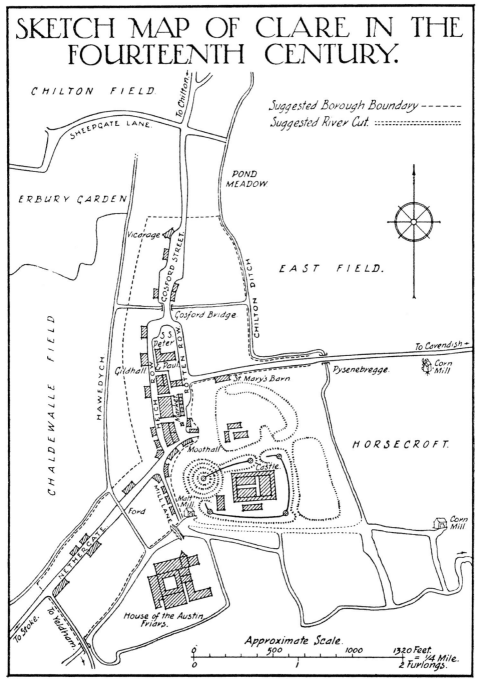

1. Sketch map of Clare in the fourteenth century, from G.A. Thornton, A History of Clare Suffolk *(Cambridge, 1928) © Jennifer and John Ward*

2. Gilbert de Clare, earl of Gloucester and Hertford (d.1314), brother of Elizabeth de Burgh, as depicted in the early fourteenth-century stained glass window in the choir of Tewkesbury abbey church. The choir was rebuilt by their sister Eleanor Despenser. Photo: Bernard Roy Osborne

3. *Seal of Elizabeth de Burgh which was attached to the statutes she gave to Clare Hall, Cambridge, in 1359. It is a vesica-shaped seal, 2½ inches by 1⅝ inches. The Lady stands in a niche holding the book of statutes in her left hand and giving the foundation charter to the Master and members of the hall with her right. Above is a half-figure of the Virgin and Child flanked by St John the Baptist and St John the Evangelist. To the left and right are the arms of Edward I and Eleanor of Castile, the Lady's maternal grandparents, and at the base her own seal which she used from 1353 with the Clare shield impaling de Burgh. (John de Burgh was her first husband and son and heir of Richard de Burgh, earl of Ulster.) © The Master and Fellows of Clare College, Cambridge*

South East View of Clare Castle, Suffolk. 1785

4. South-east view of Clare castle in the late eighteenth century, by Thomas Lyus. The top of the tower of the parish church is visible in the background. © Ipswich and Colchester Museums

Brewhouse   6 old sacks of Sandwich; 1 handmill, 5 large tubs, 6 smaller tubs, 15 vats \and/ 4 small moveable leaden vessels.

Chandlery   2 large chests, 2 smaller chests; 2 small, old and broken chests and 1 large standing chest.

Hall   2 andirons and 1 iron fork.

Ewery   2 silver measures for water weighing in total, £3 14s. 10½d.; item 2 silver basins with the Lady's arms weighing in total, £4 15s. 2d.; item 2 basins with the arms of Gloucester weighing in total, £7; towels of dinant of 3 ells, 4, 1 expended; used towels of paris each of 9 ells, 2 expended; used towels of paris of 8½ ells, 2 expended; 1 counterfeit towel of paris of 12½ ells; used towels of paris of 2½ ells, 2; 1 new over-tablecloth of paris of 15 ells; 1 worn out over-tablecloth of 9 ells.

Pantry   86 loaves remaining; item 2 silver shallow bowls with covers of which 1 [is] partly broken weighing in total £1 15s.; item 30 silver spoons with the letter E weighing in total, £1 17s. 6d.; item 2 silver-gilt spoons, in total 2s. 8d.; item 6 silver plates for fruit with the Lady's arms weighing in total, £3 19s. 2d.; item 1 leather coffer to put the said spoons in, with lock and key; 2 large baskets bound with iron; 1 knife to make cuts; item 2 tablecloths of paris in 1 piece containing in total 12 ells, 1 expended; item 2 tablecloths of paris in 1 piece containing in total 12 ells, expended; [1] torn \counterfeit paris/ tablecloth of 15 ells, expended; [next 6 entries illeg.]; 1 canvas tablecloth containing 7 ells, expended; strong over-tablecloth of Aylsham[7] containing 9 ells [illeg.]; strong over-tablecloth of Aylsham containing 10 ells [illeg.]; over-tablecloth of Aylsham containing 13 ells, expended; over-tablecloth of Aylsham of 16½ ells, delivered for the Ewery, expended; over-tablecloth of Aylsham containing 8 ells [illeg.]; 2 \used/ over-tablecloths of cloth, each containing 7 ells; 1 over-tablecloth of Aylsham containing 2 ells; 1 over-table-cloth of Aylsham containing 11 ells; 1 over-tablecloth of Aylsham containing 6 ells; 1 old over-tablecloth of cloth containing 9 ells, expended.

Buttery   220 gallons of ale remaining; item 9 tuns, 46 sesters, 1 pitcher of wine; 1 silver goblet with cover and tripod weighing in total £2 8s. 7d.; 1 ewer for the same weighing 19s. 9½d.; 1 silver cup with foot and cover weighing in total £1 11s. 6d.; 1 ewer for the same weighing 11s.; 1 silver measure containing 2 quarts weighing £2 6s. 8d.; 1 silver measure containing a cantle weighing £1 19s. 2d.; 11 silver pots weighing in total £6 15s. 10d.; 1 small silver-gilt mazer with 1 acorn; 1 silver-gilt mazer with 1 boss; 4 pewter pitchers, each containing 2 quarts; 2 pairs of kegs bound with iron with leather straps, each containing 1 gallon; 4 kegs bound with iron, each containing 2 gallons; 4 kegs bound with iron with iron chains, each containing 1 gallon; 1 pair of leather flasks containing in total 1 gallon; 2 pairs of leather flasks containing in total 4 gallons; item 1 pair of leather flasks containing in total 4 gallons; item 4 leather coffers for mazers; 1 leather coffer for putting fruit plates in; item 7 large casks for putting ale in; item 2 small casks for putting ale in; 5 little painted tankards; 3 black tankards containing 10 gallons; 2 black tankards each containing 5 gallons; 8 black tankards each containing 1 gallon; 1 tankard containing 2 quarts; 1 pair of barrels with iron [hoops]; 1 basket of withies and leather with lock and key.

Kitchen   60 live oxen from Wales; item 4 live oxen coming as gift from Sudbury; item 8 ox-hides of oxen from Wales and the gift of Master William de Brampton;

---

item 12 tanned and curried ox-hides and 8 ox-hides remaining in the salthouse; item 283 live sheep from Wales and skins and entrails of 17 slaughtered sheep; 120qr of salt at Ipswich; item ½ stick of eels; item 140 white herring; item 1 salmon; 20 whiting; 1 sheep carcass; 1qr of pork; item 436 stockfish; 23 small bacons; item 2 brass pans each containing 20 gallons; item 1 brass pan containing 18 gallons; item 160lb. of lard by estimate remaining; item 1 brass pan containing 16 gallons; 2 brass pans each containing 6 gallons; 1 \brass/ pan containing 4 gallons; item 1 \brass/ pan containing 14 gallons; item 1 brass pan containing 8 gallons; item 1 brass pan containing 5 gallons; 2 brass measures each containing 2½ gallons; 2 brass measures each containing 1 gallon; 2 brass measures each containing 1½ gallons; 2 brass measures each containing 6 gallons; 1 brass measure containing 10 gallons; 1 brass measure containing 5 gallons; 3 pots containing in all 1 gallon; 1 iron trivet with 6 feet, 9 feet long; 1 iron trivet with 6 feet, 8 feet long; 1 small iron trivet; item 1 great knife; 1 iron hammer for thrashing [m. 2] stockfish; 1 iron cauldron containing 1 gallon; item 1 cauldron containing ¾ [*gallon*]; 3 iron gridirons; 2 graters; 2 frying pans; 2 iron pegs for splitting firewood; 2 *estomours*; item 3 flesh-hooks; 2 stoups bound with iron at Anglesey and Clare; 1 large spit; item 4 spits in regular [*use*]; 2 spits for side-dishes; item 2 spits for the roasting-house; 1 net of 18½ fathoms; item 1 *fleu* of 10 fathoms; item 1 net of 6 cubits.

Poultry   5 swans remaining; item 2 rabbits; 14 capons; item 1 pair of barrels to put fish received in.

Saucery   2 barrels each of 2 gallons; 2 barrels each of 1 gallon.

Scullery   2 chargers with the Lady's arms weighing in total £4 12\s. 6d./; 2 chargers with arms of which 1 with the Lady's arms and the other with 1 cross and 1 falcon weighing in total £4 0s. 5d.; 10 silver dishes with the Lady's arms weighing in total £10 18s. 4d.; 5 silver dishes with R[*oger*] Damory's arms weighing in total £4 15s. 2½d.; 5 dishes with the letter L weighing in total £5 1s. ½d.; 2 dishes with leopards' heads weighing in total £1 18s. 2d.; 6 silver shallow bowls with leopards' heads weighing in total £1 18s. 6½d.; 4 silver shallow bowls with R[*oger*] Damory's arms weighing in total £1 2s. 3½d.; item 15 shallow bowls with the Lady's arms weighing in total £4 8s. 4d.; item 39 dishes and 21 shallow bowls of pewter.

Granary   40qr of barley and dredge at Anglesey; 35qr of malt dredge; and 15qr 7b. of malt barley remaining.

[m. 1] Marshalsea   1 cart-rope, 16 pairs of buckles for packhorses, 12 pairs of buckles for overgirths; 3 pieces of fabric for packhorses, expended; 2 pieces of fabric for the Lady's palfreys, \1 expended/; 1 piece and 1 girth for hackneys, expended; 6 new girths for packhorses; 3 old girths for [m. 2] the same, expended; 5 girths for hackneys, expended; 4 leather girths for packhorses; 1 red bridle for 1 courser; 17 pieces of Spanish iron weighing in total 496lb., expended; 9 worn out packhorse-saddles, 4 expended; and hay remaining; 10qr of oats remaining; 16 waggon-oxen without price; 2 waggons with 4 wheels bound with iron; 1 destrier for the Lady's coach called Bay de Ferrers; 1 destrier for the same called Blake Morel dead;[8] 1 destrier called Blynde Bayard, dead; 1 destrier called Doun Lymener; 1 destrier called Morel Stele, dead; 1 destrier called Bayard atte Beche dead; 1 packhorse called Rede Bay; 1 packhorse called le White Blaunchard; 1 packhorse called le Grey Ferraund de Ferrers; 1 palfrey called Bayard Beke; 1 palfrey called Powys de

---

8   The entry, 'dead', next to certain horses is in a different hand.

Wauton; 1 horse called Skewbald; 1 white and one-eyed packhorse of the Poultry; 1 red packhorse for the same; 3 carts bound with iron; 2 long cart-covers for 2 carts.

Servants and Retainers
Roll of Liveries, 17 Edward III (1343)   [TNA E101/92/23]
[m. 1] [*The first section of the Roll, concerning the knights, is torn, damaged and largely illegible. There are 15 names in the list. The number of ells refers to cloth for robes, and the terms, fur and pane, refer to fur-linings.*]
Sir John de Bardolf, 11½ ells, [*illeg.*], 3½ hoods of minever pured, [*illeg.*]; Sir William de Shardelowe, 11 ells, [*illeg.*], 3½ hoods of minever pured, [*illeg.*]; Sir Nicholas de Clare, 9 ells, [*illeg.*], 1 hood of minever pured; Sir Thomas de London, 11 ells, [*illeg.*], 1½ hoods of minever pured, [*illeg.*]; Andrew de Bures, 9½ ells, 1 fur of minever, 1 fur of popel, 1½ hoods of minever pured; Sir Warin de Bassingbourne, 9 ells, 1 fur of popel, 1 fur of [*illeg.*], 1½ hoods of minever pured, [*illeg.*].
Ladies   [*Details of hoods are illegible.*] Lady Joan de Strechesley, 13 ells, 2 furs of popel, [*illeg.*]; Eleanor Wynkesure, 12 ells, 1½ furs of budge, 1 pane of lamb, [*illeg.*]; Margery Mareschal, 13 ells, 1 fur of popel, [*illeg.*]; Suzanne de Neketon, 8¾ ells, 1 fur of popel, [*illeg.*]; Anne de Lexden, 12 ells, 1½ furs of budge, 1 pane of lamb, [*illeg.*]; Alice Cheyner, 8½ ells, 1 fur of strandling, [*illeg.*]; Elizabeth Lucas, 7 ells, 1 fur of strandling, [*illeg.*].
Clerks   Sir John St Pol, 11¼ ells, 1 fur of minever, 1 fur of popel, 1½ hoods of minever pured; Sir William de Everdon, 11½ ells, 1 fur of minever, 1 fur of popel, 1½ hoods of minever pured; Sir William de Stowe, 11¼ ells, 1 fur of popel, 1 fur of strandling, 1½ hoods of minever pured; Sir David de Wallour, 11¼ ells, 1 fur of popel, 1 fur of strandling, 1½ hoods of minever pured; Master Richard de Plessys, 11 ells, 1 fur of popel, 1 fur of strandling, 1½ hoods of minever pured; Sir Thomas de Cheddeworth, 11½ ells, 2 furs of popel, 1 fur of strandling, 1½ hoods of minever pured; Sir Robert de Stalynton, 10½ ells, 2 furs of budge, 1 hood of budge; Sir Robert Cokerell, 10 ells, 2 furs of budge, 1 hood of budge; Sir John de Lenne, 8 ells, 1 fur of budge, 1 hood of budge; Sir Peter de Ereswell, 7¾ ells, 1 fur of budge, 1 hood of budge; Sir Nicholas de Hull, 7¾ ells, 1 fur of budge, 1 hood of budge; Thomas Pulleter, 7¾ ells, 1 fur of budge, 1 hood of budge; Sir Henry Motelot, 7 ells, 1 fur of budge, 1 hood of budge; John de Boys, 7¼ ells, 1 fur of budge, 1 hood of budge; Sir William d'Oxwik, 7 ells, 1 fur of budge, 1 hood of budge; William Faunt, 7¾ ells, 1 fur of budge, 1 hood of budge; Sir Richard de Cressewelle, 7¾ ells, 1 fur of budge, 1 hood of budge; Sir John de Flete, 6½ ells, 1 fur of budge, 1 hood of budge; William Albon, 7 ells, 1 fur of budge, 1 hood of budge; Sir William [*d'Arderne*] priest of Anglesey, 7 ells, 1 fur of budge, 1 hood of budge; Sir William de Manton, 7¾ ells, 1 fur of budge, 1 hood of budge; Sir Richard de [*illeg.*], 7¼ ells, 1 fur of budge, 1 hood of budge.
Esquires   David of Athol, 5 ells, 1½ furs of budge, 1 hood of budge; Robert Percy, 5¾ ells, 1½ furs of budge, 1 hood of budge; William de Ferrers, 5¾ ells, 1½ furs of budge, 1 hood [*sic*]; Thomas Fitzwalter, 5¾ ells, 1 lambs' fur; Robert de Bures, 4¼ ells, 1 lambs' fur; Robert Mareschal, 6¾ ells, 1 lambs' fur; Thomas de la Mare, 6¾ ells, 1 lambs' fur; John de Horslee, 6½ ells, 1 lambs' fur, 1 hood of budge; Henry de Colingham, 7 ells, 1 lambs' fur, 1 hood of budge; William Lengleis, 6½ ells, 1 lambs' fur, 1 hood of budge; John Bataille, 6¼ ells, 1 lambs' fur; Robert Flemyng, 6½ ells, 1 lambs' fur; Thomas Butler, 6⅜ ells, 1 lambs' fur, 1 hood of budge; Thomas [*illeg.*], 6½ ells, 1 lambs' fur, 1 hood of budge; Andrew de [*illeg.*], 6¼ ells, 1 lambs' fur; John Gough, 6¼ ells, 1 lambs' fur; Master Roger le [*illeg.*],

6¼ ells, 1 lambs' fur; Thomas de Bassingbourne, 6 ells, 1 lambs' fur; Robert de Bassingbourne, 6½ ells, 1 lambs' fur; Henry de Dene, 6¼ ells, 1 lambs' fur; John de Claketon, 6¼ ells, 1 lambs' fur; Roger Ewyas, 6¼ ells, 1 lambs' fur; John Holdich, 6¼ ells, 1 lambs' fur; Walter de Kirkeby, 6¼ ells, 1 lambs' fur; Nicholas Nowers, 6¼ ells, 1 lambs' fur; Colinet Morley, 6¼ ells, 1 lambs' fur; Roger of the Pantry, 6¼ ells, 1 lambs' fur; Thomas de Cantebrigge, 6 ells, 1 lambs' fur; Robert Caumpe, 6¼ ells, 1 lambs' fur; Roger the Minstrel, 6¼ ells, 1 lambs' fur; John Lengleis, 6 ells, 1 lambs' fur; Giles, companion of William de Ferrers, 6¼ ells, 1 lambs' fur; Guy Span, 6½ ells, 1 lambs' fur, 1 hood of budge; Thomas Cary, 6²/4 ells [*sic*], 1 lambs' fur, 1 hood of budge; John de Ravensholme, 6²/4 ells [*sic*], 1 lambs' fur, 1 hood of budge; Thomas Priour, 6¾ ells, 1 lambs' fur, 1 hood of budge; Oliver de Burdene, 6¾ ells, 1 lambs' fur, 1 hood of budge; Richard de la Bere, 6½ ells, 1 lambs' fur, 1 hood of budge; Henry de Neuton, 6½ ells, 1 lambs' fur; John de Hertforde, 6½ ells, 1 lambs' fur, 1 hood of budge; Robert de Ellerton, 6¾ ells, 1 lambs' fur, 1 hood of budge; Roger de Blaykeston, 8 ells, 1 lambs' fur, 1 hood of budge; Robert de Thorpe, 8 ells, 1 lambs' fur, 1 hood of budge; Thomas Tochewik, 6¾ ells, 1 lambs' fur, 1 hood of budge; John Fermer, 6¼ ells, 1 lambs' fur; John Blount, 6¾ ells, 1 lambs' fur, 1 hood of budge; William Baret, 6½ ells, 1 lambs' fur; John d'Engaine, 6¼ ells, 1 lambs' fur; John Kington, 6¼ ells, 1 lambs' fur; John Turville, 6¼ ells, 1 lambs' fur; John Wake, 6¼ ells, 1 lambs' fur, 1 hood of budge; Nicholas Pik, 6¼ ells, 1 lambs' fur, 1 hood of budge; Walter Barill, 6½ ells, 1 lambs' fur, 1 hood of budge; Edmund Butler, 6½ ells, 1 lambs' fur, 1 hood of budge; Walter de Lyers, farmer of Tarrant [*Gunville, Dorset*], 6¾ ells, 1 lambs' fur; John atte Lee, 6¼ ells, 1 lambs' fur, 1 hood; Jevan ap Rhys, 6⅛ ells, 1 lambs' fur; Thomas ap Iver, 6¼ ells, 1 **[m. 2]** lambs' fur; John Seymor, 6¼ ells, 1 lambs' fur; Roger Turtle, 6²/4 ells [*sic*], 1 lambs' fur, 1 hood of budge; William de Butelsgate, 6½ ells, 1 lambs' fur; Ralph Cotel; Roger Taillour, 6¼ ells, 1 lambs' fur; William de Clopton, 6¼ ells, 1 lambs' fur; Peter Favelor, 6¾ ells, 1 lambs' fur; Walter Colpeper, 6¼ ells, 1 lambs' fur; John Goldingham, 6¼ ells, 1 lambs' fur; Robert Russel, 6¼ ells, 1 lambs' fur; William de Lavenham, 6¼ ells, 1 lambs' fur; Robert de Islep, 6¼ ells, 1 lambs' fur, 1 hood of budge; Robert Danetoft, 6¼ ells, 1 lambs' fur, 1 hood of budge; Robert de Eynesham, 6¼ ells, 1 lambs' fur; Bartholomew Thomasin, 6¼ ells, 1 lambs' fur, 1 hood; Simon de Berking, 6½ ells, 1 lambs' fur; Master Richard Carpenter, 6¼ ells, 1 lambs' fur; John Iveshale, saddler, 6¼ ells, 1 lambs' fur; Thomas Cheiner, 6¼ ells, 1 lambs' fur; Thomas Coteler, 6½ ells, 1 lambs' fur; Nigel Tebaud, 6⅛ ells, 1 lambs' fur; John Hoke, 6¼ ells, 1 lambs' fur; Roger Aubre, 6½ ells, 1 lambs' fur; Walter de Finchingfelde, 6½ ells, 1 lambs' fur, 1 hood of budge; Walter de Somerby, 6¼ ells, 1 lambs' fur, 1 hood of budge; Brundel de Petton, 6¼ ells, 1 lambs' fur; Alexander Charman, 6¼ ells, 1 lambs' fur; Hewyn, esquire of the countess of Pembroke, 6¼ ells, 1 lambs' fur; Robert Lesturmy, 6¼ ells, 1 lambs' fur; Thomas Barber, 6¼ ells, 1 lambs' fur; Henry de Honidene, 6¼ ells, 1 lambs' fur; John atte More, 6¼ ells, 1 lambs' fur; the esquire of Sir John Bardolf, 6¼ ells, 1 lambs' fur; William Hakelu, 6¼ ells, 1 lambs' fur; John Baud, 6¼ ells, 1 lambs' fur.

Serjeants   John de Chadeslee, 5½ ells, 1 lambs' fur; John Messager, 5½ ells, 1 lambs' fur; Hugh Dailleston, 5½ ells, 1 lambs' fur; Matthew the servant of David, 5¼ ells, 1 lambs' fur.

Middle clerks and Ladies of the Chamber   Sir John, priest of Bardfield, 5¼ ells, 1 fur of budge, 1 hood; Sir Henry, priest of Clare, 5¼ ells, 1 fur of budge, 1 hood of budge; Sir John, priest of Clare, 5¼ ells, 1 fur of budge, 1 hood of budge; Margaret de Neketon, 5¼ ells, 1 fur of squirrel; Christiana *la* [*?*]*Cueresse*, 6 ells, 1 fur of

70

squirrel; John de Honylegh, 5½ ells, 1 lambs' fur; Robert the Illuminator, 5¼ ells, 1 lambs' fur; the son of Adam Hogge; William de Berkwaye, 5½ ells, 1 lambs' fur. Little clerks   Agnes of the Chamber, 6 ells, 1 fur of rabbit; Magote of the Chamber, 5¾ ells, 1 fur of rabbit; Reynald, 5¼ ells, 1 lambs' fur; John de Chipham, 5¾ ells, 1 lambs' fur; Agnes of the Laundry, 6½ ells, 1 fur of rabbit; Thomas d'Oxwik, Augustine de Thrillowe, Raulyn de Ayleston, 11 ells, 3 lambs' furs; Sir Scheven de Bircham, 5½ ells, 1 lambs' fur.

Yeomen   William de Berchamsted, 5½ ells; John Butler, chamberlain, 5½ ells; Richard de Bircham, 5½ ells; John de Southam, 5½ ells; Robert de Shirewode, 5½ ells; Thomas Leseuer, 5¼ ells; Richard Chamberlain, 5½ ells; Giboun Rous, 5½ ells; Thomas de Wodham, 5½ ells; Hugh Poulterer, 5½ ells; Nicholas de Stoke, 5½ ells; Richard Petit, 5¼ ells; Thomas Scot, 5¼ ells; Gilbert Lesquiler, 5½ ells; Philip de la Marche, 5½ ells; John de Reveshale, 5½ ells; Adam Brewer, 5½ ells; Thomas le Barbour, 5½ ells; William Cospiter, 5½ ells; Richard Charioter, 5½ ells; Andrew de Braundon, 6 ells; John Chamberlain, 5½ ells; Roger de Wethersfelde, 5½ ells; Robert Crouder, 5½ ells; bailiff of Standon, 5½ ells; bailiff of Ilketshall, 6 ells; William le Peschour, 5½ ells; bailiff **[m. 3]** of Bardfield, 5½ ells; bailiff of Sudbury, 5½ ells; bailiff of Tunbridge Hall, 5½ ells; bailiff of Caerleon, 6 ells; reeve of Erbury, 5½ ells; Gilbert le Bercher, 5½ ells; bailiff of Walsingham, 5½ ells; Adam de Wetherfelde, 5½ ells; John le Venour, 5½ ells; bailiff of Wyke and Portland, 5½ ells; bailiff of Lutterworth, 5½ ells; Henry de Queye, 5½ ells; Robert le Peintour, 5½ ells; bailiff of Southwold; reeve of Hundon; Philip le Carpenter, 5½ ells; William Warnham, 5½ ells; Gautroun de Tonebrugge, 5½ ells.

Grooms   Robert of the Wardrobe, 6 ells; Robert of the Chamber, 6 ells; Roger Skinner, 6 ells; Jevan of the Wardrobe, 6 ells; John Owen, 6 ells; William de Colcestre, 6 ells; John the Brewer, 6 ells; John de Riston, 6 ells; Laurence le Porter, 6 ells; Henry le Gayte, 6 ells; Richard de Uttoxale, 6 ells; Robert Mape, 6 ells; John de Ryburghe, 6 ells; John Forider, 6 ells; John de Loundres, 6 ells; John Dyke, 6 ells; William de Berklowe, 6 ells; Richard Hauberk, 6 ells; William atte Stoure, 6 ells; William Havering, 6 ells; John de Hailles, 6 ells; Edmund Lewer, 6 ells; John Walisch, 6 ells; Ithel of the Avenery, 6 ells; Richard Loucesone, 6 ells; Richard Parker of Hundon, 6 ells; Richard Lesquiler, 6 ells; John le Hunte, 6 ells; John of the Chandlery, 6 ells; Nicholas Falconer, 6 ells; John de Garbotisham, 6 ells; William Smith, 6 ells; John Edward, smith, 6 ells; William Weblee, 6 ells; John Prat, 6 ells; Robert Garsewaye, granger of Brandon, 6 ells; John Motelot, granger of Usk; John Mape, 6 ells; Robert de Lopham, 6 ells; ~~John Seman, 5 ells~~; ~~Henry de Caerleon, 6 ells~~; Clement de Bury, 6 ells; John Batener, 6 ells; John de Chaldeforth, 6 ells; Roger le Currour, 6 ells; Richard Bisshop, 6 ells; Richard of the Chamber, 6 ells; Cnapyng Chareter, 6 ells; Adam of the Avenery, 6 ells; ~~John Havering, 6 ells~~; the gardener of Bardfield, 6 ells; the gardener of Clare, 6 ells; John Loucesone, 6 ells.

Pages. ~~Adam of the Avenery~~; John Squiler, 5½ ells; Adam of the Roasting-house, 5½ ells; John de la Mareis, 5 ells; ~~John Loucesone~~; Thomas Ponyng, 5¼ ells; William Wymbolee, 5¾ ells; ~~Ralph Charetter~~; Robert Loucesone, 5¾ ells; Henry le Hunte, 5½ ells; ~~John Wodham~~; Adam, page of the Poultry, 5½ ells; Adam, page of the Bakehouse, 5½ ells; Thomas Waynman, 5½ ells; William de Bitelesgate, 5¼ ells; page of the palfreys, 5 ells.

This roll contains the measure of cloths for the livery of Lady de Burgh, 18 Edward III (1344)[9] [TNA E101/92/26]

[m. 1] For knights   1 green cloth which measures 24 ells in length and 5½ quarter ells in breadth; another, striped, which measures 23 ells in length and 1 ell in breadth; another, green, which measures 23½ ells; another, striped, which measures 23½ ells; another, green, which measures 23 ells; another, striped, which measures 25 ells; another, green, which measures 23 ells; another, striped, which measures 24¼ ells.

Sum of cloths 8. [*Each of the cloths of colour measure 5½ quarter ells broad and each striped cloth measures 1 ell broad.*] And they contain in length 189¼ ells. [*169¼ ells expended in livery as appears in the roll of particulars.*] And there remain 20 ells.

For clerks and ladies   1 marbled cloth which measures 26 ells in length and 6½ quarter ells and more in breadth; another to match which measures 26½ ells; another to match which measures 27½ ells; another to match which measures 27¼ ells; another to match which measures 27½ ells; another to match which measures 26½ ells; another to match which measures 27 ells, 1qr less; another to match which measures 26¾ ells.

Sum of cloths 8, which measure 214¾ ells and in breadth 6 quarter ells [*illeg.*] Entirely expended in the livery.

For esquires   1 cloth of *pomiaz* which measures 24¾ ells in length and 1²/₄ ells in breadth; 1 blue striped cloth which measures 25 ells in length and 1 ell in breadth; 1 cloth of colour which measures 23½ ells; 1 striped cloth which measures 25½ ells; 1 cloth of colour which measures 24¾ ells; 1 striped cloth which measures 24½ ells; 1 cloth of colour which measures 22½ ells; 1 striped cloth which measures 24 ells; 1 cloth of colour which measures 24¾ ells; 1 striped cloth which measures 24½ ells; 1 cloth of colour which measures 23¼ ells; 1 striped cloth which measures 24½ ells; 1 cloth of colour which measures 25 ells; 1 striped cloth which measures 24½ ells; 1 cloth of colour which measures 24½ ells; 1 striped cloth which measures 24 ells; 1 cloth of colour which measures 24 ells; 1 striped cloth which measures 24½ ells; 1 cloth of colour which measures 24 ells; 1 striped cloth which measures 24¼ ells; 1 cloth of colour which measures 24 ells; 1 striped cloth which measures 24 ells; 1 cloth of colour which measures 24 ells; 1 striped cloth which measures 23 ells.

Sum of cloths 24. Each of the cloths of colour measure 1¼ ells broad, and each of the striped cloths measure 1 ell broad. And they measure in total length 582¼ ells. Expended in the livery as appears in the roll of particulars. 2 cloths remain besides the making which is in progress and charged in the amount.

For serjeants   1 yellow striped cloth which measures 23½ ells and in breadth 1¾ ells. In livery made as appears in the roll of particulars, 18 ells. There remain 5½ ells.

For middle clerks and ladies 1 cloth of apple-bloom motley which measures 22 ells, in breadth 5½ quarter ells; another which measures 22 ells; another which measures 21¾ ells.

Sum of cloths 3 which measure 65¾ ells in length and 5½ quarter ells in breadth. Of which 56 ells given in liveries as appears in the roll of particulars. There remain 9¾ ells.

For little clerks   1 cloth of green motley which measures 23 ells, in breadth 5½

---

9   There is no mention of the pages. The roll was not audited.

quarter ells; another to match which measures 23 ells; ½ cloth which measures 11½ ells.

Sum of cloths 2½ which measure in length 57½ ells and in breadth 5½ quarter ells [*illeg.*] as appears in the roll of particulars.

[m. 1d] For yeomen   1 tawny cloth which measures 25 ells; 1 striped cloth of apple-bloom which measures 24½ ells; another of colour which measures 24½ ells; another, striped, which measures 25 ells; another of colour which measures 25½ ells; another, striped, which measures 24¾ ells; another of colour which measures 24½ ells; another, striped, which measures 25 ells; another of colour which measures 24 ells; another, striped, which measures 25 ells; another of colour which measures 25 ells; another, striped, which measures 24 ells.

[*Sum 12 cloths, measuring 296¾ ells in length.*]

For grooms   1 blue cloth which measures 23½ ells, in breadth 5 quarter ells; another, striped, which measures 24½ ells, in breadth 1 ell; another of colour which measures 22¾ ells; another, striped, which measures 25¼ ells; another of colour which measures 22 ells; another, striped, which measures 24 ells; another of colour which measures 22 ells; another, striped, which measures 24¾ ells; another of colour which measures 22½ ells; another, striped, which measures 25½ ells; another of colour which measures 23½ ells; another, striped, which measures 24¼ ells.

Sum of cloths 12. Each of the cloths of colour measure 5 quarter ells in breadth, and each striped cloth measures 1 ell in breadth. And they measure in length 284½ ells. Of which 276 ells given in liveries as appears in the roll of particulars. There remain 8½.

Extract from the Goldsmiths' Account, 1333[10]   [TNA E101/91/30]

[m. 2] Divers expenses   For the expenses of Robert de Teukesbury and William atte Halle going from Clare to Walsingham and staying there for 6 days in January with 2 grooms and 2 horses, 8s. 6d. The same men's expenses [*going*] from Clare to London for 5 days, 10s. For horse-shoes, 4½d. Hire of 2 horses for Walter atte Verne and his servant coming from London to Clare and for their return to London, 5s. Robert's and Walter's expenses with 2 grooms making another [*journey*], 5s. 2d. Delivered to Walter and for his hired horses returning to London, 3s. 4d. For 1 pair of shoes given to the said Walter, price 1s. 6d. Hire of 2 horses for John de Markeby from London to Clare, 5s. Expenses of the same John de with 2 grooms and the said 2 horses, 3s. 4d. Expenses of the same 2 horses and 1 groom returning from Clare to London, 1s. 1d. Hire of 1 horse for William atte Halle from Clare to Walsingham and from there to London and from London to Malmesbury and from there to Clare, 8s. 6b. of oats bought for the said horse coming to Clare, Anglesey and London, 2s. Bread bought for the horse of Robert de Teukesbury, 2½d. Horse-shoes for the said horses [*coming*] to Clare on divers occasions, 3½d. For 1 groom hired to obtain colours, 10d. 2 horses hired for Robert de Teukesbury and John de Markeby [*going*] from Clare to Anglesey, 1s. Paid to Peter le Fevere for making divers tools, 6s. 11d. Hire of 3 horses from Clare to Anglesey on the eve of Easter for 3 goldsmiths, 1s. 6d. 2b. of oats for the same horses, 8d. Paid to 2 carpenters starting on the table, for 1 week 2s. 9d.[11] Hire of 1 carpenter from Clare for 2 days, 6d. For beds hired for the goldsmiths from London and straw for their horses coming from

---

10   The roll was not audited.
11   This table was for a religious work which is described in the rest of the entry. It would have taken the form of a panel or retable on which the images were set.

London to Clare on divers occasions, 1s. 9d. 1 groom hired from London to obtain a carpenter for the making of the table, 10d. Item hire of another groom to obtain wire and *burreys* from London, 10d. R[*obert*] de Teukesbury's expenses going to buy silver to Clare [*then*] to Coventry and returning, for 6 days, 6s. Hire of 1 horse to carry divers things from London to Clare, 3s. R[*obert*] de Teukesbury's expenses going from Clare to London for 5 days, 5s. And hire of 1 horse for the enameller from Clare to London, 1s. 6d. 2 horses hired for John de Markeby from Clare to London, 4s. The same John's expenses for this journey, 2s. 1 groom's expenses bringing 2 horses back with the horses' expenses from London, 1s. 6d. Paid to John de Markeby for making 7 images, £14 13s. 4d. And allowed to the same for the purchase of £29 6s. 8d., £1 4s. 5d. And to the same of my Lady's gift, £1. And to the same for the back of the said 7 images, £1 10s. And for the hire of an enameller staying at Clare for 28 weeks, £4 4s., taking 3s. a week. For a back for the back of the table, in part, £1 3s. 4d. Allowance for 2 horses for Walter atte Verne for 2 journeys from London to Clare, 6s. Walter's expenses coming and returning, for 8 days, 8s. Paid to Richard de Wrottyng and to his brother, carpenters, for 1 week for making part of the table, 3s. Item to the same Richard working on the said table for 2 weeks in July, 3s. And to Robert atte Brugge for the repair of the said table, 1s. And for R de Teukesbury's expenses going from Clare to London and staying there for 9 days to buy broken silver there, 9s. Item for the hire of a groom to obtain enamels from London, 1s. 2d. Paid to Roger Goldsmith of Bury St Edmunds from the feast of St John to Easter for his pay, £1.

Delivery of silver   For decoration of a belt delivered to my Lady, weight 2s. 6d. A pair of clasps for delivery to my Lady, 7d. Another pair of clasps for another delivery to my Lady, 4d. Repair of the foot of a cup, 1s. 5d. Repair of a vessel of the earl of Ulster, 2s. For the cover of a glass, 2s. 9d. And for the loss of silver of all the above works, 1s.[12] For a pentacle for the amber scent-ball, 8d. And for repair of Sir Henry de Ferrers' pot, 4d. And \for/ a box of an oak cross delivered to my Lady, 4s. 7d. And for the decoration of a belt of my Lady, 1s. 8d. And the loss of silver of these 2 works, 8d. And delivered to my Lady 6 silver dishes, weight 6s. 8d. And delivered to my Lady a cup called Tourdener, weight £1 6s. 7d. 3 clasps and 3 crests, weight £4 11s. 8d. And in the loss [*of silver*], 3s. 9d. A treacle-vase delivered to my Lady, weight 10s. 4d. Another treacle-vase for Sir John de Wauton, weight 9s. And for these works £8 were refined. And in the loss of silver in the refining, 15s. 4d. And in the loss of silver of 8 enamels which were delivered at Bury St Edmunds, 1s. 4d. And for a pair of hasps delivered to my Lady, 5d. For 2 goblets with 1 cover delivered to my Lady, weight £3 5s. 10d. In the loss [*of silver*] of this work, 2s. 9d. And for a goblet with a cover, 17s. 2d. And in the loss of silver, 9d. And for 2 mazers with 4 bands, 12s. 6d. Another mazer with a band, 3s. 4d. And in the loss of silver of the said 5 bands, 10d. And for the decoration of a belt for the earl of Hereford, 2s. 2d. And for a pair of clasps for my Lady's livery, 1s. 3d. And for another pair of clasps, 1s. 7d. In the loss of silver for the said 3 works, 4d. And for the enamels of the 3 clasps, weight 2s. 7d. more than the first. 2 bands for 2 mazers delivered to my Lady, 2s. 8d. In the loss, 2d. 2 dishes, 3s. 1d. 1 band for a mazer, 2s. 3d. In the loss of these 2 works, 3d. For the decoration of a belt for the

---

12   The loss of silver in making work for the Lady is usually noted. Precious metal was obtained from coins or old silver plate which was melted down, and its purity varied. M. Campbell, 'Gold, Silver and Precious Stones', in J. Blair and N. Ramsay, eds, *English Medieval Industries* (London, 1991), pp.110–11; J. Cherry, *Medieval Goldsmiths* (London, 2011), p.33.

bishop of London, 4s. 5d.[13] In the loss of the said work, 2d. Delivered to my Lady a pair of garters, the decoration weighing 2s. 9d. In the loss of the said work, 2d. For decoration of a belt and 3 pairs of garters, 8s. 6d. And in the loss of this work, 6d. 12 dishes £17 16s., and 12 shallow bowls, weight £4 15s. In the loss of silver of each delivery, 10d. And for 2 covers, £1 2s. 1d. In the loss of this work, 1s. For 1 foot and other repairs of a pot, 8s. 1d. In the loss of 10s. of silver refined for this, 1s. 1d. For 6 enamels for clasps [*and*] 4 for treacle-vases [?]ornamented in enamel, 2s. 1d. 1 ring with the base for a mazer, weight 2s. This mazer Robert Mareschal gave to my Lady. In the loss of this work, 3d. And delivered to my Lady for repair of a \table/, weight 2d. Delivered to my Lady 18 beads for a rosary, weight 2s. 7½d. In the loss of the said works, 9½d. For the decoration of 2 belts with enamels, weight 2s. 5d. In the loss of this work, 3d. 1 chain for a seal-purse, 2s. 3d. In the loss of this work, 2d. 1 pair of enamelled clasps for a livery, weight 1s. 3d. In the loss of this work, 2d. Delivered to my Lady 1 goblet with the cover, weight £1 5s. 10d. In the loss of this work, 1s. 7d. Delivered to my Lady 5 beads of jet for a rosary, weight 3s. In the loss of this work, 2d. Delivered to my Lady 1 pair of clasps, weight 3d. Delivered to my Lady 2 basins, weight £6 18s. 4d. In the loss of each ~~livery~~ lb., 9d. Delivered to my Lady 1 mazer with a \cockle/ shell, weight 18s. 1 pair of hasps for my Lady's livery, weight 8½d. In the loss of this work, 1s. Delivered to my Lady 1 enamelled belt, weight 2s. 9d. In the loss of the enamel, 3d. In the loss of the work, 1d. Delivered to my Lady 12 belts for Christmas of which the decoration of 4 was in enamel. In the loss of the enamel of the 4 belts, 8d. In the loss of the 8 belts in the work, 8d. For the decoration of the said 12 belts, 14s. Delivered to my Lady 2 silver varvels, weight \2s./ 9d. And in the loss of the work, 2d. 1 hasp for my Lady's livery, weight 4d. For the decoration of 1 belt of my Lady, weight 1s. 3d. In the loss of these 2 works, 2d. Delivered to my Lady 1 pax-board, weight £2 10s.

Delivery of gold. Delivered to my Lady 4 gold rings with emeralds, weight 8½d. In the loss of this work, ½d. 1 gold ring with a diamond, weight 1d. 1 pair of gold clasps for my Lady's livery, weight 9d. In the loss of this same work, ½d. Item to my Lady 1 gold clasp, weight 1s. 9d. In the loss of this work, 1d. Item to my Lady 2 gold eagles, weight 2s. 1d. In the loss of this work, 2d. And also delivered to my [*Lady*] for my Lady Bardolf's circlet 2 pieces of gold, weight 8d. And in the loss of this work, ½d. For making a gold ring, weight ½d., with a ruby for my Lady. Item for making another gold ring for the earl of Hereford, weight ½d.

The Lady's Private Expenditure: Extracts from the Lady's Chamber Account, 1352 [TNA E101/93/12]

[m. 4d] [*Week ending on 19 May*][14] Item 8 ells of red *yrame* bought for Elizabeth Mareschal, £1 8s.;[15] item 1 fur] of strandling bought for the said Elizabeth, 8s.; item 2 ermines, price 1s. 4d. each, 2s. 8d.; item for binding and whipcord bought for the ornamenting of a bed, 4d.; item for the offering of my Lady and [*her*] ladies on the day of the Ascension of our Lord, 1s. 8d.; item delivered to Master Richard Carpenter for my Lady's work in London in May, £20;[16] item given on 16 May to John Odmel who carried herons from Usk to Bardfield, 3s. 4d.; item given to the

---

13 Stephen Gravesend was bishop of London at this time.
14 The Lady moved from Bardfield to Clare via Stoke by Clare on Friday, 18 May.
15 Elizabeth Mareschal had been married the week before.
16 Master Richard de Felstede, carpenter, was responsible for building the Lady's London house in the outer precinct of the convent of Minoresses outside Aldgate.

prisoners of [*Bishop's*] Stortford the same month, 6s. 8d.; item my Lady's offering at the chapel of Stoke on 18 May, 6s. 8d; item given to Colle le Bribour of Clare on the same day, 6s. 8d.; item paid by Margery for the [*blank*] of thread, 5d.

Sum of this week £23 4s. 5d. audited

[**m. 3d**] [*Week ending on 23 June*[17]] Item for the offering of my Lady and her household on 18 June for the soul of Sir John de Burgh, 1s. 4d.;[18] item given to a groom of the countess of Pembroke on 20 June, 2s.; item 2 pieces of *volez* of paris bought for my Lady on 18 June, price 7s. each, 14s.; item 2 pieces of gold ribbon, price 8s. each, 16s.; item 2 furs of minever pured bought from Henry de Northampton, £2 6s. 8d.; item given to a groom of Sir John Bardolf carrying bream to my Lady as a present from him on the same day, 2s.; item given to the bailiff of Erbury on the same day, 13s. 4d.;[19] item to the groom keeping the palfreys, destriers amd packhorses, 3s. 4d.; item for the fulling of 7 ells of blanket for my Lady, 2s.; item for dyeing 6 ells of blanket for my Lady, 4s.; item for hiring 1 man working in the Wardrobe before the feast of Corpus Christi for 4 days, 8d.; item 1 lambs' fur for Stephen Turbeville, 1s. 6d.; item for the offering of my Lady and her household for the soul of Sir Gilbert de Clare, my Lady's brother, on 23 June, 2s. 3d.; item for the offering on the same day to Clare church, 2s.; item given to the friars of Clare on the same day, 10s.

Sum of this week, £6 1s. 1d. audited

[*Week ending on 28 July*[20]] Item given on 23 July to a servant of the duke of Lancaster who carried letters to my Lady, 5s.; item given to the masons of the Augustinian friars of Clare working on the tomb of Sir Edward de Monthermer[21] on the same day, 2s. 6d.; item given to a servant of the earl of Northampton who carried a [*?*]buck as a present to my Lady, 6s. 8d.; item given to a groom of the bishop of Connor in Ireland carrying my Lady's letters on his return to Ireland, 10s.; item for the offering of my Lady and her household on the day of St James [*25 July*] for the soul of Lady Isabella de Ferrers, 2s. 4d.;[22] item given on 25 July to Griffith Balon carrying letters to my Lady from Sir Henry Motelot,1s. 6d.;[23] item given to a groom of the bishop of Llandaff[24] carrying letters to my Lady, on the same day, 2s.; item given to the nuns of Rothwell on 26 July, 13s. 4d.; item to the reapers of wheat near Clare castle on the same day, 1s. 4d.; item given to a servant of the bishop of London[25] carrying herons to my Lady, on the same day, 6s. 8d.; item for the offering of my Lady and her household on the day of the Seven Sleepers [*27 July*]for the soul of Sir Theobald de Verdun, 2s. 1d.;[26] item given to the smith of Hundon on 27 July, 13s. 4d.; item paid for the dyeing of 48 yards of black say, 10s.; item for lamps,

---

17 The Lady was residing at Clare.
18 The Lady's first husband who died in 1313.
19 The manor of Clare was called Erbury at this time; G.A. Thornton, *A History of Clare, Suffolk* (Cambridge, 1930), pp.17–18.
20 The Lady was residing at Clare.
21 The Lady's half-brother who died at Clare in December 1339 and was buried at Clare priory.
22 The Lady's elder daughter who died during the Black Death.
23 Sir Henry Motelot was Receiver of Usk.
24 John Paschal.
25 Ralph Stratford.
26 The Lady's second husband who died in 1316.

phials, urinals and glass [?]utensils bought by my Lady, 6s. 3d.; item given to the chamberlain of Sir William de Friskeneye on the same day, 13s. 4d.

Sum of this week, £4 16s. 4d. audited

[m. 2d] [*Week ending on 18 August*[27]] Item for the offering of my Lady and my Lady of Athol[28] at the chapel of Stoke on 13 August, 6s. 9d.; item given to the poor there on the same day, 4d.; item given to the reapers of wheat in the field near Erbury on the same day, 2s.; item given to a groom of Peter de Cutyndene who carried letters from him out of Dorset, 6d.; item for the offering of my Lady and her household in Clare church on the day of the Assumption of Our Lady [15 August], 4s. 11d.; item given to 2 children who were baptised in my Lady's presence on the same day, 5s.; item given to a Friar Preacher who preached before my Lady on the same day, 10s.; item delivered to Sir Peter [*de Ereswell*] on 15 August to make daily payments to the poor, 6s. 8d.;[29] item given to the masons of the Augustinian friars on 17 August, 1s.; item given to the wife of Roger who was my Lady's courier on the same day, 1s.; item delivered to Roger the Minstrel for making 7 songs, 2s. 6d.; item to the same for removing a great stone at Colchester, 1s.

Sum total of this week £2 1s. 8d. audited

[*Week ending on 25 August*[30]] Item given to a Friar Preacher who came out of Wales to my Lady on 20 August, 5s.; item paid for the making of a bag for a knife of my Lady on the same day, 2d.; item given to the stackers of wheat in the barn of Erbury on 21 August, 6d.; item to a poor woman with 2 children on the same day, 1d.; item given to the reap-reeve of Erbury on the same day, 6s. 8d.; item delivered to Master Richard Carpenter on 22 August for my Lady's work in London, £13 13s. 7d.; item given to a Friar Preacher on the same day, 6s. 8d.; item delivered to Sir Peter de Ereswell for the making of a porch and a wall round the house of Anne de Lexden, 17s.;[31] item sent to my Lady Bardolf by Master Thomas de Friskeneye, £3; item given on 24 August to a servant of the countess of Pembroke who carried letters to my Lady, 2s.; item given on 25 August to the Augustinian friars of Clare to pray for the soul of Andrew de Waleden, 6s. 8d.; item for the offering of my Lady and her household on the same day in her chapel, 2s.; item for the offering in Clare church on the same day, 2s.; item for a long tawny cloth, bought from William de Welde, given to the bishop of Winchester, Chancellor of England, £7 6s. 8d.[32]

Sum total of this week, £26 9s. audited

---

27 The Lady was residing at Clare.
28 Elizabeth countess of Athol was the Lady's granddaughter; she was the daughter of Sir Henry and Isabella de Ferrers.
29 Peter de Ereswell was the Lady's almoner.
30 The Lady was residing at Clare.
31 Anne de Lexden, formerly one of Elizabeth de Burgh's ladies, became an anchorite.
32 William Edington was bishop of Winchester between 1345 and 1366.

IV

FOOD, HOSPITALITY AND TRAVEL

Expenditure for 17–23 December 1340 from the Counter Roll for 1340–1
[TNA E101/92/14]

[m. 2] Die Dominica xvij die Decembris: summa denariorum xvijs. xd. qᵃ; summa stauri xxxviijs. jd.; utriusque Lvs. xjd. qᵃ. Die Lune xviij die Decembris: summa denariorum xiijs. vjd.; summa stauri xxixs. vijd.; utriusque xliijs. jd. Die Martis xix die Decembris : summa denariorum ixs. viijd.; summa stauri xxiijs. jd.; utriusque xxxijs. ixd. Die Mercurii xx die Decembris: summa denariorum xxiiijs. jd.; summa stauri xlijs.; utriusque Lxvjs. jd. Expense domine cum quibusdam de familia euntis ad dominam Reginam usque Sanctum Edmundum per iij dies: summa denariorum cvs. iiijd. ob. qᵃ; summa stauri xliiijs.; utriusque vij li. ixs. iiijd. ob. qᵃ. Die Jovis xxj die Decembris: summa denariorum xixs. xd. qᵃ; summa stauri xlixs. vjd.; utriusque Lxixs. iiijd. qᵃ. Die Veneris xxij die Decembris: summa denariorum xxs. ijd. ob.; summa stauri xxxvijs. viijd.; utriusque Lvijs. xd. ob. Die Sabbati xxiij die Decembris: summa denariorum xxxviijs. xd.; summa stauri xlvs.; utriusque iiij li. iijs. xd. Summa totalis per septimanam: summa denariorum xij li. ixs. iiijd. ob. qᵃ; summa stauri xv li. viijs. xjd.; utriusque xxvij li. xviijs. iijd. ob. qᵃ.

[m. 2] Sunday, 17 December: sum of money 17s. 10¼d.; sum of stock £1 18s. 1d.; sum of both £2 15s. 11¼d. Monday, 18 December: sum of money 13s. 6d.; sum of stock £1 9s. 7d.; sum of both £2 3s. 1d. Tuesday, 19 December: sum of money 9s. 8d.; sum of stock £1 3s. 1d.; sum of both £1 12s. 9d. Wednesday, 20 December: sum of money £1 4s. !d.; sum of stock £2 2s.; sum of both £3 6s. 1d. Expenses of the Lady going with some of the household to the Lady Queen at Bury St Edmunds for 3 days:[1] sum of money £5 5s. 4¾d.; sum of stock £2 4s.; sum of both £7 9s. 4¾d. Thursday, 21 December: sum of money 19s. 10¼d.; sum of stock £2 9s. 6d.; sum of both £3 9s. 4¼d. Friday, 22 December: sum of money £1 0s 2½d.; sum of stock £1 17s. 8d.; sum of both £2 17s. 10½d. Saturday, 23 December: sum of money £1 18s. 10d.; sum of stock £2 5s.; sum of both £4 3s. 10d. Sum total for the week: sum of money £12 9s. 4¾d.; sum of stock £15 8s. 11d.; sum of both £27 18s. 3¾d.

---

[1]   This is probably a reference to Queen Isabella, widow of Edward II.

78

Expense hospitii a xvij die Decembris usque xxiij die eiusdem mensis utroque die computato. Panetria: furnita x quarteria iiij busselli frumenti que reddiderunt de ij^{m}xxxij panibus, iij bussellis j pecca floris. Et expensi ij^{m}i-j^{c}xxxiiij panes de stauro. Butteria: xxx sexteria ij pichere vini de stauro. Et viij^{c}i-iij^{xx} lagene cervisie de stauro. Coquina: v carcosa dimidium bovum, vij bacones dimidium, xj cassa dimidium multonum, j porcus and j bestia venetica de stauro. Item m^{l}viij^{c}xx allecis, xlj stokfyschi, viij lengi, xxj moruce, iij salmones j quarterium, cv^{xx}x anguille de stauro. Pulletria: iiij fesanti, vj cuniculi, iij perdrices et xviij mallardi de stauro. Marchalcia: xxxij quarteria iij busselli j tertia pars avene. Unde de incremento iiij quarteria vj busselli j tertia pars et iij pecce avene. Item iij quarteria j pecca furfure, Lxviij panes. Et xlvij ferra equorum de stauro.

probatur

Expenses of the household from 17 December to 23rd day of the same month, both days counted. Pantry: 10qr 4b. of wheat baked which rendered 2,032 loaves [*and*] 3b. 1 peck of flour. And 2,234 loaves used from stock. Buttery: 30 sesters, 2 pitchers of wine from stock. And 880 gallons of ale from stock. Kitchen: 5½ carcasses of beef, 7½ bacons, 11½ carcasses of sheep, 1 pig and 1 deer from stock. Item 1,820 herring, 41 stockfish, 8 ling, 21 cod, 3¼ salmon, 230 eels from stock. Poultry: 4 pheasants, 6 rabbits, 3 partridges and 18 mallard from stock. Marshalsea: 32qr 3⅓b. of oats of which 4qr 6⅓b. 3 pecks from increment. Item 3qr 1 peck of bran, 68 loaves. And 47 horseshoes from stock. audited[2]

Expenditure for 31 March – 6 April 1359 from the Counter Roll for 1358–9

[TNA E101/94/1]

[m. 5] Sunday, last day of March: sum of money £2 2s. 8d.; sum of stock £1 16s. 3d.; sum of both £3 18s. 11d. Monday, 1 April: sum of money £1 7s. 11d.; sum of stock £1 11s. 7d.; sum of both £2 19s. 6d. Tuesday, 2 April: sum of money £1 4s. 10d.; sum of stock £1 15s. 5d.; sum of both £3 0s. 3d. Wednesday, 3 April: sum of money 19s. 4½d.; sum of stock £1 12s. 2d.; sum of both £2 11s. 6½d. Thursday, 4 April: sum of money £1 0s. 9d.; sum of stock £1 16s. 2d.; sum of both £2 16s. 11d. Moreover Lady Bardolf's expenses going to Barnwell: sum of money 8s. 11½d.; sum of stock 7s. 10d.; sum of both 16s. 9½d. Friday, 5 April: sum of money £1 1s. 8d.; sum of stock £1 17s. 4d.; sum of both £2 19s. Saturday, 6 April: sum of money £1 6s. 1¼d.; sum of stock £1 10s. 7d.; sum of both £2 16s. 8¼d. Sum total for the week: sum of money £9 12s. 3¼d.; sum of stock £12 7s. 4d.; sum of both £21 19s. 7¼d.

Stock of this week. Pantry: 12qr of wheat baked which rendered 2,582 loaves. Of this 1,492 loaves used from stock. Buttery: 15½ sesters of wine. Item 5qr of malt wheat and 3qr of malt oats brewed which rendered 515 gallons of ale. And 635 gallons of ale used from stock. Kitchen: 2,429 herring, 49 stockfish, 11 *streitfisch*, 16 cod, 5¾ salmon, 7 pike and 2 pieces of sturgeon from stock. Marshalsea: 7qr 1½b. of oats, 468 loaves and 43 horseshoes from stock. audited

---

2   Each entry in the paragraph was audited.

Food and Expenditure for 1–7 November 1355 from the Diet Roll for 1355–6

[TNA E101/93/18]

[m. 4] Festum Omnium Sanctorum. Clare: ferculi cxvj; liberatio panum ciiij^{xx}xij; liberatio vini et cervisie xliij. Die Dominica primo die Novembris ibidem. Panetria: furnita vj quarteria frumenti que reddiderunt de m^liij^cx panes. Inde expensi iiij^cxxxij panes de stauro. In candelis emptis pro pistrina ante adventum domine jd. Butteria: v sexteria dimidium vini. Et clx lagene cervisie de stauro. In c ciphis emptis iiijs. iijd. Coquina: 1 carcosa dimidium bovum, ij bacones, ij porci, v cassa mult-onum et iij bestia venetica de stauro. In dimidio vitulo xijd. ob. Pulletria: iij fesanti, ij cigni, vij cuniculi, vj capones de stauro. In iij porcellis ijs. iijd. In xij gallinis ijs. In xij pulcinis xiiijd. In xxx columbellis xijd. ob. In iiij perdricibus xjd. In ij plovariis and j cercella vjd. ob. q^a. In j cuniculo ijd. ob. In ij^c ovis xiiijd. In iiij lagenis lactis iiijd. In j bussello dimidio frumenti pro putura xijd. ob. Scutellaria: in c discis garnitis iiijs. Marchalcia: fenum pro lviij equis, xvj hakenis de stauro. In prebenda eorundem j quarterium vij busselli dimidius avene unde de incremento ij busselli avene. Item ij^ciiij^{xx}viij panes de stauro. In vadiis xxx garcionum, iiij pagettorum iiijs. jd. In vadio j valetti iijd.

Summa denariorum xxiiijs. vd. ob. q^a; summa stauri lxxvs. iijd.; utriusque iiij li. xixs. viijd. ob. q^a. Summa Panetrie jd.; summa Butterie iiijs. iijd.; summa Coquine xijd. ob.; summa Pulletrie xs. ixd. q^a; summa Scutellarie iiijs.; summa Marchalcie iiijs. iiijd.

Feast of All Saints. Clare: 116 messes; livery of loaves, 192; livery of wine and ale, 43. Sunday, 1 November, there. Pantry: 6qr of wheat baked which rendered 1,310 loaves. Of these 432 loaves used from stock. For candles bought for the Bakehouse before the Lady's arrival, 1d.[3] Buttery: 5½ sesters of wine. And 160 gallons of ale from stock. 100 cups bought, 4s. 3d. Kitchen: 1½ carcasses of beef, 2 bacons, 2 pigs, 5 carcasses of mutton, and 3 deer from stock. For ½ calf, 1s. ½d. Poultry: 3 pheasants, 2 swans, 7 rabbits, 6 capons from stock. For 3 piglets, 2s. 3d. 12 hens, 2s. 12 pullets, 1s. 2d. 30 young doves, 1s. ½d. 4 partridges, 11d. 2 plovers and 1 teal, 6¾d. 1 rabbit, 2½d. 200 eggs, 1s. 2d. 4 gallons of milk, 4d. 1½b. of wheat for the food allowance, 1s. 1½d. Scullery: 100 decorated dishes, 4s. Marshalsea: hay for 58 horses, 16 hackneys from stock. Provender for the same, 1qr 7½b. of oats, of which 2b. from increment. Item 288 loaves from stock. Wages of 30 grooms, 4 pages, 4s. 1d. 1 yeoman's wages, 3d.

Sum of money £1 4s. 5¾d.; sum of stock £3 15s. 3d.; of both £4 19s. 8¾d. Sum of the Pantry 1d. Sum of the Buttery 4s. 3d. Sum of the Kitchen 1s. ½d. Sum of the Poultry 10s. 9d. Sum of the Scullery 4s. Sum of the Marshalsea 4s. 4d.

---

3   The Lady moved from Bardfield to Clare on 28 October.

Clare: 71 messes; livery of loaves, 133; livery of wine and ale, 34. Monday, 2 November, there. Pantry: 266 loaves from stock. Buttery: 2½ sesters of wine. And 110 gallons of ale from stock. Kitchen: 1 beef carcass, 1¾ bacons, ¾ pig, 3¼ carcasses of mutton from stock. ½ calf, 1s. Poultry: 2 rabbits, 6 capons from stock. 13 hens, 2s. 2d. 9 chickens, 1s. 1½d. 4 pullets, 4d. 15 young doves, 6¼d. 1 pheasant, 1s. 5d. 2 partridges, 6d. 4 sea-bream, 2d. 100 eggs, 7d. 1b. of wheat for the food allowance, 11d. Apples, ½d. Marshalsea: hay for 53 horses and 14 hackneys from stock. Provender for the same, 2qr 7½b. of oats of which 3b. from increment. Item 6b. 1 peck of bran and 56 loaves from stock. 1 yeoman's wages, 3d. Wages of 30 grooms, 4 pages, 4s. 1d. Item 60 horseshoes used from stock.

Sum of money 13s. 1¼d.; sum of stock £2 19s. 4d.; of both £3 12s. 5¼d. Sum of the Kitchen 1s. Sum of the Poultry 7s. 9¼d. Sum of the Marshalsea 4s. 4d.

Clare: 61 messes; livery of loaves, 146; livery of wine and ale, 39. Tuesday, 3 November there. Pantry: 270 loaves from stock. Buttery: 2 sesters 1 pitcher of wine. Item 10qr of malt barley and 6qr of malt dredge brewed which rendered 1,010 gallons of ale. Of this 106 gallons used from stock. 2lb. of candles of paris, 4d. For 1 cooper's pay mending brewing vessels for 5 days, 11½d. Kitchen: 1¼ beef carcasses, 1 bacon, 1 pig, 2 carcasses of mutton from stock. 1 calf, 2s. 9d. Poultry: 1 pheasant, 4 rabbits and 24 young doves from stock. 6 capons, 1s. 6d. 8 hens, 1s. 4d. 5 pullets, 5d. 2 partridges, 6d. 4 teal, 6d. 1 mallard, 2d. 3 piglets, 1s. 4d. 2b. of oat-flour, 1s. 8d. For Henry Poulterer's expenses at Newmarket, 3½d. Marshalsea: hay for 53 horses, 14 hackneys from stock. Provender for the same, 1qr 3b. of oats of which 1b. from increment. Item 310 loaves from [**m. 5**] stock. 1 yeoman's wages, 3d. Wages of 29 grooms, 4 pages, 3s. 11½d. Horsebread bought for John Loucesone's horse coming from Reach to Bardfield with salt, 8d. For hay and candles, 2d. Bread for Robert Loucesone's horse on the said way, 8d. Hay for Robert's horse, 1d.

Sum of money 17s. 6½d.; sum of stock £2 9s. 10d.; of both £3 7s. 4½d. Sum of the Buttery 1s. 3½d. Sum of the Kitchen 2s. 9d. Sum of the Poultry 7s. 8½d. Sum of the Marshalsea 5s. 9½d.

Clare: 61 messes; livery of loaves, 124; livery of wine and ale, 37. Wednesday, 4 November, there. Pantry: 240 loaves from stock. Buttery: 1 sester 3 pitchers of wine and 105 gallons of ale from stock. Kitchen: 230 herring, 3 stockfish, 3 *middelfisch*, 7 *cropling*, 1 ling, 5½ cod, 5 conger eels, 1½ salmon, 2 pike, 1 piece of sturgeon from stock. For 350 herring, 3s. 7d. 16 codling, 2s. 14 plaice, 8d. 90 whiting, 2s. 2d. Poultry: 9 cheeses, 1s. 3d. 360 eggs, 2s. ½d. 4 gallons of milk, 4d. Marshalsea: hay for 54 horses and 14 hackneys from stock. Provender for the same, 1qr 7½b. of oats of which 2b. from increment. Item 4qr of peas baked which rendered 990 loaves. Of these 224 loaves used from stock. A yeoman's wages, 3d. Wages of 28 grooms and 4 pages, 3s. 10d. For baking 4qr of peas at Clare, 1s. 4d. For Cnapyng's horseshoes in London by Richard le Charer, 3d. For Cnapyng's horsebread at [*Bishop's*] Stortford by Richard le Charer, 1d. For providing 3 men from Standon going with Cnapyng's cart to Dunmow, 5d. For hay for the horses of the said cart and John Loucesone's cart there, 2d. For horsebread there, 10d. For horseshoes at Thremhall, 1d.

Sum of money 19s. 3½d.; sum of stock £2 7s.; of both £3 6s. 3½d. Sum of the Kitchen 8s. 5d. Sum of the Poultry 3s. 7½d. Sum of the Marshalsea 7s. 3d.

Clare: 54 messes; livery of loaves, 142; livery of wine and ale, 32. Thursday, 5 November, there. Pantry: 246 loaves from stock. Buttery: 1 sester 2 pitchers of wine and 94 gallons of ale from stock. Kitchen: 2 quarters of beef, ½ bacon, 3 quarters of pork, ½ boar from stock. For ½ quarter of beef,1s. 6d. 3 quarters of mutton, 1s. Poultry: 3 pheasants, 1 rabbit from stock. 2 piglets, 9d. 4 geese, 1s. 4d. 3 capons, 10d. 2 hens, 4d. 4 pullets, 4d. 4 teal, 6d. 2 plovers, 5d. 3 sea-bream, 2d. 18 young doves, 7½d. 4 rabbits, 10d. Marshalsea: hay for 47 horses and 9 hackneys from stock. Provender for the same, 2qr 4b. 1 peck of oats of which 2½b. from increment. Item 4b. 1 peck of bran from stock. 1 yeoman's wages, 3d. Wages of 27 grooms, 4 pages, 3s. 8½d.

Sum of money 12s. 7d.; sum of stock £1 17s. 4d.; of both £2 9s. 11d. Sum of the Kitchen, 2s. 6d. Sum of the Poultry 6s. 1½d. Sum of the Marshalsea 3s. 11½d.

Clare: 53 messes; livery of loaves, 103; livery of wine and ale, 31. Friday, 6 November, there. Pantry: 6qr of wheat baked which rendered 1,280 loaves, 1½b. of flour. Of these 170 loaves used from stock. Buttery: 1 sester of wine and 85 gallons of ale from stock. Kitchen: 100 herring, 3 stockfish, 3 *middelfisch*, 1 *cropling*, 2 ling, ½ cod, 2 conger eels from stock. 167 herring, 2s. 2d. 13 codling, 2s. 8d. 20 plaice, 1s. 4d. 50 whiting, 11d. 1 crayfish, 4d. Marshalsea: hay for 36 horses and 10 hackneys from stock. Provender for the same, 1qr 7b. 1 peck of oats of which 2b. from increment. Item 4b. of bran from stock. 1 yeoman's wages, 3d. Wages of 27 grooms, 4 pages, 3s. 8½d. Item 76 horseshoes used from stock.

Sum of money 11s. 4½d.; sum of stock £1 11s. 3d.; of both £2 2s. 7½d. Sum of the Kitchen 7s. 5d. Sum of the Marshalsea 3s 11½d.

Moreover, 2qr of wheat baked for distribution to the poor on the Day of Souls [*2 November*] which rendered 600 loaves. Of these 420 loaves used from stock. Item delivered to the Almoner 180 loaves from stock. Kitchen: 1,000 herring from stock.

Sum of stock £1 1s. 8d.

Clare: 61 messes; livery of loaves, 113; livery of wine and ale, 21. Saturday, 7 November, there. Pantry: 206 loaves from stock. Buttery: 1 sester 1 pitcher of wine and 86 gallons of ale from stock. Kitchen: 209 herring, 3 stockfish, 3 *middelfisch*, 3 *cropling*, 1 ling, 2 cod, 4 conger eels, 1 pike from stock. For 157 herring, 1s. 10d. 63 plaice 4s. 2d. 40 whiting, 10d. 15 codling, 1s. 6d. 300 oysters, 7d. 3 sticks of eels, 1s. 9d. Conger eels received, 2s. 9d. Carrying fish from Sudbury, 3d. Poultry: 60 eggs, 3½d. 2 cheeses, 3d. 2 gallons of milk, 2d. 2b. of wheat for the food allowance, 1s. 8d. Hugh Poulterer's and Henry's expenses at Sudbury and Haverhill, 3½d. Carrying poultry from Sudbury, 3½d. Marshalsea: hay for 36 horses and 10 hackneys from stock. Provender for the same, 7b. of oats of which 1b. from increment. Item 4b. of bran and 132 loaves from stock. 1 yeoman's wages, 3d. Wages of 26 grooms, 4 pages, 3s. 7d.

Sum of money £1 0s. 5½d.; sum of stock £1 11s.; of both £2 11s. 5½d. Sum of the Kitchen 13s. 8d. Sum of the Poultry 2s. 11½d. Sum of the Marshalsea 3s. 10d.

Sum total of money for the week £5 18s. 10d.   audited

Expenditure on Feast and Fast Days at Clare, 1350–1
Feast of Pentecost [*1350*]   [TNA E101/93/4]
[m. 12d] Clare: 154 messes; livery of loaves, 222; livery of wine and ale, 66. Sunday, 16 May, there. Pantry: 560 loaves from stock. Buttery: 7½ sesters of wine and 220 gallons of ale from stock. Kitchen: 1 carcass 3½ quarters of beef, 3¼ bacons from stock. 3 quarters of beef, 9s. 2½ pigs, 8s. 1½ carcasses of mutton, 2s. 4d. 8½ calves, 11s. 2d. Poultry: 3 swans, 2 bittern from stock. 11 piglets, 7s. 4d.

31 geese, 8s. 3d. 8 lambs, 3s. 4d. 74 pullets, 7s. 8½d. 15 young doves, 5d. 600 eggs, 3s. 6d. 16 gallons of milk, 1s. For Hugh Poulterer's expenses at Haverhill and Sudbury, 4d. Marshalsea: hay for 113 horses, 17 hackneys from stock. Provender for the same, 6qr 4b. 3 pecks of oats of which 6½b. from increment. Item 6b. 1 peck of bran. Item 72 loaves from stock. 2 yeomen's wages, 4d. Wages of 40 grooms and 4 pages, 5s. 4d.

Sum of money £3 8s. ½d.; sum of stock £4 10s. 2d.; of both £7 18s. 2½d. Sum of the Kitchen £1 10s. 6d. Sum of the Poultry £1 11s. 10½d. Sum of the Marshalsea 5s. 8d.

Feast of Corpus Christi [*1350*]   [TNA E101/93/4]
[m. 13d] Clare: 217 messes; livery of loaves, 316; livery of wine and ale, 104. Thursday, 27 May, there. Pantry: 780 loaves from stock. 2 great tubs bought for the Laundry, 1s. For making 100 cups from the Lady's timber, 2s. 6d. Buttery: 18 sesters of wine and 300 gallons of ale from stock. For 42 earthenware pots, 2s. Kitchen: 1 carcass 1 quarter of beef, 3½ bacons, 5 pigs, 6 deer and 2 dishes of boar from stock. 2 carcasses of beef, 19s. 6d. 2 pigs, 8s. 3d. 7 carcasses of mutton, 14s. 11¾ calves, 17s. 2 heads and 1 dish of boar, 8s. 6d. Porpoise, 1s. Conger eels, 1s. 2 mullet, 2s. 15 mackerel, 6d. 10 whiting, 3d. Poultry: 1 swan, 6 herons, 6 bittern and 48 rabbits from stock. For 4 swans, 13s. 16 piglets, 10s. 2d. 51 geese, 13s. 9d. 33 capons, 13s. 9d. 3 hens and 3 chickens, 1s. 1d. 80 pullets, 8s. 3½d. 6 dozen young doves, 3s. 12 lambs, 7s. 6d. 1,400 eggs, 8s. 2d. 8 cheeses, 1s. 17 gallons of milk, 1s. ¾d. Cream, 1s. 1¼ gallons of honey, 1s. 9d. For the food allowance for the herons, 1s. 6d. Scullery: making 200 ornamented dishes from the Lady's timber, 4s. Hall and Chamber: For rushes purchased, 1s. 8d. Marshalsea: hay for 149 horses, 17 hackneys from stock. For provender, 9qr 4⅔b. 2 pecks of oats of which 1qr 1b. from increment. Item 16 loaves from stock. 2 yeomen's wages, 4d. Wages of 39 grooms and 5 pages, 5s. 3½d.

Sum of money £8 13s. 9¾d.; sum of stock £7 15s.; of both £16 8s. 9¾d. Sum of the Pantry 3s. 6d. Sum of the Buttery 2s. Sum of the Kitchen £3 12s. Sum of the Poultry £4 5s. ¼d. Sum of the Scullery 4s. Sum of the Hall and Chamber 1s. 8d. Sum of the Marshalsea 5s. 7½d.

Feast of the Nativity of the Lord [*1350*]   [TNA E101/93/9]
[m. 8] Clare: 126 messes; livery of loaves, 248; livery of wine and ale, 71. Saturday, 25 December, there. Pantry: 520 loaves from stock. Buttery: 7 sesters of wine and 200 gallons of ale from stock. For the purchase of 160 cups, 5s. 9d. For 160 cups bought, 7s. Kitchen: 1 carcass 1 quarter of beef, 1½ bacons, 3 carcasses of mutton, 4 deer and 1 dish of boar from stock. Item 260 herring, 9 stockfish, 6 *streitfisch*, ½ salmon, 7 pike, 3 pieces of sturgeon and 2 pieces of dolphin from stock. ½ carcass of beef, 5s. 2 pigs, 6s. 10d. 1 carcass of mutton, 1s. 4d. 2 calves, 4s. 6d. 80 plaice, 4s. 1,000 sprats, 2s. 6d. 1 large eel, 1s. 6d. 4 sticks of eels, 2s. 10 roach, 8d. 15 haddock and codling, 4s. 9d. 800 oysters, 2s. Poultry: 18 rabbits from stock. 2 swans, 5s. 5 piglets, 3s. 9d. 12 capons, 3s. 6d. 8 geese, 3s. 2 geese, 4s. 6 partridges, 1s. 7½d. 3 plovers, 7½d. 1 woodcock, 2d. 4 teal, 8d. 3 sea-bream, 2d. 2 pheasants, 4s. 2 pullets, 2d. 600 eggs, 4s. 3d. Cream, 4d. 5 gallons of milk, 5d. Expenses of Adam groom of the Poultry at Bury St Edmunds, 2d. 1 page's expenses going for rabbits at Freck-enham, 1d. Scullery: making 200 ornamented dishes from the Lady's timber, 4s. Marshalsea: hay for 82 horses and 14 hackneys and 2 oxen from stock. Hay bought for 13 horses, 2 hackneys, 7½d. Provender for the same, 5qr of oats from stock of

which 2½b. from increment. Item 3b. 2 pecks of bran and 136 loaves from stock. 2 yeomen's wages, 4d. Wages of 26 grooms, 4 pages, 3s. 7d.

Sum of money £4 8s. 3½d.; sum of stock £4 8s. 1d.; of both £8 16s. 4½d. Sum of the Buttery 12s. 9d. Sum of the Kitchen £1 15s. 1d. Sum of the Poultry £1 11s. 11d. Sum of the Scullery 4s. Sum of the Marshalsea 4s. 6½d.

Lent [*1351*]   [TNA E101/93/9]
[m. 16] Clare: 72 messes; livery of loaves, 147; livery of wine and ale, 39. Saturday, 12 March, there. Pantry: 250 loaves from stock. Buttery: 1 sester 3 pitchers of wine and 110 gallons of ale from stock. Kitchen: 415 herring, 6 stockfish, 4 *cropling*, 8 cod, 2 conger eels, 1¾ salmon, and 1 lamprey from stock. 2 plaice, 5d. 60 plaice, 3s. 6d. Conger eels received, 4s. 400 whelks, 1s. 500 oysters, 1s. 3d. 300 mussels, 3d. Expenses of Adam groom of the Poultry at Chelmsford for 1 night with 1 pack-horse, 10d. 3½ sticks of eels, 2s. 4d. Poultry: ½b. of barley, 6¾d. Suet, 6d. Hugh Poulterer's expenses at Sudbury on 2 occasions, 3½d. For 1 horse hired from Bury St Edmunds to Clare, 6d. Scullery: 1 basket bought for carrying coal, 6d. Marshalsea: hay for 41 horses, 8 hackneys and 2 oxen from stock. Provender for the same, 2qr 6b. 3 pecks of oats of which 3b. from increment. Item 1b. 3 pecks of bran from stock. 2 yeomen's wages, 4d. Wages of 22 grooms, 3 pages, 3s. For the pay of 12 horses, 1 hackney 3s. 2d. Horseshoes for Cnapyng's cart going to Freckenham, 1d.

Sum of money £1 2s. 6¼d.; sum of stock £2 8s. 5d.; of both £3 10s. 11¼d. Sum of the Kitchen 13s. 7d. Sum of the Poultry 1s. 10¼d. Sum of the Scullery 6d. Sum of the Marshalsea 6s. 7d.

Moreover for the distribution to the poor on the day of St Gregory [*12 March*].[4] Pantry: 4qr of wheat baked which rendered 1,240 loaves. Of these 504 loaves used from stock. Kitchen: 900 herring from stock.

Sum of stock £1.

The Annunciation of the Blessed Mary [*1351*]   [TNA E101/93/9]
[m. 17] Clare: 72 messes; livery of loaves, 165; livery of wine and ale, 48. Friday, 25 March, there. Pantry: 275 loaves from stock. Buttery: 2 sesters of wine and 114 gallons of ale from stock. Kitchen: 425 herring, 3 stockfish, 7 *cropling*, 4 cod, 3 conger eels, 1¾ salmon, 1 pike, ¼ turbot, 2 large eels and 110 whelks from stock. 5 plaice, 2s. 3d. 60 plaice, 3s. 6d. 1 pike, 1s. 9d. 2 large eels, 2s. 12 sole, 1s. 6d. 500 whelks, 10d. 400 oysters, 1s. 4d. Cok Havering's expenses at Dunwich and Bury St Edmunds with 1 horse for 4 days, 2s. 2d. Marshalsea: hay for 35 horses, 7 hackneys and 2 oxen from stock. Provender for the same, 2qr 1 peck of oats of which 2b. from increment. Item 1b. of bran and 92 loaves from stock. 2 yeomen's wages, 4d. Wages of 22 grooms, 3 pages, 3s. For the pay of 11 horses, 1 hackney, 2s. 11d.

Sum of money £1 1s. 7d.; sum of stock £2 2s. 10d.; of both £3 4s. 5d. Sum of the Kitchen 15s. 4d. Sum of the Marshalsea 6s. 3d.

Feast of Easter [*1351*]   [TNA E101/93/9]
[m. 19d] Clare: 122 messes; livery of loaves, 224; livery of wine and ale, 59. Sunday, 17 April, there. Pantry: 510 loaves from stock. Buttery: 6 sesters of wine and 196 gallons of ale from stock. For 100 cups purchased, 3s. 6d. Kitchen: 2

---

4   The distribution took place on the anniversary of the death of Roger Damory, the Lady's third husband.

carcasses 1½ quarters of beef and 2 bacons from stock. 2½ pigs, 8s. 6d. 1 carcass of mutton, 2s. 2d. 7 calves, 7s. 6d. Poultry: 2 swans, 8 capons from stock. 8 piglets, 2s. 8d. 6 geese, 4s. 6d. 8 hens, 1s. 4d. 8 lambs, 4s. 28 pullets, 2s. 10d. 35 young doves, 1s. 400 eggs, 1s. 8d. 3 gallons of milk, 2¼d. 2b. of wheat for the food allowance, 1s. 8d. Scullery: for making 200 ornamented dishes, 4s. 1 meat-axe, 1s. 6d. Marshalsea: hay for 58 horses, 14 hackneys and 2 oxen from stock. Provender for the same, 2qr 3½b. of oats of which 2½b. from increment. Item 3½b. of bran and 180 loaves from stock. 2 yeomen's wages, 4d. Wages of 28 grooms, 3 pages, 3s. 9d. For the pay of 15 horses, 1 hackney, 3s. 11d.

Sum of money £2 15s. ¼d.; sum of stock £3 17s. 5d.; of both £6 12s. 5¼d. Sum of the Buttery 3s. 6d. Sum of the Kitchen 18s. 2d. Sum of the Poultry 19s. 10¼d. Sum of the Scullery: 5s. 6d. Sum of the Marshalsea 8s.

Provision for those on Business Trips or staying at Clare when the Lady was away
Tuesday, 19 July 1334   [TNA E101/92/2]
[m. 4d] Moreover for the expenses of Sir John de Wauton, Sir T[*homas*] de Cheddeworth, Sir William le Blount, Richard de Wenden and others going from Bardfield to Clare and Bury St Edmunds on the Lady's business there for 2 days viz. Pantry: 112 loaves from stock. Buttery: 4 sesters of wine. 53 gallons of ale bought at divers prices without profit, 4s. 9d. Kitchen: ½ carcass of beef, 3s. 1d. ½ pig, 2s. 1¾ calves, 3s. 4d. 2½ carcasses of mutton, 5s. 8d. Poultry: 18 hens, 2s. 5d. 24 pullets, 1s. 10d. 6 young doves, 3½d. 130 eggs, 8½d. Flour, 1d. Salt, 1d. Suet, 1d. 5 gallons of milk, 5d. Scullery: Fuel, 1s. 1d. Marshalsea: hay for 22 horses purchased, 1s. 5d. Straw, 8d. Horseshoes, 3d. Expenses of John Lyrreys going ahead to Bury St Edmunds for 1½ days, 1s.

Sum of money £1 9s. 2d. Pantry from stock. Buttery 4s. 9d. Kitchen 14s. 1d. Poultry 5s. 11d. Scullery 1s. 1d. Marshalsea 3s. 4d.

Thursday, 25 January 1347   [TNA E101/92/30]
[m. 9] Moreover for the expenses of Edward Despenser, Robert Percy and others of the Lady's household being at Wimbish for the burial of Sir John de Wauton[5] viz. Pantry: 28 loaves from stock. Bread purchased, 3d. Buttery: 13 gallons of ale purchased, 1s. 1d. Kitchen: 1 quarter of bacon and ½ carcass of mutton from stock. 1 quarter of veal, 6d. Poultry: 6 hens, 9d.

[*Sum of money 2s. 7d.*] Sum of the Pantry 3d. Sum of the Buttery 1s. 1d. Sum of the Kitchen 6d. Sum of the Poultry 9d.

Monday 30 August – Friday 3 September 1350   [TNA E101/93/4]
[m. 4d] 135 messes; livery of loaves 366; livery of wine and ale, 126. Moreover for the expenses of Lady Elizabeth Athol, Sir Thomas de Cheddeworth and others of the Lady's household staying at Clare \together with expenses for the poor/, the Lady being at Hundon, from 30 August to 3 September, both days counted, viz. Pantry: 614 loaves from stock. Butter, 1d. Buttery: 1 sester 1 pitcher of wine. And 263 gallons of ale from stock. Kitchen: 1½ carcasses of beef, 1½ bacons, 4 carcasses and 1 quarter of mutton from stock. Item 3 *cropling*, 7 *streitfisch*, 2½ cod and ½ salmon from stock. 1½ quarters of beef, 2s. 6d. ½ pig, 1s. 9d. 480 herring, 8s. 8d.

---

5   Sir John de Wauton was one of the Lady's councillors. He also served as sheriff and knight of the shire for Essex, fought at the battle of Crécy and died at the siege of Calais.

58 whiting, 1s. 2d. 22 plaice and 2 sole, 1s. 2d. Poultry: 7 geese, 2s. 11d. 4 hens, 8d. 10 pullets, 11¼d. 330 eggs, 2s. 2d. 2 cheeses, 4d. 15 gallons of milk, 1s. 3d.

Sum of money £1 3s. 7¼d.; sum of stock £2 14s. 3d.; of both £3 17s. 10¼d. Sum of the Pantry, 1d. Sum of the Kitchen 15s. 3d. Sum of the Poultry 8s. 3¼d.

Thursday, 23 December 1350   [TNA E101/93/9]
[m. 7] Moreover for the expenses of William de Clopton and others at Bardfield hunting deer for 4 days accounted for viz. Pantry: 182 loaves from stock. Buttery: 2 pitchers of wine. And 48 gallons of ale from stock. Kitchen: ½ quarter of beef and 1½ carcasses of mutton from stock. Item 80 herring, 4 *streitfisch*, and ½ salmon from stock. 2 codling, 1s. 8 plaice, 5d. Poultry: 2 rabbits from stock. 3 hens, 6d. Marshalsea: hay for 19 horses and 4 hackneys. Provender for the same, 7½b. of oats.

Sum of money, 1s. 11d.; sum of stock 17s. 9d.; of both 19s. 8d. Sum of the Kitchen 1s. 5d. Sum of the Poultry 6d.

Hospitality to Family and Friends at Clare
Marie de St Pol, Countess of Pembroke, 10–11 January 1331   [TNA E101/91/2]
[m. 9] [*Clare*]. Arrival of the countess of Pembroke. 92 messes; livery of 127 loaves; [*livery*] of wine and ale [*blank*]. Thursday, 10 January. Pantry: 338 loaves from stock, 10s. Wages of the laundress, 3d. Buttery: purchase of 163 gallons of ale, 17s. 6½d. And 8 sesters 3 pitchers of wine from stock, 11s. 8d. Expenses of William Butler at Bury St Edmunds and Anglesey about his office, 2s. Kitchen: 3½ quarters of beef, 7s. 1 small bacon, 2s.; 7 carcasses of mutton, 5s. 10d.; and 1 quarter, 1 dish of boar from stock. For the purchase of 1 quarter of fresh beef, 2s. 6d.; 3 pigs, 9s. 8d.; 2 calves, 4s. 4d. Poultry, with 1 swan, 3s., and 2 curlews, price 2s., which were a gift, £1 8s. 4d. Marshalsea: hay for 64 horses, 4 hackneys from stock, 2s. 10d. 4qr 1½b. of oats, 11s. 2d. And 3b. of bran from stock. For wages of grooms and pay of 14 horses, 6s. 8d. For the expenses of 2 horses fetching Brother Richard de Conyngton and his companion from Cambridge and returning there with the same, 2s. 8\½d./.[6] For carthorses' expenses at Bury St Edmunds, 2d.

Sum of diet, £6 4s. 8d. Sum of the Pantry 10s. 3d. Sum of the Buttery £1 11s. 2½d. Sum of the Kitchen £1 11s. 4d. Sum of the Poultry £1 8s. 4d. Sum of the Marshalsea £1 3s. 6½d.

[*Clare*]: 101 messes; livery of 121 loaves, wine and 38 gallons of ale. The countess [*of Pembroke*]. Friday, 11 January. Pantry: 284 loaves from stock, 8s. 5d. Wages of the laundress, 3d. Buttery: Purchase of 116 gallons of ale, 12s. 6½d. And 7 sesters of wine from stock, 9s. 4d. Kitchen: 480 herring, 2s. 4d.; 13 stockfish, 1s. 1d.; 6 cod, 2s. 1½d.; 5 pike, 2 pieces of sturgeon, 3 slices of whale-meat, from stock. Purchase of 30 codling, 5s. 8¼d.; 50 whiting, 1s. 4d.; 800 whelks, 1s. 4d.; 600 oysters, 1s.; 3 pasties of lampreys, 1s. 4½d.; ½ salmon, 3s. 6d. Marshalsea: hay for 36 horses, 4 hackneys, 1s. 8d. 2qr 2½b. of oats, 6s. 2d. And 3b. of bran from stock. For grooms' wages and pay of 13 horses, 6s. 8d.

Sum of diet £3 4s. 9¾d. Sum of the Pantry 8s. 8d. Sum of the Buttery £1 1s. 10½d. Sum of the Kitchen 19s. 9¼d. Sum of the Marshalsea 14s. 6d.

---

6   For Richard de Conyngton, see above, p. 2.

John de Bohun, Earl of Hereford and Essex, Monday, 9 May 1334[7]

[TNA E101/92/2]

[m. 6] [*Clare*]: 62 messes; livery of loaves, 116; livery of wine and ale, 38. The earl of Hereford. Monday, 9 May, there. Pantry: 277 loaves from stock. Wages of the laundress, 5d. Buttery: 6 sesters of wine. And 100 gallons of ale from stock. Kitchen: ½ carcass of salt beef, 1½ quarters of fresh beef and 4 small bacons from stock. 1 pig, 3s. 6d. 1 calf, 1s. 4d. 1 carcass of mutton, 2s. Poultry: 6 capons, 1s. 6d. 20 hens, 3s. 4d. 36 pullets, 2s. 6d. 200 eggs, 1s. 2d. 1 kid, 1s. 1d. 8 young doves, 4d. Saucery: 1b. of flour from stock. Marshalsea: hay for 52 horses from stock. Provender for the same, 3qr ½b. of oats from stock. Wages of 3 yeomen, 2 couriers, 39 grooms, 5s. 8½d. For the pay of 11 horses and 3 hackneys, 3s. 9d.\3d./. Item 16 loaves from the Pantry for the earl of Hereford's horses.

Sum £1 6s. 1½d. Sum of the Pantry 5d. Sum of the Buttery, from stock. Sum of the Kitchen 6s. 10d. Sum of the Poultry 9s. 11d. Sum of the Saucery, from stock. Sum of the Marshalsea 8s. 11½d.

Edward III, 27–29 May 1340[8]   [TNA E101/92/12]

[m. 8d] Clare. The Lord King. 127 messes; livery of loaves, 192; livery of wine and ale, 80. Saturday, 27 May there. Pantry: 440 loaves from stock. Buttery: 20 sesters of wine, 170 gallons of ale and 21 gallons of cider from stock. Kitchen: 700 herring, 14 stockfish, 24 cod, 6 pike, 4 pieces of sturgeon and 1 lamprey from stock. 16 salt herring, 5d. 120 mackerel, 2s. 8d. 180 whiting, 2s. 9d. 19 mullet and 1 bass, 8s. 6d. 6½ sticks of eels, 3s. 3d. ½ salmon received, 2s. 3d. 8 crabs and crayfish, 1s. 4d. 300 whelks, 6d. For carriage of fish from Sudbury, 3d. Poultry: 200 eggs, 9d. Suet, 1s. Milk, 1d. 1b. of wheat for the food allowance, 9d. For the food allowance for the herons, 3d. For Hugh Poulterer's expenses at Bury St Edmunds, 2d. Scullery: 1 basket purchased to put eels in, 4d. Marshalsea: hay for 160 horses, 16 hackneys, 5 oxen from stock. Provender for the same, 11qr 3b. ⅔ peck of oats of which 1qr 4b. 1 peck from increment. Wages of 2 yeomen and 2 couriers, 8d. Wages of 38 grooms, 5 pages, 5s. 2d. Bread bought for the king's horse, 1s. 8d. For making 800 botels of hay, 8d. Item 14 horseshoes from stock expended.

Sum of money £1 13s. 5d.; sum of stock £5 15s. 3d.; of both £7 8s. 8d. Sum of the Kitchen £1 1s. 11d. Sum of the Poultry 3s. Sum of the Scullery 4d. Sum of the Marshalsea 8s. 2d.

Clare. The Lord King. 187 messes; livery of bread [*blank*]; livery of wine and ale [*blank*]. Sunday, 28 May, there. Pantry: 16qr of Hundon wheat baked which rendered 3,340 loaves and 4b. 1 peck of flour for the Saucery. 780 loaves used from stock. Buttery: 40 sesters of wine from stock. Item 8qr of malt barley [*and*] 6qr of malt dredge brewed which rendered 828 gallons of ale. 350 gallons of ale and 18 gallons of cider used from stock. 300 cups bought at Wethersfield, 9s. 12 earthenware pots, 4d. Kitchen: 3 carcasses, 1½ quarters of beef, 4 bacons, 1 pig, 4 deer, 2 beasts of the closed season, of which 1 [*was*] a gift, and 3 dishes of boar from stock. Item 4 stockfish and 4 pike from stock. \1 quarter of beef, 4s./ 5½ pigs, 14s. 6d. 3

---

7   The earl of Hereford was also at Clare on 10 May.
8   Edward III was on his way to campaign in Flanders. After his stay at Clare, he was at Ipswich on 4 June and Orwell on 22 June; from there he embarked for Flanders. His victory at the battle of Sluys took place on 24 June. C. Shenton, *The Itinerary of Edward III and his Household, 1327–45* (List and Index Society, CCCXVIII), pp.205–6.

carcasses of mutton, 4s. 6d. 13½ calves, 15s. 6d. ½ salmon, 2s. 3d. ¾ porpoise, 2s. 1½ sticks of eels, 9d. 6 crabs and crayfish, 8d. 10 mullet, 3s. 6d. Poultry: 1 swan and 3 kids from stock. Item 6 herons and 12 capons from gifts. 12 capons, 2s. 6d. 36 hens, 4s. 6d. 38 geese, 8s. 7 dozen pullets, 4s. 6d. 60 young doves, 2s. 6d. 3 kids, 1s. 9d. 3 bittern, 7s. 4 swans, 12s. 8d. 5 piglets, 2s. 6d. 5 spoonbills, 3s. 4d. 17 rabbits, 3s. 3d. 1,200 eggs, 4s. 6d. Milk, 1s. 8d. Cream, 3d. Cheese, 6d. 1b. of wheat, 9d. 2b. of oats for the food allowance, 4d. For carriage of poultry from Bury St Edmunds, 3d. Hugh Poulterer's expenses at Bury St Edmunds, 3d. Hall and Chamber: 300 nails bought for the Hall, 4½d. 6 pieces of thin rope, 3d. Marshalsea: hay for 180 horses, 16 hackneys and 5 oxen from stock. Provender for the same, 11qr 5b. of oats from stock of which 1qr 6b. from increment. Wages of 2 yeomen and 2 couriers, 8d. Wages of 39 grooms, 5 pages, 5s. 3½d. Bread for the King's horse, 1s. 8d. Item 37 horseshoes expended from stock.

Sum of money £6 6s. 3d.; sum of stock £10 8s.; of both £16 14s. 3d. Sum of the Buttery 9s. 4d. Sum of the Kitchen £2 7s. 8d. Sum of the Poultry £3 1s. Sum of the Hall and Chamber 7½d. Sum of the Marshalsea 7s. 7½d.

[m. 7d] Clare. The Lord King. 163 messes; livery of bread, 197; livery of wine and ale, 81. Monday, 29 May, there. Pantry: 480 loaves from stock. 2 baskets bought for the Pantry, 6d. Buttery: 12 sesters of wine, 224 gallons of ale and 18 gallons of cider from stock. Kitchen: 1 carcass, 2½ quarters of beef, 3½ bacons and 2 deer from stock. 2½ pigs, 6s. 2½ carcasses of mutton, 3s. 9d. 3 calves, 4s. Item 60 herring and 3 stockfish from stock. 2 cod, 7d. 6 mullet, 2s. 6d. 1½ sticks of eels, 9d. Poultry: 2 swans and 3 herons from gifts. 13 capons, 2s. 9d. 27 hens, 3s. 4½d. 60 pullets, 3s. 6d. 24 young doves, 10d. 2 herons and 4 bittern, 15s. 1 lamb, 7d. 160 eggs, 6¾d. 1b. of wheat for the food allowance, 9d. 1b. of oats for the food allowance, 4d. For the food allowance for the herons, 4d. For the carriage of poultry from Bury St Edmunds, 6d. Hugh Poulterer's expenses there, 5d. Marshalsea: hay for 106 horses, 13 hackneys and 5 oxen from stock. Provender for the same, 6qr 3b. 1 peck of oats from stock of which 7½b. from increment. Item 1qr 3 pecks of bran and 12 loaves from stock. Wages of 2 yeomen and 2 couriers, 8d. Wages of 39 grooms, 5 pages, 5s. 3½d. Wages of 8 grooms from the Lady's household for 4 days, 11 grooms for 3 days, 1 groom for 2 days and 3 pages for 3 days staying at Stoke for the King's arrival, 9s. 1½d. Item 19 horseshoes expended from stock.

Sum of money £3 2s. 1¼d.; sum of stock £4 16s. 8d.; of both £7 18s. 9¼d. Sum of the Pantry 6d. Sum of the Kitchen 17s. 7d. Sum of the Poultry £1 8s. 11¼d. Sum of the Marshalsea 15s. 1d.

Lady Isabella, the King's Daughter; Henry of Grosmont, Earl of Lancaster; Elizabeth de Burgh, Countess of Ulster; William de Bohun, Earl of Northampton, 21 May 1350[9]   [TNA E101/9¾]
[m. 5d] Clare. Lady Isabella, the King's daughter, the earl of Lancaster, the countess of Ulster, the earl of Northampton. 120 messes; livery of bread, 208; livery of wine and ale, 67. Friday, 21 May, there. Pantry: 6qr 4b. of wheat baked which rendered 1,350 loaves and ½b. of flour. Of this 460 loaves used from stock. Buttery: 13½ sesters of wine. Item 12qr of malt barley and 4qr of malt dredge brewed

---

[9]   Lady Isabella was at Clare on 20 and 21 May; Elizabeth de Burgh, the Lady's granddaughter, stayed there from 20 May to 4 June; and the earls of Lancaster and Northampton were there only on 21 May.

which rendered 900 gallons of ale. Of this 160 gallons of ale used from stock. For winnowing 64qr of malt, 1s. Kitchen: 580 herring, 14 stockfish, 13 *streitfisch*, 21 cod, 1 pike, 20 bream, 7 lampreys and 10 pieces of sturgeon from stock. 2 cod, 1s. 4d. 100 mackerel, 6s. 8d. 100 whiting, 3s. 4d. 1 turbot and 1 bream, 5s. 3 plaice, 1s. 6d. 45 plaice, 2s. 12 white herring, 6d. 6 mullet, 5s. 200 whelks, 9d. 12 crayfish and 12 crabs, 4s. Hugh Poulterer's expenses at Bury St Edmunds, 2d. Expenses of Adam, groom of the Poultry, at Chelmsford with 1 packhorse for 1 night, 9d. Poultry: 60 eggs, 3½d. 2 gallons of milk, 1½d. Cream, 1½d. Marshalsea: hay for 183 horses, 14 hackneys from stock. Provender for the same, 12qr 2b. 3 pecks of oats of which 1½qr from increment. Item 1qr 1 peck of bran from stock. For bread bought, 1s. 4d. 2 yeomen's wages, 4d. Wages of 36 grooms and 5 pages, 4s. 11d.

Sum of money £1 19s. 1½d.; sum of stock £6 7s.; of both £8 6s. 1½d. Sum of the Buttery 1s. Sum of the Kitchen £1 11s. Sum of the Poultry 6½d. Sum of the Marshalsea 6s. 7d.

The Friars [*of Clare Priory*], 9 October 1357   [TNA E101/93/20]
[m. 2] Clare. The friars with the Lady. Clare. 64 messes; livery of bread, 116; livery of wine and ale, 25. Monday, 9 October, there. Pantry: 240 loaves from stock. Buttery: 2 sesters 3 pitchers of wine and 90 gallons of ale from stock. Kitchen: ½ carcass of beef and 2¾ carcasses of mutton from stock. ½ carcass of beef, 8s. 2¼ pigs, 9s. Poultry: 4 rabbits, 5 capons and 6 chickens from stock. 5 capons, 1s. 8d. 9 hens, 1s. 6d. 16 pullets, 1s. 6d. 260 eggs, 1s. 5½d. 6 gallons of milk, 6d. 2 partridges, 7d. Cok's expenses at Wix, Isleham and Bury St Edmunds for 3 days, 1s. 3d. For 1 horse hired for Cok for 3 days, 6d. Marshalsea: hay for 41 horses and 10 hackneys from stock. Provender for the same, 2qr 6b. 1 peck of oats of which 2½b. from increment. Item 2b. 1 peck of bran and 32 loaves from stock. 1 yeoman's wages, 2d. Wages of 23 grooms, 5 pages, 3s. 3½d.

Sum of money £1 9s. 5d.; sum of stock £1 18s. 6d.; of both £3 7s. 11d. Sum of the Kitchen 17s. Sum of the Poultry 8s. 11½d. Sum of the Marshalsea 3s. 5½d.

Travel
Journey to Norfolk, 4–20 June 1347[10]   [TNA E101/92/30]
[m. 11d] Clare and Desning [*in Gazeley*][11]   91 messes; livery of bread, 111; livery of wine and ale, 30. Monday, 4 June there. Pantry: 320 loaves from stock. Buttery: 3 sesters of wine and 60 gallons of ale from stock. 51 gallons of ale purchased at divers prices, 5s. 4¾d. Kitchen: ½ carcass of beef, 2½ bacons, 1 quarter of pork from stock. 3 quarters of beef, 7s. 1 carcass of mutton, 1s. 4d. 1 pig, 2s. 8d. 4 calves, 4s. 10d. Poultry: 4 capons, 10d. 11 hens, 1s. 4½d. 34 pullets, 1s. 6d. 1 lamb, 6d. 230 eggs, 10½d.

[*Sum of money £1 6s. 3¾d.*] Sum of the Buttery 5s. 4¾d. Sum of the Kitchen 15s. 10d. Sum of the Poultry 5s. 1d.
[m. 10d] Desning and Thetford   67 messes; livery of bread, 74; livery of wine and ale, 21. Tuesday, 5 June there. Pantry: 12 loaves from stock. For bread purchased, 7s. 3d. For 1 horse hired to carry flour from Thetford to Westacre, 5d. Buttery: 2

---

10   The details of the journey, as recorded in the diet account of 1346–7, are given in full. This account was probably a draft; it did not include the Marshalsea, and, although a weekly total was given for the Kitchen's expenses, there was no figure for the sum of money spent each day.

11   Desning had been one of the principal demesne manors of the honour of Clare in Suffolk, and in the 1317 partition had been awarded to Hugh Audley and his wife Margaret, sister of Elizabeth de Burgh.

pitchers of wine and 6 gallons of ale from stock. 2 sesters, 2 pitchers of wine bought, price 8d. a pitcher, 6s. 8d. 58 gallons of ale purchased, price 1½d. a gallon, 6s. 8d. 28 gallons of ale bought, price 1d. a gallon, 2s. 2d. For carriage of ale from Gazeley to Desning, 1d. Kitchen: 1 quarter of beef, ½ bacon and 1 quarter of pork from stock. 1 carcass of beef, 10s. 1 pig, 2s. 8d. 1 carcass of mutton, 1s. 6d. 3 calves, 4s. 6d. Poultry: 5 piglets, 2s. 7d. 15 geese, 2s. 9d. 3 capons, 7½d. 1 hen, 1½d. 16 pullets, 1s. 1 lamb, 6d. 12 young doves, 6d. 300 eggs, 1s. 1\½d. Grease received, 4d. Scullery: fuel purchased, 2s. 2d. Expenses of Hugh Poulterer and others going ahead from Thetford to Swaffham for 1 night, 11¼d.

[*Sum of money £2 14s. 6¾d.*] Sum of the Pantry 7s. 8d. Sum of the Buttery 15s. 7d. Sum of the Kitchen 18s. 8d. Sum of the Poultry 9s. 6½d. Sum of the Scullery 3s. 1¼d.

Swaffham and Westacre   61 messes; livery of bread, 46; livery of wine and ale, 16. Wednesday, 6 June, there. Pantry: 6 loaves from stock. Bread purchased, 7s. 5d. Buttery: 2 pitchers of wine and 10 gallons of ale from stock. 43 gallons of ale purchased, price 1½d. a gallon, without profit, 5s. 4½d. 21 gallons of ale bought, price 1½d. a gallon, with profit, 2s. 5¼d. 2 sesters, 2¾ pitchers of wine, 7s. 2d. Kitchen: 8 stockfish, 2 pike and 12 roach from stock. 10 cod, 4s. 1½ salmon, 1s. 9d. 166 mackerel, 2s. 8d. 30 whiting, 5d. 3 mullet, 1s. 6d. 3 pike, 3s. 7d. 40 perch and 6 small pike, 8½d. 2½ sticks of eels, 1s. 4d. Porpoise, 6d. Carrying fish from Bury St Edmunds to Thetford, 1s. Carrying fish from Watton to Swaffham, 4d. H[*ugh*] Poulterer's expenses at Bury St Edmunds, 4d. Poultry: 260 eggs, 1s. ½d. Milk, 1d. Salt, 1d. 1 peck of oat-flour, 3d. Expenses of H[*ugh*] Poulterer and the groom of the Poultry at Watton, 3d. For [?]oil, 1d. Scullery: for fuel at Swaffham, 1s. 1d.

[*Sum of money £2 2s. 3¾d.*] Sum of the Pantry 7s. 5d. Sum of the Buttery 14s. 11¾d. Sum of the Kitchen 18s. 1½d. Sum of the Poultry 1s. 9½d.

Westacre   71 messes; livery of bread, 63; livery of wine and ale, 18. Thursday, 7 June, there. Pantry: For bread purchased 7s. 11d. Fuel for the Laundry, 2d. Buttery: 3 sesters of wine and 8 gallons of ale from stock. 1 sester of wine, 2s. 8d. 80 gallons of ale bought at divers prices, 8s. 3d. Kitchen: ½ quarter of beef and ½ bacon from stock. 3 quarters of beef, 9s. 2d. 2½ pigs, 6s. 6d. 1 carcass of mutton, 2s. 3 calves, 4s. For the carriage of meat from Lynn and Watton to Westacre, 1s. 2d. H[*ugh*] Poulterer's expenses at Lynn for 1 night, 5d. Poultry: 6 capons from stock. 3 piglets, 1s. 6d. 14 geese, 2s. 6d. 10 hens, 1s. 3d. 18 pullets, 1s. 24 young doves, 1s. 2 lambs, 1s. 8d. 12 rabbits, 2s. 360 eggs, 1s. 5½d. 10 gallons of milk, 1s. 1b. of oats for the food allowance, 5d. 1 peck of wheat, 3d. Saucery: Flour bought for sauce, 4d. Scullery: fuel purchased, 3s. 8d. Hall and Chamber: for rushes purchased and the cleaning of houses at Swaffham and Westacre, 8d.

[*Sum of money £3 0s. 11½d.*] Sum of the Pantry: 8s. 1d. Sum of the Buttery 10s. 11d. Sum of the Kitchen £1 3s. 3d. Sum of the Poultry 14s. ½d. Sum of the Saucery 4d. Sum of the Scullery 3s. 8d. Sum of the Hall and Chamber 8d.

Walsingham   82 messes; livery of bread 38; livery of wine and ale 14. Friday, 8 June, there. Pantry: 154 loaves from stock. Buttery: 1½ sesters of wine and 16 gallons of ale from stock. 1 sester of wine, 2s. 8d. 51 gallons of ale purchased, 5s. 11d. Kitchen: 9 stockfish, 4 pike, 1 bream and 8 roach from stock. 11 cod, 3s. 3d. ½ salmon, 7d. 110 mackerel, 1s. 9d. 100 plaice, 1s. 7½d. 160 whelks from [?]Kelling, 10d. 20 crayfish and crabs, 9d. 30 whiting, 5d. Saucery: 2 gallons of vinegar purchased, 5d.

[*Sum of money 18s. 2½d.*] Sum of the Buttery 8s. 7d. Sum of the Kitchen 9s. 2½d. Sum of the Saucery 5d.

Walsingham   96 messes; livery of bread 56; livery of wine and ale 19. Saturday, 9 June, there. Pantry: 222 loaves from stock. Buttery: 1 sester, 1 pitcher of wine and 6 gallons of ale from stock. 4 sesters, 1 pitcher of wine, 11s. 4d. 85 gallons of ale, 9s. 10d. Kitchen: 11 stockfish, 3 pike, 1 conger eel and 3 lampreys from stock. 13 cod, 3s. 120 plaice, 2s. 2d. ½ salmon, 6d. 220 mackerel, 2s. 8d. 40 crayfish and crabs, 1s. 7d. 430 whelks, 1s. 6½d. 20 *stil'*, 7d. 30 whiting, 4½d. 23 shaft-eels, 2s. 3d. 3 sticks of eels, 1s. 6d. 1 pike, 1s. Poultry: 100 eggs, 4½d. 2b. of salt, 1s. 2d. ½b. of oat-flour, 5d. Suet, 2d. For the expenses of H[*ugh*] Poulterer and the groom of the Poultry at Burnham, 1½d. Scullery: 1 bucket and 2 bowls for the Kitchen, 5d. Wardrobe: 8lb. of candles of paris, 1s. 2½d.

   Sum total of money for the Kitchen's expenses for the week £5 14s. 3d.

   [*Sum of money £2 2s. 2½d.*] Sum of the Buttery £1 1s. 2d. Sum of the Kitchen 17s. 2d. Sum of the Poultry 2s. 3d. Sum of the Scullery 5d. Sum of the Wardrobe 1s. 2½d.

Walsingham   129 messes; livery of bread, 87; livery of wine and ale 26. Sunday, 10 June, there. Pantry: 5qr of wheat baked which rendered 1,011 loaves and 1 peck of flour. Of this 306 loaves used from stock. Bread bought, 2s. Wages of Adam groom of the Bakehouse going ahead to Walsingham for 2 days, 3d. Buttery: 1 pitcher of wine and 20 gallons of ale from stock. 8 sesters of wine, £1 1s. 4d. 116 gallons of ale, 13s. 6½d. Kitchen: 1 carcass [*and*] 1 quarter of beef, ½ bacon, 3 pigs, 2 carcasses of mutton, 3 calves and 1 dish of boar from stock. ½ carcass of beef, 6s. 10d. 1 pig, 3s. 4d. 4 calves, 5s. 7d. Poultry: 3 swans, 14 capons and 12 geese from stock. 10 piglets, 5s. 8d. 18 geese, 4s. 16 hens, 2s. 4 lambs, 4s. 48 pullets, 2s. 8d. 24 young doves, 8d. Milk, 1s. 2d. 600 eggs, 2s. 6d. ½b. of wheat, 6d. 1b. of oats, 5d. Saucery: 2½ gallons of vinegar, 5d. Scullery: for fuel, 13s. 4d.

   [*Sum of money £4 10s. 2½d.*] Sum of the Pantry 2s. 3d. Sum of the Buttery £1 14s. 10½d. Sum of the Kitchen 15s. 9d. Sum of the Poultry £1 3s. 7d. Sum of the Saucery 5d. Sum of the Scullery 13s. 4d.

Holt and Gimingham   78 messes; livery of bread, 58; livery of wine and ale, 11. Monday, 11 June, there. Pantry: 6 loaves from stock. For bread bought, 9s. 9d. Soap for the Laundry, 1d. Buttery: 1 pitcher of wine and 4 gallons of ale from stock. 3 sesters of wine, 8s. 93 gallons of ale purchased, 12s. 9d. Kitchen: 3½ quarters of beef and ½ bacon from stock. 1 quarter of beef, 3s. 4d. 1½ pigs, 5s. 1 carcass of mutton, 2s. 3d. 3½ calves, 5s. 8d. Poultry: 1 bittern and 4 capons from stock. 4 piglets, 1s. 10d. 1 capon, 2½d. 16 hens, 1s. 10½d. 20 pullets, 1s. 2d. 9 young doves, 3d. 1 lamb, 1s. 160 eggs, 7½d. Scullery: Fuel purchased, 2s. 10d.

   [*Sum of money £2 16s. 7½d.*] Sum of the Pantry 9s. 10d. Sum of the Buttery £1 0s. 9d. Sum of the Kitchen 16s. 3d. Sum of the Poultry 6s. 11½d. Sum of the Scullery 2s. 10d.

Bromholm and Stalham   76 messes; livery of bread, 56; livery of wine and ale, 15. Tuesday, 12 June, there. Pantry: 60 loaves from stock. For bread bought, 5s. 6d. Fuel for the Laundry, 1d. Buttery: 1 pitcher of wine and 12 gallons of ale from stock. 3½ sesters of wine, 9s. 4d. 72 gallons of ale, 9s. Kitchen: 3½ quarters of beef, ½ bacon and 1 carcass of mutton from stock. 3 quarters of beef, 5s. 2 pigs, 6s. 3d. 3 calves, 4s. 8d. Carrying meat from Thorpe to Bromholm, 3d. Poultry: 1 bittern from stock. 4 piglets, 2s. 14 geese, 3s. 3 capons, 7½d. 13 hens, 1s. 6d. 2 lambs, 1s. 5d. 32 pullets, 2s. 3d. 9 young doves, 3d. 1 rabbit, 2d. 260 eggs, 1s. ½d. 10 gallons of milk, 10d. H[*ugh*] Poulterer's expenses at Thorpe, 1½d. Scullery: Fuel purchased, 4s. 11d. Purchase of 1 quern for the Kitchen, 1d. Expenses of John de Horslee and others going ahead from Walsingham to Gimingham, 1s.

[*Sum of money £2 19s. 3½d.*] Sum of the Pantry 5s. 7d. Sum of the Buttery 18s. 4d. Sum of the Kitchen 16s. 2d. Sum of the Poultry 13s. 2½d. Sum of the Scullery 6s.

Acle   15 messes; livery of bread, 8; livery of wine and ale, 3. Wednesday, 13 June, there. Pantry: 20 loaves from stock. Bread, 11d. Buttery: 3 gallons of ale from stock. 14 gallons of ale, 1s. 9d. Kitchen: 4 cod, 1s. 60 mackerel, 7½d. 30 whiting, 5d. 1 pike, 1s. Poultry: 100 eggs, 5d. Scullery: for the Lady's escort from Stalham to Acle, 2d.

[*Sum of money 6s. 3½d.*] Sum of the Pantry 11d. Sum of the Buttery 1s. 9d. Sum of the Kitchen 3s. ½d. Sum of the Poultry 5d. Sum of the Scullery 2d.

Thursday, 14 June, nothing, because at the cost of Sir John Bardolf.[12]

Norwich and Wymondham   40 messes; livery of bread, 21; livery of wine and ale, 12. Friday, 15 June, there. Pantry: 3 loaves from stock. Bread, 3s. 6d. Buttery: 1 pitcher of wine from stock. 58 gallons of ale, 9s. 4d. Kitchen: 4 stockfish, 1 pike and 4 roach from stock. 3 cod, 1s. 8d. 70 mackerel, 8d. 20 whiting, 2½d. 30 herring, 10d. Saucery: 1 gallon of vinegar, 8d. Scullery: fuel, 2d.

[*Sum of money 17s. ½d.*] Sum of the Pantry 3s. 6d. Sum of the Buttery 9s. 4d. Sum of the Kitchen 3s. 4½d. Sum of the Saucery 8d. Sum of the Scullery 2d.

Lopham[13]   66 messes; livery of bread, 33; livery of wine and ale, 6. Saturday, 16 June, there. Pantry: for bread, 7s. Buttery: 4 gallons of ale from stock. 1 sester of wine, 2s. 8d. 64 gallons of ale bought at divers prices, 6s. 10¼d. For carriage of bread and ale from Kenninghall to Lopham, 4d. Kitchen: 8 stockfish and 2 pike from stock. 6 cod, 3s. 4d. 2 salmon, 2s. 2d. 120 mackerel, 1s. 3d. 3½ sticks of eels, 1s. 5½d. 45 herring, 11d. 25 whiting, 4d. 2 pike, 7d. For the carriage of fish from Buckenham to Lopham, 4d. Poultry: 1 peck of oat-flour, 3d. 1 peck of peas, 2d. 160 eggs, 7½d.

Sum total of money for the Kitchen's expenses for the week £3 4s. 11½d.

[*Sum of money £1 8s. 3¼d.*] Sum of the Pantry 7s. Sum of the Buttery 9s. 10¼d. Sum of the Kitchen 10s. 4½d. Sum of the Poultry 1s. ½d.

Lopham   67 messes; livery of bread, 35; livery of wine and ale, 4. Sunday, 17 June, there. Pantry: 3 loaves from stock. Bread bought, 9s. Buttery: 1 sester, 2¼ pitchers of wine, 4s. 2d. 74 gallons of ale purchased, 9s. 1d. Kitchen: ½ bacon from stock. 1 carcass of beef, 9s. 4d. 2 pigs, 4s. 6d. 4 calves, 4s. 4d. For carriage of meat from Botesdale to Lopham, 2d. Poultry: 1 bittern from stock. 3 piglets, 1s. 3d. 6 geese, 1s. 4½d. 2 capons, 6d. 1 hen, 1½d. 20 pullets, 1s. 3d. 100 eggs, 5d. For salt, 1½d. Hall and Chamber: Rushes purchased, 11d.

[*Sum of money £2 6s. 6½d.*] Sum of the Pantry 9s. Sum of the Buttery 13s. 3d. Sum of the Kitchen 18s. 4d. Sum of the Poultry 5s. ½d. Sum of the Hall and Chamber 11d.

Lopham and Bury St Edmunds   74 messes; livery of bread, 56; livery of wine and ale, 14. Monday, 18 June, there. Pantry: 4 loaves from stock. For bread, 8s. 6d. Soap and fuel for the Laundry, 2d. Buttery: 2 pitchers of wine and 12 gallons of ale from stock. 1 sester of wine, 2s. 8d. 75 gallons of ale, 8s. 3¼d. Kitchen: ½ bacon from stock. 1 carcass, ½ quarter of beef, 8s. 6d. 2½ pigs, 7s. 1d. 1 carcass of mutton, 2s. 3d. 1½ calves, 2s. Poultry: 2 bittern from stock. 5 piglets, 2s. 6d. 18 geese, 4s. 3d. 5 capons, 1s. ½d. 2 lambs, 1s. 5d. 40 pullets, 2s. 6d. 1 bittern, 2s. 6d. 8

---

12   Sir John Bardolf married the Lady's younger daughter, Elizabeth.
13   It is not clear if the Lady stayed at North or South Lopham.

92

rabbits, 1s. 4d. 200 eggs, 10d. Milk, 9d. Saucery: garlic, 4d. Scullery: Fuel, 2s. 10d. 30 ornamented dishes, 11d.

[*Sum of money £3 0s. 7¾d.*] Sum of the Pantry 8s. 8d. Sum of the Buttery 10s. 11¼d. Sum of the Kitchen 19s. 10d. Sum of the Poultry 17s. 1½d. Sum of the Saucery 4d. Sum of the Scullery 3s. 9d.

[m. 9d] Bury St Edmunds and Desning   74 messes; livery of bread, 41; livery of wine and ale, 13. Tuesday, 19 June, there. Pantry: 6 loaves from stock. Bread bought, 7s. Carriage of bread from Newmarket to Desning, 2d. Buttery: 1½ sesters of wine, 4s. 80 gallons of ale purchased, 8s. 7¾d. Kitchen: 3½ quarters of beef, 6s. 1 pig, 2s. 7d. 3 calves, 3s. 9d. Poultry: 2 capons, 5d. 1 hen, 1½d. 16 pullets, 9d. 1 lamb, 8d. 4 rabbits, 8d. 160 eggs, 7½d. ½b. of salt, 3d. Hall and Chamber: 300 nails for the Hall, 6d. Wardrobe: 2lb. of candles of paris, 4d.

[*Sum of money £1 16s. 5¾d.*] Sum of the Pantry 7s. 2d. Sum of the Buttery 12s. 7¾d. Sum of the Kitchen 12s. 4d. Sum of the Poultry 3s. 6d. Sum of the Hall and Chamber 6d. Sum of the Wardrobe 4d.

Desning and Anglesey   74 messes; livery of bread, 39; livery of wine and ale, 16. Wednesday, 20 June, there. Pantry: 136 loaves from stock. Bread bought, 2s. 6d. Buttery: 2 sesters of wine and 66 gallons of ale from stock. 2¼ pitchers of wine, 1s. 6d. 23 gallons of ale purchased, 2s. 6½d. Kitchen: 8 stockfish and 2 pike from stock. 10 cod, 5s. 8d. 1 salmon, 1s. 19 plaice, 5s. 4d. 130 mackerel, 3s. 8d. 75 herring, 2s. 8d. Loach, 9d. 20 whiting, 5d. 50 perch and roach, 1s. 2d. 4 pike, 3s. ½ stick of eels, 3½d. 6 sole, 4d. For the carriage of fish from Cambridge to Anglesey, 3d. Poultry: 260 eggs, 1s. ½d. 5 cheeses, 7d. 1 gallon of milk, ¾d. Butter, 1d. Expenses of the groom of the Poultry at Bury St Edmunds, 1½d.

[*Sum of money £1 12s. 9¾d.*] Sum of the Pantry 2s. 6d. Sum of the Buttery 4s. ½d. Sum of the Kitchen £1 4s. 4½d. Sum of the Poultry 1s. 10¾d.

[*The Lady remained at Anglesey until Monday, 25 June, when she returned to Clare.*]

Excerpt from the Marshalsea Account concerning the Journey to Norfolk, 4–20 June 1347[14]   [TNA E101/95/8]

[m. 11] Desning and Clare [*There is no entry concerning arrivals and departures.*]

Monday, 4 June there Marshalsea Hay and grass for 81 horses and 11 hackneys from stock. For provender of the same: 74 horses on full [*diet*], 7 horses each on 8 loaves, 11 hackneys each on 4 loaves purchased. For extra provender and for reward, 2½b. of oats. \For bread bought/ for 7 destriers, 4 palfreys, 6 packhorses and 2 foals, 1s. 1d. 4qr 7½b. of oats of which 7½b. from increment. Item 56 loaves from stock. Wages of 2 yeomen, [*and*] 1 courier, 6d. And for wages of 31 grooms[*and*] 4 pages, 4s. 2½d. Pay of 2 carts going with oats, 2d. For mowing, ½d.

Thetford   Departures: 3 horses of John atte Lee, 2 horses of the prior of Ely, 1 horse of Kirkebi, 5 horses of the Lady's carts, 1 hackney of Philip Porter, 1 hackney of [*Nicholas*] Damory, 1 hackney of [[*Robert*] Mareschal. Arrivals: Dapple-grey

---

14 The excerpt has been taken from the subsidiary marshalsea account of 1346–7. The account was not audited. The heading is missing and it has been dated from internal evidence. There are two entries for each day. The shorter entry, on the left-hand side of the document, lists departures and arrivals of horses; the main entry on the right gives the horses' diet and the wages of staff. Totals were only given monthly. These entries supplement the details in the diet account of the journey to Norfolk in the summer of 1347.

la Souche, 1 horse of Thomas Mareschal. Item 1 hackney of [*William*] d'Oxwik. Departures: R groom of Kirkebi and 2 pages of Jolif.

Tuesday, 5 June there Marshalsea Hay and grass bought for 72 horses and 9 hackneys, 7s. For 1qr of oats bought at Lidgate, 4s. Item 5qr [*of oats*] from a gift. 66 horses on full [*diet*], 5 horses on 1 peck of oats and each on 3 loaves purchased, 1 horse on 8 loaves, and 10 hackneys each on 1 peck of oats. For extra provender and reward of the coach-horses, destriers, palfreys [*and*] packhorses, 1qr 1b. of oats. Bread bought for the reward of the same, 1s. 8½d. For bread for 4 packhorses of the Lady's knights, clerks and esquires, 7d. 5qr 5½b. of oats, of which 2½b. from increment. Wages of 2 yeomen [*and*] 1 courier, 6d. For wages of 30 grooms and 2 pages, 3s. 11d. Item for bread bought, 2s. 10½d. Litter bought, 1s. For axles of the coach, 7d. Ointment bought for the horses of Lady de Ferrers, ½d. Boat-hire for the Lady at Thetford, 1s.

Westacre   Departures: 1 horse for Ireland. Item 1 hackney of Balle. Arrivals: 1 horse of [*John*] Gough, 1 horse for the Ely horses. Item 1 hackney for the hackneys of Philip Porter, 1 hackney of Hugh Poulterer, 1 hackney of Wormegay.[15] Arrival: 1 page for the pages of Jolif on wages.

Wednesday, 6 June there Marshalsea Hay bought for 73 horses and 11 hackneys, 7s. 3qr of oats purchased, 10s. 14 horses on full [*diet*], 58 horses on 1 peck of oats and each on 3 loaves purchased. Item for bread bought for 1 horse, 2d., and 4 hackneys on 1 peck of oats and 7 hackneys each on 4 loaves purchased. For extra provender and reward of the coach-horses, destriers, palfreys, packhorses, [*and*] horses of knights, clerks [*and*] esquires of the Lady, 1½b. Item for bread bought for reward of the same, 3s. 9¼d. Wages of 2 yeomen [*and*] 1 courier, 6d. And wages of 30 grooms [*and*] 3 pages, 4s. Item for bread bought, 10s. 3¼d. Item for reward of the Lady's horses and paid workers at Swaffham, 1s. 6d.

Westacre   Departures: 2 horses of Thomas de la Mare. Item 1 hackney of Wormegay, 1 hackney of Hugh Poulterer. Arrival: 1 hackney of Balle. Arrival: [*John*] Gough's groom on wages.

Thursday, 7 June there Marshalsea Hay and grass bought for 71 horses and 9 hackneys, 4s. 8d. 2qr 4b. of oats, 8s. 3½d. 12 horses on full [*diet*], 54 horses on 1 peck of oats and each on 4 loaves purchased, 5 horses each on 8 loaves purchased, and 5 hackneys each on 1 peck of oats, and 5 hackneys each on 4 loaves purchased. For extra provender and reward of the coach-horses, 1½b. of oats and 2 loaves purchased. Item for bread bought for reward of the destriers, palfreys [*and*] pack-horses, 6½d. From increment 2b. 1 peck of oats. Wages of 2 yeomen and 1 courier, 6d. And for wages of 31 grooms and 2 pages, 4s. 1½d. For bread bought, 6s. 4¼d.

Walsingham[16]   Arrivals: 10 horses of Sir John Bardolf, 2 horses of John Bataille, 2 horses of William Lengleys, 2 horses of Thomas de la Mare. Item 2 hackneys of Hugh Poulterer, Bissop, 1 hackney of John Hunte scullion, 1 hackney of Balle. Arrival: [*illegible*]

---

[15] Wormegay, Norfolk, was held by Sir John Bardolf.

[16] Walsingham was one of the Lady's demesne manors, and the priory there housed the shrine of the Blessed Virgin Mary which was an important place of pilgrimage. The Lady founded a Franciscan priory there in 1347 and may well have viewed building progress during her stay. See below, pp.136–8.

Friday, 8 June there Marshalsea Hay bought for 87 horses and 16 hackneys, 4s. 5d. 4b. of oats for provender of the same, 1s. 5½d. 49 horses on full [*diet*], 1 horse on ½b. of bran and 4 loaves from stock, 37 horses on 1 peck of oats and each on 4 loaves from stock, 14 hackneys on 1 peck of oats. For extra provender and reward of the Lady's coach-horses, destriers, palfreys and packhorses, 1½b. of oats, 78 loaves from stock and 11 loaves purchased. 4qr 2b. 3 pecks of oats, 2 pecks of bran. 2qr 4b. of peas baked which rendered 530 loaves. Of these 230 loaves used from stock. Wages of 2 yeomen [*and*] 1 courier, 6d. And for wages of 31 grooms and 3 pages, 4s. 1½d. Item for bread bought, 3d. Rushes purchased for cressets, 3d. Litter purchased for 1 horse of Norhamton and Madefrey at Westacre, 1d.

Walsingham   Departures: 3 horses of Lord Bardolf, 1 hackney for the hackneys of the Poultry, 1 hackney of Balle, 1 hackney of John Hunte, 1 hackney of Richard scullion, 1 hackney of Bircham.[17] Arrivals: 1 horse of Sir John Arfych, 2 horses of ~~Damory~~ \Poer/, 2 horses of the priest of [*King's*] Lynn, 4 horses of the prior of Anglesey, 11 horses and 8 hackneys of Lady Peverel, 1 hackney of Hemlys. Arrival: Fullere on wages.

Saturday, 9 June there Marshalsea Hay bought for 104 horses and 20 hackneys, 4s. 6d. 42 horses on full [*diet*], 36 horses on 1 peck of oats and each on 4 loaves, 17 horses on 1 peck of oats and each on 1 peck of bran, 1 horse on ½b. of bran and 4 loaves, 7 horses on ⅓ and 20 hackneys on 1 peck of oats. For extra provender and reward, 3½b. of oats [*and*] 26 loaves from stock. 5qr of oats purchased. From increment ⅓qr and 3 pecks of oats. Item 5b. 1 peck of bran. And 174 loaves from stock. Wages of 2 yeomen [*and*] 1 courier, 6d. And for wages of 31 grooms and 4 pages, 4s. 2½d. For rushes bought, 8d.

Sum of oats, bran, peas, loaves and horseshoes for the month: 114qr 7⅓b. of oats; 11qr 4b. 1 peck of bran; 12qr 4b. of peas baked which rendered 2,752 loaves of which 2,347 loaves were used; 209 horseshoes from stock; wages of yeomen, couriers, grooms and pages [*blank*].

Walsingham   Departures: 7 horses of Sir John Bardolf, 1 horse of Lady Bardolf, 1 horse of [*John*] Gough, 11 horses and 8 hackneys of Lady Peverel. Arrival: 2 horses of Sir John de Ardych. Departure: Gough's groom on wages.

Sunday, 10 June there Marshalsea Hay bought for 89 horses and 12 hackneys, 4s. 6d. 30 horses on full [*diet*], 27 horses on 1 peck of oats and each on 4 loaves, 2 horses on 8 loaves, 27 horses on ⅓ and 12 hackneys on 1 peck of oats. For extra provender and reward, 132 loaves from stock. 1qr 2b. 2b. [*sic*] of oats from stock. 3qr of oats purchased, 9s. From increment 3b. \1 peck/ of oats. Wages of 2 yeomen [*and*] 1 courier, 6d. For wages of 30 grooms and 4 pages, 4s. 1d. Item for mowing grass for the destriers for 3 days, 3d. For making 500 botels of hay, 5d.

Gimingham   Departures: 4 horses of the prior of Anglesey, 3 horses of Sir John Ardych, 2 horses of W[*illiam*] Lengleys, 2 horses of the priest of [*King's*] Lynn, 2 horses of Nicholas Poer, 3 horses of Dagent. Item 1 hackney of Hemleye, 1 hackney of W[*illiam*] d'Oxwik. Arrivals: 6 horses of Lord Bardolf, 7 carthorses of Walsingham, 1 horse of Ralph de Coggeshale, 1 horse of Bartholomew de Wiche.

Monday, 11 June there Marshalsea Hay bought for 88 horses and 10 hackneys, 4s. 86 horses on full [*diet*], 1 horse on 1 peck of oats and 4 loaves, 1 horse on 8

---

17   Great Bircham, Norfolk, was one of the Lady's demesne manors.

loaves purchased, and 10 hackneys on 1 peck of oats. For extra provender and reward, 176 loaves from stock. 194 loaves from stock. Item 4qr 4b. of oats bought, 13s. 6d. Item 1qr of oats bought, 3s. 4d. From increment 3b. 1 peck of oats. For bread, 3d. Wages of 2 yeomen [*and*] 1 courier, 6d. And for wages of 30 grooms and 4 pages, 4s. 1d. Item for mowing grass for 3 destriers, ½d.

Stalham[18]   Departures: 1 horse of Colinet, 1 horse of [*John*] Horslee, 4 carthorses of Walsingham, 1 horse of Lady de Ferrers, 1 horse of Bartholomew de Wiche. Departure: Colinet's groom on wages. For the expenses of John Gough, [*John*] Horslee and others of the Lady's household at Stalham, 9d.

Tuesday, 12 June there Marshalsea Hay bought for 81 horses and 10 hackneys, 4s. 6d. 78 horses on full [*diet*], 1 horse on 1 peck of oats and 4 loaves, 2 horses each on 8 loaves purchased, and 10 hackneys each on 1 peck of oats. For extra provender and reward, 1½b. of oats, [*and*] 136 loaves purchased. 5qr of oats bought for the provender of the same, £1. From increment 2b. For bread purchased, 4s. 3d. Hay purchased, 1s. 9½d. Wages of 2 yeomen [*and*] 1 courier, 6d. And for wages of 30 grooms and 4 pages, 3s. 11d. For grass purchased for 3 destriers, 4d. For litter bought, 1s. 9d.

Journey from London to Clare, 10–25 September 1358   [TNA E101/93/20]
[**m. 8d**] London and Woodford   65 messes; livery of bread, 83; livery of wine and ale, 8. Monday, 10 September, there. Pantry: 208 loaves from stock. Buttery: 36 gallons of ale from stock. 3 sesters of wine purchased, 6s. 35 gallons of ale bought at Ilford, 5s. 10d. Carriage of the said ale from Ilford to Woodford, 8d. Kitchen: 1½ quarters of beef, ½ bacon, and 2 carcasses, 1 quarter of mutton from stock. 3 quarters of beef, 8s. 8d. 2 carcasses of mutton, 4s. 1 pig [*and*] 1 quarter, 6s. 9d. ½ calf, 1s. 3d. Poultry: 3 rabbits from stock. 12 capons, 6s. 2d. 14 pullets, 1s. 9d. 9 young doves, 6d. 200 eggs, 1s. 8d. Scullery: Fuel bought at Woodford, 2s. 6d. Marshalsea: hay bought for 53 horses and 20 hackneys, 8s. Provender for the same, 3qr 2²/₃b. 2 pecks of oats of which 1²/₃b. from increment. Item 10 loaves from stock. Horsebread bought, 3s. Straw, 2s. Carriage of 2qr 1b. of oats from Stepney to Woodford, 1s. 14 hackneys hired from Standon for the Lady's household for 3 days, 7s. 4 yeomen's wages, 8d. Wages of 26 grooms, 5 pages, 3s. 8d.

Sum of money £3 11s. 1d.; of stock £1 4s. 8d.; of both £4 15s. 9d. Sum of the Buttery 12s. 6d. Sum of the Kitchen £1 0s. 8d. Sum of the Poultry 10s. 1d. Sum of the Scullery 2s. 6d. Sum of the Marshalsea £1 5s. 4d.
Woodford and North Weald   52 messes; livery of bread, 83; livery of wine and ale, 13. Tuesday, 11 September, there. Pantry: 194 loaves from stock. Buttery: 25 gallons of ale from stock. 2 sesters, 1 pitcher of wine, 4s. 6d. 40 gallons of ale bought at North Weald, 4s. 7½d. Kitchen: 1 quarter of beef, 3 quarters of bacon, 1½ carcasses of mutton from stock. 1 quarter of beef, 2s. 10d. ½ pig, 2s. 9d. 3 carcasses of mutton, 6s. ½ calf, 1s. 3d. ½ stick of eels, 8d. Poultry: 3 rabbits from stock. 11 capons, 5s. 6d. 1 chicken, 2d. 12 pullets, 1s. 6d. 1 lamb, 1s. 9 young doves, 6d. 200 eggs, 1s. 8d. Scullery: Grene's expenses going from London to Standon to drive sheep to North Weald, 3d. Robert Tymme's expenses going from London to Woodford and from there to North Weald, for 3 days, 4d. Marshalsea: hay for 44

---

[18]   The Lady visited the shrine of the Holy Rood at Bromholm; see above, p.91.

horses, 6 hackneys from stock. Provender for the same, 3qr 2b. 3 pecks of oats. 4 yeomen's wages, 8d. Wages of 25 grooms, 5 pages, 3s. 6½d.

Sum of money £1 17s. 9d.; of stock £1 7s.; of both £3 4s. 9d. Sum of the Buttery 9s. 1½d. Sum of the Kitchen 13s. 6d. Sum of the Poultry 10s. 4d. Sum of the Scullery 7d. Sum of the Marshalsea 4s. 2½d.

North Weald[19]   75 messes; livery of bread, 88; livery of wine and ale, 15. Wednesday, 12 September, there. Pantry: 216 loaves from stock. For bread bought in London, 6d. Buttery: 25 gallons of ale from stock. \2/½ sesters of wine from stock. 70 gallons of ale bought at Epping, 11s. 8d. Kitchen: 7 stockfish, 5 *streitfisch*, 6 cod, 1 salmon and 4 lampreys from stock. 346 herring, 6s. 3d. 5 cod, 4s. 2d. 2 pike, 3s. 8d. Small fry, 1s. 1 trout, 6d. Henry Poulterer's expenses at Woodford and Ware, 1s. 1½d. Poultry: 260 eggs, 2s. 1d. 7 gallons of milk, 7d. Cok's expenses at Waltham, 1d. Saucery: 2 gallons of vinegar, 1s. 4d. 3½ gallons of verjuice, 2s. 4d. Marshalsea: hay for 58 horses, 9 hackneys from stock. Provender for the same, 4qr 3⅓b. of oats. Item 28 loaves from stock. 4 yeomen's wages, 8d. Wages of 25 grooms, 5 pages, 3s. 6½d.

Sum of money £2 4s. 6d.; of stock £1 16s.; of both £4 0s. 6d. Sum of the Pantry 6d. Sum of the Buttery 16s. 8d. Sum of the Kitchen 16s. 8½d. Sum of the Poultry 2s. 9d. Sum of the Saucery 3s. 8d. Sum of the Marshalsea 4s. 2½d.

London   Moreover, the expenses of Sir William de Manton and others of the Lady's household being in London on 10 and 11 September, the Lady being at North Weald. Pantry: 52 loaves from stock. Buttery: 30 gallons of ale from stock. 10 gallons of wine for ullage of 3 tuns of wine in London, 5s. Ale bought in London, 1d. Kitchen: ½ bacon and ½ carcass of mutton from stock. 1 quarter of beef, 2s. 8½d. ½ pig, 2s. 6d. Poultry: 4 geese, 1s. 11d. Saucery: garlic purchased, ½d. Marshalsea: hay for 14 horses, 6 hackneys from stock. Provender for the same, 1qr of oats and 14 loaves from stock.

Sum of money 12s. 3d.; of stock 11s. 3d.; of both £1 3s. 6d. Sum of the Buttery 5s. 1d. Sum of the Kitchen 5s. 2½d. Sum of the Poultry 1s. 11d. Sum of the Saucery ½d.

[*The Lady remained at North Weald on 13–16 September.*]

[**m. 7d**] North Weald and Roding[20]   59 messes; livery of bread, 107; livery of wine and ale, 23. Monday, 17 September, there. Pantry: 235 loaves from stock. Buttery: 2 pitchers of wine. And 20 gallons of ale from stock. 2½ sesters of wine purchased, 5s. 62 gallons of ale bought at Roding, 9s. 3½d. Kitchen: 1 quarter of beef, 1 bacon and ½ carcass of mutton from stock. ½ carcass of beef, 5s. 8d. 1½ pigs, 7s. 6d. 3 carcasses of mutton, 5s. 2d. ½ calf, 1s. 9d. Poultry: 4 capons, 12 pullets and 3 young doves from stock. 9 capons, 4s. 6d. 8 pullets, 10d. 200 eggs, 1s. 8d. Expenses of Henry Poulterer at Dunmow and the Poultry's packhorse, 1½d. ½b. of oat-flour, 6d. 2 partridges, 1s. 4d. Scullery: expenses of Scot Ewer and Walter going ahead to Laver and Roding, 2d. Robert Tymme's wages going ahead from North Weald to Roding, for 1½ days, 2¼d. Wardrobe: 3lb. of candles of paris, 6d. Marshalsea: hay bought for 60 horses and 18 hackneys, 7s. Provender for the same, 4qr 7⅔b. 2 pecks of oats from stock. 3 yeomen's wages, 6d. Wages of 22 grooms, 4 pages, 3s. 1d. Expenses of 4 grooms and 7 horses of the prior of Stoke and 1 horse of Englisch going from Stoke to London, North Weald and Bardfield on divers occa-

---

19   The Lady was probably staying with Robert Mareschal, member of her council.
20   It is not clear which of the Roding villages the Lady stayed at.

sions, 2s. 6½d. Expenses of \14/ horses from Standon returning from Woodford to Standon, 6d.

Sum of money £2 17s. 9¾d.; of stock £1 10s. 5d.; of both £4 8s. 2¾d. Sum of the Buttery 14s. 3½d. Sum of the Kitchen £1 0s. 1d. Sum of the Poultry 8s. 11½d. Sum of the Scullery 4¼d. Sum of the Wardrobe 6d. Sum of the Marshalsea 13s. 7½d. Roding and Bardfield   70 messes; livery of bread, 101; livery of wine and ale, 22. Tuesday, 18 September, there. Pantry: 220 loaves from stock. 36 loaves, 1s. 6d. Buttery: 2 sesters of wine. And 35 gallons of ale from stock. 25 gallons of ale bought at Roding, 4s. 2d. 39 gallons of ale bought at Bardfield, 4s. 6d. Kitchen: ½ carcass of beef, 1 bacon, 3 quarters and 1 carcass of mutton from stock. 3 quarters of beef, 8s. 6d. 1 pig [and] 1 quarter, 5s. 4½ carcasses of mutton, 7s. 6d. Poultry: 9 young doves from stock. 3 capons, 1s. 6d. 6 geese, 2s. 6d. 17 pullets, 1s. 11d. 9 young doves, 6d. 3 partridges, 2s. 5 gallons of milk, 5d. 220 eggs, 1s. 9½d. 1 groom's expenses obtaining pike at Ware, 2d. Carriage of poultry from Dunmow, 3d. Henry Poulterer's expenses at Dunmow, 2d. Scullery: expenses of Thomas Scot and Testepyn, 2d. Marshalsea: hay for 61 horses, 20 hackneys from stock. Provender for the same, 1qr 7½b. of oats of which 2b. from increment. Item 418 loaves from stock. 3 yeomen's wages, 6d. Wages of 25 grooms, 4 pages, 3s. 5½d. For 8 hackneys hired for the Lady's household from North Weald to Bardfield, for 3 days, 4s.

Sum of money £2 10s. 6d.; of stock £1 17s. 8d.; of both £4 8s. 2d. Sum of the Pantry 1s. 6d. Sum of the Buttery 8s. 8d. Sum of the Kitchen £1 1s. Sum of the Poultry 11s. 2½d. Sum of the Scullery 2d. Sum of the Marshalsea 7s. 11½d.

[*The Lady remained at Bardfield for the rest of the week, until Monday, 24 September.*]

[m. 6d] Bardfield and Birdbrook   49 messes; livery of bread, 67; livery of wine and ale, 19. Monday, 24 September, there. Pantry: 156 loaves from stock. Buttery: 2½ sesters of wine. And 20 gallons of ale from stock. 40 gallons of ale bought at Baythorne End, 5s. 1d. Kitchen: 1 quarter of beef, 3 quarters of bacon, 2 carcasses of mutton and ½ deer from stock. 1 quarter of beef, 2s. 3d. 3 quarters of pork, 3s. 2d. 3 quarters of mutton, 1s. 2d. ½ calf, 1s. 4d. Poultry: 3 geese, 1s. 1½d. 3 capons, 1s. 25 young doves, 1s. ½d. 100 eggs, 7½d. 3 gallons of milk, 3d. 4 partridges, 2s. Marshalsea: hay for 52 horses, 25 hackneys from stock. Provender for the same, 1qr 7½b. of oats of which 2b. from increment. Item 352 loaves from stock. 2 yeomen's wages, 4d. Wages of 24 grooms, 5 pages, 3s. 5d. 4 hackneys from Bardfield hired for the Lady's household [*to go*] to Clare, for 2 days, 1s. 4d. 15 hackneys hired from Clare to Bardfield to fetch the Lady's household, for 1 day, 2s. 6d.

Sum of money £1 6s. 7½d.; of stock £1 8s. 10d.; of both £2 15s. 5½d. Sum of the Buttery 5s. 1d. Sum of the Kitchen 7s. 11d. Sum of the Poultry 6s. ½d. Sum of the Marshalsea 7s. 7d.

Stoke and Clare   80 messes; livery of bread, 86; livery of wine and ale, 18. Tuesday, 25 September, there. Pantry: 246 loaves from stock. Buttery: 4 sesters of wine. And 95 gallons of ale from stock. 7 gallons of ale bought at Stoke, 1s. 2d. 100 cups purchased, 4s. 4d. Kitchen: 2½ quarters of beef, 1 bacon, 3 carcasses [*and*] 3 quarters of mutton from stock. ½ carcass of beef, 4s. 9d. 1½ pigs, 6s. 1 carcass, 1 quarter of mutton, 2s. Poultry: 1 partridge and 18 young doves from stock. 9 geese, 3s. 3d. 2 capons, 8d. 3 pullets, 3¾d. 4 partridges, 1s. 6d. 12 young doves, 6d. 2 piglets, 2s. 260 eggs, 1s. 6¾d. 3 gallons of milk, 3d. Expenses of 1 packhorse of the Poultry for 2 days, 3d. 2b. of oat-flour, 2s. 1 groom's expenses with 1 horse at Newmarket, 2d. Marshalsea: hay for 54 horses, 11 hackneys from stock. Provender for the same, 4qr 1b. 1 peck of oats of which 4b. from increment. Item 20 loaves from stock. 2 yeomen's wages, 4d. Wages of 24 grooms, 5 pages, 3s. 5d.

Sum of money £1 14s. 5½d.; of stock £2 3s.; of both £3 17s. 5½d. Sum of the Buttery 5s. 6d. Sum of the Kitchen 12s. 9d. Sum of the Poultry 12s. 5½d. Sum of the Marshalsea 3s. 9d.

Clare   59 messes; livery of bread, 48; livery of wine and ale, 8½. Moreover, the expenses of some of the Lady's household at Clare, the Lady being at Bardfield, for 3 days ending on 23 September viz. Pantry: 174 loaves from stock. Buttery: 80 gallons of ale from stock. Kitchen: 1 quarter of beef, 1 bacon and 1 carcass [and] 1 quarter of mutton from stock. ½ carcass of beef, 5s. 1½ carcasses of mutton, 2s. 6d. Poultry: 3 piglets, 2s. 6d. 6 geese, 2s. 12 young doves, 6d. Cok's expenses at Clare and Haverhill for 2½ days, 1s. 1b. of wheat for the food allowance, 7½d. 1 peck of oat-flour, 3d. Scullery: expenses of John de Donmowe and Grene going ahead to Clare for 1½ days, 3½d. Marshalsea: hay for 64 horses and 12 hackneys from stock. Provender for the same, 3qr 3b. of oats of which 3b. from increment. Item 234 loaves from stock.

Sum of money 14s. 8d.; of stock £1 14s. 8d.; of both £2 9s. 4d. Sum of the Kitchen 7s. 6d. Sum of the Poultry 6s. 10½d. Sum of the Scullery 3½d.

V

ESTATES AND LORDSHIP

The Value of the Lands of Elizabeth de Burgh, 1338–9[1]   [TNA SC11/roll 801]
[m. 2d] The Bailiwick of Clare
The manor of Walsingham is worth £55 13s. Of this, from rents and farms, £23 14s. 5¼d. From wool, £2. From profit of livestock, £4. From perquisites of the courts, £11 11s. ½d. From other issues and profits with profits of the mills which are not at farm [*blank*]. And it renders from profit of cultivation, but as loss £1 8s. 6d. And there remain there 2 carthorses, 6 draught animals, 1 bull, 12 cows, 140 sheep, 1 sow.
And there were sown there the year before 10qr 4b. of wheat which yielded this year, with an estimated 14qr which remains in a stack in the barn, 43qr 6b., 1qr 6b. more than the fourth grain. 3qr 6b. of rye sown, yielding, with an estimated 4qr remaining in a stack to be threshed, 12qr 5b., 1qr 3b. more than the third grain. 8qr 2b. of peas sown, yielding, with an estimated 6qr which are in a stack, 20qr 2b., 3b. less than 2½ grains. 47qr 4b. 3 pecks of barley sown, yielding 176qr 2b., 10qr more than 3½ grains. 14qr of oats sown, yielding 51qr 5b., 2qr 5b. more than 3½ grains.
The manor of Bircham is worth £6 14s. 2d. Of this, from rent and farms, £4 0s. 5½d. From wool, perquisites of courts and other issues, £2 13s. 8½d. And it renders from profit of cultivation, but as loss, 12s. And there remain there 2 draught animals, 119 sheep.
And there were sown there the year before 5qr 4b. of rye, yielding this year 25qr 3b., 5b. more than 4½ grains. 12qr of barley sown, yielding 51qr 1½b., 3qr 1½b. more than the fourth grain. 10qr 4b. of oats sown, yielding 32qr 4b., 1qr more than the third grain.
The manor of Claret is worth £26 8s. 9d. Of this from rents, £10 15s. 8½d. From wool, £2 10s., from profit and [*sale*] of livestock with the issue of the lambs, £6 12s. 8d. From perquisites of courts [*damaged*]. From other issues and profits [*blank*]. And it renders of profit of cultivation, but as loss, 2s. And there remain there 2 carthorses, 4 draught animals, 4 oxen, 1 bull, 12 cows, 4 steers and heifers, 5 bullocks, 3 calves, 3 rams, 111 mother ewes, 36 unmated ewes.
And there were sown there the year before 15qr 1b. of wheat, yielding 56qr 5b., 3qr 5½b. more than 3½ grains. 1qr 7b. of maslin sown, yielding 13qr 7b., 1½b. more than 7½ grains. 1qr 4b. of rye sown, yielding 8qr 4b., 4b. less than the sixth grain. [*damaged*]qr 4b. of beans and peas **[m. 3d]** sown, yielding [*damaged*]qr, 2b. more

---

1   This valuation covers all the lands held by Elizabeth de Burgh in England and Wales. For a summary of the whole document, see G.A. Holmes, *The Estates of the Higher Nobility in Fourteenth-Century England* (Cambridge, 1957), pp.143–7.

than 2½ grains. 3b. of barley sown, yielding 1qr 6b., 1b. less than the fifth grain. 7½b. of dredge sown, yielding 3qr 1b., 2½b. more than the third grain. 22qr of oats sown, yielding 85qr 5½b., 2qr 2½b. less than the fourth grain.

The manor of Hundon is worth £97. 2s. 6d. Of this, from rents and farms, £21 6s. 4¾d. From the profit of cultivation, £4 9s. 4d. From wool, £10. From profit and sale of livestock [blank]. From perquisites of courts, £3 7s. From other issues [blank]. And there remain there 4 carthorses, 12 draught animals, 19 oxen, 2 bulls, 48 cows, 13 steers and heifers, 12 bullocks and heifers, 12 calves, 43 sheep, 187 hoggets, 40 unmated ewes, 169 lambs, [marginal total, 439 sheep], 61 pigs, 33 piglets.

And there were sown there there [sic] the year before 62qr 7b. of wheat, yielding 230qr 3b., 9qr 2½b. more than 3½ grains. 7qr 5b. of beans and peas sown, yielding 41qr 7b., ½b. less than 5½. 87qr 3b. of dredge and oats sown, yielding 380qr 6b., 12qr 3½b. less than 4½ grains.

The manor of Erbury[2] is worth £110 9s. Of this, from rents, farms and customs [blank]. [Several lines left blank for the rest of the entry.] And there remain there 5 carthorses, 17 draught animals, 24 oxen, 1 bull, 20 cows, 4 bullocks and heifers, 5 calves, 12 rams, 376 mother ewes, 120 unmated ewes, 24¾ sacks of wool, [marginal total, 508 sheep].

And there were sown there the year before 61qr 6b. of wheat, yielding, with an estimated 140qr remaining in the barn to be threshed, 201qr 3b., 16qr 1b. more than the third grain. 1qr 4b. of maslin sown, yielding an estimated 10qr 4b. in the stack, which is the seventh grain. 3qr 5b. of rye [sown], yielding, with an estimated 10qr in the stack, 23qr, 1qr 2b. more than the sixth grain. 6qr 2b. of beans and peas sown, yielding, with an estimated 16qr 2b. in the stack, 44qr 4b., 6b. more than the seventh grain. 13qr 2b. of barley sown, yielding 77qr 3b., 2qr 1b. less than the sixth grain. 2qr 4b. of dredge sown, yielding 14qr, 2b. more than 5½ grains. 85qr 4b. of oats sown, yielding, with an estimated 30qr in the stack, 331qr ½b., 10qr 7½b. less than the fourth grain.

The manor of Woodhall with the mills of Sudbury is worth £25 6s. Of this, from the profit of cultivation, £6 18s. From wool, £3 10s. From other issues with the profits of the mills which are not at farm [blank]. And there remain there 2 carthorses, 6 draught animals, 4 oxen, 118 lambs.

And there were sown there the year before 19qr 5b. of wheat, yielding 77qr 5b., 7b. less than the fourth grain. 2qr 1b. of rye sown, yielding 10qr 2b., 5½b. more than 4½ grains. 1qr of peas sown, yielding 3qr 1b., 1b. more than the third grain. 8qr of barley sown, yielding 41qr 5b., 1qr 5b. more than the fifth grain. 3qr of dredge sown, yielding 17qr 1b., 7b. less than the sixth grain. 17qr 7b. of oats sown, yielding 47qr 1½b., 2qr 4b. more than 2½ grains.

The manor of Ilketshall is worth £30 2s. 7d. Of this, from rents and farms [blank]. [Several lines left blank for the rest of the entry.] And there remain there 8 draught animals, 2 foals, 10 oxen, 1 bull, 24 cows, 5 bullocks and heifers, and 139 sheep.

And there were sown there there [sic] the year before 10qr 4b. of wheat, yielding 34qr 1b., 2qr 5b. more than the third grain. 1b. of rye sown, yielding 1qr, which is the eighth grain. 10qr 1½b. of peas sown, yielding 34qr 6b., 7b. 1 peck less than 3½ grains. 10qr 6½b. of barley sown, yielding 50qr 3b., 1qr 5b. 1 peck less than 4½ grains. 24qr 7b. of oats sown, yielding 88qr 2½b., 1qr 2b. more than 3½ grains.

The manor of Standon is worth £94 11s. [Several lines left blank for the entry.] And

---

2   I.e. the manor of Clare.

there remain there 3 carthorses, 8 draught animals, 3 foals, 21 oxen, 2 bulls, 21 cows, 8 steers and heifers, 7 bullocks and heifers, 6 calves, 236 sheep, 31 hoggets, [marginal total, 267 sheep], 28 pigs, 22 piglets.

And there were sown there the year before 35qr 5b. of wheat, yielding this year, with an estimated 40qr in the stack to be threshed, 165qr, 4qr 5½b. more than 4½ grains. 3qr 4b. of peas sown, yielding, with an estimated 4qr in the stack, 19qr 2b., which is 5½ grains. 3qr 4b. of barley sown, yielding 23qr 5b., 7b. more than 6½ grains. 3qr of dredge sown, yielding 19qr 6b., 2b. more than 6½ grains. 40qr 6b. of oats sown, yielding, with an estimated 10qr in the stack to be threshed, 97qr 5b., 4qr 2½b. less than 2½ grains.

[m. 4d] The manor of Bardfield is worth £80 14s. [*Several lines left blank for the entry*.] And there remain there 4 carthorses, 18 draught animals, 14 oxen, 1 bull, 35 cows, 7 steers and heifers, 5 bullocks and heifers, 8 calves, 6 rams, 60 mother ewes, 120 unmated ewes, 160 lambs, [marginal total, 346 sheep], 43 pigs and 52 piglets. And there were sown there the year before 58qr 1b. of wheat, yielding 188qr 6b., 14qr 3b. more than the third grain. 1qr and 7b. of maslin sown, yielding 10qr 7b., 3b. less than the sixth grain. 3qr 4b. of peas sown, yielding 14qr, 2b. more than 4½ grains. 3qr 4b. of barley sown, yielding 22qr 3b., 3b. less than 6½ grains. 3qr of dredge sown, yielding 10qr 2b., 2b. less than 3½ grains. 83qr 4b. of oats sown, yielding 230qr 4b., 22qr 5½b. more than 2½ grains.

Tunbridge Hall   There are there 4 carthorses, 4 draught animals, 10 oxen, 24 cows, 6 steers and heifers, 4 bullocks and heifers, 6 calves, 243 sheep and 6 piglets.

Stebbing   There are there 4 carthorses, 18 draught animals, 15 oxen, 34 cows, 4 steers and heifers, 7 bullocks and heifers, 7 calves, 7 rams, 213 mother ewes, 124 lambs [marginal total, 244 sheep; *recte* 344], 19 pigs, 35 hoggets and 44 piglets.

The borough of Clare is worth £15 16s. 3d.

The bailiwick of Suffolk with the vill of Southwold[3] is worth £26 17s. 10d.

The bailiwick of Norfolk is worth £23 16s. 3d.

The bailiwick of Essex is worth £58. 6s. 2d.

The borough of Bardfield is worth £9 5s.

[*Marginal totals*] The sum of sheep in the said bailiwick [*of Clare*], 2,813. The sum of the said value, £661 2s. 6d.[4]

Account of Henry de Neuton, Receiver of Clare, from Michaelmas, 16 Edward III, to the morrow of Michaelmas next following, 17 Edward III, 1342–3

[TNA SC6/1110/10]

[m. 1] Arrears   The same man is debited with £8 13s. 7½d. of the arrears of Robert Pentriz formerly receiver there. And he answers for £270 13s. 9d. of the arrears of the last account for the preceding year.

Sum £279 7s. 4½d.

Standon   The same answers for £92 received from William Buntyng, serjeant there, by 5 tallies. And for £1 received from the same William, without tally.

Manor of Bardfield   And for £28 10s. received from William, serjeant of the manor of Bardfield, by 3 tallies. £1 3s. 4d. received from the same William on his account,

---

3   The money received by the bailiwicks came from rents, farms and perquisites of courts; see below, pp.127–8.

4   The sum total of all the bailiwicks held by Elizabeth de Burgh in England and Wales came to £2,583 15s. 7d.

without tally. 6s. 8d. received from the same for money paid to Laurence Janitor there for his pay, without tally.

Borough of Bardfield   And for £6 10s. received from Peter Alfred, bailiff of the borough of Bardfield, by 2 tallies. 13s. 4d. received from the same by the hands of Sir John de Thrillawe, without tally. 3s. 4d. received from John Pountfrett, formerly bailiff, in payment of his arrears, without tally.

Walsingham   And for £2 12s. received from Edmund Wymer, serjeant of Walsingham, of his arrears from the time when he was serjeant of Stebbing, of which £2 by tally, with 1 tally remaining.

Claret   And for £17 received from William Cole, serjeant of Claret, by 2 tallies.

Woodhall   And for £35 received from Richard atte atte [sic] Pole, serjeant of Woodhall, by 2 tallies.

Erbury   And for £44 1s. received from John Segor, reeve of Erbury, by 2 tallies. 3s. 4½d. received from the same for 73 small works, price ½d. per work, and 4 great works, price 1d. per work, expended in the castle, without tally. £2 5s. 6d. received from the same for 22qr 6b. of oats for provender, without tally. 7s. 6d. received from the same for straw bought by him to roof the kennel,⁵ without tally.

Hundon   And for £55 10s. 5d. received from Roger Garbedons, reeve of Hundon, by 4 tallies.

Essex   And for £51 8s. received from John atte Mor, bailiff of Essex, by 3 tallies. £1 14s. received from the same before the account, without tally. £2 18s. received from the same John on this account, without tally.

Marshalsea⁶   And for 12s. received from Robert de Redeswell, bailiff of the Marshalsea, by the hands of Walter de Ware, without tally. 8s. received from the same on account by the hands of John atte Mor, without tally.

Borough of Clare   And for £18 received from Robert de Rokwod and Hugh de Godleston, bailiffs of the borough of Clare, by 2 tallies. £2 received from the same Robert and Hugh on account, without tally. £3 received from Robert and Hugh before the account at the term of St Andrew, without tally.

Borough of Sudbury   And for £20 received from John de Rumwode, now bailiff of the borough there, by 3 tallies. £1 received from the same John on his account, without tally. 5s. 7¼d. received from Robert Bantyng, formerly bailiff there, of his arrears, without tally. £3 received from John Brian, last bailiff there, of his arrears, by 1 tally remaining. £1 9s. 11¼d. received from the same John of his arrears, without tally.

Justiceshall   And for 7s. received from Peter de Gaiesle, formerly serjeant of Justiceshall, of his arrears, without tally.

Issues of the garden of Clare   The same [answers] for £1 4s. received from osiers of the issues of the garden of Clare sold this year.

Issues of the garden of Bardfield   And for 6s. received from osiers sold in the garden of Bardfield by the hands of Sir John de Thrillawe, chaplain there, as appears in the account of William, bailiff there.

[Marginal note: Memorandum that the Abbot of Waltham owes for 2 Michaelmas terms, viz. £2 each term.]

    Sum £394 19s.   audited

---

5   This was probably for the Lady's hunting dogs; see below, p.104.
6   The bailiwick of the Marshalsea included fees acquired by the Clares from the Marshal family inheritance in the thirteenth century.

Sale of wool   From 1 sack of white wool of Caythorpe sold for making the Lady's cloth by Matilda Maynard, £6 13s. 4d. From 5½ stone of black wool of Caythorpe sold for making cloth by the said Matilda, £1 8s. 2¼d. From 12 sacks of wool and 7 stone sold to Thomas de Canterbirs, draper and citizen of London, £61 5s., at £5 a sack.

Sum £69 6s. 6¼d.   audited

Sum of all receipts and arrears £743 12s. 10¾d.   audited

Expenses in Clare castle For pay and wages of divers carpenters, sawyers, masons, plasterers and divers other workmen working on Clare castle for the time of this account, making a new building between the hall and the kitchen, with solar and divers chambers in the same for the Scullery, Saucery, Larder, Oven-house and other buildings for offices, and \also/ divers new pentices under the walls of the castle between the chamber called Colingham's chamber and the gate of the castle. With the making of divers fireplaces in the same[*damaged*] making another new building in the outer bailey of the castle for the Lady's huntsmen and dogs, and repairing divers other [*damaged*] in the castle, with tiles, lime, straw, lead, timber, iron nails and divers other items purchased for the aforesaid [*as appears*] in the particulars sown to this roll and examined, £34 2s. 1½d.[7] For 73 small works, price ½d. per work, and 4 great works, price 1d. per work, bought from the reeve of Erbury and [*expended in the castle*], 3s. 4½d.

Sum £34 5s. 6d.   audited

[m. 2] Expenses in the manor within the park of Bardfield For divers expenses incurred in the repair of buildings of the manor within the park of Bardfield, with divers items bought for this, and repairing the gutters of the enclosure of the same manor for the time of this account, as appears from the particulars of Sir John de Thrillawe, chaplain, made there, £2 19s. 6¼d.[8]

Sum £2 19s. 6¼d.   audited

Pay and wages   For pay and wages of Sir John de Thrillawe, chaplain in the manor within the park for the year except 9 weeks at the Lady's table, the lady staying there from 22 February to 24 April this year, £2 17s. 8d. [*damaged*] of Laurence Janitor there for 43 weeks and 1 day, £1 17s. 9d. And not more because he was at [*the Lady's table*] for 8 weeks and 6 days, the lady staying there. Item for 1 groom's wages helping in the garden and doing other work [*damaged*] in the manor this year, 5s. Wages of the gardener of the castle, 10s. a year. Wages of 1 other gardener there, 6s. 8d. a year.

Sum £5 17s. 1d.   audited

Fees   For the fee of John de Hertford, steward, £20 a year. For the fee of Henry de N[*euton*] receiver, £6 13s. 4d. a year. ~~In remuneration made to the same Henry~~ ~~[damaged] made with the Lady, £3 6s. 8d.~~ For the fee of Sir Henry [*constable of the castle, £1*].

Sum £27 13s. 4d.   audited

[m. 1d] Expenses For the expenses of Sir Andrew de Bures going to London in October, staying there on the Lady's business concerning Caerleon and Weymouth, and returning, for 8 days, with £2 9s. 2d. paid for the charter of confirmation of the liberty [*illegible*] of Usk and Caerleon, and for having the Lord King's commission by 1 sealed bill for the business concerning Weymouth, £4 7s. 6d. For the

---

7   The particulars are found on membranes 3, 4 and 6 of this account.
8   The particulars are found on m.5 of this account.

expenses of the said Sir Andrew and John Bataille going to London on the Lady's business concerning the Countess Marshal, staying and returning, for 11 days, together with obtaining 3 writs, as appears by 1 sealed bill, £3 3s. 2d. Paid to 2 men being at Justiceshall during the previous year's harvest beyond harvest-service, for their wages, 6s. \and not accounted for in the same year/. Carrying 1 letter to William Buntyng, serjeant at Standon, about coming to Clare to make the view of his account, 3d. Item paid to Thomas Molecatcher taking moles in the garden and the outer bailey of the castle at the term of All Saints [1 November], 2s. For his wages taking moles in the manor this summer, 3s. Carrying the Lady's letter to Sir William Botvulyn about business concerning the church of Newton, 4½d.[9] For 2 cows bought for the Lady's Chamber in summer, £1 1s. 1½d. For remuneration made to John Tebaud for weighing the Lady's wool at Clare to deliver to Thomas de Canterbirs, 2s. For the expenses of Sir Andrew de Bures and the auditors of accounts at London on the Lady's business for 2½ days, together with their expenses coming from Farnham at the term of St Martin [11 November], £1 9s. 8d.

Sum £10 15s. 1d. audited

Pardon   Pardon to Sir John de Thrillawe concerning faggots carried away in Bard-field park and sold to the receiver the previous year by the Lady's letter, 7s. 6d. Pardon to Nigel Tebaud concerning wool sold to him, £1.

Sum £1 7s. 6d. audited

Delivery of money   Delivered to Sir Robert de Stalynton, the Lady's receiver, £527. 5s., by 15 acquittances. To the same for 1 sack of white wool [and] 5½ stone of black wool of Caythorpe delivered to Matilda Maynard to make cloth for the Lady, without acquittance, £8 1s. 6¼d. Item to the same Sir Robert for 12¼ sacks of wool of the bailiwick of Clare delivered to Thomas de Canterbirs, citizen and draper of London, without acquittance, £61 5s.

Sum £596 11s. 6¼d. audited

Sum of all expenses and liveries £679 9s. 6½d. And he owes £64 3s. 4¼d. Of this, Robert Pentriz, formerly receiver there, owes £8 13s. 7½d. Thomas de Whate-feld is bound to acquit him of £7 18s. 5d. from wool sold to him. Thus Robert owes 15s. 2½d, and Henry de Neuton, now receiver, £55 9s. 8¾d. And on this he is allowed $^{2}/_{3}$ of the expenses of grooms and horses of the abbot of Dereham and prior of Walsingham staying at Clare for 3 days and 3 nights on going to Wales to bring the Lady and her household from there to Clare. And £3 2s. of the expenses of Sir Andrew de Bures and John Bataille in London on divers occasions on the Lady's business, of which £1 for a charter of the Lord King about having licence to appropriate the church of [Great] Gransden [Hunts.] for the nuns of Denny. And £5 12s. 2d. allowed him at the Lady's order for certain secret acts done by him by command of the Lady. Thus he is allowed £8 16s. 5d. And he owes £46 13s. 3¾d.

Account of John Segor, Reeve of Clare, from Michaelmas, 10 Edward III, to the morrow ~~of the feast~~ of Michaelmas next following, 11 Edward III, 1336–7

[TNA SC6/992/25]

[m. 1] Arrears   The same man is debited with £7 2s. 2½d. of the arrears of John Wulwy, formerly reeve there. And £4 7s 1¼d. of the arrears of the last account.

Sum £11 9s. 3¾d. audited

---

9   Possibly All Saints, Newton near Sudbury, where 14th-century glass in the east window has the Botvulyn shield.

Rent of assize From rent of assize for the term of St Andrew [*30 November*], £1 0s. 5½d. From the term of the Annunciation of the Blessed Virgin Mary [*25 March*], £3 0s. 9¾d. From the term of the Nativity of St John the Baptist [*24 June*], 14s. 10¼d. And from Michaelmas term, £3 11s. 2¾d.

From Gilbert Scheldrake's new rent for a purpresture, 1d. at Easter and Michaelmas terms. From Henry Pack, 1d. of new rent at the said terms. From William Tailor, ¼d. for Michaelmas term. From Gilbert Scheldrake ½d. for increment of rent at the same term. From Alice who was Walter atte Touneshend's wife from increment \of rent/ of 2 acres of land acquired from William Pully, ½d., this year 5. From 2 ploughshares of rent there sold for Michaelmas term, 1s. 6d.

Sum £8 9s. 1½d.   audited

Poultry rents 25 capons of rent sold at Easter, 6s. 3d., price 3d. a capon. 31 hens of rent at Christmas sold, 5s. 2d., price 2d. a hen. And 302 eggs sold at Easter, 1s.

Sum 12s. 5d.   audited

Farms From 13½ acres of land in Horsecroft let to John le Saucer by the Lady's deed, £1 10s. 4d. at Easter and Michaelmas terms. From 26 acres of land and 2 acres of meadow, which Amice Huberd held for life, let to the said John by the Lady's deed, £1 7s. 8d. at the said terms. From 12 acres of land let to John Tom in East Field, nothing, because the said John left it and it is grazed by the Lady's sheep. From 40 acres of land, meadow and pasture which Richard Carpenter held of the Lady for life at Fornham,[10] nothing, because Roger Pantler holds the said tenement by the Lady's lease for doing his service to the Lady.

Sum £2 18s.   audited

Issues of the manor and sale of works From plough-service remitted and sold for the terms of Christmas, Easter and St John the Baptist, £6 3s., and not more because the reeve and reap-reeve hold ¾ virgate and have an allowance of 6s. From the remission and sale of making 30qr 2b. of malt barley [*and*] 30qr 2b. of malt oats for Christmas term, 15s. 1½d., for a qr of malt barley 4d. and for a qr of malt oats 2d. From John son of Alexander Quilter to have licence to hang his hides in the water next to the old mill, 6d.[11] From toll \on the water held in severalty by the Lady's/ letter, 1s. 4d. From 1 enclosure sold at the gate of the manor, 5s. From thornwood sold to Matilda Mone, 1s. From eels caught at the watermill and in the pond this year, 3d. From the issues of the dovecote, 6s. 8d. From 1 barrel of cider sold, 7s. 3d. And from 1 other barrel sold, 5s. And from 2 barrels of cider sold to the Lady's household, 14s. From wax and honey of 3 beehives sold this year, 3s. 6d. From hay in the garden sold this year, 7s., and not more because it is grazed by the Lady's cows for lack of a buyer. From green beans sold this year, 2s. 5d. And 4d. worth of land of the sheepfold sold this year, 2s. 4d. From leeks sold this year, 10d. From 1qr 3b. of hard apples sold, 3s. 2½d. From pears sold, 1s. From onions and garlic, nothing this year. From fullers' teasels, nothing because they remain to be sold. From madder sold this year, £1 3s. 6d. From canvas sold, 1s. 4d. From 8 old timbers of the sluice-gates sold, 12s. From the profit of pigs \sustained by the dairy/ this year, 5s. 8d.

Sum £12 2s. 8d.   audited

---

10 It is not clear if this land was in Fornham St Martin or Fornham All Saints.

11 John Quilter was listed as a tanner in 1337 (below, p.122). Soaking hides in water was part of the tanning process.

Sale of works   From 848½ and ¼ small works sold, £1 15s. 4¼d., price of work ½d. From 21 great works sold, 1s. 9d., price of work 1d.

Sum £1 17s. 1¼d.   audited

Sale of pasture   From cows grazing on the stubble this year, 10s. 4d. From sheep-pasture, nothing this year because it is grazed by the Lady's sheep. From the pasture in the bailey, old vinery and under the castle-wall between the keep and the great gate, between the Dernegate and the Redgate, and the pasture over the moat under the castle-wall, valued at £1, nothing because it is grazed by the oxen of the waggon. From the pasture above the pond between the new mill and the malt-mill sold this year, 1s. 6d. From the pasture round the castle-mound and under the walls to the new tower, no response, because Richard de Taleworth who has custody of that part of the castle in time of war has the pasture for his fee and for waitefee, £1 17s. which the same Richard pays every other year, for which the bailiff of Essex is debited in his account. From \the pasture of/ Chalfpyttel and Houndewalle, nothing this year because it is grazed by the plough oxen and draught animals, and the Lady's sheep. From the pasture in Hogelowestret this year, 1s. 6d., and not more because it lies fallow. From the pasture at Le Wychez, 3s. From the pasture at Waltonstret, 2s. From the pasture of Hawesdych nothing this year because it is grazed by the Lady's cows. From the pasture of Galwstret nothing this year because it is grazed by the Lady's cows. From the pasture of Wynton, 3s. 6d. From the pasture of Berdesleye and Longeslade this year 2s. From the pasture of Roundemerch and Rouwemerch, nothing this year because it is grazed by the Lady's lambs and cows. From fallow land nothing this year because it is all grazed by the Lady's sheep. From nettles round the fish-pond sold, 1s. From hay of 50 acres of meadow sold to the Lady's household, £16 13s. 4d. at 6s. 8d. an acre.

Sum £17 18s. 2d.   audited

Sale of grain   From 19½qr of wheat sold for provisions of the Lady's household, £5 4s., at 5s. 4d. a qr From 94½qr of wheat sold to the said household, £23 12s. 6d., at 5s. a qr From 2qr of wheat sold to the said household, 6s. 8d. From 30qr of rye sold, £5, at 3s. 4d. a qr From 26qr of rye sold, £3 18s., at 3s. a qr From 4b. of peas sold to the said household, 1s. 6d. From 8qr 7½b. of peas sold, £1 10s. 9½d., at 3s. 4d. a qr From 3b. of barley sold, 1s. 10½d. From 73qr 2b. of oats sold, £8 10s. 11d., at 2s. 7d. a qr From 80qr 4b. of oats to the said household, £10 1s. 3d., at 2s. 6d. a qr From 26qr 3b. of malt sold to the said household, £5 13s. 6½d. £5 14s. 3½d., at 4s. 4d. a qr From 22qr 2b. of malt sold to the said household, £4 9s., at 4s. a qr From 4qr 2b. of malt of the mill sold, 18s. 5d., at 4s. a qr.

Sum £69 8s. 2½d.   audited

Sale of livestock   From 1 carthorse sold, 19s. From 2 old draught animals sold, 4s. 8d. From 3 oxen sold to the Lady's household, £2, price per head 13s. 4d. From 1 other ox sold, 16s. From 1 other ox sold, 12s. From 1 other ox sold, 11s. From 1 other ox sold 15s. 6d. From 1 cow sold about the feast of St Matthew [*21 September*], 6s. From 1 calf sold, 1s. 8d. And 1 other calf sold, 9d. And 8 calves of issue sold, 8s. 1d. From 17 ewes in danger of death sold, 16s. ½d. From 62 ewes sold, £3 2s. And 2 unmated ewes in danger of death sold, 8d. From 9 lambs sold, 2s. 3d. From 3 wool-fells sold, 1s. 6d. And 4 sheepskins sold, 4d. From 9 lambskins, 6d. From 24 capons sold, 5s. From the hide of 1 draught animal which died of murrain, 1s. From the hide and flesh of 1 ox which died of murrain sold, 3s. From the hide and entrails of 1 ox which died of murrain sold, 4s. 6d. From the farm of 4 geese, 4s. From the farm of 12 hens, 6s.

Sum £12 1s. 5½d.   audited

Dairy produce   From the dairy produce of the cows \of the herd/ this year, £1 17s. 7d. From the dairy produce of 240 ewes this year at 2d. a head, [£2]. And not more because 96 were dry viz. some because of old age, and the rest because they were hoggets.

Sum £3 17s. 7d.   audited

Perquisites of the court   From fines and perquisites of the court and leet this year, £3 14s. 6d.

Sum £3 14s. 6d.   audited

Sold on account   The same is debited with £1 5s. 3d. for divers things sold on account.

Sum £1 5s. 3d.   audited

Sum total of receipts with arrears £145 13s. 9½d.   audited

Payment of rents   Paid to Richard Tydy, Laurence son of Gilbert, Matilda Thurston, William Beard and John Gynner for 8 acres 1 rood of land and ½ acre of meadow which Roger Fylloth and Alice his wife held freely of the same, 8¾d. a year, \and the land came into the Lady's hands by escheat, now John atte Pirie, the Lady's villein, holds it at the will of the Lady and his rent is debited above./ In acquittance of the smith's rent for making the ironwork for the ploughs, 1s. 4d. a year. In default of rent of 1 acre of land which John Crawe held and now is in the Lady's demesne, 6d. a year. In default of rent of 5 acres 3 roods of land in Horsecroft of the holding once of Peter Huberd because it is in the Lady's hand, 8½d. a year. In default of rent of the right of way between the old fish-pond and Cavendish once held by John de Essex because it is in the Lady's hand, 6d. a year. In default of rent of 5 acres 3 roods of meadow called Howesmed because it is in the Lady's hand, 1s. 11d. a year. In acquittance of John Segor's rent because he is reeve this year, 2s. 3d. In acquittance of rent of John Scheldrake because he is reap-reeve this year, 4s. 6d.

Sum 12s. 5¼d.   audited

Tithe   Paid for the tithe of pasture-herbage and [?]underwood sold above this year, 1s. 7d. For tithe of green beans, madder, beehives and other small items sold in the garden this year, 4s. 2¼d. 3s. 11¼d.

Sum 5s. 6¼d.   audited

[m. 2] Costs of ploughs   For 54 pieces of iron bought at Reach fair, 18s. 6d., at 4d. each, plus in total 6d. 36 pieces of iron bought at Stourbridge fair, 12s., at 4d. each. 11 measures of steel bought at the said fairs, 8s. 3d., at 9d. each. 6qr of sea-coal purchased, 6s. 16 plough-irons purchased, 2s. 8d. 16 straddle-clouts bought, 2s. Making 3 ploughshares of the Lady's iron, 6d. Making 8 drails of the Lady's iron, 1s. For 4 new ploughs newly made of the Lady's timber, 1s. Fitting 6 ploughs with a head, 1s. Making 4 ox-yokes of the Lady's timber, 4d. Shoeing 16 draught animals for the year, 12s. Shoeing 4 draught animals at the time of sowing wheat, 9d. Shoeing 2 draught animals for the year, 1s. 11d. Shoeing 20 oxen on their front feet, 3s. 4d. \Shoeing 5 oxen on their hind feet, 10d./ 1 quart of ointment to anoint the necks and feet of the oxen, 3d. For the cost of 1 boon-work of 29 ploughs at the time of sowing wheat and oats, 4s. 10d., at 2d. a plough. 1 carpenter's wages felling timber for plough-beams and heads at Hundon for 5 days, 1s. 3d.

Sum £3 18s. 5d. And so much this year because of the dearness of iron and a fifth plough at the time of sowing wheat.   audited

Costs of carts   1 pair of new iron-hooped wheels purchased, 11s. 1d. 80 large nails bought for mending old wheels, 1s. 11½d. 3 iron bands purchased, 3d. 2 winding bands bought, 1d. 4 frets bought for binding hubs, 2d. 40 cart-clouts bought, 2s. 6d. 16 large cart-clouts bought, 2s. 16lb. of fat and grease bought to grease the carts,

2s. For putting 2 spokes in 1 iron-hooped wheel, 6d. 4 dowels bought for the same, 3d. 4 winding bands bought for the same, 2d. 400 nails bought for removals and replacements, 6d. Fitting axles to tumbrels and other carts for the year, 1s. For enlarging hubs, 1d. Repairing the wheel of 1 tumbrel with 1 spoke, 4d. 4 pairs of traces bought, 1s. 8d. 1 collar bought, 7d. Mending 5 collars twice, 10d. 2 reins bought, 2d. 2 hurters, 1½d. 2 ropes measuring 13 fathoms bought for the carts, 8d. 1 cart-rein bought, 2d. Shoeing 4 carthorses for the year, 6s.

Sum £1 13s. 1d.   audited

Purchase of grain and stock   8qr 1b. of wheat bought for seed, £2 8s. 9d., at 6s. a qr. 12½qr of wheat purchased for the same, £3 10s. 10d., at 5s. 8d. a qr. 5qr of wheat bought for the same, £1 7s. 6d., at 5s. 6d. a qr. 4½qr of wheat bought for the Lady's household provisions, £1 2s. 6d., at 5s. a qr. 4qr of oats purchased, 10s., at 2s. 6d. a qr. 1 carthorse, £1 0s. ¼d. 1 ox purchased, 13s. 4¼d. 2 cows bought after calving, £1 0s. 1d. 1 cow bought at Ridgewell fair, 10s. 6d. 1 other cow bought about the feast of St Matthew [*21 September*], 10s. ¼d. 6 ewes bought before lambing and shearing, 12s. 2¾d.

Sum £13 5s. 9½d.   audited

Costs of buildings   For 1 roofer's wages roofing over the walls opposite the dove-cote for 9½ days, 3s. 2d., taking 4d. a day for himself and his boy. The same man's wages roofing over the hay-barn for 24½ days, 8s. 2d., at 4d. a day. The same man's wages roofing and fitting ridge-pieces over the forge for 6 days, over the ox-house for 3 days, over the great barn for 27½ days, over the walls round the garden and in the manor for 11½ days, and over the bean-store for 9 days, 19s., taking as above. For carpentry repairs in the hay-barn, 1s. 1 carpenter's wages making 1 door for the dairy for 2 days, 6d. Iron nails bought for the same, 1d.

Sum £1 11s. 11d.   audited

Costs of mills   For 60 ells of canvas bought for the windmill, 6s. 3d., at 1¼d. an ell. For 1 door iron newly made for the same with iron of the forge, partly purchased, 10d. For the carpenter making 1 new axle and 1 sail-yard for the said mill and installing them, 6s. For 13 pairs of forks bought for the sails of the said mill, 2s. 100 spikenails bought for the same, 4d. 4 bands of iron bought to bind the said sail-yard, 8d. For repairing the spindle of the ~~new~~ \new/ mill, 7d. For 27 iron rods bought to repair the pick [*for dressing millstones*] and installing them, 1s. 6d. 2 pairs of trendle-wheels made, 1s. For binding the same, 4d. For the contract with 1 carpenter making 1 pair of new sluice-gates for the malt-mill, £4. 700 spikenails bought for the same, 2s. 4d. 400 larger nails purchased purchased [*sic*] for the same, 9d. Wages of 153 men quarrying for 1 day making a new place for the said sluice-gates, and digging for clay and ramming it, and hauling timber for the same, and dragging the old sluice-gates from the water, £1 5s. 6d., each taking 2d. a day. 2 men's wages for 2 nights bailing water at the sluice-gates and throwing it away, 6d. For the contract with 1 man digging the new pond and filling in the site of the old sluice-gates, £5 6s. 8d.

Sum £11 15s. 3d.   audited

Small necessaries   5b. of salt bought for pottage of the paid workers, 1s. 5½d. \this year/. 2b. of salt bought for the dairy, 7d. 4 sacks bought, 2s. 4d. 2 new winnowing fans bought, 1s. 6d. 2 shovels, 2 spades, 2 forks bought, 6d. For fitting the same with ironwork, 8d. 1 barrow bought, 6d. For 1b. of beans bought for seed for the garden, 7d. 2qr of teasel seed bought, 3d. and garlic and onions bought, 3d. For ~~vine~~ \onion/seed, 1d. 2 small locks bought for the door of the barn, 5d. Making 4 perches of new wall opposite the pound by order of the Lady, 2s. Repairing and binding 1 barrel \for putting cider in/, 9d. Mowing 4 acres of straw to roof the buildings, 2s. For 1 lock bought for the gate of the pound, 2½d.

    Sum 14s. 1d.   audited

Costs of the fold   4 gallons of tar bought, 1s. 4d. 4 gallons of butter bought for the same, 2s. 2 gallons of fat for the same, 1s. 8d. 3 feeding-racks purchased, 32 feet long, 9d. 3lb. of candles bought to have light in the sheepfold, 6d. 104 hurdles bought for the fold, 4s. 4d. 1 man's wages for 2 days mending the old hurdles, 4d. For washing and shearing 346 ewes, 3s. 11½d.

    Sum 14s. 10½d.   audited

Mowing   For mowing 4 acres of meadow in Pedekesholm, 5 acres 3 roods in Housemed as piece-work, 4s. ¾d., at 6d. an acre. Spreading \and tossing/ the hay, 2s. ¼d., at 2½d. an acre. Spreading the hay of 10½ acres \of meadow/ in Stone, 31 acres 1 rood in the old fish-pond, 29 acres 3 roods in Melnemed, and 6½ acres in Chaldewalle as piece-work, 3s. 3d., at ½d. an acre. Mowing the second crop of 2 acres of meadow in the old fish-pond, 10d. Spreading and tossing the hay of the same, 5d. For the cost of the custom for their rams after the mowing of the meadows, 1s.

    Sum 11s. 7d.   audited

Costs of harvest   For baking 2qr 6½b. of wheat for the food for the boon-work of reaping and binding the Lady's corn, for 1 day with 2 meals, 11¼d. For relish purchased for their drink viz. ale 8s., meat 8s. 6d., cheese 5s. Wages of 2 men hired from the Gules of August [*1 August*] to Michaelmas [*29 September*] for 8 weeks and 2 days to stack the Lady's grain in the barn, and making 1 stack of peas and roofing it, and partly roofing the paid workers' house, and putting a ridge on the walls round the pound, and doing other necessary jobs in the manor, 18s. for their food and wages. For the pay of the reeve and reap-reeve for 5 weeks in the harvest this year, 8s. 9d., each taking 1½d. a day. 1lb. of candles bought to have light in the barn at night, 2d. Henry of the Wardrobe's pay supervising the reaping and custody of the grain for the said time, 8s. 9d., taking 3d. a day by letter of the Lady.

    Sum £2 18s. 1¼d.   audited

Wages   Yearly wages of the second carter, 6s. Yearly wages of 2 shepherds, 10s. 1 boy's wages helping at lambing-time \this year/, 6d. Yearly wages of the dairy-maid making pottage for the paid workers, 2s. Yearly wages of 3 millers, 4s. 6d. Robert Gardener's yearly wages, 10s. Wages of 1 woman making dairy produce from Easter to Michaelmas, 2s. 1 cowherd's wages, 2s. 6d.

    Sum £1 17s. 6d.   audited

Supervisory expenses   For the expenses of the bailiff \Lengleys/ for his coming to supervise the manor \at different times/, 5s. 8½d. For the expenses of the same taking the view of account of his whole office, 11s. For the expenses of the same and others supervising and removing the Lady's wool, 2s. 8d.

    Sum 19s. 4½d.   audited

Foreign [*expenses*]   Paid for the tax of the fifteenth, £1.

    Sum £1.   audited

Delivery of money   Delivered to Henry de Thrillawe receiver by 2 tallies, £14 12s. 2d. Delivered to Richard atte Hache reeve of Hundon, £3 2s. without tally. Delivered to John Darre clerk of the Lady's Wardrobe by 1 acquittance, £19 9s. 8½d. \2½d./. To John de Lenne clerk of the Lady's Wardrobe by 1 acquittance, £57 11s. 7d. Delivered to the said John for the Lady's household provisions, as the price of 2qr of wheat, 6s. 8d. by 1 acquittance.

    Sum £95 1s. 7½d.   audited

[m. 3] Sum of all expenses and deliveries, £136 19s. 6¾d. And he owes [£8] 14s. 2¾d. Of this he is allowed 1s. 5½d. of items allowed to him on account [*damaged*] £1 4s. postponed \because the Wardrobe is responsible/ from 8 swans used in the Lady's household and sold on [*damaged*] of John de Lenne Lady's Wardrober. And he owes £7 8s. 9¼d. [*damaged*] formerly reeve £7 2s. 2½d. And John de Segor now reeve [*damaged*].

[m. 1d] [*Grain account*]Wheat   Of the issues of old grain by tally against Henry of the Wardrobe, 38qr 3b. [*illegible*] And of issues by 1 tally against the same H[*enry*] 55qr 2½b. of which 5qr 7½b. from the same. And the rest of the issues by 1 tally against the same H[*enry*] 33qr 3b. From the same by 1 tally against John le Chamberleyn 44qr 3b. of which 8qr 3b. from Pykyng. Received from Richard atte Hache for seed 32½qr. And from Richard serjeant of Woodhall 4qr. Purchased for seed 25qr 5b. From the issues of 2 mills by tally against Henry de Thrillawe 22qr 3b. And bought for the Lady's household in the harvest 4½qr. From the issue of new grain by tally against Henry of the Wardrobe [*illegible*]qr 6b.

Sum 262qr ½b.

Of this for seed [*illegible*] 2b. less in total, 3qr 3b. \7b./ For tithe of the mills 2qr 1b. 3 pecks [*illegible*] at 12 weeks. Livery given to Richard gardener of the castle for the year except 6 weeks [*illegible*] taking as above. Livery of the said Richard's boy for the year except the said 6 weeks 3qr 2b. 1 peck, taking 1qr for 14 weeks. Livery of William [?]Coscenel fisherman for the year except for the said 6 weeks 5qr 6b. taking 1b. a week. Livery of Gilbert the shepherd for the year for overseeing the Lady's sheep 4qr 2½b. taking 1qr for 12 weeks. Livery of Thomas Catoun 2qr of wheat a year by the Lady's letter. Given to Richard [*illegible*] carpenter making the sluice-gates of the malt mill by agreement 1qr of wheat mixed with 7b. of rye as below to make maslin. Maslin for liveries [*illegible*] 41qr 5½b. For bread baked for food of 180 men for the harvest boon-works as if for reaping and binding for 1 day 60 acres of wheat, and 46 men with 23 carts carrying the Lady's grain as boon-work, each of whom had 2 loaves from 560 loaves, 2qr 6½b. Sold for the Lady's household provisions, 116qr. Given to Roger Skinner of Clare by the Lady's letter, 1qr.

Sum as above. And he is quit.   audited

Maslin   Received from wheat as above for making maslin for seed, 7b. From rye as below, 7b. From the issues of the mills by tally against Henry de Thrillawe 18qr 6b. \19qr/. From the farm of Boyton mill, tithe deducted, 8qr.

Sum 28qr 6b.   audited

Of which for seed on 3 acres of land in Schrotele field and on 2 acres 3 roods in le Wynton, 1qr 6b., at 2½b. an acre minus in all ½ peck. 2qr to Thomas Catoun by the Lady's letter. For maslin for the liveries of the paid workers, 16qr 6b.

Sum 20qr 4b. There remain 8qr 2b. of maslin.   audited

Rye   10qr remaining. From all issues by 2 tallies against Henry of the Wardrobe 70qr 7b.

Sum 80qr 7b.   audited

Of this for seed on 9½ acres in Schrotele field, on 4 acres 1 rod at le Wynton, and on 1 acre 3 roods at le Melnefeld 4½qr, at 2b. an acre plus in all 1b. 1 peck. Delivered for making maslin as above for seed, 7b. Delivered to Richard atte Hache reeve of Hundon 4qr 7b. by tally. Delivered to the serjeant of Claret 1qr 1b. by tally. For maslin for the liveries of the paid workers 10qr 2b. Sold, 56qr. Given in increment, 2qr 6b. Given to William Gerold at the Lady's order 4b.

Sum as above. And he is quit.   audited

111

Peas Of the issues of the old grain by 1 tally against Henry of the Wardrobe 12qr 1½b. Of the issues of the barn by tally against the said Henry, 10qr.

Sum 22qr 1½b.   audited

Of this for seed on 23 acres of land in Chaldewalle field 5qr 6b., at 2b. an acre. For seed on 16 acres in the same field 2qr, at 1b. an acre and not more because sown with oats. Delivered to Richard atte Hache reeve of Hundon 3½qr by tally. For mixed corn for the liveries of the paid workers 1qr 1b. Sold for the Lady's household provisions, 4b. For the peacocks' provisions, 3b. Item sold 8qr 7½b.

Sum as above. And he is quit.   audited

Vetch Of the issues \of ½ acre of vetch/ nothing this year because expended by the carthorses in the hay. And he is quit.   audited

Barley From the whole issues by 1 tally against the said Henry 23qr 1b. Of this for seed on 36 acres of land in Chaldewalle, and on 7 acres of land at le Wych, 21½qr at 4b. an acre. 1qr 2b. mixed for dredge seed. 3b. sold.

Sum as above. And he is quit.   audited

Dredge Received from barley as above for seed, 1qr 2b. And 6b. of oats for the same.

Sum 2qr.   audited

And sown on 4½ acres of land in Chaldewalle at 3½b. an acre, plus in all 1 peck. And he is quit.   audited

Oats Of issues by 1 tally against the said Henry 262qr. From issues by 1 tally against John le Chamberleyn 7qr. From the issues in 1,108 sheaves by the lesser hundred received for provender of the oxen, 13qr 6½b. by estimate, with 10 sheaves to 1b. Bought for the carthorses' provender and flour for pottage, 4qr.

Sum 286qr 6½b.   audited

Of this for seed on 86 acres 3 roods of land in Chaldewalle field and not more because 3 roods lie fallow, on 100½ acres of land in East Field and not more there because 94½ acres lie fallow \both from recent and old [*time*]/, 72qr 2b. at 3b. an acre plus in all 2qr 1 peck. Item for seed on 16 acres of land sown with peas in Chaldewalle field, 4qr at 2b. an acre. Mixed with barley for dredge seed as above, 6b. For provender of 4 carthorses from Michaelmas to the Gules of August [*1 August*] for 305 nights, 19qr ½b., taking ½b. a night, for this year only because of continuous labour \over carrying [?]faggots and the timber of the new sluice-gates/. For provender of the same obtaining charcoal at Reach fair twice, 3b. \over and above their set provender/. For provender of the draught animals at the time of sowing wheat, 7½b. For the provender of 16 draught animals from 1 January to 3 May, the first day counted, for 122 nights, 15qr 2b., taking 1b. a night. For the provender of 20 oxen for the said time, by estimate in sheaves, 13qr 6½b. For flour and pottage of the paid workers for the year 6qr \this year/. For the support of the swans \in the castle/, 5b. Sold for the Lady's household provisions, 153qr 6b.

Sum as above. And he is quit.   audited

Malt Of the issues of the mills by 1 tally against Henry de Thrillawe 55qr 1b. From the same issues for grinding 101½qr of malt, 3qr 5b. for the Lady's household.

Sum 58qr 6b.   audited

Of this for tithe 5qr 7b. Sold for the Lady's household 48qr 5b. 4qr 2b. sold.

Sum as above. And he is quit.   audited

Liveries of the paid workers Received from wheat as above, 41qr 5½b. of which 10qr from Pykyng instead of mixed corn. \From mixed corn 16qr 6b./ From rye, 10qr 2b. From peas, 1qr 1b.

Sum 69qr 6½b.   audited

Of this in livery to 2 carters and 8 ploughmen for the year, 51qr 6b., each taking 1qr for 12 weeks. Livery to 2 ploughmen from Michaelmas for the 6 weeks following at the time of sowing wheat, 1qr, taking as above. Livery to 1 carter carting dung from 4 May to 21 July for 11 weeks, 7b. Livery to 1 boy helping the shepherd look after the ewes from 8 February to 3 May for 12 weeks, 6b. Livery to another boy at lambing-time for 5 weeks, 2½b. Livery to 2 boys spreading the furrows at the time of sowing wheat for 9 weeks, 1qr 1b. Livery to the dairymaid making the paid workers' pottage for the year, 3qr 2b., taking ½b. a week. Livery to 3 millers for the year 6qr 3½b. of maslin of the mills. Livery to 1 boy keeping the cows and bullocks from 9 November to Michaelmas for 46 weeks, 2qr 7b. Livery to 1 maid making dairy produce from 20 April to Michaelmas for 23 weeks, 1qr 3½b., taking ½b. a week.

Sum as above. And he is quit. audited

[m. 2d] Stock account

Carthorses   4 remaining; 1 purchased; 1 received from the Lady's foals.
Sum 6. audited
1 sold.
Sum 1. And there remain 5 carthorses. audited

Draught animals   21 remaining; received from Hynton 4.
Sum 25. audited
Of these 2 sold; 2 died of murrain; 1 delivered to the serjeant of Standon, 1 to the serjeant of Sudbury, 1 to the reeve of Hundon, 1 to the serjeant of Claret.
Sum 8. And there remain 17 draught animals. audited

Oxen   29 remaining; 1 added; 1 purchased; 1 received from the reeve of Hundon.
Sum 32. audited
Of these 1 died of murrain; 3 sold for the Lady's household provisions; 4 sold; 1 delivered to the reeve of Claret; item 1 died of murrain.
Sum 10. And there remain 22 oxen. audited

Cows   3 remaining; received from Hynton 2; 2 from the reeve of Hundon; 1 from the reeve of Claret; 3 added; 2 purchased after calving; 1 purchased at Ridgewell fair; 1 from heriot after the death of William Wacheloc; 1 purchased about Michaelmas.
Sum 16. Of these 1 sold. And there remain 15 cows. audited

Steers   1 remaining; 3 added from the bullocks.
Sum 4. audited
Of these 1 added to the oxen.
Sum 1. And there remain 3 steers. audited

Heifers   Received from the reeve of Hundon 3; 1 added.
Sum 4. audited
Of these 3 added to the cows. And there remains 1 heifer. audited

Bullocks   4 remaining; 5 added from the calves.
Sum 9. audited
Of these 3 added to the steers and 1 to the heifers.
Sum 4. And there remain 5 male bullocks. audited

Calves   Received from the reeve of Claret 5; from the issues this year, 11.
Sum 16. audited
Of these 5 added to the bullocks; in tithe 1; sold 10.
Sum as above. And he is quit. audited

Rams   14 remaining; received from the reeve of Hundon after shearing 10.
Sum 24. audited

Of these 1 died of murrain before shearing; delivered to the reeve of Hundon 13 before shearing.

 Sum 14. And there remain 10 rams.   audited

Ewes 301 remaining; 118 added; from purchase before lambing and shearing 6; 3 taken from stock before lambing and shearing.

 Sum 428.   audited

Of these 17 sold in danger of death before lambing and shearing; 2 died of murrain after lambing and before shearing; 1 stolen by a thief before lambing and shearing; 62 sold before lambing and shearing because of old age; 4 died of murrain after shearing; 4 delivered to the reeve of Hundon after shearing.

 Sum 90. And there remain 338 ewes.   audited

Unmated ewes 118 remaining; received from Hundon after shearing 10; received from the serjeant of Bardfield after shearing 94.

 Sum 222.   audited

Of these 118 added to the ewes as above; 2 in danger of death sold after shearing.

 Sum 120. And there remain 102 unmated ewes.   audited

Lambs Of issue 326 336 and not more because 22 12 were barren; received from the serjeant of Woodhall 80; received from Robert Wulwy reeve of Claret 98.

 Sum 514.   audited

Of these 6 died of murrain before weaning; in tithe 32; delivered to the reeve of Hundon 240 male lambs; given to the shepherd 2; 1 died of murrain; 9 sold; delivered to the serjeant of Bardfield 224.

 Sum as above. And he is quit.   audited

Fleeces Of the issue of the ewes, 346 fleeces. Received from William Buntyng serjeant of Standon, 176 fleeces weighing 64 stone, the stone [*containing*] 7lb. From Richard atte Hache reeve of Hundon, 327 fleeces weighing 134 stone. From Robert Wulwy serjeant of Claret, 103½ fleeces weighing 32 stone. From Richard atte Pole serjeant of Woodhall 87 fleeces weighing 31 stone. From Richard Warner serjeant of Bardfield, 275 fleeces weighing 90 stone 2lb., the stone [*containing*] 7lb. And 1,101 fleeces weighing 5½ sacks received from Richard Porter reeve of Caythorpe. And 162 fleeces weighing 44 stone, the stone [*containing*] 7lb., received from John atte Lye reeve of Holton. And 181 fleeces weighing 31½ stone, the stone [*containing*] 7lb., received from Edmund Edward reeve of Farnham.

 Sum 1,314½ 2,758½ fleeces.

Of these 34 in tithe of the issue of wool of this manor.

 Sum 34. And there remain 1,280½ fleeces weighing 453 stone 2lb., the stone [*containing*] 7lb., that makes 8½ sacks 11 stone 2lb. And there remain 2,724½ fleeces weighing 15½ sacks 8 stone 5½lb., the stone [*containing*] 7lb.   audited

Wool-fells 1 ram and 2 ewes died in the said murrain.

 Sum 3. And sold. And he is quit.   audited

Sheepskins 4 ewes died in the said murrain after shearing.

 Sum 4. And sold. And he is quit.   audited

Lambskins 6 lambs died of the said murrain before weaning and 1 after weaning; 2 received from Claret.

 Sum 9. And sold. And he is quit.   audited

Stray swans The same man is debited with 4 stray swans in the water round the castle.

 Sum 4. And there remain 4 stray swans.   audited

Geese 5 remaining including 1 gander.

 Sum 5. And there remain 5 geese including 1 gander.

Capons   24 remaining; 25 in rent; 12 castrated.

Sum 61.   audited

Of these the 25 in rent sold; item 24 sold.

Sum 49. And there remain 12 capons.   audited

Cocks and hens   2 cocks and 12 hens remaining; 33 from rent.

Sum 47.   audited

Of these in acquittance of the reeve and reap-reeve, 2; 31 sold.

Sum 33. And there remain 2 cocks and 12 hens.

Pullets   From purchase for making capons, 12; from issue nothing because the hens at farm.

Sum 12. And accounted for in making capons. And he is quit.   audited

Swans of issue   From issue this year 14.

Sum 14.

Of these in tithe, 1. ~~In provisions for the Lady's household, 8~~ \because he is acquitted/.
Sold on account, 8 valued at £1 4s. And there remain 5 cygnets.   audited

Eggs   From rent, 307 eggs. Of these, in acquittance of the reeve and reap-reeve, 5.
302 sold. And he is quit.   audited

Hides   2 draught animals and 2 oxen from the said murrain.

Sum 4.   audited

Of these 1 hide of a draught animal and 2 ox-hides sold; 1 white-tawed for harness.

Sum as above. And he is quit.   audited

Plough-shares   From rent, 2. And sold. And he is quit.   audited

Pieces of iron   36 pieces of iron and 40 slabs remaining; 54 pieces of iron bought
at Reach fair; and 36 pieces of iron bought at Stourbridge fair.

Sum 126 pieces of iron and 40 slabs.

Of these expended on the ironwork of ploughs this year, 73 pieces of iron and 40
slabs. And there remain 53 pieces of iron.

Measures of steel   5 measures of steel remaining; purchased at the said fairs, 11.

Sum 16.   audited

Of these expended on the ironwork of ploughs, 11½ measures. And there remain
4½.   audited

Cider   7 barrels of cider remaining; from making from the issue of the garden this
year, 1 barrel and 2 small barrels containing 60 gallons.

Sum 8 barrels and 60 gallons.   audited

Sold for the Lady's household provisions, 2; sold 2.

Sum 4. And there remain 4 barrels and 2 small barrels of 60 gallons. audited

Apples   4½qr remaining; from issue of the garden this year, 1qr.

Sum 5½qr.   audited

Of these delivered in the castle 2qr by tally against Henry of the Wardrobe. 1qr 6b.
sold. From putrefaction, 6b. And there remains 1qr of apples.   audited

[m. 3d] [*Small*] works, ½d. Of the issue of 16⅛ virgates of land between Michaelmas and Pentecost for 36 weeks this year for which each works 5 works a week,
which results in 80½+⅛ works, 2,902¼ works. Of the issue of 5 akermen for the
same time of whom each owes [*2 works*] a week, 360 works. Of the issue of 6
cotmen for the above time of whom each owes 1 work a week, 216 works.

Sum 3,478¼ works.   audited

Of these for the allowance of the reeve and reap-reeve holding ¾ virgate for all
the above time, 135\¼/ works. In acquittance of the works of the smith who is an
akerman for the same time, 72 works. In acquittance of the works of the said 15
virgates +¼+⅛ of a virgate of land and 4 akermen and 6 cotmen for the 2 festival

weeks viz. Christmas and Easter, for each, 2½ works. In acquittance of the works of the said 15 virgates+¼+⅛ of 1 virgate of land for 10 festival days within the said time viz. the Apostles Simon and Jude [*28 October*], St Martin [*11 November*], St Katherine [*25 November*], ~~the Conception of the Blessed Virgin Mary~~ \St Nicholas [*6 December*]/, Epiphany [*6 January*], St Matthias [*24 February*], the Annunciation of the Blessed Virgin Mary [*25 March*], St Mark the Evangelist [*25 April*], the Apostles Philip and James [*1 May*], and the Ascension, 105 works ~~and ¼~~. In acquittance and relaxation of the same \for ploughing/ 121 acres of land in winter and 121 acres of land in Lent, 484 works viz. 2 works for an acre. And given for plough-service to each [*damaged*] In acquittance of the same works for making 30qr 2b. of malt barley and 30qr 2b. of malt oats, 121 works, 2 works for a qr. For threshing and winnowing 71qr 3½b. of wheat, 70qr 7b. of rye [*damaged*] For threshing and winnowing 22qr 1½b. of peas, 23qr 1b. of barley, 121 works, 3b. for a work. In [*threshing and winnowing*] 269qr of oats [*damaged*] for 269 works, 1qr for a work. For cutting and collecting 20 acres of stubble to roof divers buildings, 60 works. For spreading furrows [*damaged*] of wheat, peas and oats this year, 26 works. For making and opening watercourses at the time of sowing wheat, 21 works. In 123 acres [*damaged*] Collecting withies at Hundon for the fold, 4 works. Digging clay for the new sluice-gates of the mill, 8 works. For wheat [*damaged*] for seed and for the Lady's household, 68 works. Sold 848½+¼ [*works*]. Sold on account [*damaged*]

Sum as above. And he is quit. audited

[*Harvest*] works   Of the issue of 16⅛ virgates of land between Pentecost and \the morrow of/ Michaelmas for 16 weeks this year of which each works for [*10 works a week*], 2,580 works. Of the issue of 5 akermen for the same time of which each does 2 works a week, 160 works. Of the issue of 6 cotmen for the same time of which each does 1 work a week, 96 works.

Sum 2,836 works, price of work 1d.
Of which in acquittance of the reeve and reap-reeve holding ¾ virgate of land for the above time, 120 works. In acquittance of the smith who is an akerman for the same time, 32 works. In acquittance of the works of the said 15 virgates+¼+¹/₈ virgate of land, 4 akermen and 6 cotmen for Pentecost week, 160 +7½ works. In acquittance of the works of the said 15 virgates +¼+⅛ virgate of land for 9 festival days falling in the same time viz. the Nativity of St John the Baptist [*24 June*], the Translation of St Thomas the Martyr [*7 July*], St Mary Magdalen [*22 July*], St James [*25 July*], St Peter ad Vincula [*1 August*], the Assumption of the Blessed Virgin Mary [*15 August*], the Beheading of St John the Baptist [*29 August*], the Nativity of the Blessed Virgin Mary [*8 September*], and Michaelmas [*29 September*], this year 138¼ works. In acquittance of the works of the same for plough-service of 130 acres of land by estimate [*damaged*] 2 works for an acre. Hoeing the Lady's grain this year, 440 works. Mowing 9 acres 1 rood of meadow in Stone this year, and not more there because [*damaged*] it was grazed, 31 acres 1 rood in the old fish-pond, 29 acres 3 roods in Melnemed, 5 acres 3 roods in Chaldewalle, 304 works, 4 works for an acre. In aid for stacking hay in the barn, nothing this year. Carting 560 cartloads of dung in Stone field to the length of 8 furlongs [*damaged*] 224 works, 2 works for 5 acres. For spreading the said dung nothing this year because [*it was done*] by the paid workers. For reaping and binding 38 acres of wheat, [*damaged*] acres 3 roods of maslin, 15½ acres of rye, 39 acres of peas and *bolemong*, 43 acres of barley, 4½ acres of dredge, [*damaged*] for an acre 3 works. For reaping and binding 355 acres of wheat and oats, 710 works, for an acre 3 works. 21 works sold.

Sum as above. And he is quit. audited

Account of William Paycok and William Dunkeslee, bailiffs of the Borough of Clare, from the Feast of St Michael the Archangel 31 Edward III until the morrow of the said feast next following, 32 Edward III, 1357–8   [TNA SC6/993/17]

[m. 1] Arrears   The same is debited with £5 from a fine of William Brokhole for trespasses against the Lady. And £5 5s. 8¼d. from the arrears of Hugh de Godeston and Thomas Bory, formerly bailiffs there. And they answer for 2s. ¼d. of \old/ arrears of the same William Paycok and William Dunkeslee, formerly bailiffs there.

Sum £10 7s. 8½d.   audited

Rent of assize   From rent of assize there at the term of the Annunciation of the Blessed Virgin Mary [*25 March*] with new increments of rent at the same term as appears in the account roll of year 26 [*1352*] of the present king, £2 1s. 11½d. From rent at the term of the Nativity of St John the Baptist [*24 June*] ½d. From rent of assize there at the term of Michaelmas with new increments of rent at the same term as appears in the said account roll, £2 6s. 10d. From new rent of John Grym, barber, for a purpresture of land lying next to the lane called Rotten Row at the term of Easter, ¼d. From Peter Smith's increment of rent for a purpresture next to the castle moat opposite his tenement at the customary term, 4d. a year. From William Havering's increment of rent for 4 pennyworth of land which came into the Lady's hands as an escheat after Peter Hubert's death at the said term, ¼d. From new rent of John Pollard and Alice his wife for a purpresture opposite his messuage acquired from Walter Bory at the said term, 2d. From William Paycok's new rent for a purpresture between his messuage where he lives and the royal highway in the Nethergate at the term of the Annunciation of the Blessed Virgin Mary, ½d. From Gilbert atte Style's new rent for a purpresture next to his tenement where he lives in the Nethergate at the said term of the Annunciation of the Blessed Virgin Mary, ¼d. From Thomas Baron's new rent for 1 plot of land opposite his tenement acquired from Peter Smith 10½ feet long and 5 feet wide at the term of Christmas, this year the fourth, 1d. a year. Of Thomas Davon's new rent for 1 waste plot next to the castle ditch 37 feet long and 8 feet wide at the term of Easter, this year the third, 1d. a year. From new rent of Jevan Tailor from Wales for a purpresture next to the castle moat opposite the said Jevan's messuage to the east 20 feet long and 30 feet wide to be held at the Lady's will at the said term, this year the second, 1d. a year. From Robert Bory's new rent for a 3½ feet enlargement of 2 stalls in the market next to John Parker's stall at the usual terms, this year the first, 4d. a year.

Sum £4 10s.¼d.   audited

Chevage   From Richard Boket's chevage nothing because he is dead. From the chevage of Alexander de Neuton, William Raulyn, John atte Medwe, Thomas Baron and Henry Brynkelee for having the liberty of the vill, 1s. 3d. a year at the terms of Easter and Michaelmas, from each of them 3d. From the chevage of John Bot, William Frethik and John Pollard at the said terms, 6d. a year, from each of them 2d.

Sum 1s. 9d.   audited

Farms   From the farm of 1 messuage once of John Mayduyt being in the Lady's hands for lack of tenants, let to Robert Skynnere for the whole of Robert's life at the usual terms 2s. 1d. a year. From the farm of 1 plot of land lying between Peter Smith's tenement and the castle moat 44 feet long and 42 feet wide let to John Warde and Matilda his wife and John's heirs at the Lady's will at the four usual terms, this year the seventh, 4d. a year. Of the farm of Clare market, £6 a year.

Sum £6 2s. 5d.

Perquisites of courts   From fines and perquisites of 16 courts and 1 leet held there this year, £8 14s. 2d.

Sum £8 14s. 2d.   audited

[*Marginal note*] Memorandum concerning 1 small book of extracts at the said courts for which the bailiffs of the vill are answerable next year.

Sum of all receipts with arrears £29 16s. ¾d.   audited

Default of rent   In default of rent of 1 messuage with appurtenances once of John Mayduyt which came into the Lady's hands in time of plague for lack of heirs and at farm as appears above, 2d. a year.

Sum 2d.   audited

Turn over

[m. 1d] Delivery of money   Delivered to Humphrey de Waleden, receiver of Clare, of the arrears of Hugh de Godeston and Thomas Bory, formerly bailiffs there, £5 5s. 8¼d. by tally. Item delivered to the same Humphrey by the hands of William Paycok and William Dunkeslee, the present bailiffs there, £13 by tally.

Sum £18 5s. 8¼d.   audited

Sum of allowances and deliveries, £18 5s. 10¼d. And they owe £11 10s. 2½d. of which £5 due from William Brokhole for a fine for divers trespasses against the Lady which is respited at the Lady's order over his good behaviour until etc. And William Paycok and William Dunkeslee now bailiffs there owe £6 10s. 2½d. Profit of the borough this year £19 8s. 2¼d.

The Court of the Manor of Clare, 20 October 1338 and 7 April 1349
Court held on 20 October 1338   [TNA SC2/203/26]

[m. 1] Chilton[12]   Curia ibidem tenta die Martis proxima post festum Sancti Luce Evangeliste anno regni regis Edwardi tertii a conquest xij.

Essonia. Johannes in le Mor de communi [*secta*], per Ricardum filium Ricardi. Williemus le Gos versus Ricardum le Hert de placito transgressionis, per Thomam filium Ricardi.

Misericordia iijd. Ricardus Thihel ponit se in misericordia pro licencia concordanda cum Roberto Brion de placito transgressionis plegius ballivus.

Misericordia ijd. De primis plegiis Johannis Payn quia non habuerunt eum ad respondendum Henrico Alfred de placito debiti. Et preceptum est facere eum venire per meliores. Et predictus Henricus optulit se et habet diem.

Misericordia ijd. Willelmus le Breuster ponit se in misericordia pro dampno facto in pastura domine cum uno boviculo plegius Willelmus Sorel.

Chilton   Court held there on Tuesday next after the feast of St Luke the Evangelist 12 Edward III

Essoins. John in le Mor from common suit, by Richard son of Richard. William le Gos against Richard le Hert in a plea of trespass, by Thomas son of Richard.

Amercement 3d. Richard Thihel puts himself in mercy for licence to settle out of court with Robert Brion in a plea of trespass, pledge the bailiff.

Amercement 2d. From the first pledges of John Payn because they did not produce him to answer Henry Alfred in a plea of debt. And it is ordered to make him come by better [*pledges*]. And the said Henry appears and has a day.

Amercement 1d. William le Breuster puts himself in mercy for damage done in the Lady's pasture with 1 bullock, pledge William Sorel.

---

12   The manor of Clare was sometimes referred to in the court rolls as the manor of Stoke with Chilton.

Finis iiijd. Alicia atte Halle finem facit pro ingressu habendo in uno cotagio perquisito de Alicia Berde de feudo domine in Stoke.

Fine 4d. Alice atte Halle pays a fine to have entry to 1 cottage acquired from Alice Berde of the Lady's fee in Stoke.

Finis iijd. Willelmus le Walch finem facit pro ingressu habendo in uno cotagio perquisito de Willelmo le Hosebund de feodo domine in Stoke.

Fine 3d. William le Walch pays a fine to have entry to 1 cottage acquired from William le Hosebund of the Lady's fee in Stoke.

Fines pro secta vs. ixd. Alicia que fuit uxor Willelmi cum Barba, vjd., Johanna Wynter, vjd., Robertus Brion, vjd., Stephanus Sheldrake, vjd., Johannes Fretherik, iijd., Stephanus filius Willelmi Wathelok, iijd., Semanus Sheldrake, vjd., Ricardus Rolf, vjd., Willelmus Gynne, Ricardus Pally, iijd., Robertus Cokener, iijd., Willelmus le Parker, iijd., Willelmus Stonhard, vjd., Christophorus Page, vjd., Johannes Sevar, vjd. finem faciunt pro respecto secte curie habendo usque festum sancti Michaelis proximum futurum.

Fines for suit of court 5s. 9d. Alice who was wife of William with the Beard 6d., John Wynter 6d., Robert Brion 6d., Stephen Sheldrake 6d., John Fretherik 3d., Stephen son of William Wachelok 3d., Seman Sheldrake 6d., Richard Rolf 6d., William Gynne, Richard Pally 3d., Robert Cokener 3d., William le Parker 3d., William Stonhard 6d., Christopher Page 6d., John Sevare 6d., pay the fine to have respite of suit of court until next Michaelmas.

Preceptum est. Preceptum distringere Johanni filio Thihel pro ingressu in uno cotagio perquisito de Willelmo Walch de feodo domine in Stoke.

Order to distrain John son of John Thihel for entry to 1 cottage acquired from William Walch of the Lady's fee in Stoke.

Braciatores vs. ixd. De Katerina le Berde, js., uxore Michaelis Bertram, iijd., Alicia atte Halle, vjd., Elena Knappyng, js., Alicia Bylgold, vjd., Johanna le Breuster, vjd., Alicia Page, js., uxore Semani Sheldrake, vjd., uxore Stephani Page, vjd., braciatores pro assisa fracta. De Johanne Wulwy, iijd., Ricardo Brion, iijd., Petro in le Medwe, iijd., tassatoribus cervisie quia non fecerunt officium suum in misericordia.

Brewsters 5s. 9d. From Katherine le Berde 1s., the wife of Michael Bertram 3d., Alice atte Halle 6d., Elena Knappyng 1s., Alice Bylgold 6d., Joan le Breustere 6d., Alice Page 1s., the wife of Seman Sheldrake 6d., the wife of Stephen Page 6d., brewsters, for breaking the assize. Amercement 9d. From John Wulwy 3d., Richard Brion 3d., Peter in le Medwe 3d., ale-tasters, in mercy because they did not do their office.

Memorandum quod duo boves, duo bovetti et due juvence \qui appretiantur ad xls./ capti fuerunt in tenementis que fuerunt Johannis de Goldington pro Lijs. de redditu a retro deliberati sunt Waltero Crabbe, Willelmo Paycok, Rogero Page et Ricardo le Couherde usque proximam curiam tunc ad returnandum ad manerium de Clarett vel ad respondendum domine de predicto pretio.

Memorandum that 2 oxen, 2 steers and 2 heifers, valued at £2, taken in the tenements that used to be John de Goldington's for £2 12s. arrears of rent, were handed over to Walter Crabbe, William Paycok, Roger Page and Richard the Cowherd until the next court, then to be returned to the manor of Claret or to answer to the Lady for the aforesaid price.

Memorandum quod due vacce que appretiantur ad xvjs. capte fuerunt in tenementis que fuerunt Johannis de

Memorandum that 2 cows, valued at 16s., taken on the tenements that used to be John de Goldington's for £2 12s.

Goldyngton pro Lijs. de redditu a retro deliberate sunt Roberto de Chilton usque proximam curiam tunc ad returnandum ad manerium de Clarett vel ad respondendum domine de pretio predicto.

arrears of rent, were delivered to Robert de Chilton until the next court, then to be returned to the manor of Claret or to answer to the Lady for the aforesaid price.

Misericordia vjd. Juratores presentant quod Willelmus Crowe cepit iij garbas frumenti in autumpno de blado domine. Et quod Willelmus Gynne Webbe recepit predictum bladum ideo in misericordia.

Amercement 6d. The jurors present that William Crowe took 3 sheaves of wheat at harvest-time from the Lady's corn. And that William Gynne weaver received the said corn, so in mercy.

Summa xiijs. xd.

Sum 13s. 10d.

Chilton Extract from the court held there on Tuesday, 7 April, 23 Edward III, 1349[13]   [TNA SC2/203/28]

[m. 6] Day At the request of the parties a day was given to William de Chilton plaintiff and John Tyrel defendant \for licence to settle/ in a plea of debt at the next court without essoin.

It is still ordered to distrain Hugh Brom to answer the Lady concerning the fine for entry on 1 plot of land acquired from Thomas le Bowyer of the Lady's fee in Chilton.

Order Item to distrain John Spillet and John le Clerk of Bulleghe to reply to the Lady for trespass in Alsytheney.

Item to keep in the Lady's hands 1 plot of land that John Palli junior obtained from William le Wryghte of the Lady's fee in Chilton and to answer for the issues etc.

The whole homage has a day to certify the court concerning several trespasses in Pekesholm under penalty of ½ mark. And they now say that they cannot inquire about several trespasses there. So they are quit of the said penalty.

It is ordered to take into the Lady's hands 1 messuage with appurtenances in Chilton of which Roger Punge died seised etc. So it was ordered to keep the said tenement in the Lady's hands and answer for the issues etc. [Sentence added] It is ordered to keep Richard Punge until of age to do [fealty] to the Lady.

Day John atte Pyrei still has a day at the next court to hear judgement about the matter that he says he should not do if he married without the court's licence etc.

Relief 3½d. Alice Page who held 1 acre 3 roods of molmen land of the Lady by service of 3½d. has died. After her death it was found that Richard her son is the next heir and of full age. And he gives the Lady 3½d. in relief. And he does fealty.

It is ordered to take into the Lady's hands all the lands and tenements of which Geoffrey Pye died seised in Horsecroft and they are taken etc. So it is ordered to keep the said tenements in the Lady's hands etc.

Item it is ordered to take into the Lady's hands all the lands and tenements of which Christina Kempe died seised etc. And it was found that Joan her daughter is her heir etc. who is now dead. So it is ordered to take the said tenements into the Lady's hands and to answer for the issues etc.

Item it is ordered to take into the Lady's hands 1 messuage and 11 acres of land after the death of John Payn. And they are taken etc. And it is now found that William Payn is his heir etc. but remains away. And that the said tenement, worth 10s. a year,

---

13 All the court rolls of the manor of Clare for the spring and summer of 1349 are damaged and partly illegible.

owes heriot but he has no beast that can be taken from Erbury. And it is ordered to retain the said tenement in the Lady's hands and answer for the issues etc.

A cow taken as heriot Item 1 messuage and 15 acres of unfree land and 1 messuage and 3 acres of free land are taken into the Lady's hands after the death of John Sevare. And 1 cow, price 6s. 8d. is taken as heriot. And it is found that Agnes his daughter is his next heir, aged 1 year. It is ordered to keep these tenements in the Lady's hands because of the minority etc.

[*The rest of the entries for this court are damaged.*]

The Court of the Borough of Clare: Leet held at Clare on Tuesday before the Feast of the Apostles Philip and James, 11 Edward III, 29 April 1337 [TNA SC2/203/42] [m. 7] Fine 10s. The capital pledges present to the Lady 10s. of cert-money.

Amercement 6d. Item that William le Piper of Hundon committed house-breaking against William Brokhole and wounded the said William Brokhole for which the same William justly raised the hue and cry. Pledges, William Panecrek, John Tony.

[*Amercement*] 6d. Item that Stephen le Webbe assaulted Henry Gamelin on the royal highway and drew blood from Henry, for which Stephen's wife unjustly raised the hue and cry \on Henry/. Pledges, William Brokhole and John Wegg.

[*Amercement*] 6d. Item that William de Chilton assaulted John Scerle on the royal highway for which John justly raised the hue and cry \on William/. Pledges, William Sorel and John Asselote.

[*Amercement*] 6d. Item that William de Chilton assaulted and beat William Karpenter on the royal highway. Pledges, Hugh de Godelistone and John Dunkeslee.

[*Amercement*] 6d. Item that William Karpenter assaulted William de Chilton on the royal highway for which William de Chilton's wife justly raised the hue and cry. Pledges, Roger Syward and John Dunkeslee.

[*Amercement*] 6d. Item that John Stile assaulted John Egr' on the royal highway. Pledges, John Aylith, Henry Gamelin.

[*Amercement*] 1s. Item that Walter Chaure junior assaulted and beat John de Stokis on the royal highway for which the said John justly raised the hue and cry. Pledges, John Poke, Hugh de Godelistone.

Amercement 1s. Item that John de Stokis committed house-breaking against John de Pentelowe for which the same John de Pentelowe justly raised the hue and cry. Pledges Philip Poke and John Hegeyn.

Amercement 6d. Item that John Bacon \junior/ assaulted John Witlok on the royal highway and beat him. Pledges, John Bacon, Roger Grym.

Pardoned because of poverty. Item that John Witlok wounded John Bacon on the royal highway for which \Katherine/ mother of John Bacon justly raised the hue and cry. Pledges, William Pachelis and John Folke.

Item that William Bacon junior assaulted Margery le Chapman on the royal highway for which Margery justly raised the hue and cry. Pledges, John Wegg and John Bacon.

[*Amercement*] 6d. Item that William Bacon senior committed house-breaking against Alice Dalman and beat her for which the said Alice justly raised the hue and cry. Pledges, John de Ovintone and John Asselote.

[*Amercement*] 6d. Item that William Bacon carried away from the home of William in le Hale \by night/ 1lb. of candles for which the said William Bacon unjustly raised the hue and cry. Pledges, John Bacon and John Asselote.

[*Amercement*] 1s. Item that Walter Smith committed house-breaking against John

Stile for which the said John justly raised the hue and cry. Pledges, Peter Smith, John Hegeyn.

[*Amercement*] 6d. Item that Mauricia le Meller assaulted Agnes le Ry on the royal highway for which Agnes justly raised the hue and cry. Pledges, Robert Bakhous and John Asselote.

[*Amercement*] 1s. Item that John Cole assaulted John Facoun for which \Alice/ daughter of John Facoun unjustly raised the hue and cry. Pledges, Richard of the Wardrobe and John Dunkeslee.

[*Amercement*] 6d. Item that William with the Beard beat and drew blood from John Skinner of Stoke on the royal highway. Pledges, John Poke and William Sorel.

[*Amercement*] 6d. Item that Roger Syward beat Agnes le Crawe on the royal highway. Pledges, William le Schepherde and John Dunkeslee.

[**m. 7d**] The names of those selling unwholesome meat: John Bory 6d., Walter Chaure junior 6d., William Bory 6d., John Arnold 3d., Peter Beaucher 6d., William de Chilton 6d., Walter Chaure senior 6d., William Dylkis 6d., Laurence Chenoun 6d., Hamond Chenoun 3d., Thomas Finch 6d., Laurence Finch 6d., Henry Alfred 3d., Thomas Helewis 6d.

Tanners: John Huberd 6d., Peter Huberd 6d., John Syward 6d., William Paycok 6d., John Robilard 6d., John Grey 6d., John Quilter.

Hucksters: Cecilia Folke 3d., Elena Turbil 3d., Joan Bory 3d., Alice Say 3d., Alice de Stokis 3d., Katherine Baton 3d., Denise le Celer 3d., Matilda Mone 3d., Margery le Seler 3d., Christina de Yeldham 3d., Alice Raffrey 3d., Joan Chiping 3d.

Forestallers: Elias Bonting 6d., John Maynard 6d., William Fretherek 6d., Richard Rogeroun 6d.

Brewers [*illegible*]: Joan Tony 6d., Alice de Brokhole 6d., Alice Huberd 1s., Margaret Aylith 1s., Beatrix in le Hale 1s., Margery Sorel 1s., Alina Abraham 1s., Christina Huberd 6d., Joan atte Style 6d., Joan de Bolleyehalle 6d., Joan Everle 1s., John Quilter 6d., Alice Mone 1s., Matilda Pye [*illegible*], Denise de Rocwod 6d., Matilda Grey 1s., Margery of the Wardrobe 1s., Sarah de Pentelowe 1s., Matilda Crund 6d., Florence de Stremesham 6d., Agnes Broun 6d., Katherine de Clare 6d., Matilda Scot 6d. are brewers and sell contrary to the assize, so in mercy.

Bakers 4s. John Aylith 2s., Thomas Mone 1s., Maurice Miller 6d., Roger le Baxtere 6d. are bakers and sell contrary to the assize, so in mercy.

Amercement 6d. It is presented by 12 jurors *ex officio* that John Tony is a forestaller baker, so in mercy.

Amercement 2s. Item it is presented that the wife of Peter Smith brewed and sold contrary to the assize, so in mercy.

Amercement 3d. Item it is presented that the wife of John son of Alexander Quilter is a regrator and sells contrary to the assize, so in mercy.

Amercement ½ mark. All the capital pledges are fined for the said concealment.

[*Amercement illegible*] From Walter Crabbe, capital pledge, because he did not have John son of William Panecrek in his tithing, 3d. From Roger Syward, capital pledge, because he did not have John le Pottere [*illegible*]. From Thomas Mone, capital pledge, because he did not have William de Pentelowe, 3d. From John Hegein, capital pledge, because he did not have Robert Panecrek, Thomas Gascoyne and William Bavent in his tithing, 3d. each. From Robert atte Bachous, capital pledge, because he did not have William de Bodekesham and John son of William le Sutere. From Peter Smith, capital pledge, because he did not have Thomas de Wrattyng and

William Taylour, 3d. From William Paycok, capital pledge, because he did not have William son of Geoffrey with the Beard and John Beneyt of Ovington, 3d.[14]

Sum £3 4s. 2d.

[*Added at the end of m. 7d*] William Sorel beat and drew blood from William de Chilton on the royal highway, pledges John Hegein and John [*illegible*].

The Court of the Honour of Clare

Court of the honour of Clare held on Wednesday, the eve of the feast of the Apostles Simon and Jude, 7 Edward III, 27 October 1333 [TNA SC2/212/49]

[m. 1] Suffolk Fine 1s. 6d. Joan de Waldyngfeld pays a fine for having respite of suit of court until next Michaelmas.

Fine 2s. Richard Breaute pays a fine not to be distrained since Michaelmas for the suit of court demanded from the tenement of Walter son of Humphrey.

Fine 2s. Robert de Badele pays a fine for having respite of suit of court until Michaelmas.

Fine 6d. Thomas le Heyward pays a fine to have entry to 1 cottage acquired from Cassandra his mother of the Lady's fee in Wratting.

Fine 3d. Henry de Brunne pays a fine to have entry to 1 cottage acquired from Peter Miller of the Lady's fee in Wratting.

Fine ½ mark. Robert de Peyton and Andrew [*de*] Bures give the Lady for a fine not to be charged for suit of court which John de Munteny owes for a tenement in Waldingfield until next Michaelmas.

Fine 6d. Margery Turpet pays a fine to have entry on 1 acre of land acquired from Richard Bunne of the Lady's fee in Burstall.

Amercement 1s. The first pledges of Nicholas Sygo in mercy because they did not produce him to answer Peter Maynard in a plea of trespass with 2 complaints. It is ordered for them to be replaced by better [*pledges*].

Amercement 6d. The first pledges of Nicholas Sygo in mercy because they did not produce him to answer Simon son of William Maynard in a plea of trespass. And let them be replaced by better [*pledges*].

Amercement 6d. William Hythe did not prosecute John Campeden in a plea of trespass with 2 complaints. So he and his prosecution pledges in mercy.

Amercement 6d. From the earl of Oxford for default of suit of court.

Essex Fine 3s. 4d. John Taylour pays a fine to have entry on 7 acres of land acquired from Roger Megge of the Lady's fee in Thaxted.

Fine 1s. John Huchun pays a fine to have entry on 3 roods of wood and 1 rood of meadow acquired from John Bloumester and Luke de Naylyngherst of the Lady's fee in Halstead.

Fine 2s. Robert de Lessedewelle pays a fine to have entry on 4 acres of land acquired from William Cawe of the Lady's fee in Bulmer.

Amercement 3d. John Gok did not prosecute John le Reve in a plea of covenant, so he and his prosecution pledges in mercy. And the said John should go *sine die*.

Fine 1s. 8d. Matilda who was the wife of Richard de Saunford pays a fine to have respite of suit of court until Michaelmas.

It is ordered to attach John le Fermer to answer Peter le Someter of Pentlow in a plea of taking and detaining animals. And the said Peter is there and has a day. And it is ordered to attach John Muriel of Bottisham \distrained by 1 horse/ to answer

---

14 Some of the individual amercements are now missing.

Thurstan de Redeswell in a plea of debt with 3 complaints. And the said Thurstan is there and has a day.

Amercement 6d. From the tenants of Walter son son [*sic*] of Humphrey for default of suit of court.

Norfolk   Fine 1s. 3d. William Geldenelde pays a fine to have entry on 2½ acres of land acquired from Geoffrey atte Mor of the Lady's fee in Threxton.

Fine 2s. Richard Sayle pays a fine to have entry on 4 acres of land acquired from Robert Pope chaplain of the Lady's fee in Ashley.

Amercement 6d. John de Brunham did not prosecute the prior of Walsingham in a plea of trespass. So he and his prosecution pledges in mercy.

Amercement 6d. Geoffrey Devereye did not prosecute Ralph le Shepherde in a plea of trespass, so he and his prosecution pledges in mercy.

Amercement 3d. Ralph de Fyncham did not prosecute John atte Tounesende in a plea of trespass, so he and his prosecution pledges in mercy.

Amercement 3d. Nicholas de Ryngested did not prosecute John de Wulhous in a plea of trespass, so he and his prosecution pledges in mercy.

Amercement 3s. 4d. The first pledges of Richard son of Simon in mercy because they did not produce him at this court to make fine for entry on the manor of Pensthorpe with 12 knights' fees acquired from Nicola his mother. And let them be replaced by better [*pledges*].

Amercement 2s. The first pledges of Robert Dawes in mercy because they did not produce him to answer the Lady concerning the collection of the bailiff's amercements in the leet of Griston. And let them be replaced by better [*pledges*].

Amercement 4s. 6d. William de Barsham 6d., William Pouer 6d., John de Waubourne 3d., Roger Bacun 3d., Edmund Bacun 3d., John Dunde 6d., Robert Knyth 3d., John Walter 6d., Simon le Barker 3d., Thomas le Blexster 3d., John le Coupere 6d., Robert Bryde 3d., Richard Fraunke 3d. were summoned in the inquiry between John de Kellyng chaplain plaintiff and Walter de Holewell defendant in 2 complaints and they were not [*present*] etc., so in mercy. And it is ordered etc.

Amercement 3s. 3d. William Symund 6d., John Godwyne 3d., John Clerice 3d., John le [?]Coweward 3d., Alexander Waryn 3d., Robert Lesset 3d., Robert de Bungeye came previously, John Palmere 3d., John Bysshop 3d., John atte Mor 3d., Thomas Cacchevache 6d., Gerard le Chapman 3d. were summoned in the inquiry between John son of Richard plaintiff and Roger Caccheve defendant in a plea of trespass with 3 complaints. And it is ordered etc.

Fine 2s. Edmund de Goneville pays a fine to have respite of suit of court until Michaelmas.

Fine 1s. Matilda de Berford pays a fine not to be distrained before Michaelmas for demand of suit of court from the tenements that were of William de Berford.

Amercement 2s. From the tenants of William de Berford's land 6d., Thomas de Nerford pardoned, the tenants of Roland Romely's land 6d., Roger Cacchevache 6d., the tenants of the lands that were of Thomas de Hyndryngham pardoned by the Lady, John Howard 6d.

Suffolk   Relief £2 10s. It is found by inquiry that Thomas Passelewe who has died held of the Lady on the day he died divers tenements in Gazeley, Needham and Higham by service of ½ knight's fee and by suit of court every three weeks. And they say that Thomas Passelewe is the son and heir of the said Thomas and of full age. And he gives for relief etc. And it is ordered to distrain the said Thomas for homage and fealty.

Amercement 6d. From the tenants of the lands of Thomas Passelewe for default.

From the tenants of the lands that were of Walter son of Humphrey for the same. Amercement cancelled because of fine.

Order [*Illegible*] complains of Walter Potekyn in a plea of covenant, prosecution pledges John de Dunkeslee and the bailiff, so it is ordered to attach [*him*].

Order   Thurstan de Redeswell \he is produced/ complains of Peter le Taylour of Hundon in a plea of detinue, and the said Peter is summoned and does not come, so to be attached etc.

Fine 3s. 4d. John le Boteler pays a fine to have respite of suit of court till Michaelmas.

Order   It is still ordered to distrain Thomas de Cornerth knight for entry on tenements acquired of the Lady's fee in Poslingford. Item Robert de Peyton knight for the same. Item Roger Est for tenements in Ryngesele. Item Richard de Berkelowe for tenements in Kentford. Item Andrew de Halle for tenements in Stoke.

[**m. 1d**] John le Rotour and Cecily his wife were attached to answer Alan Baret \and Cecily his wife/ in a plea of detinue of 1 tapestry. They complain that on Monday after the feast of the Nativity of St John the Baptist in the fourth year of the present king Edward [*1331*] in Heacham next to Snettisham the said ~~Alan~~ Cecily handed over to the said Cecily wife of the said John 1 tapestry price 10s. to be delivered to the said Alan and Cecily whenever they wished to ask for it. The said Alan on Tuesday before the feast of St Nicholas in the sixth year of the present king Edward [*1332*] \asked/ the said John and Cecily to deliver the said tapestry to them and they would not deliver it but kept it etc. to the loss of the said Alan and Cecily of £1, and on this they produce their suit. And the said John and Cecily come and defend etc. And they say that they are guilty of nothing etc. and ask for an inquiry. So it is ordered to make the jury come.

Order It is ordered to carry out all orders not carried out in this court.

Affeerers: Henry de Honeden, William Engleys, William de Honeden.

   Sum £5 1s. 4d.; whereof Norfolk £1 2s. 10d.; Essex 8s. 9d.; Suffolk £3 9s. 9d.

Letter attached to the proceedings of the court of the honour of Clare held on Wednesday the eve of the Conception of the Blessed Virgin Mary 8 Edward III, 7 December 1334   [TNA SC2/212/49]

[**m. 11**] Elizabeth de Burgh Lady of Clare greets John de Hertford our steward of Clare. Because Thomas Passelewe has not been obedient, our bailiffs of our fees in Suffolk distraining him for relief for ½ knight's fee in Gazeley, and on this he has not been obedient because he only holds ¼ fee and William de Henmal the other ¼. We order you to enquire diligently if he holds the said ½ fee or ¼, and have us certified at the next court after Michaelmas so that he can be charged what is right, and in the meantime put in respite the demand for the said relief and for his homage. Be with God. Written at Clare on 11 September.

Court of the honour of Clare held on Wednesday after the feast of the Conversion of St Paul, at the beginning of 24 Edward III, 27 January 1350[15]   [TNA SC2/213/10]

[**m. 3**] Norfolk   The Lady granted to Thomas Crane of Walsingham custody of 1 messuage and 3 acres with appurtenances in Great Walsingham which were taken into the Lady's hands because of the minority of Stephen, son and heir of John

---

[15]   This court record is less well written than the earlier rolls and gaps were left in the layout, possibly reflecting administrative confusion in the aftermath of the Black Death.

Burgeys, who is 3 years old, together with Stephen's marriage, to have and to hold the said wardship and marriage with their profits until Stephen is of full age and to do the Lady the due and customary services. And he gives the Lady for the wardship £1 6s. 8d.

Farm 1s. 1 cottage containing in all 1 rood of land, once of Alan Smith, which is of the Lady's fee in Cley, is taken into the Lady's hands after Alan's death. This cottage is situated between the messuage once of William le Melnere and the land of William Smith. The cottage was taken into the Lady's hands as her escheat because there is no heir or anyone to succeed. So the said tenement is let to John son of Geoffrey Clerk of Cley for 1s. a year to be paid at Easter and Michaelmas in equal portions, to have and to hold to the said John and his heirs for ever by the same farm.

Fine 10s. Nicholas Trussebut pays a fine of 10s. to have entry on 1 messuage and 20 acres of land acquired from Walter Heresser of the Lady's fee in Shouldham.

Relief, £2 10s. John de Griston died seised of certain tenements of the Lady's fee in Griston and after his death his heir gives the Lady £2 10s. relief.

Relief, £2 10s. John de Boyland died seised of certain tenements of the Lady's fee in [*Little*] Ringstead by service of ½ knight's fee. After his death Richard de Boyland is his heir. And he gives the Lady £2 10s. relief.

Relief £2 10s. Blamich Lovel died seised of certain tenements of the Lady's fee in Walpole by service of ½ knight's fee. After his death Beatrix Lovel \his sister and heir/ gives £2 10s. relief.

Sum £9 6s. 8d.

Suffolk   The Lady grants to John son of John Sly ½ acre of land with 2 cottages built on it, with appurtenances, in Mildenhall. To hold and to have the said tenement with its appurtenances to the said John for the whole of his life. Rendering for it 2s. 6d. a year at the 4 usual terms in equal portions. And he gives the Lady 6d. for entry-fine.

Matilda Hern held of the Lady \1 messuage/ [*and*] 7 acres of land in Tuddenham. These were taken into the Lady's hands because of the minority of John, Matilda's son and heir who is 15 years old. And the said tenements with the heir are handed over to John Mallyng and Agnes his wife to keep until the heir is of full age for 15s. cash down.

Sum 15s. 6d.

Essex   Amercement 1s. The first pledges of [*blank*] wife of Philip le Despenser in mercy because they did not produce her to answer the Lady concerning an entry-fine for a tenement acquired from the same Philip of the Lady's fee in Toppesfield.

Amercement 3d. The first pledges of Matilda who was wife of Thomas le Ferour in mercy because they did not produce her to answer Simon Sauser in a plea of debt.

Amercement 3d. Thomas Dyke did not prosecute Robert le Parker in a plea of trespass. So he and his prosecution pledges in mercy.

Fine 5s. Ralph and John, sons of Thomas de Boyton, pay a fine of 5s. to have entry on 15 acres of land acquired from the same Thomas of the Lady's fee in Hempstead.

Amercement[16]   John le Bourchier owes suit of court and makes default. So in mercy.

Sum 6s. 6d.   audited

---

[16]   No sum of money is given.

Account of William Lengleys junior, bailiff of the honour of Clare in the county of Suffolk, from Michaelmas 12 Edward III to the morrow of Michaelmas next following 13 Edward III, 1338–9   [TNA/SC6/1110/6]

[m. 1] Arrears   The same is debited with £8 8s. 1¼d. of the arrears of his last account of the preceding year.

Sum £8 8s. 1¼d.   audited

Rents and farms   From the farm of tenements in Bury St Edmunds nothing hence-forth because Suzanne de Neketon has the same tenements of the Lady's gift for life. From 15s. 4d. rent a year in Mildenhall. £1 rent a year in Lelleseye. £1 rent of lands and tenements of John de Ingham in Cowlinge at Michaelmas term. 4d. rent from the tenement once of Richard de Cornerth at the same term. 6d. rent from the tenement once of Robert de Bradefeld in Lelleseye at the same term. 6d. rent from the tenement once of Richard de Cokefelde at the same term. 2s. rent from Robert de Abethorp for 1 sore sparrowhawk at the feast of St Peter ad Vincula [*1 August*]. From the farm of Southwold nothing this year because it is in the Lady's hands and the bailiff there is answerable for the issues this year. £1 from a yearly rent in Priditon because of the minority of the heir of John de St Philibert. From the farm of the custody of Thomas de Burgh's lands in Hawkedon because of the minority of Thomas's heir, nothing because William de Laufare, the Lady's Butler has the custody of the Lady's gift until the full age of the heir.

Sum £3 18s. 11d.   audited

Issues of the tenements in Mildenhall   From £1 5s. 4d. received from herbage of the meadow sold at Mildenhall this year. 17s. received from 8qr 4b. of barley remaining on his last account of the previous year from the farm of 8 acres of land with liberty of the fold in Mildenhall sold for the provisions of the Lady's house-hold, price 2s. a qr.

Sum £2 2s. 4d.   audited

Perquisites of courts   £8 0s. 3d. from the perquisites of courts this year. 3s. received from the perquisites of the leet of Denston this year.

Sum £8 3s. 3d.   audited
Sum total of receipts and arrears £22 12s. 7¼d.   audited

Fee   For the fee of the bailiff this year, £1 6s. 8d.

Sum £1 6s. 8d.   audited

Pardon to William Bret of a fine by the Lady's letter, 6s. 8d.

Sum 6s. 8d.   audited

Delivery of money to John de Lenne Wardrober of the Lady for 8qr 4b. of barley sold for the provisions of the Lady's household, 17s. by 1 acquittance. Item to Henry de Thrillawe receiver of Clare, £19 16s. by 1 acquittance.

Sum £20 13s.

Sum of all expenses and deliveries £22 6s. 4d. And he owes 6s. 3¼d. He answers for this in his account of the bailiwick of Essex.

Profit this year £12 17s. 10d.

[m. 1d] Barley   The same man answers for 8qr 4b. of barley remaining from his last account. And for 8qr 4b. of barley received from the farm of 8 acres of land and the liberty of 1 fold in Mildenhall at Michaelmas term, this year the second, let for 7 years, to be paid every year at Michaelmas at the end of the year.[17] From the farm of 1 acre of land there that lies waste and is of no value.

---

[17]   Michaelmas was the end of the financial year.

Sum 17qr
Of this 8qr 4b. sold as below. And there remain 8qr 4b. of barley.   audited

Letter from Elizabeth de Burgh to the auditors, 12 February 1343

[TNA SC6/1109/9]

[m. 1] Elizabeth de Burgh, Lady of Clare, to the auditors of our accounts, greeting. It has been testified before us and our council by our dear esquire John de Hertford, our steward of Clare, and by others of our council that £11 2s. of the amercements of divers people who were amerced in our leet of Guilden Morden in the time of William Lengleys junior formerly our bailiff cannot be levied because the people who committed the trespass for which they were amerced had nothing in our lordship by which they could be attached, and that 15s. 10d. of the amercements of outsiders amerced in our leet of Bottisham because they overcharged the marsh there with their beasts also cannot be levied for the above reason. We [*therefore*] order that all the above money be allowed to the said William on his account and that he be accounted quit by warranty of this. May God keep you. Written at Clare on 12 February, 17 Edward III.
Allowed.

VI

PATRONAGE AND INFLUENCE

Almsgiving
Distribution to the Poor, 1331–2   [TNA E101/91/27]
[m. 4] For 23qr 2b. of wheat bought for distribution to the poor on 2 occasions this year, £8 15s. 6d., as in the roll of particulars. 14,100 red and white herring for the same poor, £4 1s. 3½d.

Distribution to the Poor for the Soul of Sir Edward de Monthermer, 1339[1]
                                        [TNA E101/92/12] **[m. 9]**
Furnished for the distribution to the poor for the soul of Sir Edward de Monthermer on 11 December 8qr of wheat from Erbury which rendered 2,497 loaves. And they were expended. Item expended 4,280 herring from stock.

Distribution to the Poor, 1358–9   [TNA E101/94/1]
Saturday, 27 October. Moreover paid to 848 poor people at Clare, Hundon and Bardfield for the [*previous*] month, £3 10s. 8d. [*The same entry was made on Saturdays, 24 November, 22 December, 19 January, 16 February, 16 March, 13 April, and 11 May.*] Saturday, 8 June: Moreover paid to 540 poor people in London and 84 poor people at Standon for the [*previous*] month, £2 12s.[2] [*The same entry was made on Saturdays, 6 July, and 3 August*]. Saturday, 31 August: Moreover delivered to the Almonry for distribution and paid to 548 poor people in London and 84 at Standon. Sum of money £2 12s.; of stock 8s.; of both £3. Sunday, 29 September: Moreover expenses of 4,900 poor people in the parts of Clare, 2,255 horses and 175 hackneys there. Sum of money £35 19s. 2½d.; of stock £24 15s. 5d.; of both £60 14s. 7½d.
                                        audited

Wardship and Education
Extract from the Wardrobe and Household Account, 5–6 Edward III, 1331–2
                                        TNA E101/91/27]
[m. 4] The Lady's Chamber   The same man accounts for 22 pairs of shoes bought for the Lady, shoes for Roger Damory, Robert Sturmy and Robert de Wyveton who are in the Lady's wardship, linen cloth for the same, nails, hooks, candlesticks and other small items for the children, £1 16s. 2d.

---

[1] The Lady's half-brother who died of his wounds in December 1339 early on in the Hundred Years War; he was buried in Clare priory.
[2] The Lady spent the summer months in London in her house in the outer court of the Minoresses' convent outside Aldgate. The demesne manor of Standon was on her route from Clare to London.

Expenses of student-clerks The same accounts for the commons[3] of Peter de Ereswell, clerk, William d'Oxwik, John Chelrey and Hugh de Colingham living in the Bench in London, of Thomas Doubrigge and John de Teukesbury, students at Oxford, with £1 for the salary of the master of the same, £17 8s. 2¼d. as contained in the book of particulars. And for cloth, linen, hose and shoes for the same clerks, £2 9s. ½d.

Sum £19 17s. $2^3/_4$d.

Extract from the Wardrobe and Household Account, 1336–7   [TNA E101/92/4]
[m. 9] Foreign expenses   For the expenses of 2 grooms and 2 horses fetching the little clerks at Cambridge, 1s. 1d. For the expenses of 2 horses and 1 groom taking the little clerks to Cambridge with the same clerks' expenses on the way, 1s.

Licence for Elizabeth de Burgh to make a Grant to University Hall, Cambridge, 1336[4]   [TNA C66/187]
[m. 33] Licence [notwithstanding the statute of mortmain]. The King to all people to whom the present letters come, greeting. Wishing to show special grace to the master and scholars of University Hall, Cambridge, we have granted and given licence on behalf of us and our heirs as far as in us lies to our beloved kinswoman Elizabeth de Burgh that she may give and assign the advowson of the church of Litlington in the county of Cambridge to the aforesaid master and scholars to have and to hold to them and their successors for ever. And we have given special licence to the same master and scholars that they may receive that advowson from the said Elizabeth and appropriate the said church and hold it appropriated to their own uses to them and their successors for ever according to the present letters. Not wishing that the said Elizabeth or her heirs or the said master and scholars or their successors by reason of the said statutes should be molested or oppressed over this in any way by us or our heirs, yet saving the due and customary services to the chief lords of the fee. In witness of this we have had these letters patent drawn up. Witnessed by the King at Westminster on 12 March.

Licence for Elizabeth de Burgh to make a Grant to Clare Hall, Cambridge, 1346   [TNA C66/217]
[m. 22] The King to all people to whom the present letters come, greeting. Know that when we formerly granted and gave licence by our letters patent on behalf of us and our heirs as far as in us lies to our beloved kinswoman Elizabeth de Burgh that she could give and assign the advowson of the church of [Great] Gransden in the county of Huntingdon, which is held of us in chief as is said, to our beloved dean and chapter of the church of St Paul in London to have and to hold to the same dean and chapter and their successors for ever, as is more fully contained in our letters, and now Elizabeth has petitioned us, since this has not been put into effect, that we should permit her to give and grant the advowson of the said church to our beloved in Christ the master and scholars of Clare Hall in Cambridge to have and to hold to

---

3 I.e. food and drink.
4 For the context of the two licences, see A.C. Chibnall, *Richard de Badew and the University of Cambridge 1315–1340* (Cambridge, 1963), pp.37–41. University Hall was founded by Richard de Badew, the university chancellor, in 1326. Ten years later, the Lady was approached for financial help and in response granted the advowson of Litlington church. The Lady secured full rights as patron in 1346 and from this time the name Clare Hall was used for the foundation.

the same master and scholars and their successors for ever. We wishing to consent to Elizabeth's petition have granted and given licence to Elizabeth on behalf of us and our heirs as far as in us lies that she may give and grant the advowson of the said church to the aforesaid master and scholars to have and to hold to them and their successors of us and our heirs for ever. We have also granted of our special grace and given licence to Elizabeth on behalf of us and our heirs as far as in us lies that she may give and grant the advowson of the church of Duxford, which is not held of us as is said, to the aforesaid master and scholars to have and to hold to them and their successors for ever. Similarly we have given special licence to the same master and scholars that they may receive the advowson of the said churches from Elizabeth and appropriate those churches and hold them thus appropriated to their own uses to them and their successors for ever according to the present letters notwithstanding the statute of mortmain. Not wishing that Elizabeth or her heirs or the said master or his successors by reason of the aforesaid should be molested, troubled or oppressed in any way by us or our heirs, justices, escheators, sheriffs or other bailiffs or officials whosoever, yet saving to us and our heirs and the other chief lords of that fee the due and customary services. In witness of this we have had these letters patent drawn up. Witnessed by the King at Portchester on 15 June.

The Lady's Interventions on behalf of Herself and Members of her Council
Commission of *oyer and terminer* for Elizabeth de Burgh, 17 February 1343
[TNA C66/209]
[m. 32d] The King to his beloved and faithful men, Andrew de Bures and Warin de Bassingbourne, greeting. Since it has been given to us to understand \by the fine of £1/ that many goods and chattels of our beloved kinswoman, Elizabeth de Burgh, of no small worth, found at Clare in Suffolk, Walsingham in Norfolk, Bardfield in Essex and Brandon in Hertfordshire[5] by several malefactors and disturbers of our peace were feloniously taken and carried away, to the serious loss of our kinswoman and contrary to our peace. Not wishing that the said felonies should remain unpunished, we have assigned you to enquire by the oath of honest and lawful men of the said counties, from whom the truth of the matter may be better known, concerning the names of the malefactors who perpetrated the aforesaid [*offences*] and of their followers, receivers and maintainers, and concerning other articles touching the truth more fully. And so we order you to provide for those inquiries. [*The malefactors were to be arrested and imprisoned, and would appear before the commissioners and the juries summoned by the sheriffs.*]

Commission of *oyer and terminer* for Elizabeth de Burgh, 4 December 1357, for £1
paid in the hanaper [TNA C66/253]
[m. 5d] The King to his beloved and faithful men, William de Shareshull, William de Notton, Nicholas Damory and John \de/ Cavendish, greeting. We have received a serious complaint from Elizabeth de Burgh that when she had certain cattle taken by William Brokhole, her serjeant, at Barton [*Mills*] next to Mildenhall for customs and services due to her, and the same William wanted to drive those cattle from there to Elizabeth's manor of Clare and impound them there according to the law and custom of our realm of England, John Shardlow knight and Katherine his wife, William the parson of Barton church, William the parson's cook of Barton, John

---

5   It is likely that Standon, Hertfordshire, was meant; Brandon was a demesne manor in Warwickshire.

Wodereve chaplain, William de Brandon chaplain, Philip de Horkele, John Gerveys, Ivo de Ingham, Bartholomew Holme of Mildenhall and William Ketele of Mildenhall, and some other malefactors and disturbers of our peace pursued William Brokhole from the said vill of Barton to Herringswell with force and arms, with the hue and cry raised, and rescued the said cattle there, and attacked William Brokhole there and beat, wounded, imprisoned and maltreated him so that he despaired of his life, and kept him in prison there in the stocks until the same Elizabeth made a fine with the said John etc. for £5 to have her serjeant freed. From this, the same Elizabeth lost the serjeant's service for a long time, and they took and carried away Elizabeth's goods and chattels found there to the value of £40, and committed other outrages against her to her serious loss and contrary to our peace. And since we do not wish the said trespasses so perpetrated to remain unpunished, we have assigned three or two of you, of whom one is to be the said William or William. We wish our justices to enquire by the oath of honest and lawful men of Suffolk, from whom the truth of the matter may be better discovered, concerning the names of the said malefactors who together with the said John etc. perpetrated the said trespasses and concerning the truth of those trespasses more fully, and to hear and determine the same trespasses according to the law and custom of our kingdom of England.[6]

Petition on behalf of Robert de Scales granted, 10 April 1317   [TNA C66/147]
[m. 17] The King to all his bailiffs and faithful men to whom the present letters come, greeting. Know that at the request of our beloved kinswoman, Elizabeth de Burgh, we have granted on behalf of us and our heirs as far as in us lies to our beloved Robert de Scales that he should have this liberty for life viz. that he should not be put on any assizes, juries or inquests, and that he should not be made our sheriff, coroner or other official against his will. And so we order you not to molest or oppress [him]. In testimony of this we have had these our letters patent drawn up. Witnessed by the King at Clarendon on 10 April, by writ of privy seal.

Petition on behalf of Andrew de Bures granted, 8 August 1343   [TNA C54/174]
[m. 22d] The King to his Treasurer and Barons of the Exchequer, greeting. Since at the request of our beloved kinswoman, Elizabeth de Burgh, on whose business our beloved and faithful Andrew de Bures is engaged, and who for that reason cannot appear in person before you at the Exchequer on the octaves of Michaelmas next, according to the notice you gave him, to render his account for the last time when he was one of the collectors of wool in Suffolk, granted to us by the community of our realm of England, to answer to us there concerning what is demanded from him by summons of the Exchequer and from the time when he was supervisor of weights and measures in the said county, together with others appointed by our commission. We have granted the same Andrew that he can make the report on this occasion by suitable attorneys. And so we order you to admit Richard de Cressewell and William de Longele whom the said Andrew in our presence made his attorneys in his place to make the report, or one of them if both cannot be present in Andrew's place, and not to molest or oppress the same Andrew in anything by reason of his not coming to the Exchequer at the said octaves on this occasion. Witnessed by the King at Corfe on 8 August.

---

6   The next entry in the Patent Rolls comprised a commission with the same commissioners on behalf of William Brokhole.

Petition on behalf of Warin de Bassingbourne granted, 22 May 1348

[TNA C66/225]

[m. 38] The King to all his bailiffs and faithful men to whom the present letters come, greeting. Know that of our special grace and at the request of our beloved kinswoman, Elizabeth de Burgh, we have pardoned Warin de Bassingbourne, sheriff of Cambridge, whatsoever appertains to us for the escape of the undernamed prisoners viz. Walter Verdon of Draycote and John de Turvey, convicted clerks, Adam Pigas of Waresley, Oliver Kempe of Bury St Edmunds, John de Roudon, John Culpoun of Orton Longueville and John Baret of Stotfold, approvers, and Thomas de Glatton of Ramsey, Alexander Bocher of Impington, John Magottessone of Dullingham, Ralph de Geddyng and Ralph son of Adam of Ridgewell from the prison in Cambridge castle while the same Warin had custody of the prison and of the same prisoners. Not wishing that the same Warin should be troubled or oppressed in anything concerning the aforesaid by us or our heirs or our officials whosoever. In testimony of this we have had these our letters patent drawn up. Witnessed by the King at Westminster on 22 May, by writ of privy seal.

Licence for a Grant to John de Lenne, 12 December 1351[7] [TNA C66/235]

[m. 5] The King to all to whom the present letters come, greeting. Know that of our special grace and in return for £10 which Elizabeth de Burgh will pay us we have granted and given licence on behalf of us and our heirs, as far as in us lies, to the same Elizabeth and to John Bardolf and Elizabeth his wife that they may give and grant the manor of Ilketshall in the county of Suffolk with its appurtenances, which is held of us in chief, to John de Lenne, to have and to hold to the same John de Lenne for life of us and our heirs by the due and customary services, by rendering yearly to the same Elizabeth de Burgh for her lifetime £20 at Easter and Michaelmas in equal portions. So that if the same Elizabeth dies in John de Lenne's lifetime, then the same John de Lenne will render every year the said £20 to the said John Bardolf and Elizabeth and the heirs of Elizabeth, John's wife, at the above feasts, and so that after John de Lenne's death the said manor with appurtenances will revert to the said Elizabeth, John Bardolf and Elizabeth, and the heirs of Elizabeth, John's wife, to have and to hold of us and our heirs by the said services for ever. And similarly we have given special licence to the same John de Lenne that he may receive and hold the said manor and its appurtenances of Elizabeth, John Bardolf and Elizabeth for life of us and our heirs by the aforesaid services, by rendering to the said Elizabeth de Burgh for her lifetime and after her death to John Bardolf and Elizabeth his wife £20 at the above feasts. So that after John de Lenne's death the said manor with appurtenances will revert wholly to the said Elizabeth, John Bardolf and Elizabeth, and the heirs of Elizabeth, John's wife, as is aforesaid in the wording of the present letters. Not wishing that John de Lenne or the said Elizabeth, John Bardolf and Elizabeth or the heirs of Elizabeth, John's wife, by reason of the aforesaid should be interfered with, molested or troubled in any way by us or our heirs, our justices, escheators, sheriffs or other bailiffs whosoever. In testimony of this we have had these our letters patent drawn up. Witnessed by the King at Westminster on 12 December. And the said £10 has been paid in the hanaper.

---

7   Ilketshall and Clopton, Suffolk, were granted to Elizabeth de Burgh by Edward III in return for Kennington and Vauxhall, Surrey, which had been granted to Roger Damory and Elizabeth jointly by Edward II. Elizabeth Bardolf was their daughter and therefore heiress to the property; *CChR*, IV, pp.426–7.

Patronage of Religious Houses: Clare priory
Grant to the Priory of Augustinian Friars at Clare by Roger Damory and Elizabeth
de Burgh, 26 October 1320   [BL Harley MS 4835]
[fol. 7r] On Sunday before the feast of All Saints in the fourteenth year of the reign
of King Edward son of King Edward. The agreement between Sir Roger \Damory/
and Elizabeth his wife on one side and the prior and convent of the order of St
Augustine of Clare on the other side viz. that with the assent and consent of the
Provincial Prior P̶r̶i̶o̶r̶ of the same order in England and of the said prior and convent
of Clare they have granted on behalf of themselves and their successors that two
friars should live in Clare castle, singing daily masses, as long as the said Roger
and Elizabeth live, without any difficulty or contradiction. And the said Roger and
Elizabeth wish and grant that the prior and convent should receive every year ten
quarters of wheat from the barn of the said Roger and Elizabeth at Clare and ten
quarters of malt from the issues of the mill next to the friars by the hands of the
reeve of the same as long as they live as is aforesaid viz. at the feasts of Easter and
Michaelmas in equal portions. And if it should happen that the said friars should
cease from the said celebration with the agreement of the prior and convent, they
will receive none of the said wheat or malt but are excluded from all [legal] action
over this. In testimony of this they have put their seals alternately on the parts of
the indenture.

Extract from the Wardrobe and Household Account, 1331–2   [TNA E101/91/27]
[m. 4] Expenses of the friars   The same man accounts for ½ black cloth, 11½ ells
of blanket, 24 ells of worstead [and] 6 ells of linen for the habits of 2 friars of the
order of St Augustine living in the Lady's household, and 20 pairs of shoes bought
for the same, dyeing cloth, [and] sewing cloaks, scapulars and tunics for the same,
with 2 pairs of spurs, £4 3s. 1d., as contained in the book of particulars.
    Sum, £4 3s. 1d.

Anglesey Priory
Establishment of a Chantry, 28 February 1332[8]
                            [Monasticon Anglicanum, VI, i, pp.395–6]
This indenture testifies that when the most excellent Prince and our Lord Sir Edward,
illustrious King of England, third from the Conquest, by his letters patent granted
and gave licence to his beloved kinswoman, Elizabeth de Burgh, and she could give
and assign 20 librates of rent, coming from the manor, messuage and 24 acres of
land which formerly were hers, in the vill of Lakenheath, and also from the manor
of the prior of Ely, in the same vill, to her beloved in Christ, the prior and convent
of Anglesey, to be received from the hands of the prior of Ely and his successors
for ever, to have and to hold to them and their successors of the said Elizabeth
and her heirs in free, pure and perpetual alms. And [the King granted and gave
licence] to the same prior and convent of Anglesey that they could receive the said
20 librates of rent from the said Elizabeth and could hold to them and their successors of Elizabeth and her heirs in free, pure and perpetual alms, as is contained in
the Lord King's letters. We therefore, the prior and convent of Anglesey, seised of
the said rent by licence of the Lord King and by Elizabeth's gift and assignment in

---

8   For mortmain licences connected with this grant, see CPR, 1327–30, pp.61, 243; CPR, 1330–4,
    pp.39, 101, 159.

the above form, have granted on behalf of us and our successors that we are bound to find in our house two suitable secular chaplains to be chosen by us, the prior and convent of Anglesey and our successors, to celebrate divine service every day at the altar of the Holy Cross in our church of Anglesey for ever for the good state of Elizabeth while she lives and for her soul when she has departed from this light and also for the souls of her ancestors and heirs and all the faithful departed. And also, in order to establish the said chantry for ever, we, the said prior and convent of Anglesey, have granted on behalf of us and our successors that we would find the said chaplains a suitable house within the enclosure of our priory, and find them sufficient and adequate food at our table and provide for each of them their robes and other necessaries out of the said rent of £20 of silver at the feasts of Michaelmas and Easter every year in equal portions, or if it seems to us more expedient we have granted for us and our successors every year that we would render to the said chaplains at that time twelve marks to be received for ever out of the said rent from our hands and those of our successors at two terms of the year in equal portions, namely yearly at the feasts of Michaelmas and Easter, unless we can agree on a smaller sum with the said suitable chaplains. And if it should happen that the said chaplains, or one of them, are ill so that they, or he, cannot celebrate divine service, we bind ourselves and our successors to conduct the said chantries by our religious brothers of our house until he, or they, are better, or if it should happen that the said chaplains or one of them die or are ill – may this never happen – so that we cannot appoint the secular chaplains before the feast of Michaelmas then next following, we bind ourselves and our successors to carry out the said chantries or chantry by our brothers in the aforesaid form until the feast of Michaelmas then next following, at which time we bind our secular chaplains or secular chaplain to provide for their lapse when it happens. And if it should happen that we or our successors fail to support the said chaplains, as is aforesaid, either for 3 weeks or a month to close down the said chantry contrary to the aforesaid form, then we and our successors are bound to grant to the said Elizabeth, her heirs or assigns £20 a year to be received yearly in equal portions at the said two terms of the year, namely Easter and Michaelmas, from all our lands and tenements in Bottisham which are of Elizabeth's fee; and that the said Elizabeth and her heirs or assigns may distrain in all our lands and tenements for the arrears of the said rent. And we, the said Elizabeth, wish and have granted on behalf of us and our heirs that the residue of the total rent of £20 should remain for ever to support the office of kitchener of the said house, for the increase of dishes of the prior and convent, and to support the said prior and convent and their successors over the burdens and necessaries of the house in equal portions, according to the disposition of the prior and convent of the time. And we, the said Elizabeth de Burgh, have granted on behalf of us and our heirs that if the said manor, messuage and land from which the rent of £20 comes, or part of the same manor, messuage and land, should be recovered from the prior and convent of Ely or their successors by us or our heirs or others whosoever, through our failing or that of our heirs by reason of prior right or [legal] action, as a result of which the prior of Anglesey or his successors cannot get or obtain the said rent or part of the same rent from the hands of the prior of Ely, then the prior and convent of Anglesey and their successors for ever should be quit of the said chantry in return for the proportion of rent thus annulled, and from the portion of the said £20 in which the prior and convent of Anglesey are bound to us and our heirs, as above, from the tenements they hold of us in Bottisham. In testimony of this matter, both Elizabeth and the prior and convent of Anglesey alternately affix their seals. Witnesses: Sir Henry de

135

Ferrers, Sir John de Cambridge, Sir Alexander de Walesham, Sir John de Wauton, Sir Thomas de Cheddeworth, Robert de Fenkeriche and others. Given at Anglesey on Saturday next after the feast of St Matthias the apostle, in the sixth year of the reign of King Edward, third after the Conquest.

Changes made to the Chantry, 24 April 1355

[Monasticon Anglicanum, VI, i, p.396]

This indenture, made between the most honourable lady, Lady Elizabeth de Burgh, Lady of Clare, on one side, and the prior and convent of the house of Anglesey on the other side, testifies that when the aforesaid prior and convent were charged for ever with finding two chaplains to celebrate divine service in their church of Anglesey for the said Lady Elizabeth and her ancestors in return for certain rent granted them for this by the said Elizabeth for ever, to be taken from the prior and convent of Ely from certain lands and tenements in Lakenheath in the county of Cambridge [*sic*] which the prior and convent of Ely hold by gift for ever of the said Lady Elizabeth. And at the new request of Lady Elizabeth, the aforesaid prior and convent of Anglesey have granted by their deed to Master Robert de Spaldyng a yearly pension of £5, to be taken for his lifetime from year to year at the feasts of Michaelmas and Easter in equal portions. The said Elizabeth wishes and grants for herself and her heirs that the said prior and convent of Anglesey be discharged of finding one chaplain for the time when they remain charged with the said pension of £5 for the said Master Robert in the above form. And to meet the full pension of £5, the said Lady Elizabeth wishes and grants for herself and her heirs to the said prior and convent of Anglesey 8s. 1d. rent a year which she used to take from the hands of Agnes Geffrei, her tenant in the vill of Bottisham. And that the said prior and convent of Anglesey should have and hold their lands discharged of 11s. 11d. rent a year which they hold of the said Lady Elizabeth in the vill of Bottisham for the time that they remain charged with the pension of £5 for the said Master Robert, abovenamed, in the aforesaid form. Saving in every way to the said Lady Elizabeth and her heirs all other services due from the said prior and convent of Anglesey and Agnes Geffrei, her tenants, for the lands and tenements which they hold of the said Lady Elizabeth in the vill of Bottisham. In witness of this matter the aforesaid Lady Elizabeth on one side and the prior and convent of Anglesey on the other side have alternately fixed their seals to these indentures. Given at Bardfield on 24 April, in the twenty-ninth year of the reign of King Edward, third since the Conquest.

Walsingham Priory and the Foundation of a House of Franciscan Friars
Mortmain Licence for making a Franciscan foundation, 1 February 1347

[TNA C66/220]

[m. 28] The King to all to whom the present letters come, greeting. Know that when our beloved Elizabeth de Burgh, inflamed by the fervour of charity and devotion, was disposed with the Lord's support to found a house for the habitation of friars of the order of Friars Minor in the vill of Walsingham, we, commending Elizabeth's pious intention and so that we might join with her in so pious an undertaking, primarily wishing to support Elizabeth in pursuing this, by our special grace have granted and given licence on behalf of ourselves and our heirs, as far as in us lies, to the said Elizabeth that she may found a house of this kind on a certain plot in the said vill for the fitting habitation of this type of friars minor, and give and assign that plot with appurtenances to the friars of the said order to have and to hold to them and their successors for ever. And similarly we have given special licence

136

to the same friars that they can receive the said plot with appurtenances from the said Elizabeth to hold to them and their successors for habitation of this kind for ever, as is aforesaid, according to the present letters, notwithstanding the statute of mortmain. Not wishing that the said Elizabeth or her heirs or the said friars or their successors by reason of the aforesaid or of the said statute should be interfered with or oppressed in any way over this by us or our heirs. Yet saving to the capital lords of that fee the due and customary services. In testimony of this we have had these our letters patent drawn up. Witnessed by the Keeper at Reading on 1 February, by writ of privy seal.

Petition of the Prior and Canons of Walsingham to Elizabeth de Burgh[9]

[BL Cotton MS Nero E vii, fols 160r–161r]

[fols 160r–161r] To the honourable and venerable Lady of Clare, if it should please your ladyship, her humble priests, the prior and canons of her priory of Walsingham, demonstrate that if any place within the parishes of Great or Little Walsingham should be granted to the friars minor or any other order of mendicants to build on, and by virtue of that grant they put up a building and live there, innumerable losses and injuries will occur as a result to the said priory, as will be shown more openly on inspection of the underwritten articles.

First it must be observed that by the construction of buildings and walls within the said parishes the fruits of the earth and of the place, from which tithes are accustomed to be paid, will be destroyed. And the said place and the land thus built on will be ruined, so that from henceforth tithes will not come, and thus permanent injury is done to the aforesaid parish churches.

Item another danger of greater weight must be observed, that the said friars in building, inhabiting and celebrating services within the said parishes, will attract to themselves the parishioners of the same churches, and turn their hearts away from their parish churches, as with masses and hearing confessions; so that where the same parishioners, out of the devotion which they bore towards their parish churches, used to hear masses in the same churches, and on that occasion used to help the same churches with many benefits, and made their confessions to their parish chaplains to whom the cure of their souls is committed, they will completely abandon the churches themselves and the parish chaplains for the aforesaid and other matters in which the same parishioners were and are bound to the said churches.

Item it must be observed that whereas the said parishioners used to hear their masses almost every day in their parish churches, at which churchings of women and burials of men commonly occurred, and made their offerings out of devotion at these churchings and burials, they will move away from these services in their parish churches as a result of the enticement and smooth and deceitful words of the said friars.

Item it must be observed that the aforesaid friars on the aforesaid occasion convert many other parochial rights to their own singular and common uses, to the

---

9   The petition is undated, but is likely to have been sent to the Lady when her plans first became known and certainly before she received the mortmain licence of 1 February 1347. French and Latin versions of the petition were copied into the cartulary of Walsingham priory; the Latin version contains an additional paragraph. The petition is printed in J. Lee-Warner, 'Petition of the Prior and Canons of Walsingham, Norfolk, to Elizabeth, Lady of Clare, *c*.1345', *Archaeological Journal*, XXVI (1869), pp.166–73.

injury of the said parish churches, since the same friars can have nothing of their own or in common, according to their assertion.

Item it must be observed that the gates of the monastery of the prior and canons of Walsingham, on account of the attack of thieves and threats often made against the monastery, are shut at night for the safety of both people and property; during the night, as long as the time of pilgrimage lasts, access for people is available and the people await the daytime to make offerings, but in all likelihood they would not do this if they had recourse to the buildings of the friars.

Item it must be observed that all the spiritual and temporal goods, conferred on the same prior and convent, would not suffice for half a year to support its burdens as now, if it lacked the said offerings in future.

Item it must be observed that if the said friars stated that they wanted to give security against loss of the aforesaid, this would be by means of relics, sureties or oath, and these precautions do not suffice in this case because ecclesiastical rights are inestimable, and on this point the said friars are exempt persons. And if the said precautions were entered into, it would not help the said prior and convent, nor any rector of the church with any Ordinary [*Bishop*] unless only with the Pope or his legate, and it would be impossible for the said prior and convent or rector to bring a suit for any injury done to their church concerning these matters. For the fruits and proceeds of their church would not be sufficient for this, and therefore the same church would remain without remedy over this for ever.

Item it must be observed that the said friars cannot acquire new places for themselves without licence of the Apostolic See. And if they do this, they are excommunicated, so let it be guarded against in this case.

Item it must be observed that the said friars intend to build and inhabit the place within the said parishes, or one of them, not only for their own advantage but more for the damage and ruin of the said parish churches and the said priory, because at Burnham [*Norton*], four leagues distant from the said parishes of Walsingham on one side, there is a full house of Carmelite friars, and at Snitterley[10] on the other side, five leagues distant from the same parishes, another house of friars of the same order, which occupy the neighbouring parts sufficiently, and therefore in no way could the friars build anew in the said places for their advantage, unless this was turned to infinite loss for the said priory.

Therefore in view of the losses and injuries and other matters coming about by chance through the building and habitation of the said friars in the said parishes, may it please the honourable Lady aforesaid, the venerable patron of the aforesaid priory, to postpone this plan with the insight of charity, and graciously to help and maintain her said priory in its rights, liberties and benefits, as it was helped and maintained by her and her ancestors, lest in the building of the aforesaid friars the conception of new charity may result in the perpetual wasting of the said priory founded earlier with the utmost devotion of charity. And if the aforesaid venerable Lady has conceived in her mind such devotion of the new charity, which would result in permanent injury to her said priory, as to grant the building of the said friars in the said places, her humble priests, the prior and canons aforesaid, ask humbly that out of charity she consider that proposal worthy of being revoked.

---

10 In Blakeney.

The Abbey of Denny

Mortmain Licence for the Abbey of Denny, 28 January 1343[11]   [TNA C66/209]

[m. 42] The King to all to whom the present letters come, greeting. Know that when the Lord E[*dward*], formerly King of England, our father, by his letters patent of his special grace granted and gave licence on behalf of himself and his heirs to our beloved kinswoman, Elizabeth de Burgh, that she could give the advowson of the church of [*Great*] Gransden in the county of Huntingdon, which is held of us in chief as is said, and assign it to the dean and chapter of St Paul's church, London, to have and to hold to them and their successors for ever, and for the dean and chapter to be able to receive the said advowson from the said Elizabeth and appropriate that church and to hold it appropriated to their own uses to them and their successors for ever, and the said Elizabeth has now petitioned us that she has not yet given the advowson of the said church to the said dean and chapter nor assigned it by virtue of the above grant, and asked that we would wish to grant her that she may give and assign the advowson of the said church to our beloved in Christ, the abbess and sisters Minoresses of Denny,[12] to have and to hold to them and their successors in return for doing, fulfilling and maintaining certain religious works appertaining to the advowson for ever. We, wishing to agree to her petition have granted and given licence on behalf of us and our heirs, as far as in us lies, to the same Elizabeth that she can give and assign the advowson of the said church to the said abbess and sisters, to have and to hold to them and their successors in return for carrying out, doing and sustaining certain religious works appertaining to the advowson, as is aforesaid. And similarly we have given special licence to the same abbess and sisters that they can receive the said advowson from the said Elizabeth, and appropriate that church, and hold it appropriated to their own uses to them and their successors for ever, as is aforesaid, according to the present letters, notwithstanding the statute of mortmain. Not wishing that the said Elizabeth or her heirs or the aforesaid abbess and sisters or their successors by reason of the aforesaid or of the said statute should be interfered with, molested in any way or oppressed by us or our heirs, justices, escheators, sheriffs or other bailiffs or officials whosoever. Yet saving to us or our heirs or other capital lords of that fee the due and customary services. In testimony of this matter we have had these our letters patent drawn up. Witnessed by the Keeper at Kennington on 28 January, by letter of the Keeper.

Letter concerning the Defence of the Realm, 16 April 1360   [TNA C54/198]

[m. 35] The King to his beloved and faithful John de Sutton and his fellow-commissioners of array of men-at-arms and archers in the county of Essex, greeting. We have been petitioned on the part of our beloved kinswoman, Elizabeth de Burgh, that since she with a great number of armed men-at-arms and archers and all her household is living with great power in her castle of Clare (near the sea-coast in the said county, where grave dangers from the attacks of our enemies are threatened every day) for the salvation and defence of the coastal land in those parts against the attacks of the said enemies if they dared to attack those parts; and she will substitute

---

[11]   This mortmain licence did not take effect. In 1346, the Lady received a licence to grant the advowson of the church of Great Gransden to Clare Hall, Cambridge. See above, pp.130–1.

[12]   The abbey of Denny, Cambs, was converted into a convent of Minoresses by Marie de St Pol, countess of Pembroke; she received the licence to do this from Edward III in 1339 (J. Ward, ed. and trans., *Women of the English Nobility and Gentry* (Manchester, 1995), pp.202–3. The Minoresses were Franciscan nuns, following the Rule established by Isabella, sister of Louis IX of France.

and appoint Thomas le Butler as arrayer and leader of all her men who are arrayed and always prepared to set out against our said enemies when any danger shall happen to threaten from their attacks in the said parts; and she would sustain the toil and excessive costs daily for that cause. For this consideration you are not to compel Elizabeth to find certain men-at-arms and archers to stay in other places on the coast continuously by heavy distraints and much disturbance to Elizabeth's great damage and injury. We wish her to be provided with a remedy. And because we do not wish her to be unduly oppressed, we order you not to meddle in any way with the array of armed men-at-arms and archers of the said Elizabeth and her tenants of the manors of Great Bardfield and Claret in the said county, [*and*] you should find other armed men-at-arms or archers to stay on the sea-coast by no means near the parts adjoining the said castle while the said dangers last. So that her said men always be held arrayed and ready and prepared to set out with you and our other faithful men of those parts, under the leadership of the said Thomas or another reliable man appointed by Elizabeth herself, wherever and whenever any danger from the attacks of the said enemies shall happen to threaten. Witnessed by the Keeper at Reading on 16 April.

A similar royal writ is directed to Edward de Montagu and his fellow-commissioners of array in the county of Suffolk for Elizabeth's manors of Clare, Hundon, Stradishall, Denston and Sudbury in the said county of Suffolk.   Witnessed as above.

VII

THE WILL OF ELIZABETH DE BURGH, 1355

Elizabeth de Burgh's Testament and Last Will, drawn up in French on 25 September 1355[1]

[Lambeth Palace Library, London, Islip's Register, fols 164v–166v; printed by J. Nichols, *A Collection of All the Wills of the Kings and Queens of England* (London, 1780), pp.22–43]

[**fol. 164v**] In the name of the Father, the Son and the Holy Spirit, Amen. I, Elizabeth de Burgh, Lady of Clare, ordain and make my testament and last will with my full memory on 25 September in the year of the Incarnation of Our Lord Jesus Christ 1355, in the form and manner following. First I leave my soul to God and to his sweet mother St Mary and to all the saints of Heaven, and my body to the earth to be buried at the house of Minoresses outside Aldgate in London. Item I bequeath for light around my body on the eve and day of my burial 200lb. of wax of which I wish and ordain that all the surplus of the light that shall be expended shall be divided among the poor churches of the area, with the consent of the above house, according to the discretion of my executors. Item I bequeath and ordain for the expenses of burying my body on the eve and day of my burial and for the distribution to the poor on the same day, £200. And I wish and ordain that my body should not remain above ground more than fifteen days after my death in which time the solemnities of my burial are to be carried out without further delay.

And after my burial I wish and ordain that my debts are paid first, and after my debts are rendered and paid I wish first that the services of my servants are paid in the following manner: first to Sir Nicholas Damory 6 chargers, 12 dishes, 1 silver cup with a cover and 1 silver salt-cellar. To Robert Mareschal, 12 silver dishes and 2 silver cruets partly gilt. To Suzanne de Neketon, 12 silver dishes, 2 new silver cruets, 1 silver clasp enamelled with my arms, and my best robe with all the garments. To Anne de Lexden, £20 sterling, 1 chalice, 1 silver clasp enamelled with my arms, 12 silver dishes, and my black robe with all the garments. To Elizabeth Torel, 1 silver cup with crenellated cover, and 2 silver basins with spout and with the bottom enamelled, and my second-best robe with the garments. To Margaret Banchon, 4 silver ewers, and my third-best robe with all the garments. To Colinet Morley and Isabel his wife, 1 silver-gilt cup with crenellated cover, 8 large shallow bowls, 36 smaller shallow bowls, and to the said Isabel my fourth-best robe with all the garments. To John de Southam and Agnes his wife, 4 silver pots, 1 silver cup, 1 alabaster goblet with silver-gilt decoration, 1 small silver basin in the form of a dish, and to the said Agnes 3 garments of my fifth-best robe, namely coat, surcoat and

---
[1]   I have divided the will into paragraphs.

cloak with lining. To Alison de Wodeham, 6 silver plates, 1 silver powder-pot, and all the remainder of my sixth-best robe except what is bequeathed to Joan Horslee for the loss of a ring. To Johanette Drueys, 6 silver plates and 2 silver-gilt spoons and 1 spoon of blanched silver. Item to divide between the said Alison and Johanette my 2 robes of tiretain. To Sir John de Lenne, 1 mazer with crenellated cover decorated with silver-gilt, 1 silver chalice, 1 confessor's vestment of chequered silk with all the apparel. To Sir Peter de Ereswell, 1 enamelled silver-gilt box, 1 chalice, 1 pair of candlesticks, 2 basins, 1 holy water pot with a sprinkler, 1 bell, and 1 silver-gilt clasp with precious stones, my 2 books of antiphons in an old volume, 2 graduals in an old volume, 1 vestment of red and indigo camaca with all the apparel, and 6 of the best surplices of my chapel which he wishes to choose. To Sir Henry Motelot, 6 basins, 1 silver plate with a foot, 1 vestment of red and tawny camaca with all the apparel, and 1 mazer with the cover decorated with silver-gilt. To **[fol. 165r]** Sir William de Manton, 3 silver pots, 15 pieces of silver, and 1 silver scallop. To Brother John de Haselbech, 5 marks. To Brother Robert de Wisebech, 5 marks. To Sir William Albon, the better of 2 single vestments of white camaca. To Sir John de Chipham, the other single vestment of white camaca. To Sir Edward Sothword, £5. To Sir John de Huntyngdon, £5. To Sir William de Berkwey, 1 vestment of camaca, the field dark tawny, with all the apparel. To Sir William de Wykkewane, 2 silver spoons, 1 pair of silver candlesticks with decoration, and 1 goblet of beryl with silver-gilt decoration. To Sir William Aylmer, £5. To Sir William de Ditton, 1 box of blanched silver, 1 silver-gilt chalice, 2 cruets, 1 pax, 1 silver candlestick for the holy candle, 1 vestment of camaca with a black field. To Sir Henry Palmer, 1 silver-gilt pax, 34 silver spoons, 2 silver chargers, 1 striped vestment of 2 camacas with all the apparel. To Sir William Coke, £3. To Brother John the hermit, 1 little silver bell, 1 gold spoon, and 2 silver ewers. To Sir John de Kirkeby, £3. To Richard de Waterden, £3. To John de Clare, £20 sterling. To John Bataille, 2 silver-gilt cruets, 2 large pots and 2 smaller pots of silver, and 12 silver dishes. To Robert Flemengs, 2 silver ewers, and 1 silver dish with a very broad foot for the almonry. To Joan Horslee, 3 garments of my sixth best robe, namely the coat, surcoat and cloak with lining. To Walter de Kirkeby, 1 pair of silver basins, 1 holy water pot, and 1 silver-gilt sprinkler. To Nicholas Nowers, £10. To John Gough, 1 silver ewer, partly gilt, and 4 silver cups. To Humphrey de Waleden, 2 silver chargers [*and*] 2 plates with feet partly enamelled to match. To Thomas Charman, 1 ewer and 12 silver dishes. To Richard de Kingeston, 1 little silver pot, 1 cup of jasper, 1 goblet of plain silver. To Alexander Charman, 3 pairs of basins. To Richard de Buskeby, 1 tablet, 2 *chaufepoyntz* of which 1 is gilt, and 1 large silver pot. To John Messenger, £5. To Master Philip Lichet, 10 marks. To Stephen Derby, £3. To John de Knaresburgh, 20 marks. To William Beneyt, 2 silver chargers. To Richard de Wodeham, £5. To John Motelot, 1 candlestick partly of silver, 2 holy water pots, and 2 sprinklers. Item to Thomas de Lynton, £3. Item to Firmyn de Shropham, £2. To John de Henle, £2. To Walter de Coleshull, £5. To William de Stone, £4. To Stephen Skinner, £2 10s. To William de Colecestre, 6 silver cups. To Thomas Montjoye, £5. To Thomas Scot, 1 basin and 3 silver ewers. To John Larderer, 10 marks. To Hugh Poulterer, 10 marks. To Richard the Pastrycook, £3. To John de Dunmowe, £3. To Henry Poulterer, 5 marks. To Cok Havering, £4. To John Brian, £5. To John Whiteheved, £5. To John Brewer, £5. To John de Rushton, £5. To John Chandler, 1 plain silver-gilt goblet, 1 little ewer of silver. To Richard Watchman, £3. To Richard le Charer, £4 and the ladies' coach with the equipment belonging to it. To Justin Forester, 5 marks. To Richard Forrider, £3 10s. To John de Kent, £3. To John de Reveshale, £2. To John le Venour, formerly residing with me, £2. To Richard de Waltham, £3. To John Parker of Southfrith, £1. To John Parker, bailiff of Erbury, £2. To Roger Garbedons, £5. To Richard Segor, £5. To Richard atte Pole, £2. To William Edward, £2. To Simon Parker of Trelleck, £2. To Adam Baker, £2. To William Gruffuth, £3. To Thomas Aylmer, £1. To Esmon Edward of Farnham, £2. To John Bacon, bailiff of Burton [*sic*], £1. To Nicholas Artour, bailiff of Cranborne, £3. To John Goffe, bailiff of Wyke, £2. To Thomas Palmer, reeve of Stoke Verdon, £5. To Adam ap Wyllym, bailiff of New Grange, £2. To Richard Cook, bailiff of Liswerry, £3. To Richard Toyere, reeve of Troy, £2. Item to Robert of the Chamber, £2. To John de Wardon, 2 pieces of silver. To Nicholas le Ewer and Isabel his wife, 5 marks. To John de Redyng, £2. To Thomas de Henham, £2 6s. 8d. To John Testepyn, 2 marks. To Richard groom of the Chamber, 2 marks. To Thomas le Purtreour, 2 marks. To Richard de Lanyngton, £2. To John groom of the Buttery, 2 marks. To Adam of the Bakery, £5. To William Bacon, £2. To Robert Wulwy, £1. To Perot de Holand, £1 13s. 4d. To John Caton, £3. To John Loucesone, £3. To Robert Loucesone, £3. To Henry Cnapyng, £3. To Richard of the Forge, 2 marks. To Robert of the Chandlery, 2 marks. To Walter Hunte, 2 marks. To William Joliffe, 2 marks. To John Saddler, £1. To all the pages of my household who wear my livery, £10 to divide between them, according to the disposition of my executors.

Item I bequeath for masses to be sung for the souls of Sir John de Burgh, Sir Theobald de Verdun and Sir Roger Damory, my lords, for my soul, and for the souls of all my good and loyal servants who have died or will die in my service, £140. And I wish that this be done in the first year after my death as quickly as can be carried out well in the most convenient places according to the ordinance of my executors. Item I bequeath 100 marks in order to find 5 men-at-arms for the Holy Land to be given to anyone who would be faithful and suitable who wishes to take up the duty, if a common expedition is mounted within 7 years of my death, to be devoted to the service of God and the destruction of His enemies, for the souls of my lords, Sir John, Sir Theobald, Sir Roger, and mine.[2] And it is my will and final intention that if no common expedition is mounted to the said land within the aforesaid years that after this time has elapsed the aforesaid 100 marks should be divided and given to other alms and works of charity, as in part for the relief of houses of men and women religious possessioners who have fallen into poverty by chance of divers misfortunes, to pray for the aforesaid souls, the souls of all my benefactors and of all Christians. Item I bequeath to the Holy Land to help Christians to maintain the law of God, 6s. 8d.

Item I bequeath to the house of the Sisters Minoresses outside Aldgate in London, £20, 1 crystal reliquary, 1 large silver-gilt chalice, and 2 [?]costly cruets, 1 vestment of white cloth of gold with whatever belongs to the said vestment, and 3 clasps with a thousand pearls, together with my russet robe with all the garments. Item I bequeath to the same place for a memorial the vestment of black cloth of gold with whatever belongs to it, 5 cloths of gold, 1 bed of black tartarin with 8 hangings and whatever belongs to the same bed, of which 4 hangings belong to the above black vestment. Item to the same place 6 large hangings of fine wool of 1 of my other black beds, and 12 large hangings of fine wool of 1 of my other black beds, and 12 green hangings with the border powdered with owls. **[fol. 165v]** Item to Sister

---

2   The Lady's interest in a crusade to the Holy Land may stem from the fact that her mother, Joan of Acre, daughter of Edward I and Eleanor of Castile, was born in the Holy Land in 1272 during her father's crusade.

Katherine de Ingham, abbess of the same place, £20. Item to each sister of the same abbey on the day of my burial, 13s. 4d. Item to 4 brothers of the same place on the said day, to each $^1/_2$ mark.

Item I bequeath to my hall called Clare Hall in Cambridge, £40 in money, 1 silver-gilt censer, 6 chargers, 39 shallow bowls, 1 boat for the almonry to help them to build. Item I bequeath to my said Hall for a perpetual memorial to the profit of my chaplains in the college, 2 silver-gilt chalices with 2 small spoons, 2 cruets, 1 gilt and enamel decorated box for the body of our Lord,[3] and 1 censer with a silver boat for incense. Item to the same place, a vestment of red camaca embroidered with gold imagery with whatever belongs to the said vestment, 1 vestment of black camaca for requiems with 1 cope and whatever belongs to the said vestment, 1 vestment of white tartarin striped with gold for Lent with all the apparel, and 1 cloth for the sepulchre,[4] 1 vestment of blue camaca diapered with dark tawny with 2 albs and whatever belongs to the said vestment, 1 vestment of white samite also for Lent, and all the furnishings of my chapel except those which are bequeathed to Sir Peter, and the larger container of the two, fashioned like a sparrow-hawk, for the body of our Lord. Item I bequeath to my said Hall 2 good books of antiphons each with a gradual in the same volume, 1 good book of saints' lives, 1 good missal well noted, another missal covered with white leather, 1 good Bible covered with black leather, 1 book by Hugutio,[5] 1 Legend of the saints, 1 pair of Decretals,[6] 1 book of *Quaestiones*,[7] and 32 quires of a book called *Of the Cause of God against Pelagius*.[8]

Item I bequeath to the cathedral church of St Paul [*London*] a new vestment of white camaca with whatever belongs to it for a memorial. Item I bequeath to St Thomas of Hereford an image of our Lady of silver-gilt to be attached to his shrine, and to the cathedral church there 1 vestment of indigo satin, namely a chasuble, 2 tunicles, 1 cope embroidered with imagery and powdered with archangels. Item I bequeath to the work of the church of Walsingham 1 silver-gilt and enamelled cup with a tripod, and £4 in pennies, and 2 cloths of gold.[9] Item to the house of Stoke [*by Clare*], 12 silver-gilt spoons, and 1 *drag'* with a silver foot, partly gilt, and 2 cloths of gold.[10] Item to the house of Anglesey, 10 marks, and the vestment of a red cloth of gold of [*?*]taffeta[11] with 3 crests, partly silver-gilt, for the copes.[12] Item to the house of Royston, £3, and 2 cloths of gold.[13] Item to the house of Tewkesbury,

---

3 The host which the priest consecrates during mass.
4 A reference to the Easter sepulchre, Jesus' tomb after the Crucifixion. In a medieval church, the Easter sepulchre was situated to the north of the high altar; the host was placed in it on Good Friday and taken out on Easter Sunday.
5 Hugutio was an exponent of the Decretals.
6 Two collections of Decretals, i.e. two works on canon law.
7 Questions of theology expounded in the universities.
8 Written by Thomas Bradwardine, archbishop of Canterbury, d.1349.
9 This is probably a reference to the priory of Augustinian canons at Walsingham of which the Lady was patron.
10 The priory of Stoke by Clare was founded in Clare castle in 1090 by Gilbert of Tonbridge, the son of Richard son of Count Gilbert, founder of the Clare family in England. It was transferred to Stoke in 1124, and was a cell of the Norman Benedictine abbey of Bec. The Clare family, including the Lady, held the patronage.
11 'Raffata' in the manuscript.
12 Anglesey priory was a small house of Augustinian canons, founded about 1200 by Richard de Clare, earl of Hertford. The Lady resided there from time to time into the 1340s and was the patron.
13 The priory of Royston was established for Augustinian canons. The Lady was patron.

2 reliquaries, 1 cross with Mary and John, and 2 cloths of gold.[14] To the house of Amesbury, £10 and 2 cloths of gold.[15] To the house of Cranborne, £1 and 2 cloths of gold.[16] To the house of Tonbridge, £5 and 2 cloths of gold.[17] To the house of Tintern, 1 vestment of white *saeryn* cloth with whatever belongs to it, and 2 cloths of gold.[18] To the house of ladies of Usk, 10 marks, and 2 cloths of gold.[19] To the house of Croxden, £5, and 2 cloths of gold.[20] To the house of Chipley, £2 and 1 cloth of gold.[21] To the house of [*Bury*] St Edmunds, 3 cloths of gold.[22] To the hospital of St John in Cambridge, £2.[23] To the house of monks in Thetford, 10 marks and 1 cloth of gold.[24] To the house of ladies in Swaffham, 12 silver dishes, and 2 cloths of gold.[25]

To the parish church of Clare, £3, and 1 cloth of gold. To the parish church of Bardfield, £3, and 1 cloth of gold. To the parish church of Standon, £3, and 1 cloth of gold. To the parish church of Bottisham, £2, and 1 cloth of gold.

Item to the friars of St Augustine of Clare, £10.[26] To the friars minor of Babwell, £5.[27] To the friars preacher of Thetford, £2. To the 4 orders of friars of Lynn, £8.[28] To the 4 orders of friars of Norwich, £8. To the friars minor of Walsingham, £5.[29] To the four orders of friars in Yarmouth, £8. To the friars of St Augustine in Orford, £2. To the friars preacher of Dunwich, £2. To the friars minor of Ipswich, £2. To the friars minor of Colchester, £2. To the friars preacher of Sudbury, 10 marks. To the friars preacher of Chelmsford, £2. To the friars minor of Ware, £2. To the Carmelite friars of Maldon [*no sum of money*]. To the 4 orders of friars in London, £8. To the 3 orders of friars in Canterbury, £6.[30] To the friars minor of Cambridge, £2. Item to the same friars for their work, £5, and the other 3 [*orders*] of friars in Cambridge, £6.

---

14 The Benedictine abbey of Tewkesbury was closely associated with the earls of Gloucester in the twelfth and thirteenth centuries. The Clare family succeeded to the earldom of Gloucester in 1217 and became patrons of the abbey. Earls Gilbert (d.1230), Richard (d.1262), Gilbert (d.1295), and Gilbert (d.1314) were buried in the abbey church. The patronage in 1317 was awarded to Hugh le Despenser the younger and his wife Eleanor de Clare. The Lady stayed at Tewkesbury on journeys to and from Usk, and with her father and brother buried there presumably wanted to maintain her connection with the abbey. See above, Plate 2.

15 The Lady lived at the nunnery of Amesbury after the death of her second husband, Theobald de Verdun, in 1316, and her daughter Isabella was born there on 21 March 1317.

16 Cranborne priory was Benedictine. The Lady was patron.

17 Tonbridge was a small priory of Augustinian canons, founded about 1190 by Richard de Clare, earl of Hertford.

18 Tintern was founded as a Cistercian abbey in 1131 by Walter fitz Richard, younger son of Richard son of Count Gilbert, founder of the Clare family in England. Walter's lands passed to Gilbert and Richard Strongbow, and in the late twelfth century to the Marshal family.

19 The Benedictine nunnery of Usk was founded about 1170 by Richard Strongbow, descended from a younger line of the Clare family. The Lady was patron.

20 Croxden was a Cistercian abbey in Staffordshire; Theobald de Verdun, the Lady's second husband, was buried there.

21 Chipley was a small Augustinian priory on the outskirts of Clare.

22 I.e. the Benedictine abbey of Bury St Edmunds.

23 St John's hospital was converted into St John's College, Cambridge, in 1509–11.

24 This was a Cluniac foundation.

25 Swaffham Bulbeck, Cambs. This was a Benedictine nunnery.

26 Clare priory was founded by the Lady's grandfather, Richard de Clare, earl of Gloucester and Hertford, in 1248.

27 This priory was at Bury St Edmunds.

28 I.e. the four orders of the Dominicans, friars preacher; Franciscans, friars minor; Carmelites and Augustinians.

29 This house was founded by the Lady.

30 I.e. Dominicans, Franciscans and Augustinians.

To the friars minor of Bedford, £2. To the friars of St Augustine of Huntingdon, £2. To the 4 orders of friars of Northampton, £8. To the 4 orders of friars of Stamford, £8. To the friars minor of Grantham, £2. To the 4 orders of friars of Oxford, £8. To the friars minor of Worcester, £3. To the friars in Hereford, £4.[31] To the 4 orders of friars in Bristol, £8. To the 2 orders of friars of Cardiff, £6.[32] To the 4 orders of friars of Gloucester, £8. To the friars preacher and minor of Salisbury, £4. To the friars minor of Dorchester, £2.

Item I bequeath to Lady Elizabeth my daughter [*sic*], Countess of Ulster,[33] all the debt which my son, her father, owed me on the day he died. Item I bequeath to my said daughter for seed-corn 407qr of wheat, rye and maslin for the winter sowing-season on the manors of my inheritance in the bailiwick of Clare, namely, Standon, Bardfield, Claret, Erbury, Hundon, Woodhall, Bircham and Walsingham; in the bailiwick of Dorset, namely, Cranborne, Tarrant Gunville, Pimperne, Steeple, Wyke and Portland; and in Wales, namely, Troy, Trelleck, Llangwm, New Grange,[34] Llantrissent and Tregrug.[35] Item 61qr of beans, peas, and vetches on the same manors for the Lent sowing-season. Item 204qr of barley and dredge for the same season. Item 529qr of oats for the same season. Item cart-horses for the above manors, 23; item draught-animals, 94; of oxen for the ploughs, 248; together with the dead stock in the said manors such as carts, ploughs, ox waggons, hay and straw.

Item I bequeath to my daughter Bardolf[36] my bed of green velvet striped with red with whatever belongs to it together with 1 coverlet of dark cloth lined with minever pured, 1 half-coverlet to match, and 1 kerchief of indigo samite lined with [*?*]blanket, and 1 coverlet of tawny medley lined with gris. Item I bequeath to my said daughter 1 great hall of worstead [*hangings*], the field tawny, with parrots and blue cockerels, and whatever belongs to it. Item I bequeath to my said daughter my great coach with the equipment, curtains and cushions and whatever belongs to it. Item I bequeath to Sir John Bardolf and to my said daughter his wife jointly in my manors of Caythorpe and Clopton 26qr of wheat for seed-corn for the winter sowing-season, [*and*] 7qr 4b. of maslin and rye. Item for the Lent sowing-season, 17qr 4b. of peas, 37qr 4b. of barley, 9qr 4b. of dredge, 22qr 1b. of oats; 4 carthorses, 12 draught-animals, 22 oxen, together with my carts and ploughs which belong to the said manors, and all their equipment. Item I bequeath to my young daughter, Isabel Bardolf,[37] to help her to marry 1 goblet of plain gold, 2 large ornaments partly enamelled, and 12 large silver shallow bowls, my bed of sendal, with a coverlet of ash-grey medley lined with minever. Item to Agnes her sister to help her to marry 1 silver cross, 2 candlesticks, 2 salt-cellars, 1 cup, 1 large dish for the almonry, 1 goblet of embossed silver, 1 incense-boat, 1 censer, 1 clasp with the **[fol. 166r]** Annunciation, and 6 new chargers of silver. Item to the said Agnes, a bed of indigo of which the hangings and coverlet are of velveteen, with what belongs to it, and a blue coverlet lined with gris.

Item I bequeath to Sir William de Ferrers[38] in my manor of Lutterworth seed-

---

31 I.e. Dominicans.
32 I.e. Dominicans and Franciscans.
33 Elizabeth, countess of Ulster, was the Lady's granddaughter and principal heir; she was married to Lionel, second surviving son of Edward III.
34 New Grange manor belonged to Usk.
35 Tregrug alias Llangibby.
36 Elizabeth daughter of the Lady and Roger Damory.
37 The Lady's granddaughter.
38 The Lady's grandson, son of her daughter Isabella and Sir Henry de Ferrers.

corn for the said manor, namely, 11qr 6b. of wheat, 6qr 4b. of rye, 2qr of maslin, 13qr of beans and peas, 13qr of barley, 2qr of dredge, 29qr of oats; 4 carthorses, 6 draught-animals, 18 oxen, together with the carts and ploughs and all the equipment. Item I bequeath to Sir Thomas Furnivall[39] grain for seed-corn on my manors of Farnham[*Bucks*], Sere,[40] Stoke Verdon [*Staffs*] and Wilsford [*Wilts*], namely, 35qr 2b. of wheat, 12qr 4b. of rye and maslin, 10qr 6b. of peas and vetches, 45qr 4b. of barley and dredge, 34qr 7b. of oats; 2 carthorses, 16 draught animals, 28 oxen, together with the carts, ploughs and all the equipment. Item I bequeath to my daughter the countess of Athol[41] my 2 beds of tawny, the large and the small, with whatever belongs to them. Item 1 coverlet of bronze cloth in grain, with a half-pured lining, and 1 kerchief of dark tawny camaca with a half-pured lining.

Item I bequeath to my lord the King for his college of Windsor[42] 1 gold cup with a foot for the body of our Lord, and 1 of silver-gilt with 3 little angels on the cup. I bequeath to my lord the Prince[43] a gold tabernacle with the image of Our Lady and 2 little angels of shaped gold, 1 large silver-gilt cross with Mary and John, and 2 large paxes of silver-gilt and enamel, and 1 gold ring with a ruby. Item I bequeath to the duke of Lancaster[44] my little psalter covered with gold *arcail*, and 1 square cross with a piece of the true cross which is in a gold enamelled case. Item I bequeath to Lady Marie de St Pol, countess of Pembroke, 1 little gold cross with a sapphire in the centre, and 1 gold ring with a diamond. Item I bequeath to Joan de Bar, countess of Warenne, 1 gold image of St John the Baptist in the desert.

And I wish and ordain that, if I do not reward any of the aforesaid persons as in wardships, marriages, grants of lands, rents, gifts of money, any loan or other benefit beyond the certain covenant with my aforesaid servants, namely between the date of this testament and the day of my death, that with reference to reward of wardships, marriages, grants of land, rents, gifts of money and loans, if any person is included in part of the payment in this my testament, no person excepted, except only those who will undertake the charge and execution of this my testament, their reward will be found, together with their names and the total sum of money which I vouchsafe to each person, in a remembrance sealed with my seal in place of the sum of money above, the parcels of gold and silver are assigned to the aforesaid persons and divers houses. Item I wish and ordain that the delivery of all the parcels, named and bequeathed, saving only the money, is carried out by my executors to each person according to what I have declared in the above remembrance; I wish that the parcels should be had and held as included in this [*document*] and of the same consequence and value as they were written word for word in this my testament. And if it happens that any of the parcels of gold and silver bequeathed to my household are ordained for another benefit during my lifetime after the date of this testament, so that the same parcels are not found after my death because of the change made by me, I wish that due amends be made to the same person in money or in another parcel of my goods to the [*same*] value. And everyone should know

---

39 Sir Thomas Furnivall married one of the daughters and coheiresses of Theobald de Verdun, the Lady's second husband; part of his inheritance was assigned to the Lady as dower.
40 This place has not been identified.
41 The Lady's granddaughter, daughter of Henry and Isabella de Ferrers; she married David de Strathbogie, earl of Athol.
42 The college of St George, founded by Edward III in 1348.
43 The Black Prince, eldest son of Edward III.
44 Henry of Grosmont.

that it is my will and last ordinance that each person to whom I have bequeathed plate or other parcel of silver, except money, be the sum lesser or greater, should have according to his portion 17lb. in weight of precious metal to £20 sterling, and, if by chance any person's portion is more than the sum of money bequeathed to him, the said person should make amends to my executors for the surplus, and, if any person should have less for his portion than the above weight, I wish that compensation should be made to him for what is lacking. And if my executors are informed that I have not made full satisfaction to my aforesaid servants or to others of my servants not included in this my testament for their work at the present time, in the past or in the future, I wish and ordain that, out of the residue of the plate of my chapel and wardrobe, apart from what is bequeathed, there be made to them a reasonable reward according to the good discretion of my executors, and the said residue be not put to other profit, sold or delivered until my last will is fully carried out. And if it happens by chance, which God forbid, that any of those close to me, friends, or any other man to whom I have bequeathed anything, or any other in their name should hinder and trouble my executors so that they cannot peacefully administer all my goods, movable and immovable, according to their charge and the content of this my last will, I wish and ordain that the bequest to the said persons of any condition should be null and void, so that they do not receive part or parcel of this my bequest or of my other aforesaid goods, except the peril which comes to wrongful occupiers of the goods of the dead and disturbers of their last wills. Item if through necessity a cutback must be made, I wish it to be made as much from the goods that I have bequeathed to the said Lady Elizabeth, my daughter of Ulster, Sir John Bardolf and my daughter his wife, Sir William de Ferrers, Sir Thomas Furnivall, and my daughter of Athol, as from all the others included in this my testament. And because divers hindrances are often made through malice, and man's subtlety is greater than was usual before this time, I wish and ordain that all those to whom I have bequeathed anything in this my testament should give acquittances to my executors as much for all manner of actions, complaints and demands which they have or could have against my executors, as for the bequests made to them and paid by the aforesaid executors. And if the said legatees refuse and do not want to make such acquittances according to the content of this my ordinance, I wish and ordain that the bequests made by me to them should be held null and unwritten. Item I ordain that my executors give acquittance and full liberation to Sir John Leche for 1,000 marks which he owes me by his deed of obligation, so that he is to make general acquittance to my executors for all manner of actions which he has or could have towards them as executors.

And as for the residue of all my goods and chattels which will remain after the execution of this my testament, I wish and ordain that a distribution be made by my executors in the following manner, namely to relieve poor religious possessioners, both ladies and others who have fallen into misfortune, partly for poor gentlewomen who are burdened with children, to help poor parish churches and to repair and improve their furnishings, partly to find and support poor scholars at school, to repair bridges and causeways, poor people who used to have a household, poor merchants who by chance have been ruined, and to be concerned with and help poor prisoners; the rest is to be used for other works of charity with reference to the good discretion of my executors, according to what they will see best to do for the salvation of my soul.

And to carry out and accomplish fully and faithfully this my last will and testament, I ordain, appoint and name my executors written below, namely, Sir Nicholas

Damory, Sir John de Lenne, Sir **[fol. 166v]** Henry Motelot, John Bataille, Sir Peter de Ereswell, Robert Mareschal, and Sir William de Manton, principal and chief [*executors*]; Sir Henry Palmer, Richard de Buskeby, Thomas Charman, Alexander Charman, Humphrey de Waleden, Richard de Kyngeston, John Motelot, and Sir William de Berkwey, secondary [*executors*]. And I wish and ordain that the afore-said Sir Nicholas, Sir John, Sir Henry Motelot, John Bataille, Sir Peter, Robert, Sir William de Manton, Sir Henry Palmer, Richard, Thomas, Alexander, Humphrey, Richard de Kyngeston, John Motelot and Sir William de Berkwey administer all my goods and chattels touching this my testament in the following form and manner and not otherwise: namely that of my goods which shall be sold in all parts to perform my will, the sellers in the counties of Norfolk, Suffolk and Essex should be Sir William de Manton, Humphrey de Waleden, and Thomas Charman. Item in the lord-ship of Usk and elsewhere in parts of Wales, the aforesaid Sir Henry Motelot and Alexander; in the counties of Dorset, Wiltshire and the Chilterns, Sir Henry Motelot, Richard de Kyngeston, and John Motelot. Item in the counties of Lincoln, Leicester and Warwick, Richard de Buskeby and Sir William de Berkwey. And the money raised from all my goods and chattels aforesaid is to be delivered by indenture to Sir William de Manton, Sir Henry Palmer and Richard de Buskeby, and the same Sir William, Henry and Richard are to be accountable for their receipt to the afore-said Sir Nicholas, Sir John, Sir Henry Motelot, and my other principal executors. And by the ordinance of the said Sir Nicholas, Sir John, Sir Henry Motelot, John Bataille and the other principal and chief executors, all the bequests will be made; other distributions which will be carried out and all other things for which they are responsible are to be performed and settled. In witness of these things I have affixed my seal to this my last will. Given at Clare on the day and year aforesaid.

[*Probate of the said testament in the presence of Simon Islip, Archbishop of Canter-bury, in the church of the Sisters Minoresses of the order of St Clare outside Aldgate, London, on 3 December A.D.1360.*]

APPENDIX

The Household Accounts of Elizabeth de Burgh

Elizabeth de Burgh's household accounts are to be found in the National Archives, London. The majority can be dated, either from the heading or from internal evidence. The undated rolls are included at the end of the list. The accounts usually ran for the medieval financial year, from Michaelmas (29 September) to Michaelmas, but some are incomplete and others cover a shorter period. Those marked * are published here in full or as excerpts.

E101/94/20 is listed in *List of Exchequer Accounts, Various* (TNA *Lists and Indexes*, XXXV, 1912) as a Clare household account of the reign of Edward III, but it differs from the other Clare diet accounts in layout and terminology. It has therefore been omitted.

TNA reference	Date	Description
E101/94/9	?1320	Diet account, incomplete
E101/95/11	3 October 1324	Indenture between John de London, clerk of the Wardrobe and Robert de Pentriz, receiver of Clare
E101/91/11	1325–7	View of account of the Wardrobe and Household, of John de London, clerk of the Wardrobe
E101/91/12*	28 September – 19 October 1326	Household expenses
E101/91/15	9 December 1327 – 17 January 1328	Subsidiary account: expenses of the Lady's daughters and household at Clare
E101/91/16	October 1327	Subsidiary account: journey to Anstey
E101/91/17	1327–30	Wardrobe and Household account of Hugh de Burgh, clerk of the Wardrobe
E101/91/18	27 April 1328 – March 1329	Subsidiary account: expenses of William de Burgh, earl of Ulster
E101/91/19	19–25 October 1328	Subsidiary account: journey to Anstey
E101/91/20	30 December 1328 – 2 April 1329	Subsidiary account: officials' journey to and stay at Usk
E101/91/21	Michaelmas 1328 – 29 July 1329	Account book of John de London, clerk of the Wardrobe
E101/94/8	July [?]1329	Subsidiary account: journey to Anstey
E101/91/22	1329–30	Chamber account of John de London, clerk of the Lady
E101/91/23	1329–30	Indenture between John de London and Hugh the clerk
E101/91/24	1330–1	Wardrobe and household account of Hugh the clerk
E101/91/25*	Michaelmas 1330 – 6 April 1331	Diet account
E101/91/26	1331–2	Draft wardrobe and household account of Hugh de Burgh, clerk of the Wardrobe

151

E101/91/27*	1331–2	Wardrobe and household account of Hugh de Burgh
E101/91/28*	1 October 1332	Indenture between Hugh de Burgh, clerk of the Wardrobe, and William le Blount
E101/91/29	1 October 1332	Indenture between John de London, clerk of the Lady, and William le Blount
E101/91/30*	1333	Subsidiary account: goldsmiths' expenses
E101/92/1	1333–4	Subsidiary account of the brewers
E101/92/2*	27 March – Michaelmas 1334	Diet account
E101/92/3	4 February – Michaelmas 1336	Wardrobe and household account of John Darre, clerk of the Wardrobe
E101/92/4*	Michaelmas 1336 – 23 March 1337	Wardrobe and household account of John Darre, clerk of the Wardrobe
E101/92/5	22 March – Michaelmas 1337	Counter roll
E101/92/29	30 September 1337 and 20 January 1338	2 indentures between Robert de Stalynton, clerk of the Lady, and John de Lenne, clerk of the Wardrobe
E101/92/6	Michaelmas 1337 – 11 January 1338	View of account of John de Lenne, clerk of the Wardrobe
E101/92/7	March–Mich. 1338	Wardrobe and household account
E101/91/14	[?]1337–8	Diet account. No marshalsea expenses
E101/92/8	20 April – Michaelmas 1338	Counter roll
E101/92/9	1338–9	Wardrobe and household account of John de Lenne, clerk of the Wardrobe
E101/92/10	30 September 1339 and 21 May 1340	2 indentures between Robert de Stalynton, clerk of the Lady, and John de Lenne, clerk of the Wardrobe
E101/92/11*	1339–40	Wardrobe and household account of John de Lenne, clerk of the Wardrobe
E101/92/12*	Michaelmas 1339 – July 1340	Diet account
E101/92/13	1340–1	Wardrobe and household account of William de Manton, clerk of the Wardrobe
E101/92/14*	Michaelmas 1340 – August 1341	Counter roll
E101/92/15	30 November 1340 – Michaelmas 1341	Kitchen account
E101/92/17	20 June – Michaelmas 1341	Subsidiary account: diet account of Henry de Colingham and the Household at Clare
E101/92/16	Michaelmas 1341 – 20 January 1342	View of account of William de Manton, clerk of the Wardrobe
E101/92/18	Michaelmas 1341 – 9 February 1342	Counter roll
E101/91/13	March–Michaelmas [?] 1342	Counter roll
E101/94/7	Michaelmas 1341 – 28 January 1342; 1 June – 21 September 1342	Subsidiary account: expenses of the Marshalsea

E101/92/19	7 October 1341	Indenture between Robert de Stalynton, clerk of the Chamber, and William de Manton, clerk of the Wardrobe
E101/92/20	Michaelmas 1341 – 2 June 1342	View of account of William de Manton, clerk of the Wardrobe
E101/92/22	9 June – Michaelmas 1342	Diet account
E101/92/21	Michaelmas 1342 – 26 January 1343	View of account of William de Manton, clerk of the Wardrobe
E101/92/23*	1343	Subsidiary account: roll of liveries
E101/94/6, m.1,2	Michaelmas – 16 November [?]1343	Subsidiary account: expenses of the Marshalsea
E101/92/24	1343–4	Diet account
E101/92/25	22 July – 11 August 1344	Counter roll
E101/92/26*	1344	Subsidiary account: roll of cloths for liveries
E101/92/27	1344–5	Wardrobe and household account of William de Manton, clerk of the Wardrobe
E101/92/28	10 November 1344 – Michaelmas 1345	Counter roll
E101/94/6, m.3 and 95/8*	1346–7	Subsidiary account: expenses of the Marshalsea
E101/92/30*	1346–7	Diet account. No marshalsea expenses
E101/93/1	1 October 1348	Indenture between Sir William d'Oxwik, clerk of the Chamber, and William de Manton, clerk of the Wardrobe
E101/93/2	1348–9	Diet account
E101/93/3	Michaelmas 1348 – April 1349	Counter roll
E101/94/17	April–Michaelmas 1349	Counter roll
E101/93/4*	1349–50	Diet account
E101/93/5	1349–50	Chamber account of William d'Oxwik, clerk of the Chamber
E101/93/6	1349–50	Wardrobe and household account of William de Manton, clerk of the Wardrobe
E101/93/7	1349–50	Indenture between William d'Oxwik, clerk of the Chamber, and William de Manton, clerk of the Wardrobe
E101/93/8	1350–1	Chamber and wardrobe and household account of William de Manton, clerk of the Wardrobe and Chamber
E101/93/9*	26 October 1350 – 8 September 1351	Diet account
E101/93/11	8 May – Michaelmas 1351	Counter roll
E101/93/10	1351–2	Counter roll
E101/95/12	1351–2	Chamber expenses, incomplete
E101/93/12*	1351–2	Chamber account of the Lady's private expenditure
E101/93/13	22 October 1351 – 16 September 1352	Diet account

E101/93/14	Michaelmas – 10 November 1352	Counter roll
E101/93/16	1353–4	Subsidiary account: expenses of the Marshalsea
E101/93/15	1353	Part of a roll of payments and gifts
E101/93/17	1354–5	Diet account. No marshalsea expenses.
E101/93/18*	1355–6	Diet account
E101/93/19	1355–6	Chamber and wardrobe and household account of William de Manton, clerk of the Wardrobe and Chamber
E101/93/20*	1357–8	Diet account
E101/94/1*	1358–9	Counter roll
E101/95/9	1358–9	Diet account
E101/94/2	1358–9	Chamber and wardrobe and household account of William de Manton, clerk of the Wardrobe and Chamber
E101/94/10	1322–60	Diet account, incomplete
E101/94/12	1322–60	Indenture
E101/94/14	1322–60	Draft counter roll
E101/94/16	1322–60	Draft account of household departments
E101/94/19	1322–60	Diet account, incomplete
E101/95/1	1322–60	Draft counter roll
E101/95/2	1322–60	Diet account, incomplete
E101/95/3	1322–60	Counter roll, incomplete
E101/95/4	1322–60	Subsidiary account, incomplete: expenses of the Marshalsea
E101/95/5	1322–60	Subsidiary account, incomplete: expenses of the Marshalsea
E101/95/6	1322–60	Diet account, incomplete
E101/95/7	1322–60	Diet account. No marshalsea expenses
E101/95/10	1322–60	Household expenses, fragmentary
E101/95/13	1322–60	Diet account, incomplete
E101/510/13	1322–60	Counter roll, incomplete
E101/510/14	1322–60	Draft counter roll, incomplete

GLOSSARY

Most of the terms used in the household accounts can be found in the *Oxford English Dictionary*. Medieval Latin, Anglo-Norman and Middle English dictionaries are also very useful. For specialist areas, there are valuable glossaries in works such as the following:

J.L. Fisher, *A Medieval Farming Glossary of Latin and English Words taken mainly from Essex Records*, second edition revised by Avril and Ray Powell (Essex Record Office, Chelmsford, 1997)

Household Accounts from Medieval England, ed. C.M. Woolgar, 2 volumes, British Academy Records of Social and Economic History, new series, XVII, XVIII (Oxford, 1992–3), I, pp.71–102

Manorial Records of Cuxham, Oxfordshire, c.1200–1359, ed. P.D.A. Harvey (Oxfordshire Record Society, L, 1976; Historical Manuscripts Commission), pp.774–801

D. Stuart, *Manorial Records. An Introduction to their Transcription and Translation* (Chichester, 1992)

E.M. Veale, *The English Fur Trade in the Later Middle Ages* (second edition, London Record Society, XXXVIII, 2003), pp.216–29

D. Viner, *Wagons and Carts* (Shire Publications, Botley, Oxford, 2008)

D. Yaxley, *Glossary of Words found in Historical Documents of East Anglia* (Dereham, 2003)

advowson: the right of patronage over parish churches and certain monasteries.

affeerer: one who assesses fines in court proceedings.

akermen: unfree, villein tenants, performing less week-work than the virgaters, and also additional work at harvest.

alb: long, sleeved robe of white linen, worn under the chasuble or cope by the priest celebrating mass and his assistants.

alkanet: a European plant producing a red dye.

amercement: a financial penalty levied by a court. It is comparable to the modern word, fine.

anchorite: a man or woman who leaves society to live a solitary life devoted to religious exercises and contemplation. Anchorites were often attached to religious houses or parish churches.

antiphons: antiphons comprised verses from the Bible which were sung at the beginning or end of a part of the mass.

appropriation: the annexation of a benefice, usually a parish church, by a religious house, so that in future the house would enjoy all the benefice's tithes and sources of income. In such cases, the religious house was expected to appoint a vicar to the benefice and allocate certain revenues to him.

approver: a person who admits to committing a felony and gives evidence against his accomplices.

assize of bread and ale: the regulation of the price of bread and ale as laid down in the assize issued by the king. This regulation took place at the court leet.

bailiwick: a grouping of estates, often on a geographical basis, for the purposes of administration and exploitation.

basinet: a small light steel helmet with a visor.

bis: the back of the winter skin of the Baltic squirrel, but the name was also used for the whole squirrel skin.

blanket: a coarse woollen cloth.

bolemong: a mixed fodder crop.

botel: a bundle of hay.

budge: imported lambskins. The name comes from Bougie in North Africa, but in the fourteenth century was also used for lambskins from other parts of the Mediterranean.

bullock: a young ox, usually in its second or third year.

camaca: a fine fabric, probably silk.

camelin: a woollen fabric mixed with silk or other fibres.

candle of paris: a tallow candle.

cantle: a heaped measure of grain.

capon: a cock which has been castrated in order to improve the meat.

cart-clout: an iron plate to protect the woodwork of the cart.

cera pullana: wax imported from Poland. The Middle English word *pullane* means Polish.

cert money: cert money was offered at the court leet by the capital pledge of the tithing so that the tithing's members would not be called by name.

chaplain: a secular chaplain was a priest who was not a member of a monastic or friars' order.

charger: a large dish.

chasuble: a sleeveless vestment, rectangular or elliptical in shape, with a central opening to go over the head.

chevage: an annual payment from unfree villein tenants living outside the manor.

citronade: candied lemon, or lemon preserved in syrup.

comfit: a round sweetmeat comprising a piece of spice, a seed or a piece of fruit covered with sugar.

cope: a cloak worn by the clergy.

cotmen, cottars: unfree villein tenants who were smallholders; they performed less week-work than akermen, and also additional work at harvest.

cresset: an iron basket hung in a building and holding rushes to supply light.

cubeb: a small Indonesian berry, somewhat resembling pepper in taste. It was used as a medicine.

deaute: a kind of salve or ointment for horses.

demesne manor: a manor exploited by the lord himself, as opposed to manors held by his vassals. The term, demesne, is also used to describe the lord's own land on the manor, as distinct from the peasant holdings.

destrier: a warhorse. The word, courser, was used as an alternative.

distraint: the taking of chattels in order to enforce a judicial decision.

dowel: a wooden pin used to join two pieces of wood together.

dower: the land held by a woman of the nobility or of tenants by knight service after the death of her husband. From *c.*1200, it amounted to one-third of her husband's land; this amount was laid down in Magna Carta.

dowry: the sum of money paid by the bride's father to the bridegroom's father.

drail: a piece of iron projecting from the plough-beam, to which the oxen or horses were hitched.

dredge: mixed grain (oats and barley).

ell: a linear measurement of 45 inches, 1¼ yards, or 1.143 metres.

enfeoffment to use: the grant of lands to a group of people known as feoffees who held the lands to the use of a named beneficiary.

entail: a grant of land laying down a specific line of succession.

entreme: a light dish, served between courses.

escheator: the royal official who was responsible for land which came into the king's hands temporarily or permanently. The escheator was responsible for taking inquisitions *post mortem* and proofs of age, and for allocating dower. From the fourteenth century, it was usual to appoint a member of the county gentry.

essoin: the excuse for not attending court. The excuse had to be for a good reason, and the suitor was allowed three essoins which were numbered in the court roll.

ewer: a vessel with a spout to contain water. The Ewery was the household office where the vessels and table-linen were stored, and where the official prepared for his duties.

fathom: a measure of length, of about six feet.

felloe: a section of the rim of a cartwheel.

femme sole: literally, a woman on her own, without male protection. Widows counted as *femmes soles*, and were entitled to run their estates, bring lawsuits, and make their own policy decisions.

fevere, fever: an iron-worker, often making high-class articles.

fine: an agreement with the king or a lord for which a sum of money was paid.

forestaller: a person who buys merchandise before it comes to market, and then sells it at the market at a higher price.

fother: a unit of weight for lead.

fret: the hoop fitted to the hub of a wheel.

fuller: a man who fulls cloth i.e. scours and beats it in a mixture of water and fullers' earth to tighten up the weave and make the cloth stronger. The process was mechanised with the introduction of the fulling mill in the thirteenth century.

garnet-hinge: a type of hinge, shaped like the letter T, and laid horizontally.

God's penny: payment of 1d. indicating that the purchase was made on credit.

goshawk: a bird similar to but larger than the sparrowhawk. It takes rabbits, geese, cranes, pheasants and partridges.

gradual: a book containing graduals and other antiphons sung at mass. The gradual was sung after the epistle had been read.

gris: the grey back of the winter skin of the Baltic squirrel.

grisel: grey.

grope: an iron clamp, or a type of nail.

grover: grover refers to the whole skin of the Baltic squirrel.

Gules of August: 1 August.

hackney: a horse used for riding.

hame: part of the collar of a carthorse.

hanaper: office in the royal chancery.

heifer: a young cow which has not yet had a calf.

herber: medieval term for a pleasure-garden.

heriot: on the death of an unfree tenant, his best beast was handed over to the lord as heriot.

hobyn: a nag.

hogget: either a hog, usually in its second year, or a sheep between one and two years old.

honour: a lordship, centred on the lord's chief castle, comprising the lord's demesne

157

manors and the knights' fees held by his vassals. The honour court was held at the castle. The lord had the right to levy feudal incidents from his vassals: wardship and marriage when the heir succeeded to a fee under the age of 21; and relief, at the rate of £5 for a knight's fee, when the heir took up the holding.

host: the wafer, consecrated by the priest celebrating mass; it was believed that the wafer was transformed into the Body of Christ at the consecration.

huckster: a petty trader.

hue and cry: when a crime was committed, the hue and cry was raised to pursue and catch the felon, so that he, or she, could be produced in court.

hundred: a subdivision of the county with its own court; it was used as a judicial and administrative unit.

hurter: an iron plate between the axle and wheel of a cart.

increment: the extra grain received from a heaped measure, as against a measure which had been levelled off.

inquisition *post mortem*: this was compiled after the death of a tenant-in-chief by the Crown, or after the death of a vassal by the honour's officials. It comprised a survey of all the tenant's lands, and information about the heir.

jesses: in falconry, the jesses consist of two leather straps which are fitted round the hawk's legs, and are used to keep the hawk on the falconer's gloved fist.

jointure: land held jointly by husband and wife, and held by the wife for life in the event of the death of her husband.

lanner falcon: the lanner was smaller than the peregrine falcon and originated in Africa. It was used to take smaller game birds.

last: the equivalent of twelve barrels of cod or herring.

liberty: an area where the lord had special judicial privileges. The specific privilege was described as a liberty or franchise.

librate: the term used with reference to land, indicating its value. Thus three librates of land were worth £3.

litter: bedding for horses.

madrian: a type of spice or sweetmeat.

marshalsea: the household department including the stables and the forge. It dealt with all matters concerning the horses.

maslin: mixed grain (wheat and rye).

mazer: a bowl made of maple or a hard wood, often decorated and mounted in silver.

mess: the amount of food served to a group of people, normally numbering two or four, who were served together at mealtimes. The word also denoted a dish of food.

minever: the white belly skin of the Baltic squirrel with a little grey left round the white. Minever pured refers to the white belly skin with all the grey removed.

missal: mass-book, containing all the liturgical variants, so as to enable the priest to celebrate mass throughout the year.

molmen: unfree villein tenants, with light labour services. The size of their holdings varied.

morel: dark brown.

multure: payment, usually in kind, to the lord of the mill for grinding corn.

murage: a levy, granted by the Crown, to raise money to repair town walls.

murrain: a disease affecting livestock. Its exact nature is uncertain.

octave: a week, eight days, after a specified date.

oriel: a large bay window projecting from a building. The bay itself might be used as a closet or private space within a large room such as the hall or chapel.

oyer and terminer: a judicial commission to hear and determine a particular case, often concerning trespass.

pane: a number of skins sewn together to make up a fur lining.

pannage: payment in return for the right to pasture pigs in the lord's woods.

pantler: the official in charge of the Pantry which was mainly responsible for the supply of bread to the household.

pargeting: ornamental plasterwork on the inside or outside of a building.

pax or pax-board: a small tablet or board, often decorated, kissed by the priest during mass, and then passed round the congregation to be kissed. This replaced the earlier kiss of peace.

pentice: a sloping roof projecting from the outside wall of a building and placed over a door, window or passage-way.

pervant: the bar (in a cart) to which the traces are attached.

pinaculum: a pinnacle. The term was used in connection with work on jewellery and tombs.

plumber: a man who works in lead.

plunket: light blue.

popel: the early summer skin of the Baltic squirrel.

pound: a fenced enclosure for keeping livestock which had been confiscated by the lord and his officials as a distraint.

pourparty: the share of an inheritance. In cases where two or more women succeeded to a feudal estate, the lands were equally divided between them.

primer: a book of hours, containing a shortened version of the divine office, especially the Office of Our Lady, the Virgin Mary, the Office for the Dead, penitential psalms, the litany, and prayers. The owner could add to the prayers.

purpresture: an encroachment or enclosure on someone else's land. In the case of the Lady, this was usually allowed in return for payment.

pyx: the container for the consecrated hosts in the church.

quindene: a fortnight, fifteen days, after a specified date.

reap-reeve: the manorial official responsible for the harvest.

reeve: the villein who was responsible for running a demesne manor. Alternatively, a bedel or serjeant could be in charge.

regrator: a retailer who bought goods in the market and later sold them there at a higher price.

relief: payment by a military tenant on succeeding to a fee. The rate laid down by Magna Carta was £5 for a knight's fee.

rent of assize: a rent paid annually to the lord by manorial and borough tenants.

robe: a suit of clothes for a man or woman.

royal pastry, *pasta real*: a type of sweet pastry.

samite: a rich silk fabric, with a diagonal weave making it look like satin.

saucer: a shallow bowl.

say: a type of silk or satin.

scapular: a short cloak worn by clerics.

seisin: possession of land.

sendal: a silk fabric; the early name for taffeta.

shearman: a man who shears the woollen cloth in order to produce a fine nap.

solsele: marigold-colour; the term was used in connection with dyeing cloth.

steer: a young ox, usually in its third or fourth year.

stick of eels: twenty-five eels.

stockfish: stockfish came from the Baltic and were cured by splitting the fish and drying them without salt. *Streitfisch, middelfisch and rakelfisch* were all types of stockfish. *Cropling* were an inferior kind of stockfish.

straddle-clout: an iron plate on the plough, protecting the end of an axle.

strake: an iron strip or tyre on the wheel of a cart.

strandling: the autumn skin of the Baltic squirrel.

stud: a small vertical timber post in a timber-framed building, one storey in height to which laths were attached.

tally: a receipt for payment. The term, acquittance, was also used to mean a receipt.

tartaryn: a rich silk fabric.

tenant-in-chief: a man or woman who held directly of the Crown by knight service.

tercel: a male falcon, particularly a male peregrine falcon.

timber: a bundle of 40 skins.

tiretein: a woollen fabric mixed with cotton or linen, and of mediocre quality.

triaclier: a vase for treacle (pharmaceutical).

tunicle: a tunic worn by clerics assisting the priest in celebrating mass.

ullage: the replacement in the cask of liquid which has evaporated.

varvel: a metal ring, often made of silver, with the owner's name engraved on it. The ring was attached to the end of a hawk's jess, and it connected the jess with the leash.

vassal: the vassal held land of a lord in return for performing homage and swearing fealty to him. His holding was termed his fief or knight's fee, and ranged from a fractional fee to a fee owing, in theory, the service of several knights. Originally, he owed military service and castleguard, suit at the honour court, and relief on his succession, but from the thirteenth century his relationship with his lord was mainly financial.

veiroun: skewbald.

vestment: a garment worn by the priest, deacon and subdeacon during the celebration of mass, namely the chasuble, or the chasuble with other mass garments.

view of frankpledge: many lords had the right to hold the view twice a year on their manors in order to check on the tithings in which men over the age of twelve were grouped for policing purposes. Each tithing was placed under a head man, or capital pledge. In addition to checking the tithings, minor law and order offences were dealt with. A lord who had this franchise was said to have exercised leet jurisdiction.

virgater: unfree villein tenants, performing week work and additional boon work at harvest-time.

waitfee: a commutation payment for the performance of castleguard.

warranty: guarantee of tenure.

winding bands: iron tyres or bands for repairing or strengthening cartwheels.

SELECT BIBLIOGRAPHY

MANUSCRIPT SOURCES

British Library, London
   Cotton MS Nero E vii
   Harley MS 1240
   Harley MS 4835
Lambeth Palace Library, London
   Islip's Register, fols 164v–166v
The National Archives, London
   Chancery Inquisitions Post Mortem
      C134/42–4; C135/152/5
   Chancery Miscellanea
      C47/9/23–5
   Court rolls
      SC2/171/44–9; 178/37–45; 203/38–56, 87–8, 107, 112–15; 204/2–4; 212/36–52; 213/1–15
   Exchequer Accounts Various
      See the Appendix, p.151 above
   Ministers' Accounts
      SC6/836/7–12; 838/4–30; 839/1–2; 868/19–23; 869/1–13; 930/3–29; 992/10–25; 993/1–17; 996/6; 999/20, 22; 1004/17–28; 1006/9–20; 1008/2–16; 1109/19; 1110/4–20, 26–9; 1111/1–6
   Rentals and Surveys
      SC11/799, 801

PRINTED PRIMARY SOURCES

Bailey, M., ed. and trans., *The English Manor, c.1200–c.1500*, Manchester Medieval Sources (Manchester, 2002)

Calendar of Chancery Warrants, 1244–1326 (London, 1927)

Calendar of Close Rolls, 1307–64, 15 vols (London, 1892–1910)

Calendar of Entries in Papal Registers relating to Great Britain and Ireland: Papal Letters, 1305–62, 2 vols (London, 1895–7); *Petitions to the Pope, 1342–1419* (London, 1897)

Calendar of Fine Rolls, 1307–69, 7 vols (London, 1911–23)

Calendar of Inquisitions Post Mortem, 1300–1360, 7 vols (London, 1908–21)

Calendar of Miscellaneous Inquisitions, 1307–77, 2 vols (London, 1916–37)

Calendar of Patent Rolls, 1307–61, 16 vols (London, 1891–1911)

Chartularies of St Mary's Abbey, Dublin, ed. J.T. Gilbert, 2 vols, Rolls Series (London, 1884–6)

Chronicle of Pierre de Langtoft, ed. T. Wright, 2 vols, Rolls Series (London, 1866–8)

Court Rolls of the Abbey of Ramsey and of the Honor of Clare, ed. W.O. Ault (New Haven and London,1928)

Cronica Maiorum et Vicecomitum Londoniarum, ed. T. Stapleton, Camden Society, old series, XXXIV (London, 1846)

Flores Historiarum, ed. H.R. Luard, 3 vols, Rolls Series (London, 1890)

Foedera, Coventiones, Litterae, ed. A. Clarke, J. Caley, J. Bayley, F. Holbrooke and J.W. Clarke, 4 vols, Record Commission (London, 1816–69)

Harvey, P.D.A., ed., *Manorial Records of Cuxham, Oxfordshire, c.1200–1359* (Historical Manuscripts Commission and Oxfordshire Records Society, L, 1976)

Heywood, J., *Early Cambridge University and College Statutes* (London, 1855)

Holmes, G.A., 'A Protest against the Despensers, 1326', *Speculum*, XXX (1955), pp.207–12

Inquisitions and Assessments relating to Feudal Aids, 1284–1431, 6 vols (London, 1899–1921)

Lee-Warner, J., 'Petition of the Prior and Canons of Walsingham, Norfolk, to Elizabeth Lady of Clare, c.1345', *Archaeological Journal*, XXVI (1869), pp.166–73

Monasticon Anglicanum, ed. J. Caley, H. Ellis and B. Bandinel, 6 vols (London, 1817–30)

Nichols, J., *A Collection of all the Wills of the Kings and Queens of England* (London, 1780)

Ridgard, J., ed., *Medieval Framlingham: Select Documents, 1270–1524* (Suffolk Records Society, XXVII, 1985)

Rotuli Parliamentorum, I and II (London, 1783)

Vita Edwardi Secundi, ed. N. Denholm-Young (London, 1957)

Ward, J., ed. and trans., *Women of the English Nobility and Gentry, 1066–1500*, Manchester Medieval Sources (Manchester, 1995)

Woolgar, C.M., ed., *Household Accounts from Medieval England*, British Academy Records of Social and Economic History, new series, XVII, XVIII (Oxford, 1992–3)

SECONDARY SOURCES

Altschul, M., *A Baronial Family in Medieval England: the Clares, 1217–1314* (Baltimore, 1965)

Archer, R.E., 'Rich Old Ladies: the Problem of Late Medieval Dowagers', in A. Pollard ed., *Property and Politics: Essays in Later Medieval English History* (Gloucester, 1984), pp.15–35

Archer, R.E., '"How Ladies ... who live on their manors ought to manage their households and estates": Women as Land Holders and Administrators in the Later Middle Ages', in P.J.P. Goldberg, ed., *Women in Medieval English Society* (Stroud, 1997), pp.149–81

Bailey, M., *Medieval Suffolk. An Economic and Social History, 1200–1500* (Woodbridge, 2007)

Barnadiston, K.W., and Scarfe, N., eds, *Clare Priory. Seven Centuries of a Suffolk House* (Cambridge, 1962)

Blair, C.H., 'Armorials on English Seals from the Twelfth to the Sixteenth Centuries', *Archaeologia*, LXXXIX (1943), pp.1–26

Blair, J., and Ramsay, N., eds, *English Medieval Industries* (London, 1991)

Bothwell, J., Goldberg, P.J.P., and Ormrod, W.M., eds, *The Problem of Labour in Fourteenth-Century England* (York, 2000)

Bourdillon, A.F.C., *The Order of Minoresses in England* (Manchester, 1926)

Boyer, M.N., 'Medieval Suspended Carriages', *Speculum*, XXIV (1959), pp.359–66

Campbell, B.M.S., 'Grain Yields on English Demesnes after the Black Death', in M. Bailey and S. Rigby, eds, *Town and Countryside in the Age of the Black Death. Essays in Honour of John Hatcher* (Turnhout, 2012), pp. 121–74

Chibnall, A.C., *Richard de Badew and the University of Cambridge, 1315–40* (Cambridge, 1963)

Clark, J., *The Medieval Horse and its Equipment* (Woodbridge, 2004)

Davis, J., *Medieval Market Morality. Life, Law and Ethics in the English Marketplace, 1200–1500* (Cambridge, 2012)

Davis, J., 'Selling Food and Drink in the Aftermath of the Black Death', in M. Bailey and

S. Rigby, eds, *Town and Countryside in the Age of the Black Death. Essays in Honour of John Hatcher* (Turnhout, 2012), pp.351–95

Dyer, C., *Standards of Living in the Later Middle Ages* (Cambridge, 1989)

Emden, A.B., *A Biographical Register of the University of Cambridge* (Cambridge, 1963)

Frame, R., *English Lordship in Ireland, 1318–61* (Oxford, 1982)

Hailstone, E., *The History and Antiquities of the Parish of Bottisham and the Priory of Anglesey in Cambridgeshire* (Cambridge Antiquarian Society, 1873)

Hamilton, J.S., *Piers Gaveston, Earl of Cornwall* (Detroit, 1988)

Harvey, J., *English Medieval Architects. A Biographical Dictionary down to 1550* (London, 1954)

Harvey, J., *Medieval Gardens* (London, 1981)

Holmes, G.A., *The Estates of the Higher Nobility in Fourteenth-Century England* (Cambridge, 1957)

Hyland, A., *The Horse in the Middle Ages* (Stroud, 1999)

Jenkinson, H., 'Mary de Sancto Paulo, Foundress of Pembroke College, Cambridge', *Archaeologia*, LXVI (1915), pp.401–46

Kaeuper, R.W., 'Law and Oder in Fourteenth-Century England', *Speculum*, LIV (1979), pp.734–84

Langdon, J., *Horses, Oxen and Technological Innovation. The Use of Draught Animals in English Farming from 1066 to 1500* (Cambridge, 1986)

Mertes, K., *The English Noble Household, 1250–1600. Good Governance and Politic Rule* (Oxford, 1988)

Moore, E.W., *The Fairs of Medieval England. An Introductory Study* (Pontifical Institute of Medieval Studies: Studies and Texts, LXXII, 1985)

Mortimer, R., 'The Beginnings of the Honour of Clare', *Proceedings of the Battle Conference on Anglo-Norman Studies*, III, ed. R.A. Brown (1980), pp.119–41

Mortimer, R., 'Land and Service: the Tenants of the Honour of Clare', *Anglo-Norman Studies: Proceedings of the Battle Conference*, VIII, ed. R.A. Brown (1985), pp.177–97

Musgrave, C.A., 'Household Administration in the Fourteenth Century with special reference to the Household of Elizabeth de Burgh, Lady of Clare' (London University M.A. thesis, 1923; unpublished)

Newton, S.M., *Fashion in the Age of the Black Prince. A Study of the Years 1340 to 1365* (Woodbridge, 1980)

Ormrod, W.M., *The Reign of Edward III. Crown and Political Society in England, 1327–77* (London, 1990)

Ormrod, W.M., *Edward III* (New Haven and London, 2012)

Oxford Dictionary of National Biography (Oxford, 2004)

Phillips, J.R.S., *Edward II* (New Haven and London, 2010)

Piponnier, F., and Mane, P., trans. Beamish, C., *Dress in the Middle Ages* (New Haven and London, 1997)

Prestwich, M., *Edward I* (London, 1988)

Prestwich, M., *Plantagenet England, 1225–1360* (Oxford, 2005)

Raban, S., *Mortmain Legislation and the English Church, 1279–1500* (Cambridge, 1982)

Salzman, L.F., *Building in England down to 1540. A Documentary History* (Oxford, 1967)

Stuart, D., *Manorial Records. An Introduction to their Transcription and Translation* (Chichester, 1992)

Sutton, A.F., 'The Early Linen and Worsted Industry of Norfolk and the Evolution of the London Mercers' Company', *Norfolk Archaeology*, XL (1987–9), pp.201–25

Sutton, A.F., *The Mercery of London. Trade, Goods and People, 1130–1578* (Aldershot, 2005)

Thornton, G.A., *A History of Clare, Suffolk* (Cambridge, 1928)

Underhill, F.A., 'Elizabeth de Burgh, Connoisseur and Patron', in J.H. McCash, ed., *The Cultural Patronage of Medieval Women* (Athens and London, 1996), pp.266–87

Underhill, F.A., *For her Good Estate. The Life of Elizabeth de Burgh* (Basingstoke, 1999)

Veale, E.M., *The English Fur Trade in the Later Middle Ages* (second edition, London Record Society, XXXVIII, 2003)

Ward, J., 'The Honour of Clare in Suffolk in the Middle Ages', *Proceedings of the Suffolk Institute of Archaeology*, XXX (1964), pp.94–111

Ward, J., 'Fashions in Monastic Endowment: the Foundations of the Clare Family, 1066–1314', *Journal of Ecclesiastical History*, XXXII (1981), pp.427–51

Ward, J., 'The Place of the Honour in Twelfth-Century Society: the Honour of Clare, 1066–1217', *Proceedings of the Suffolk Institute of Archaeology and History*, XXXV (1983), pp.191–202

Ward, J., *English Noblewomen in the Later Middle Ages* (London, 1992)

Ward, J., 'Elizabeth de Burgh, Lady of Clare (d.1360)', in C.M. Barron and A.F. Sutton, eds, *Medieval London Widows* (London, 1994), pp.29–45

Ward, J., 'Elizabeth de Burgh and Usk Castle', *Monmouthshire Antiquary*, XVIII (2002), pp.13–22

Ward, J., 'Noble Consumption in the Fourteenth Century: Supplying the Household of Elizabeth de Burgh, Lady of Clare (d.1360)', *Proceedings of the Suffolk Institute of Archaeology and History*, XLI, part 4 (2008), pp.447–60

Woolgar, C.M., *The Great Household in Late Medieval England* (New Haven and London, 1999)

Woolgar, C.M., Serjeantson, D., and Waldron, T., eds, *Food in Medieval England* (Oxford, 2006)

INDEX OF PEOPLE AND PLACES

Names of people have been standardised; where there are variants in the text, these are grouped under the main heading. Place-names are given in the modern form; if they have not been identified, they have been put in italics.

165

168

INDEX OF SUBJECTS

180

THE SUFFOLK RECORDS SOCIETY

For nearly sixty years, the Suffolk Records Society has added to the knowledge of Suffolk's history by issuing an annual volume of previously unpublished manuscripts, each throwing light on some new aspect of the county's history.

Covering 700 years and embracing letters, diaries, maps, accounts and other archives, many of them previously little known or neglected, these books have together made a major contribution to historical studies.

At the heart of this achievement lie the Society's members, all of whom share a passion for Suffolk and its history and whose support, subscriptions and donations make possible the opening up of the landscape of historical research in the area.
In exchange for this tangible support, members receive a new volume each year at a considerable saving on the retail price at which the books are then offered for sale.

Members are also welcomed to the launch of the new volume, held each year in a different and appropriate setting within the county and giving them a chance to meet and listen to some of the leading historians in their fields talking about their latest work.

For anyone with a love of history, a desire to build a library on Suffolk themes at modest cost and a wish to see historical research continue to thrive and bring new sources to the public eye in decades to come, a subscription to the Suffolk Records Society is the ideal way to make a contribution and join the company of those who give Suffolk history a future.

THE CHARTERS SERIES

To supplement the annual volumes and serve the need of medieval historians, the Charters Series was launched in 1979 with the challenge of publishing the transcribed texts of all the surviving monastic charters for the county. Since that date, nineteen volumes have been published as an occasional series, the latest in 2011.

The Charter Series is financed by a separate annual subscription leading to receipt of each volume on publication.

CURRENT PROJECTS

Volumes approved by the Society's council for future publication include *Wills of the Archdeaconry of Suffolk, 1627–1628*, ed. Marion Allen; *William Morris and the Restoration of Blythburgh Church*, ed. Alan Mackley; *The Diary of John Clopton, 1648–50*, ed. John Pelling; *Papers of the Rookwoods of Stanningfield, 1606–1761*, ed. Francis Young; in the Charters Series, *The Charters of the Priory of St Peter and St Paul, Ipswich*, ed. David Allen; and *Bury St Edmunds Town Charters*, ed. Vivien Brown. The order in which these and other volumes appear will depend on the dates of completion of editorial work.

MEMBERSHIP

Membership enquiries should be addressed to Mrs Tanya Christian, 8 Orchid Way, Needham Market, IP6 8JQ; e-mail: tcachristian@gmail.com

The Suffolk Records Society is a registered charity, No. 1084279.